Chaucer and Langland

Chaucer and Langland

Historical and Textual Approaches

GEORGE KANE

University of California Press
Berkeley and Los Angeles

First Published 1989 by
The University of California Press, 2120 Berkeley Way,
Berkeley, California 94720, U.S.A.

© George Kane 1989

Library of Congress Cataloging in Publication data

Kane, George
 Chaucer and Langland: Historical and Textual Approaches/
 George Kane.
 P.   CM.
 ISBN 0-520-06316-3
 1. English Poetry—Middle English.   1100–1500—History and Criticism.
 2. Chaucer, Geoffrey. D. 1400—Criticism and Interpretation.   3.
 LANGLAND, WILLIAM. 1330?–1400? Piers the Plowman.   I. Title
 PR313.K3 1989
 821 ' .1 ' 09—DC19

Printed in Great Britain

Contents

Acknowledgements

For permission to reproduce items already published I am under the following obligations: to University College London for 'The Autobiographical Fallacy in Chaucer and Langland Studies' (the R. W. Chambers Memorial Lecture for 1965); to the Accademia Nazionale dei Lincei for 'Chaucer and the Idea of a Poet' (1976); to Pilgrim Books for 'Langland and Chaucer: an Obligatory Conjunction' (*New Perspectives in Chaucer Criticism*, 1981), for 'Chaucer, Love Poetry and Romantic Love' (*Acts of Interpretation: the Text in Its Context 700–1600*), and for 'John M. Manly and Edith Rickert' (*Editing Chaucer: the Great Tradition*, 1984); to Oxford University Press for 'Music Neither Unpleasant Nor Monotonous' (*Medieval Studies for J. A. W. Bennett*, 1981), and for 'The Text of *The Legend of Good Women* in CUL MS Gg. 4. 27' (*Medieval Studies Presented to Norman Davis in Honour of his Seventieth Birthday*, 1983); to Medieval Institute Publications of Kalamzoo for 'The Perplexities of William Langland' (*Essays in Honor of Morton W. Bloomfield*, 1982); to Duke University Press for 'Poetry and Lexicography in the Translation of Piers Plowman' (*Medieval and Renaissance Studies* 9, 1982); to the English Association for 'Criticism, Solecism: Does It Matter?' (called 'Some Reflections on Critical Method' in *Essays and Studies*, 1976); to the New Chaucer Society for '"Good" and "Bad" Manuscripts: Texts and Critics' (*Studies in the Age of Chaucer*, 1986); and to the Center for Medieval and Early Renaissance Studies for 'Outstanding Problems of Middle English Scholarship' (*Acta IV, The Fourteenth Century*, 1977). 'The Literating Truth', the University of London's John Coffin Memorial Lecture for 1979, was published by Athlone.

Preface

All these essays are occasional pieces, written to no programme and without conscious adoption of any theoretical position. Many of their topics reflect interests generated by my teaching of graduate students in the United States. Such coherence as they possess is conferred by the critical movements of the last couple of decades, in the light of which, because of my age and the accidents of my education, they are now period pieces.

When I was an undergraduate it was stylish to be seen with a copy of Eliot's *Selected Essays* under one's arm. About that time the *Poetics* and Longinus came my way in Greek courses: the two kinds of elegant thinking between them seemed to make all secure. When my first book was unfavourably reviewed in *Scrutiny* because I had 'nothing to say' the effect, albeit in the immediate instance chastening, was beneficial because it turned me to the New Critics. And, rejoicing in these, to my delight I found that there was no genuine conflict between their manners of proceeding and my own belief that a writer is best understood and valued in his historical setting. Over the years I have tried to teach my students that fine sensibility, elegant thinking, command of languages and historical knowledge are not merely compatible, but actually congenial associates. But I cannot remember formulating the convictions on which that effort must have been based until a couple of years ago.

They are very simple. My attitude to literary works of art is unashamedly elitist. My taste tells me that some texts, however this is to be explained, are more salient, more distinguished than others. Thus I cannot equate Lydgate with Chaucer in any particular except volume of output. My judgement tells me that some readings of texts are more correct, more accurate in an absolute sense, than others: criticism, like what it criticizes, can be good or bad. Therefore a critic, it seems to follow, is 'privileged' too: he, correspondingly, has a responsibility of intelligence which includes intellectual honesty and the avoidance of solecism whether through disregard of the language of the text in any sense of that word, or of the historical circumstances in which it originated, or of the logic of inference.

It has become vogue to challenge or express scepticism about at least the first two of those convictions, and the last is much neglected. I will record that I have found nothing in post-structuralist or any other, subsequent criticism of intellectual cogency to induce me to discard them, far less to condone bad critical writing. Indeed they seem to me to be enabling postulates, with a value not unlike that of the hypothesis in the days of the first nominalism. It is hard for me to conceive how anyone can in honesty profess to teach literature without respecting them.

I write this without arrogance in the assurance that those from whom I have learned, far too many for more than a general expression of great debt, also wrote or write from that position. I count myself lucky in the scholars before and in my time, from whom I learned more than I can possibly acknowledge, and in the traditions of values, learning and intellectual integrity which they stood and stand for.

I also count myself lucky in the succession of accidents that brought the two poets of my title together in my interest. The association has been strenuous at times; nevertheless I have found them, in their combination of similarities and differences, the best company a man could wish for.

George Kane

1

The Autobiographical Fallacy
in Chaucer and Langland Studies

There is some great poetry which conveys to its readers the liveliest impression of a personality in and behind it. If, in such a case, the poet's life is adequately documented, by diaries, letters, contemporary accounts, 'conversations', and so on, the personality which we feel in his writings appears to us a reflection of what we otherwise know about him, and we tend to search those writings for insights into the processes by which this is known, actual experience has been transmuted into poetry. But when biographical documentation is lacking, and when at the same time the poetry creates in its reader a strong sense of a distinctive, individual authorial presence, that poetry can take on the aspect of a source of information about the poet. This has been the case with Chaucer and Langland. Out of their poetry these two men have emerged as legendary national figures: the one, roly-poly, whimsical, but also a shrewd observer, hiding his perceptivity behind a pretence of genial condonation; the other a lanky, embittered malcontent in a rusty cassock, striding arrogantly about the Malvern Hills, or, variously, the City of London. Those figures are, of course, fanciful popular simplifications, which need not be taken seriously. But, in my opinion, correspondingly unverifiable conceptions of the two poets inhabit the area of professional Chaucer and Langland scholarship, and these will be my subject today.

The life-records of Chaucer relate mainly to his career as a royal servant; the various facts of office and employment tell us relatively little about the man as a private individual; and of Langland we actually have no information beyond his paternity and, possibly, his birthplace. Yet it seems to us that we know them both. There are not many studies of Chaucer where discussion is not rounded out by the author's impression of a Chaucerian personality, inferred from his poetry; and all the 'biographies' of Langland have been constructed on the assumption that he has recorded his life history in his poems.

My argument will be that our notions of the personalities of these two poets, and our sense that we 'know' them as men, are attained by inferences both logically dubious in themselves, and unauthorized by the literary history of the fourteenth century. These are distinct considerations. They seem to me, however, to support one another. For I believe that in the second, the particular literary circumstances of our poets, lies both the explanation of our strong impulse to identify them, and the reason why we do this at our peril.

I begin with our logic. We deduce the attitudes and intentions of Chaucer and Langland from their poetry; from the content of works or parts of works where the poets themselves seem to figure we deduce the occurrence of particular events in their lives, or their circumstances. Out of the sum of such deductions we fashion individuals apt (in our various views) to have written the poetry out of which we have created them. This seems a most natural process; it arises from an impulse almost impossible to resist. But viewed as reasoning it appears perfectly circular, and it is altogether subjective. For the judgement we exercise in creating these personalities and reconstructing their undocumented lives, or the undocumented parts of these, rests on complexities of preconception in ourselves which we could not hope to identify and disentangle. Our inferences are, for one thing, reached by *a posteriori* rationalization; for another unverifiable. Yet even when one accepts this disqualification the poetry continues to exercise a compulsion to make them.

The situation is both difficult and tantalizing. The nature of literature being what it is, we can scarcely dispense with the use of internal evidence in its study. We must constantly make inferences from texts: about a poet's reading; about his opinions and values; about his creative methods; about the events of his life. Some of these classes of inference can be tested. Thus we can fairly conclude from an apparent echo in an author's work that he has read a particular book if we know: that the book was available to him; that the echo could not equally well be of another book with similar content; that the verbal or notional resemblances between putative source and echo could not easily be coincidental. For testing inferences about his opinions and values we use our sense of his tone and our knowledge of external standards in effect in his time. Inference about topicality we can check by its historical possibility, by the aptness of the apparent reference, and by the consideration whether it has any conceivable literary or social point. Inferences about creative methods we measure against our whole understanding of the processes of literature, acquired during more general observation. Conclusions reached by such inferences must often remain presumptive, since it is no part of the study of literature that its problems are necessarily soluble. But if reached by sound methods they can be useful and illuminating. Such procedures of inference contain their own rationale; and in terms of that rationale they are subject to judgement and correction by our colleagues.

But in the case of poets about whom little or no biographical information has survived, and whose works therefore are the only possible source of information about them, is there any logic, any rationale, by which biographical inference from these works may be safely conducted? Are there tests by which such inference can be checked? To me this seems improbable, even if those poets have written largely or entirely in the first person, and appear to figure, as themselves, in their writings. A poet represents himself in a poem as a fat man; can we, with genuine logical necessity, infer that he actually was corpulent? Can we absolutely exclude the ancient joke of naming by opposites, a kind of *lucus a non lucendo?* He repeatedly professes inexperience, or lack of aptitude, or lack of success as a lover.[1] Do we accept this as autobiography, or call it a conventional pose, or take the position that we cannot possibly know? Or he represents himself as slow-witted, and we reject this as impossible. What criteria can we apply? There are, it seems to me, three situations in which we might make inferences from texts about such undocumented matters respecting the life and personality of an author: because they are indicated by, and referable to external biographical knowledge, in which case they fall into another class; or because they match impressions created by his poetry as a whole; or because they fit an ideal image of the poet already formed, and to a large extent subconsciously, by our reading of and about him. I would put it to you that inferences made in at least the third of these situations, while not necessarily wrong, are not logically necessary.

The weakness of biographical inference unsupported by external knowledge lies in its subjective character. When we profess to have detected the poet 'revealing himself' in his works, or when we postulate that certain experiences or attributes ascribed by a poet to himself in his writing are autobiographical, we apply only one criterion: our preconception of appropriateness in the particular instance. This could conceivably be wholly correct; it might be fairly accurate; it might be totally wrong. Who is to say? By exercise of selection in our identification of the moments of self-revelation, or of autobiographical attributes, we beg the question: the instance is appropriate because it seems appropriate. And while we may have hit it right, this is not logic. Let us consider the opposite situation, where biographical data exist which appear incongruent to the image of the poet set up by his works: a Chaucer so responsive in his poetry to the pathos in the lives of women, apparently figuring in a case of rape; the deeply imaginative Malory according to the records a freebooter, in and out of prison all his life for violent crime. An instinctive reason is, 'but we *know* our author;[2] he cannot have behaved in this way; there must be some mistake'. So we retranslate *raptus* as 'abduction', and we look for a second Thomas Malory. By such conviction, in its positive or negative forms, we idealize our poets. We forget that the personalities of themselves which they project in their works may conceivably be disingenuous, for those personalities may be an element in the design of the works, a part of the poets' technique. It is hardly safe to posit that the poets will, all that often, reveal themselves unconsciously. The line of our images of the poets were, after all, created by the poets themselves; they may be self-dramatizations, they were not necessarily designed as autobiography.

This caveat is not new.[3] Kittredge uttered it as long ago as 1915 with a particular reference to Chaucer;[4] in Langland studies the advocates of multiple authorship were quick to appeal to it.[5] It is repeated at intervals,[6] and then ignored; the practice of biographical inference persists. Our two poets at least seem irresistibly to induce it, sometimes even in those who have themselves pronounced the caution. A line spoken by the dreamer called Geoffrey in *The House of Fame* suggests that the actual Chaucer has a shrewish wife.[7] Or, otherwise, he had a contemporary reputation as a bookworm.[8] Or he was a fat man,[9] with an 'unromantic face and figure', an 'unromantic personality';[10] his repeated references to his own inexperience in love were designed to protect him, when he read love-poetry aloud, from the chaff of his social superiors.[11] Or love as a subject for poetry, and indeed the popular poetic form of the love-vision, 'were radically uncongenial to his temperament. . . . He married, of course; but possibly the only woman with whom he was ever deeply in love was his own Criseyde. . . . it is not merely a favourite little joke of his

. . . that he is an outsider in matters of love. That recurrent disclaimer . . . expresses something fundamental in his nature.'[12] Or, alternately, Chaucer was for eight years actually in love with an unattainable noble lady.[13] Or where, in *The Parliament of Fowls*, Chaucer wrote of having seen Venus 'north-north-west' when he began to versify his dream, he was referring to an actual woman who, looking over his shoulder, stood in that direction from him as he sat at his desk—'Whether the lady deserved identification with Venus or not I have no means of knowing', the proposer adds with scholarly reserve.[14] Or the legal terminology of his *Franklin's Tale* reflects Chaucer's experience when he was summoned for rape by Cecily Champagne.[15] He was in sympathy with the alchemists, an adept in their science, and had possibly discovered the secret of secrets.[16] Alternately he may have been a dupe of the alchemists, and reduced himself to poverty in search of the philosophers' stone.[17]

These are, to be sure, extreme examples of unsupported biographical inference, and it would be hard to take some of them very seriously. Nevertheless they illustrate both the strength of the inducement to such inference, and the intrinsic impossibility of determining its correctness. Take Chaucer's references to his unsuccess as a lover: they might be autobiographical or they might not; without external information we could not conceivably know. As it turns out, someone discovers that the eight years of his hopeless passion verbally echo a love of equal length in his model, Machaut.[18] And those apparently melancholy lines in *The Parliament of Fowls* where the dreamer, seeming to voice deep personal discontent, says *bothe I hadde thyng which that I nolde, and ek I nadde that thyng that I wolde*, prove to be a quotation from Boethius, in whose text it seems intended to describe the general human condition.[19] And the identification of the object of Chaucer's 'hopeless love' as Joan of Kent appears to have been carried out by selective use of evidence, and to involve contradictions of a kind which would rule it out.[20] And someone discovers that almost all his alchemical knowledge, of which Manly confidently wrote that it 'could have been the fruit only of a profound and prolonged devotion to the subject',[21] was actually available to him in a single author, whose content he closely reflects.[22] Thus certain particular speculations receive a check. But such corrections are fortuitous; they depend on external information. The process of free biographical inference contains within itself no element to control its accuracy, and therefore no means by which its logical necessity or even its probability can be checked. It has no rationale. It is essentially imaginative, affective, subjective, pure speculation.

I have spoken so far about Chaucer; but *Piers Plowman* studies afford instances of even wilder aberrations of biographical inference. I must in charity no more than mention the worst offender; he did not have a scholar's training and his enthusiasm for Langland exceeded his capabilities. I will say only that *New Light on Piers Plowman* is the ultimate demonstration of the fallacy, with respect both to far-fetched identification of the autobiographical in the poem, and to absurdly subjective criteria of behaviour appropriate to the poet.[23] But many *Piers Plowman* scholars (I shamefacedly include myself) have at some time and in some way thought or argued in terms of the fallacy; to find one secure against it, and also believing in single authorship, is the exception.[24] The situation is not without its comedy. An article surveying, with great parade of judiciousness, forty years of *Piers Plowman* scholarship, argues that when the dreamer in the B version recounts a youthful lapse into unregeneracy this cannot be autobiographical because 'it is not credible that the conscientious author of A fell victim to the sins of the flesh after writing A'.[25] Arming us against one element in the fallacy, the author of this article demonstrates the other in his appeal to a manifestly questionable subjective notion of appropriate behaviour. Sitting in judgement he too registers, however absurdly, the powerful impact of what has been aptly called 'the imagination inhabiting *Piers Plowman*'.[26] The brutal fact is that all 'biographies' of Langland[27] are constructed on the basis of the fallacy. Some of them seem wise, perceptive, full of insight; they may be full of truth; but all are purely speculative; all are, in the present state of knowledge, unverifiable.

The predicament created by the strong sense of the author's personality in the poetry of Chaucer and Langland extends beyond biography into criticism, where attempts to explain this salient circumstance of their poetry have resulted in a variety of perplexed and conflicting propositions. These range from the elementary to the supersubtle, and some, it may be observed, explain nothing. Our understanding of Chaucer's poetry is, for example, not greatly advanced by the assertion that 'Chaucer's direct and indirect self-characterizations are meant to be funny'.[28] Not much more enlightening is the proposal that the illusion of Chaucer's presence in his poetry may have no further purpose than to create 'a little mild fun' among friends.[29] The suggestion that Chaucer's 'self-mockery' is 'an essential ingredient' in his allusions to himself 'if they are not to become offensive'[30] fails to explain why he should persist in such allusions. About the precise object of these allusions there is no agreement: someone writes, it is 'Geoffrey Chaucer in person' who figures in *The Canterbury Tales*, [31] or *The House of Fame* and the Prologue to *The Legend of Good Women*;[32] someone else, it is 'himself that he is representing, however posed and semi-dramatic.[33] 'His audience . . . would not leap unaided to the assumption that he was speaking in a fictive personality.[34] But, to another view, the first-person narrator is a *persona*, 'a naïve, uncomplicated reporter of experience';[35] Chaucer the Pilgrim and Chaucer the Poet represent a 'deliberate artistic dualism'.[36] The 'obtuseness' of the dreamer in *The Book of the Duchess* was designed by the poet to signify his own inability to do justice to his subject.[37] Or, even, the dream reported by the narrator of *The Book of the Duchess* (who claims, also, to have put it into rhyme) has a 'therapeutic function'; it is 'an effort of the psyche to resolve an intolerable emotional situation by repudiating it through this disguise'.[38] Or, at another extreme, 'Chaucer does not seem to have been much interested in his narrator, much less to have been trying to express through him his own personality.[39]

The inconclusiveness and conflicting nature of such attempts to explain the mode of being and the significance of the author's personality in his poetry are complementary aspects of the same situation which generates the logically unauthorized but nevertheless persistent biographical inference. For they also turn on the question in what particulars and to what extent the author has revealed his actual self, his attributes and life, in his poetry. And if I am right in thinking that this question is unanswerable except where checks from external evidence are possible, then presumably in the absence of such evidence no generally acceptable explanations could be achieved. But such evidence may exist. I believe that one kind of it is to be found in the literary history of the fourteenth century, and that this both confirms the fallaciousness of free biographical inference about Chaucer or Langland and clarifies the position of the author in their poetry.

The first reason why the author of a fourteenth-century narrative poem was present in his poetry was because he delivered it orally, if not in all instances at least often enough for this circumstance to form in him an attitude to his public, which he conceived of as an audience, and thus to affect his tone.[40] A poet would not have to be learned to appreciate what Geoffrey de Vinsauf formulated for the public speaker: *In recitante sonent tres linguae: prima sit oris, Altera rhetorici vultus, et tertia gestus*;[41] he would instinctively sense the power of his living presence. But he would hold the attention of his public.[42] by more than merely histrionic means: by relating himself to them and to his subject; personally vouching for his story; professing ignorance and incapacity; expressing criticism of his sources; registering his own response to the action; making moralizing observations, and so on. It may well be, as Lüdeke has suggested of Chaucer, that consideration of these possibilities would be enough to lead a fourteenth-century poet to write the reciting narrator into his narrative.[43] There are two other circumstances which would induce the poet to identify himself with his narrator. The first is the absence, in fourteenth-century England, of any convention of detached, impersonal narrative. A tale implied a teller; and this was, by implication as well as by his vocal use of the first person, the poet. The second is that any considerable poet of the time would be writing for a coterie, that set of people, comprising his patrons and their associates, to whom he read, and thus in effect presented and published his work.[44] This situation implied the identification of author and narrator, at least in the case of a new work; acceptance of such identification was the easiest course for the poet.

In the particular sort of narrative poetry which we call the dream-vision, practised by Chaucer and Langland, and the main source of biographical inference about them, the situation of the narrator was particularly intricate. The special characteristics of the dream-vision poem establish it as a distinct literary kind, which had acquired, by the fourteenth century, a set of clearly discernible conventions. I cannot find that these were ever formulated in the middle ages, and the kind certainly fits none of the recognized categories of narrative. It is not *fabula*, the wholly fictitious, altogether incredible story; not *historia*, the account of events remote but true; not *argumentum*, the account of fictitious yet conceivably possible incidents.[45] The kind was developed, as far as I can discover (its whole history has still to be written), empirically, by a succession of practitioners on the primary model of Guillaume de Lorris and his continuator. On the double suggestion of that model the dream-vision became a vehicle for subjects ranging from the amatory or social, through satire, to eschatology. If any external influences affected it they did so, in my opinion, only very remotely, and without the knowledge of the poets who employed the kind.[46] This existed by virtue of its own conventions, which were evidently well understood. By the time Chaucer and Langland received them they were developed to the degree where they expressed the intrinsic potentialities of the kind.

I should perhaps make clear my understanding of that hard word 'convention'. I use it to mean a literary practice which, because it is evidently convenient or useful, has been followed often enough for its use to be identifiable as such. It may come to imply certain symbolisms; to confer certain licences on its users; to raise certain expectations in their public; and to give this public certain directions of response. By that definition the dream-vision kind has conventions which relate to the situation of its author, and thus to my subject this evening.

Dream-vision poems are by their nature personal poems.[47] They take the form of reports by a first-person narrator who professes to have himself experienced the dream he recounts. He always figures in the report as an observer, and often as a participant. The personages in the dream with whom he converses or is otherwise engaged range from the necessarily fictional (because they are allegorical or fantastic), through the possibly actual, to those who are actual in the sense that they bear the names of historical people. Similarly the incidents that the dreamer reports observing or taking part in are of all kinds, from the conceivably possible to those which (because of their nature) are necessarily fictional. The dreamer-narrator commonly announces that he is the one who has made or will make the dream into rhyme. If he is named he invariably (to the best of my knowledge) bears the name of the author. He is addressed or referred to by that name; or he reveals it himself, when asked; or records it in a coda, either openly or in a cryptogram. And where the authorship of a dream-vision poem and the circumstances of the author are known it very often proves the case that the dreamer of the poem possesses not merely the name, but also other historical attributes of that actual author. It is thus a convention of this literary kind for the dreamer to share identity with the poet, whether simply by being represented as a writer, or nominally, or more than nominally. To some greater or lesser extent the author of a dream-vision poem fashions his dreamer-narrator in his own image.[48] This convention of identity between narrator and poet extends, moreover, to narratives recounting waking experience. I need mention only *Confessio Amantis*, a report of fantastic events by a narrator named John Gower, who does not tell us that he fell asleep and dreamed what he experienced. The implications of the convention with respect to the narrator extend to *The Canterbury Tales*, which work, if we view it as a whole compound of incidents, is strictly speaking just as impossible as are the speaking lions and falcons of Machaut.

The conventional identification of dreamer-narrator and author may well have begun as a direct consequence of the circumstance of publishing by recitation. Inevitably it was put to use. One of its primary functions, perhaps also the most elementary, was to publish the author's name, to afford him a means of signing his poem, as Chambers recognized.[49] Before long it became, from a circumstance 'given' and relatively insignificant, an operative factor in the poem. Its potentialities were apparent even to a medieval rhetorician: Matthieu de Vendôme in the twelfth century casts a part of his *Ars Versificatoria* in the form of a dream vision which he has experienced, so that, he writes, *jocosae narrationis amminiculo docilitas exuberet, respiret attentio, redundet benivolentia, resonetur audientia, taedii redimatur incommodum, uberior disciplinae suppullulet appetitus.*[50] The dream which follows hardly accomplishes this, but his purpose at least shows some sense of literature. In a general way the implied or explicit personal presence of the dreamer in the poem would vivify the allegory and induce imaginative acceptance. By the immediacy of the report, dreamer and poet being conventionally identified, by the implied proposition, 'This happened to me', the author would make the conventionally requisite claim to historical authenticity; and from the sense of actuality, of the dreamer having a full personality through his identification with the poet during the physical act of recitation, a kind of verisimilitude would extend to the least probable incidents of the dream.

These potentialities of the dream-vision kind were recognized, it seems a fair presumption, by even the least distinguished of its users. The two great fourteenth-century English poets who employed it put it to still further, and formidably complex uses. For one thing they developed the irony implicit in the conventional identification of dreamer and poet. The character of this irony has been disputed, but it seems inconceivable to me that it could ever be totally missed. The fact of the literary occasion, the artificial circumstance of the narrative being in verse, the degree to which the reported dream must surpass any actual dream in organization, coherence, and circumstantial character, the known use of the dream setting for fictional representation, all would presumably signal to even the least intelligent hearer the necessary existence of at least some kind of distinction between the entities of poet and dreamer.[51] But in our poets the irony extends beyond the mere matter of identification. Both relate it to the further irony implicit in the interplay of literal and allegorical; both adopt (I suspect) an ironic attitude to the social distance between themselves and their patrons, and to an inversely corresponding distance with respect to learning and creative power. Both evidently recognize a humorous element in the identification, which they intensify by their representation of the characters of their dreamers. Both employ the identification as an instrument of involvement: at the simplest level to make their hearers respond with the thought 'There he goes again, pretending,' and follow this with the question. 'To what end? What am I supposed to perceive, detect, understand?[52]

But also, if I am any judge, both poets became themselves imaginatively involved in the personages of their dreamer-narrators. To the extent that these dreamers were projections of their poets they will have seemed to possess substantive existence; to have become dramatic personalities with their own imaginative reality; to be implicated, as dramatic personalities will, in situations beyond their control or manipulation. They became—because cognition of such personages is progressive as information about them is imaginatively conceived or, in communication, perceived—subject to chronology, thus acquiring lives and histories. Such a process may well link the dreamer of *The Book of the Duchess* to the nameless reporting voice of *Troilus and Criseyde* and to Chaucer the pilgrim. We can actually observe its operation in the three versions of *Piers Plowman*: the dreamer of the A version, at first scarcely realized, beginning to show signs of having a temperament and character in the latter part of that poem; the same dreamer in the B version gradually taking shape as a sharply defined personality; and then, his traits having been established in B as occasion suggested, appearing in the last version fully formed, his character and the circumstances of his life represented at length near the beginning of this version.

Such, then, in Langland's poetry and much of Chaucer's, is the situation of the author and his narrator. To an indeterminable extent the two share an identity; but they are also, necessarily, distinct entities with different modes of existence: the fictional entities important to their authors as imaginative creations, and to the audiences as challenging objects of interest. The complexity of these two situations is, as far as I know, unparalleled in the fourteenth century, and for that reason alone the generalizations which have been made about the 'poetic I' in medieval literature would not easily apply to them. Each narrator is a phenomenally elaborate product of the creative imagination, anything else but 'a rhetorically autobiographical figure';[53] and from all indications it was not, in their two cases, 'a trifling matter who the empirical person behind this "I" [the narrator] actually was'.[54] The 'habit of confusing the empiric with the poetic I', though this hardly describes the situation adequately, far from being 'in general unknown' in the middle ages as has been maintained,[55] was a major factor in the dynamism of the poetry of Chaucer and Langland. The speaking person in their works is both more and less than the poet; in him creator and thing created simultaneously merge and are distinguished; these two have, however urgent may be the invitation to identify them, distinctive modes of being. For all their confidential asides to the audience, their apologies for digression, the dreamers and narrators of Chaucer and Langland are, if I may use jargon, constructs. They bear the poets' names, and speak of writing down their dreams. But things happen to them which could not, except in imagination, have happened to the poets; thus their ultimate reality is imaginative only. They are manipulated by the poet. When it suits his purpose they surrender the speaking voice to him without signal, just as readily as on other occasions they licence him to report for truth the most extravagant incidents, to adopt as his own the most preposterous attitudes. Their nature is enigmatic.

The poets invite us to identify the narrators with themselves, and then, by the character of what is narrated, caution us not to carry out the identification. This they do consciously, creating an ambiguity which they then variously exploit: the enigma is deliberate. It may be that its most elementary function was to pose a form of *demande*: 'Say if you can how much of this is actually true of me'. The vogue of the *demande*, and the addiction of various fourteenth century poets to verbal puzzles, make this a distinct possibility. In that simple way, for a start, the narrator would be a function of the relation between the poet and his contemporary, immediate audience. More profoundly, the narrator would serve to focus that sustained challenge of poetry to define the relation between artistic reality and historical actuality which is a factor in its power of engagement. There seems every likelihood that our two poets were instinctively aware of this, even relished the insoluble questions that they were offering their audiences. Nowadays the intriguing possibility of self-revelation is one main source of the hold of Chaucer and Langland over us. In their own time, the conflicting invitation to identify and caution against doing so will have set up a distinctive tension, established a special kind of intimacy between poet and public, a bond of understanding, or at least the illusion of one, which is, for literary purposes, the same thing. For, however much any member of his audience might know about the poet's external circumstances, he would seem to receive through the exposed personality of the dreamer a sense of closer association, of insight into the poet's inner self, again perhaps illusory, but corresponding also in degree of depth to the poet's involvement in the dreamer. His feeling that he 'knew' the poet might be as much a fictive impression as his experience of those parts of the poem where the narrator did not figure. But the direction of that feeling to an actual living and speaking man would diminish the distance between the actual and the literary experience and thus intensify the latter. The limited identity of the poet in time and space, and the unbounded life of the narrator in the world of the poet's imagination, would seem to cease to be discrete. Today, at a long remove, the volumes of inconclusive discussion register a corresponding effect; restored to contemporary terms they would signify excited interest—the indispensable first objective of the oral narrator. And when a modern critic writes of the narrator of *The Canterbury Tales* that 'he is almost the only figure in his "drama" who is fully realized psychologically, and who truly matters to us',[56] he records what may be one of Chaucer's most spectacular successes: to have given this reader the illusion of being admitted to a confidence which was, at the outset, withheld.

The situation arising out of the conventions of the dream-vision, and extending to other fourteenth-century poetry narrated in the first person, is then that there exists an inferentially necessary distinction of a designedly indeterminable character between the life and circumstances of the poet, whose imagination and language have brought narrator and narrative into existence, and that narrator, apparently speaking with the poet's voice, even named after him, to whom necessarily fictitious things happen in a structure of fiction. One part of the poet's technique is to suggest that these personalities

are identical, another part to imply the caution that we fix on particulars of identity at our peril. This situation by its nature denies any
necessary truth to externally unsupported biographical inference
from the poet's works. All logical considerations apart, it confirms
the fallacious character of such inference. Whatever sense of reality a
dreamer or narrator awakens in us, we have no historical authorization, just as we have no good logic, for imputing that dreamer's
particular attributes and circumstances and attitudes to the actual
poet. Meanwhile, by reference to the convention, it is almost
certainly the case that the dreamers and narrators of Chaucer and
Langland are not fictions in any total sense; that they do mirror to
some extent the actual men who created them. The question is to
what extent and in what respects they are fictions, and that question,
having been made designedly difficult for contemporaries in the first
instance, has as far as we are concerned become unanswerable.

We can then, as things are, have no biography of Langland, only
speculative 'lives', without historical necessity. The general
probability that there is autobiography in his poems becomes, in
respect of any particular detail, only a possibility, for the
establishment of which there is neither logic nor support from literary
history. We cannot know, if this matters, whether Chaucer got on
badly with his wife. There are some compensations, and not small
ones. In the case of *Piers Plowman* the indication of the convention is
powerfully for single authorship[57]—but that is another story. Applied
to Chaucer's poetry it seems to show, once and for all, that we have no
entitlement to take the words and attitudes of his narrators at their
face value. But as far as the lives of these poets go we are in the
hardest position of scholarship: obliged, in the face of tantalizing
biographical possibilities, to acknowledge that we cannot, and
strictly speaking should not try to, establish these.

2
Chaucer and the Idea of a Poet

There was a stage in the history of Chaucer scholarship when it was fashionable to describe his career as consisting of three periods, the first French, the second Italian and the third English. Merely because that categorization came to seem too simple, easy and rigid, it fell into disfavour. But there are two other, more serious reasons why it was bad. The first is that if the term is to mean anything Chaucer's 'English period' began with his original decision to write in English rather than in French or in Latin, or in all three languages like his contemporary John Gower. Another is that the three-part division, by placing Italian in the middle, suggests that the importance of Chaucer's Italian cultural experience decreased in his later years, whereas in fact what he learned from the Italian poets, by way of both theory and practice, was a continuing force throughout his career.

It seems more accurate to divide Chaucer's career into two periods set apart by a radical change in his *idea* of a poet: in the first he was content with the status and functions of a court poet and to that extent not his own master; in the second, which cannot be described by any single term, he had outgrown that status. Of course my division also is an oversimplified one. But I think it worth considering for its possible contribution to the understanding of the poet. For instance it corresponds significantly to sharp differences of tone about certain topics, notably the relation of the sexes and its representation in the convention of *fine amour*, between his demonstrably earlier and his later poetry. These differences of tone must by definition have originated in changed attitudes to both his subjects and his audiences, and those attitudes, in turn, derived from his conception of the proper functions and status of poets, and thus necessarily relate to his *idea* of a poet.

That Chaucer was much concerned, if not actually preoccupied, with the *idea* of the poet, his status, functions and appropriate skills, would be likely a priori merely from the circumstance that he knew himself to be one of the first poets, if not the first, to be writing in English with significant awareness of near-contemporary and contemporary literature in other vernaculars. But there is particular evidence of his concern in the high degree of self-consciousness that he exhibits in his poetry, specifically through the effect created there of a personality purporting to be that of the poet. That effect undoubtedly originated in the convention of dream-vision poetry whereby the poet gives to the narrator of the dream his own name and identity and even other of his attributes. But Chaucer developed the convention extremely and carried it over into poetry not of the dream-vision in kind, until the narrator of his poems comes almost to preoccupy the reader. The impression of authorial presence cannot be an accidental consequence of the poet's egotism but is necessarily deliberate and contrived. The more or less fictitious personality which Chaucer projects into his poetry must relate, positively, or negatively, or intermediately by distortion, to the actual poet's sense of identity and function.

That situation raises four questions. What kinds of theoretical information and what models might have contributed to Chaucer's formation and modification of his *idea* of a poet? What are the actual grounds for identifying a change in that *idea*? What might have been the reasons for the change? And what kind of poet was Chaucer at the end of it?

The answer to the first question must begin with the circumstance that in 1360, when Chaucer was between 17 and 20 years old, there were no English writings in which he could have found theoretical discussion of the poet as a class of individual, or indeed of poetry. As to models, there were no English poems of any distinction which could have served him in his situation. There was no national English literary tradition. Poetic activity was mainly regionally isolated, and the contact that individual poets, some of considerable distinction to judge by their works, had with other poets or poetry was mainly a matter of chance.

Such chance, however, greatly favoured Chaucer. As a Londoner, and connected with the Court from 1357 onward, he was situated both at the centre of English communication and most advantageously for foreign contacts. He seems, also, to have received as good an education as a layman could get in his time. That set of circumstances gave him Latin, and fashionable as well as

Anglo-Norman French. Thus he was both placed where, in all England, a man would most likely hear of what he ought to read, and had the languages to read it as well. The further circumstance that in his adolescence there occurred the first great upsurge of English national feeling is indirectly but still markedly significant for its powerful inducement to emulation, in particular to competition with French poetry, and for the effect of that inducement on his sense of identity.

What Chaucer's formal education taught him about poets and poetry can be simply listed: a sense of grammar, the basis of all learning; such understanding of rhetoric as the textbooks available in fourteenth-century England could convey; mastery of those aspects of logic which apply to the persuasiveness of statements; and the notion that the composition of poetry could be taught and learned, that poetry was schoolwork and a school subject. That would have been a joyless set of lessons had not there been examples in his textbooks of grammar and rhetoric from the best classical Latin poetry, as well as books of selections or *florilegia*, and had he not encountered the actual works of some classical Latin poets. From those he will have seen that poetry is not an academic exercise. In this respect English poetry also might have helped: not the romances, which will have seemed inferior to their French archetypes, but the lyric poetry. For, while early and mid-fourteenth century English lyrics lacked the social assurance of corresponding French poetry, they were superior in verbal music, in a melodic quality generally lacking in the French. That music Chaucer appears to have made his own and never to have lost. A contemporary writes that the whole country was full of love poems and songs which Chaucer composed in his youth.[1] One recalls how his Squire was gifted both in composing music and in writing lyrics for it.

The technical feature in which pre-Chaucerian English poetry was mainly deficient compared with the French was the lyric of fixed form. Not that English poetry lacked variety of stanza forms: those forms it had acquired from Provençal poetry during the Angevin connexion of the twelfth century and had carried over into fourteenth-century use principally in political and satirical verse. One single fixed lyric form, a poem for dancing, the carole, had by 1360 been introduced from Northern France and naturalized. But it was apparently Chaucer who introduced the fashionable song forms, balade, rondel and virelai into English practice. In the *Prologue* to

The Legend of Good Women he ascribes the composition of many such lyrics to himself.[2] By his early concern with the formal structure of verse, which he retained all his life, Chaucer was realizing the concept of the poet as technician, an important aspect of the *idea* of court poet.

His models in that particular were initially two French poets, Nicole de Margival, who was active about 1300, and Guillaume de Machaut, who died in 1377. Chaucer apparently knew the one entire poem by de Margival, *Le Dit de la Panthère*, which has survived, and will have noted how it named and exhibited nine distinct lyric forms within its dream-vision frame.[3] His borrowings from and imitations of Machaut appear relatively extensive. Simply because Chaucer made evident use of that poet's work English scholars have tended to overrate him: he can be very long-winded and his humour is laboured. His French contemporaries valued him more justly as a composer of music first and a versifier second. Indeed his poetry shows the fine technical finish associated with musician-poets, and in that particular he was a good model for the young Chaucer.

Machaut was also a highly successful court poet, most of whose longer works are a record of his relations with successive patrons. The concept of court poet with its implications of subservience can seem repugnant in our time. In the Middle Ages this was not necessarily the case; the submission of loyalty and service in return for support and security need not seem degrading; to please a patron need not involve loss of self-respect. There is one poem by Chaucer, *The Book of the Duchess*, usually dated 1369, where he unmistakably writes as court poet for an identifiable patron. The extent to which that poem borrows from Machaut suggests how closely Chaucer studied his model's conduct of the relation between poet and prince. In such a relation the critical point would be when its continuation must unbearably affront the poet's intelligence, or moral sense, or self-respect. In Chaucer's case that moment was yet to come. In his middle twenties he seems to have been able to sustain the role and even to enjoy representing its elegant attitudes, and himself as their exponent.

One set of postures which a court poet had to represent and appear to promote was that of *fine amour*, of elegant love. Appropriately to do so he had to pose as the devotee of the God of Love, as the servant of that god's servants, and as himself an aspiring (usually un-successful) lover. For all this there were plenty of models, mostly deriving from the archetypal first part of the *Roman de la Rose*, including the poems of Machaut. Again it seems likely that the young Chaucer took pleasure in successfully mastering that poetic idiom. But it was essentially absurd, as its intelligent exponents had understood and recorded from the very outset of its vogue in Provence, and it will not have been long before Chaucer's superior intelligence found •thàt absurdity oppressive. Even in his early reading of the *Roman de la Rose* he will certainly have been struck by thc intellectual inferiority of the first, the romantic part, and by the superior correspondence of the satirical second part to actuality.

Chaucer never ceased to absorb French literary culture, but after its first powerful effect upon him in the decade from 1360 to 1370 his obligation to it was more for additional detail of information than for enlargement. As new poems by Machaut circulated, and as Froissart displayed his imitations of Machaut in England, so Chaucer learned not new poetic attitudes to new subjects, but a wider variety of attitudes to the same subjects, more refinements of the same situations. A new generation of French poets, including Chaucer's contemporaries Deschamps and Granson, did not change this. Granson's poetry was skilful and pretty but without significant content. Deschamps, the most intelligent of the four I have named, did break out of the repertory of dream-vision and compliment poetry. Moreover he wrote a little manual of poetic composition, *L'Art de Dictier*,[4] which expresses several important principles: that the phonetic value of poetry is an element in its emotional effect; that there can be a correlation between rhyme schemes and the intellectual content of a poem; that words can be arranged more, or less musically; and that to produce musical verse calls for an inborn aptitude which cannot be taught by even the best teacher, and which needs only *un petit de regle* to fulfil itself.[5] Chaucer had that aptitude to a higher degree than Deschamps and no doubt sensed those principles without ever formulating them. Nevertheless, if he read the *Art de Dictier* it was good for him to find them expressed authoritatively there by another expert versifier in another language. But Deschamps, for all that, was a court poet. His *Art de Dictier* begins, indeed, by asserting that the composition of poetry as a branch of the liberal arts is reserved to *fils de noble homme et astrait de noble lignie*,[6] to a man ofhigh breeding and good descent. Chaucer as the son of a man in trade, a commoner, would not be able to take that assertion seriously.

For larger ideas of the poet and his art, for models of a kind not to be found in French, and for a final extension of his verse technique, Chaucer was indebted to Italy, specifically to Dante, Petrarch and Boccaccio. From the extensive borrowings and imitations identified in his poetry it is certain that he read the *Divina Commedia* and was acquainted with a considerable amount of both the prose and poetry of Petrarch and Boccaccio. While he may well have learned Italian before he ever set foot in Italy[7] it is likely that he acquired his knowledge of those three poets, and probably copies of works by them, during the 1370s when, from documentary evidence, he was in Italy at least twice on the king's business.

In Italy he will certainly have found an immensely stimulating intellectual climate. Because of Dante's achievement vernacular poetry had acquired a new status: men were speaking and writing of him and of his poetry in terms such as had previously been reserved for ancient Latin writers. There was recognition of the distinction of the poet as a class of individual. He was a rare being. The impulse which drove him to composition was described as *fervor*, a frenzy. There was discussion of that intoxicating concept, inspiration. The vernacular poet could immortalize himself by his poetry as had the ancients. He belonged to a European tradition which stemmed from them. But the fulfilment of his role demanded exacting qualifications and imposed responsibilities.

If Chaucer came upon Boccaccio's *De Genealogia Deorum Gentilium* he will have found those and other, related notions gathered up in the seventh chapter of its fourteenth book. If he did not actually handle the work he will still have heard in Italy the kind of conversation in which such notions figured. He will have measured himself, the court poet, in terms of them. Reading the *Divina Commedia* will have taught him the limitations of the French poetry on which so far he had modelled his own: its prolixity, its lack of intensity, its relative poverty of topics. By contrast here now were new, exciting ideas and values, and experience of a poetry more powerful than at the beginning of his own poetic undertaking he could even have imagined, a demonstration of how little he had achieved, and a new, grander scope for achievement. The Italian experience will have been chastening, but in compensation it enriched his knowledge of the ancient world and offered him a sense of community with its poets. There were also technical lessons: the most important a demonstration of the effectiveness of the five-stress line, which with sure instinct he adopted, first in stanzaic and then in couplet form.

Chaucer's Italian lessons, of the vernacular poet's status, dignity and obligations, and of the force which really serious poetry could generate, furnished criteria by which to measure the role of the court poet. From these it will now have appeared to him that writing mainly for the pleasure of patrons, in the modes which they fancied, and on prescribed topics which amused them, was an inferior activity. In particular the court poet's main topic, elegant love or *fine amour*, will now come to seem frivolous, deficient in seriousness and truth.

It is in Chaucer's attitude to this same poetic topic, and to its prose equivalent, the actual relation of the sexes, that the change in his idea of a poet seems to me identifiable. My identification rests upon his treatment of the love story in his longest completed work, *Troilus and Criseyde*, written in the middle 1380's. In that poem Chaucer examines the literary idealization of sexual love represented by *fine amour* in terms of a man's obsessive love for a woman whom circumstances force into inconstancy, and finds the sort of love which is appropriate to be idealized as *fine amour* illusory and destructive.

Chaucer's conduct of the examination amounts to a sustained display of remarkable insight into the motives that govern the behaviour of men and women in such situations. The insight in itself would not of course be evidence of any change in his attitude to the idea of a poet. Even the earliest exponents of *fine amour* had perfectly well understood the unreality of the mode and conventions in which they wrote. But they had sustained the pretence: they generally kept their idealized poetry and their scurrilous or anti-feminist writings distinct and separate. Correspondingly Chaucer's early court poetry was straightforward. The novel and striking feature of Chaucer's examination of *fine amour* in *Troilus and Criseyde* was the manner in which, by only pretending to observe the pretence of idealization, he tested the convention in terms of itself. What he did was to use the ameliorative terms of *fine amour* and to subscribe ostensibly to its values, while representing the actual sexual relationship with total psychological realism. The result was both outrageous to and condemnatory of *fine amour*, which he thus made to appear deficient in essential truth.

The first and principal evidence of Chaucer's prior dissatisfaction with the conventions of *fine amour* is his choice of the subject he represents in *Troilus and Criseyde*: a woman who though of angelic

beauty and high moral excellence (so the poem tells us) was nevertheless unable to remain constant to the man, himself also greatly
excellent, who loved her to distraction. The second is Chaucer's
representation of the love story through a dramatically projected
first-person narrator whose imperceptions and misconceptions constitute a factor in its meaning. That narrator is so grievously confused
about moral values that he thinks of praying to the God of
Christianity for the success of those who live by the poetic religion of
the god of erotic love. His memory is so short that having begun his
story by announcing its unhappy ending, he quickly forgets this and
become involved emotionally to the extent that the advent of the
catastrophe at the end appears to surprise him. His discernment is so
poor that even while proclaiming the excellence of Criseyde he seems
to imply question of her motives and integrity. The third is Chaucer's
representation of the two lovers as brought together by the procurer,
Pandarus. Conventionally he is the 'confidant' of *fine amour*, which
circumstance should have obscured the moral aspects of his agency.
But Chaucer departs from his source to make him Criseyde's young
uncle, which is shocking, represents him as aware that his service to
Troilus is unsavoury, and by one dark incident seems to suggest that
there is some kind of reprehensible complicity between uncle and
niece. The fourth is expressing, at the end, in Christian moral terms,
outright condemnation of the excessive and delusory love of created
beings. I mean none of this to belittle the magnificent representation
of the splendours and miseries of human love that the poem constitutes. My point is that it shows Chaucer no longer able to acquiesce
in his own heart in the pretences of *fine amour*, in the sham required
of the court poet.

His change of attitude appears to have been neither sudden nor
comfortably accommodated. If one looks back from *Troilus and
Criseyde* there are signs of it in *The Parliament of Fowls*, a dream-
vision poem dated about 1381 and showing much influence of Dante
and Boccaccio. The poem is not easy, mainly because the relation of
its three parts is not explicit. The reader has to relate them like the
panels of a triptych, and they can have the appearance, then, of
comparative studies of several concepts of love. The first panel of the
'triptych' considers it philosophically; the second, deriving from
Boccaccio's *Teseida*, is an allegorization of libido with unmistakable
moral overtones; the third represents a small number of the
extravagances of *fine amour* in terms of a courtship of birds of exalted

nobility. The whole poem has the look of an attempt to appraise sexual ethics without reference to either Hebraic tribal customs or the emotional exaltation of chastity deriving from the Pauline Epistles, simply in terms of comparative unselfishness, self-regulation, good taste and personal dignity, that is by wholly secular standards. In the third part, where the exalted and ineffectual courtship is represented, and there are suggestions of topical reference, the superior grace and elegance of the noble birds are obvious, but there are also vulgar opinions and comments expressed by plebeian birds which often make better sense. The poem could be viewed as an exercise in preparation for the full-scale study of *Troilus and Criseyde*.

Chaucer's next poem after *Troilus and Criseyde*, the *Prologue to the Legend of Good Women*, dated about 1386, enacts in a dream-vision the social predicament of a court poet who has actually expressed his disenchantment with *fine amour* in his poetry. The device Chaucer uses, borrowed from either Machaut or Froissart, if not from both, is to represent the dreamer-poet as under accusation of blasphemy, heresy and apostasy by the God of Love. The dreamer-poet's defender against those charges is Alcestis, the paragon of all womanhood, in whom a topical reference to Chaucer's patroness Queen Anne has been detected. The *Prologue* has such exquisite beauty and sweetness of tone as to rule out any possibility that Chaucer would have wished to offend his patroness, but not withstanding its courtesy and unmistakable affection for Alcestis-Anne it is wholly uncompromising. Alcestis is made to defend the poet against the God's accusations, but the grounds that she brings forward for pardoning him lack both relevance and any force. She says the accusations may not be true; the foolish poet, as an obsessive versifier, cannot resist writing about any topic that comes his way; he did not actually realize what he was doing; he was only translating and adapting and so not responsible for what was said; he has written so much anyway; he has done the best he can, etc. The eagerness of Alcestis in proffering such a bundle of poor excuses can be read as Chaucer's recognition of the kindness of the patroness. But the excuses remain poor or inapplicable notwithstanding, and bearing in mind that the historical poet wrote all the parts and manipulates all the puppets this must signify by irony that same poet's refusal to take at all seriously any charges of offence by him against *fine amour*. The fashion in which the dreamer-narrator thanks Alcestis, 'May the God above reward you for having caused the God of Love to relent his anger toward me', simply by recalling the ascendancy of Christian moral considerations, reduces the courtly game of eros to profane absurdity.

Those three poems, of which the sequence is certain, and which belong to the middle of Chaucer's career, that is to the period between 1380 and 1389, evidence his courteous but thoughtful and decisive rejection of *fine amour* and of the court poet's obligation to promulgate it in a posture of servant of the God of Love and his servants. They mark the major change in Chaucer's idea of a poet. Accounting for that change will necessarily to some extent be speculative; it must touch questions of artistic and personal integrity, of a sense of identity, and of self-respect.

There are some certainties to take into account. One is how badly French poetry will have emerged from comparison with that of Dante, an operation which could not fail to seem a juxtaposition of the trivial and the splendid. The *Divina Commedia* was concerned with issues of absolute moment; its style was vibrant with intellectual energy; it rose, and not seldom, to sublimity, a quality which Chaucer's borrowings and attempts to imitate show that he recognized. For a single detail of contrast we have Machaut, the admired model of the French school, writing in a time when war had made his country into a desert, able to complain apparently without shame how difficult this made travelling to visit one's mistress.[8] The intellectual content of fourteenth-century French poetry was mainly derivative of thirteenth-century thought, or else was slight and thin; the subjects were frequently trifling; the effects frequently prosaic. The fourteenth-century French poets themselves seem to have lacked a sense of relative values, or else to have been ignoring them. Whatever humanistic conceptions of the rarity of poets as human beings, of their exalted status, of the seriousness of their function and of the superior truth of their art Chaucer may have acquired from Italian culture, the poets and poetry of France in his time will have measured up to them poorly at best.

A second certainty is that by 1385 the frivolity of the elegant shams of court poetry will have been finally impressed upon Chaucer by the condition, both political and spiritual, of his own country. The manifestations of that condition were as complicated and extensive as the causes in which they originated and I can here only sum them up by describing their effect as a general and fundamental anxiety about the future, whether of individual souls, or of the Church, or of England, or indeed of Christendom. Both the permanence and the validity of institutions and beliefs which for many centuries had conferred a sense of security were being called into question. In those conditions the exercise of his talent, which by 1385 Chaucer must have known to be of the first order, merely for the diversion of his nineteen-year old patroness or her even younger and already evidently wayward and irresponsible husband the king, for pampered children it might have seemed, cannot have enhanced his self-respect.

By 1385 also Chaucer cannot have avoided measuring his own adequacy to the responsibilities imposed on a poet, both by the idea of his status and by the special nature of his gifts, against William Langland's *Vision of Piers Plowman*, composed in the 1370s, which rapidly attained wide currency, and possibly even became notorious through the adoption of the name of its hero by the insurgent peasants of 1381 as a rallying cry.

Piers Plowman is not an easy poem; I do not suppose that Chaucer found its peculiar manner of expressing concern about contemporary issues anything but perplexing. At the same time he cannot have mistaken its seriousness, the depth of the anxiety it expressed, and its power. In the particular of uncompromising dedication to the values which its poet considered absolute *Piers Plowman* of all English poems comes nearest to the *Divina Commedia*. Like Dante, moreover, Langland had the rare poetic gift of sublimity. Here then, Chaucer found a poem in his own language, indeed in an unstylish upcountry metre, yet nevertheless matching in some qualities the great Italian work that he himself could never manage to imitate successfully for more than a few lines at a time. *Piers Plowman* will have disturbed Chaucer in at least three other ways. The first is by its poetic excellence, which nothing in his previous reading can have prepared him to expect from a poem in English. The second is by the very unusual combination of devout religiosity, intellectual integrity and linguistic virtuosity from which its power derives. The third is by its content. For where the *Divina Commedia*, by enabling an intense aesthetic experience of a harmonized system of theological and political doctrines, had the capacity to reassure and to comfort, *Piers Plowman* was calculated to have a contrary effect. Its poet was certainly devout, and expressed total abhorrence of heresy. But the poem touches very many, if not most, of the potentially subversive theological ideas current in the Europe of its time, and some of them it can dispose of only by violent, even abusive condemnation coupled with the injunction to avoid the sin of questioning God's mysterious ways: doubt must not be abolished by intellection but be suppressed by an act of faith. And the best comfort that *Piers Plowman* the poem can offer is the conviction that since it is inconceivable for divine grace to fail mankind, therefore grace will necessarily be forthcoming.

In that poem Chaucer found grave and immediately contemporary issues treated in English by a poetic talent of the first order. The poem confronted those issues directly and, to judge from the outspokenness of the criticism it expresses, did so without regard to the poet's self-interest. Chaucer's experience of reading it will have brought home clearly to his judgement the limitations of poetry designed merely or mainly to afford, by ingenuities of elegance, distraction from an uncomfortable present and escape into worlds of pretence. He will also have sensed what acceptance of those limitations might imply about the integrity and self-respect of poets who, being capable of better things, were content with the lesser enterprise.

To those certainties I will now add a possibility, that Chaucer's sense of his own standing as a court poet, as the poet of ladies, might have been diminished by reading Guillaume de Machaut's *Le Voir Dit*, 'the true poem', which was written in 1363–4.[9] That poem Machaut presents as an autobiographical account. He tells how he received a letter from a young gentlewoman who had never seen him, professing that she had fallen in love with him for the excellence and reputation of his music and verse, how in due course they met, how a relationship of *fine amour* developed between them, how once for his comfort she allowed him some considerable degree of intimacy (this part of the story he veils in an allegory), how they were estranged and then reconciled. He claims to have written the poem as it were day by day as a record of their affair, and inset in it there are lyrics which the two exchanged as occasion arose. Machaut names the girl by anagram (a device he often uses): she was Peronelle of Armentières. A historical person of that name has been identified.[10]

No interpretation of this poem does any credit to Machaut. If it were simply a verse record of a sexual fantasy, then to introduce a real person as its subject would be shocking. If the poem were a deliberate travesty of *fine amour*, to put a real person into it would be brutally cruel. If the story is autobiographical as its editor believed,[11] then the poem is in very bad taste.

Other considerations apart the poem offends against two principles of *fine amour*—a term which Machaut introduces into its text often enough to establish the convention as his context. Simply by existing the poem can be held to violate the great principle of discretion, of secrecy; but Machaut seems actually to have let other people see it; 'several great lords', he reports, asked for a sight of it and he agreed.[12] And second, by his report of the girl's emotional surrender and physical kindness to him he appears as a sexual boaster, an *avauntour*: guilty of another terrible crime against *fine amour*. The poem is actually smug in its detail of her loving correspondence. It reports how she writes to the poet that she will do all she can to please him.[13] She calls him her heart, her love and everything she desires.[14] 'I shall apply', so he sets her down as having written, *& cuer & corps & une partie de mon honneur . . . à faire de quanque je saray qui vous porra donner joie & confort*, that is, 'both heart and body, with a part of my honour (or does this mean chastity?) to do to the best of my understanding what will be able to give you happiness and comfort'.[15] After these offences there remained only one capital sin against *fine amour* to commit, namely inconstancy. Our court poet, even though he appears innocent of this last sin, shows up badly.

Moreover his behaviour realistically viewed is that of a stock target of medieval satire, *senex amans*. Machaut, when all this happened, was well over 50 years old, afflicted with gout and a hypochondriac, with defective vision in one eye. He also happened to be rather small, and self-conscious about his stature. The girl was 18 years old and quite tall. Machaut seems not to have sensed what an undignified figure he was cutting by his own report, both in general and of particulars like the occasion when Peronelle sent him parts of a headdress she had worn at a sentimental meeting and he proceeded to behave like the green girl in the *chanson de croisade*,

Si près de mon cuer les mettoie
Et de mon corps, com je pooie.[16]

There are enough satirical representations of besotted old men in Chaucer's poetry to indicate that he would be alert to this aspect of *Le Voir Dit*.

Seen as the work of a court poet *Le Voir Dit* appears a disgraceful exhibition: there is a further circumstance in the light of which it was actually scandalous. Machaut was in holy orders; at one time he actually held three canonries and a perpetual chaplaincy.[17] Just precisely what all that implies about his clerical status I have not yet managed to establish, but canons were technically required to be celibate and a chaplaincy, implying pastoral duty, suggests that he was an ordained priest. Now whatever the spiritual condition of France may have been in the 1360s and 70s, in England at that time criticism of clerical delinquency was continuous, loud and severe. An English reader of *Le Voir Dit* would not have been amused by a priest's or even a clerk's report of how, kneeling beside a girl's bed, he spoke the following devotion,

> Venus, je t'ay tousjours servi
> Depuis que ton ymage vi . . ..
> Tu ies ma dame & ma deesse.[18]

or his telling how he met the girl in church, how they kissed behind the pillars, and how he afterwards found it hard to concentrate on his devotions,[19] or by his parodies of the litany to the Virgin Mary in praising the girl,[20] or worst of all by reading how, suspicion having arisen between them, he finally recovered his trust of her through her confessor telling him her confessional secrets.[21]

How strong is the possibility that Chaucer read *Le Voir Dit* and reacted as I have suggested? It has recently been proposed that Chaucer 'evidently knew most of Machaut's numerous works'.[22] Editors of Chaucer have identified some possible echoes of *Le Voir Dit* in his poems and I could add a few, but none of this is conclusive. It is more impressive to observe how the mature Chaucer pointedly adopts certain attitudes directly opposed to those of Machaut in *Le Voir Dit*, in view of his readiness to copy from his other works. For instance Machaut will register anxiety whether a woman can think of loving a man of his unlikely shape, but Chaucer rejoices that his unaptness sets him at liberty. 'Look', he proclaims in a lyric, 'how fat I am! Love has not taken away *my* appetite, and I do not intend that He shall'.[23] Machaut pronounces that a poet can write authentically about love only from experience; Chaucer (incidentally a more perceptive observer of the behaviour of lovers than Machaut) insists that he is without experience and is only writing of what he finds in books, in his authorities. The list could be extended. Chaucer, as if anxious not to resemble Machaut in this, calculatedly projects an impression of his own unaptness for love.

Still nothing is proved by this, any more than by the circumstance that there are satirical fourteenth-century poems in both French and English about dissolute canons who hold benefices without heed for their pastoral obligations.[24] Nor is there proof in the circumstance that Chaucer's contemporary John Gower represents in *Confessio Amantis* how for an older man to be caught up with a young woman is a sickness from which he must wish to be cured.[25] It is more striking that Chaucer's other contemporary William Langland twice gives the name Peronelle to a woman connected with a dissolute priest, and indeed once calls her Peronelle of Flanders: of the three places in France named Armentières one was, at the time when Langland was writing, in the County of Flanders.[26] There is a further circumstance, that Machaut's Peronelle in one of her letters to him alludes to a romance where there is a personage called Peronne de Flandres, which might conceivably have suggested the association.[27]

Whether or not *Le Voir Dit* and unfortunate Peronelle became a scandal, if Chaucer saw the poem at all he certainly recognized how the status of poet was degraded by its spectacle of the aging, decrepit Machaut seeking rejuvenation as one last emotional adventure, and applying the shams of *fine amour* to embellish his unashamed account of his relation with a girl one third his age.

There is a judgment of *fine amour* which Chaucer sets into the *Manciple's Tale*, although the story does not need or call for it.

> Ther nys no difference, trewely,
> Bitwixe a wyf that is of heigh degree,
> If of hir body dishonest she bee,
> And a povre wenche, oother than this—
> If it so be they werke bothe amys—
> But that the gentile, in estaat above,
> She shal be cleped his lady, as in love,
> And for that oother is a povre womman,
> She shal be cleped his wenche or his lemman.[28]

'There is truly no difference between a woman of exalted rank and a poor servant girl who are unchaste except that the social superior is described in romantic terms, and the other in coarse abusive lan-

guage because she is a poor woman.' What is remarkable about this
passage is not the perception—that is not new—but the gratuitous-
ness and the strength of its expression. It must signify that Chaucer
had when he wrote it ceased to be willing to acquiesce in the
pretences of *fine amour*. There is disagreement about the date of the
Maniple's Tale. In the *Merchant's Tale*, which is agreed to be 'late',
Chaucer represents those pretences as positively ugly, in a totally
disenchanted account of a young woman deceiving her old husband.
It is the deceitfulness which offends him most. See how outrageously
he represents it: just before the woman betrays her husband she
swears to him, in tears, 'I have a soul to care for, and my honour, and
the tender flower of my womanhood which I put in your trust, and I
pray to God that if the day dawns on which I am false to you, I may die
most hideously. I am', she says, *'a gentil womman and no wenche'*.[29]
One can hear an echo in those words.

There Chaucer is ironic. At the end of *Troilus and Criseyde*, the
poem where he recorded his sense of the inadequacy of the *idea* of the
court poet and his commitment to *fine amour*, his stance of the poet as
moralist is unmistakable. The injunction to young persons to turn to
the love of Christ is deeply moving but also very plain. This might
suggest that concern for moral issues has now become a part of
Chaucer's new *idea* of a poet. He does not, however, maintain the
stance of poet as moralist for the rest of his career. And I would call
that stance at the end of *Troilus and Criseyde*, in its application of
standards of Christian morality to *fine amour*, more a declaration of
independence of that mode than a dedication of his art to the cause of
morality. He has asserted a liberty which will characterize his subsequent work; he is going to write, now, for himself. But the sense of
liberty does not express itself in attitudes of defiance. It is, rather,
maintained through a system of variable irony which functions by the
ingeniously contrived personality of the narrating voice, the quasi- or
else pseudo-authorial 'I' of the story-teller.

Within his new liberty Chaucer was free to experiment with a wide
variety of expressions of the poet's activity; and thereafter his
writing, as far as it can be dated, shows with increasing frequency
evidence of his pleasure in the investigation. We see the poet as
philologist and rhetorician, the poet as a man of letters, an obsessive
reader who owns a large library, all of 60 books, the poet as natural
philosopher, or as moral philosopher, above all the poet as
increasingly expert technician. In those roles, which correspond

remarkably to Boccaccio's prescription of the skills required of a poet, Chaucer experimented, borrowed and innovated with fluctuating seriousness but with a constant virtuosity of expression that was to command the admiration of the next generation of English poets and to initiate the English poetic tradition. I suspect, however, from the number and variety of Chaucer's experiments, that he never did succeed in reconstituting a whole *idea* of a poet to his satisfaction.

Indeed the nature of his cultural experience and its timing together were calculated to devalue one kind of poetic identity without providing another to replace it. There are two main circumstances which will have hindered the replacement. The first will have been the overwhelming pressure of fourteenth-century English ecclesiastical, social and political conditions to the moral orientation of the interest of any person both serious and honest with himself, the second the prevalent anti-intellectualism which discouraged speculative thinking. Certainly Chaucer felt the pressure to moral concern, and it is evident from the texture of the *Canterbury Prologue* and of a number of the tales that he was doctrinally equipped to examine behaviour in moral terms. As to speculative philosophy, his Clerk may have had twenty volumes of Aristotle by him, but Chaucer's own philosopher was the unadventurous and reassuring Boethius.

So in the end Chaucer did return to the moral stance, and I think wholeheartedly, but at the cost of some pride in his achievement. There can be no doubt about his commendation of the saintly Parson of the Canterbury pilgrimage. In describing the Parson the pilgrim-narrator ceases to be obtuse; his attidues and his terminology become those of the professional ecclesiastical reformer, remarkably echoing Langland; his confusion about wordly and spiritual values vanishes. Speaking now with the author's voice he represents the Parson as full of grace, and implies that a return to that condition, a spiritual regeneration, is what England needs. One might judge from Chaucer's accounts of some of the other pilgrims that he had doubts whether such a regeneration would come. But the tone of his representation of the Parson, no less than his own contrition and prayer to be forgiven for his poetry, record his hope for it nevertheless. The expression of that hope matches the cry for grace at the end of *Piers Plowman*. Chaucer's poet, finally, is a fourteenth-century soul needing to be saved.

3
Chaucer, Love Poetry, and Romantic Love[1]

By Chaucer's love poetry I mean the dramatic love lyrics embedded in his narrative works and such of the narratives themselves as are concerned with emotional as well as physical arousal in the relation of the sexes, therefore love poetry objectively understood.

The immediate and obviously primary factor in the shaping of that love poetry is what a fairly recent book tells us to swallow our historical scruples and go on calling 'courtly love.' This it describes as 'a comprehensive cultural phenomenon: a literary movement, an ideology, an ethical system, a style of life, and an expression of the play element in culture.'[2] The description is too broad to be serviceable, too miscellaneous and too positive. I will offer another: what Chaucer once called 'fyn lovynge,'[3] and what in the Auchinleck *Floris and Blauncheflor* is called *fin amour* (establishing the expression as Middle English),[4] was a shifting nexus of forms of thought and expression, associatively linked and reciprocally evocative in particular sets of ways, developed to express a fairly narrow class of emotions in the relation of the speaker of a poem with a woman or of lovers in a narrative; the forms of thought and expression being first found in any density in the twelfth-century lyrics called Provençal; having the appearance of conventionally established rhetorical and stylistic correlatives; but in the poetry first of Provence, and then the imitating cultures, represented as accepted values in the milieu where the relationship was set.

Chaucer was interested in the manifestations of this phenomenon transmitted to him and represented himself as puzzled by the lack of definition in his understanding of it. *In nouncerteyn*, says Troilus (*TC* 1.337–8, jibing at lovers to keep his countenance, *ben alle youre observaunces, But it a sely fewe pointes be* ('Your rites and observances are all matters of uncertainty except, maybe, a few trifling particulars'). Chaucer seems to have sensed that the phenomenon had a history: the language of love changes with time and place, his narrator suggests early in the second book of *Troilus*, *for to wynnen love in sondry ages, In sondry londes, sondry ben usages* (lines 27–8). He was familiar with the commonplaces about the perplexing character of love. To match Bernart de Ventadorn's *Ai las! tan cuidava saber/d'amor, et tan petit en sai*,[5] or Walther von der Vogelweide's *Saget mir ieman, waz ist minne?*[6] there is the question in his third *Compleynt of Mars*, '*To what fyn made the God that sit so hye,/Benethen him, love other companye?* 'What was God's lofty purpose in creating upon earth love or the relation of the sexes' when they have no power to confer lasting happiness (lines 218–19)? His *locus classicus* will have been Jean de Meun's long list of paradoxes lifted from or imitating Alanus: love is a hateful peace, a security set in anxiety, despairing hope, wise madness a joy full of misery, bitter sweetness, and so on.[7] He knew the clichés: the power of love, the folly of resisting it, how it improves the lover.[8] He could have resolved the paradoxes philosophically or dismissed them by theological means.

That he chose rather to make literary capital of them and their contexts of convention—for which we must give thanks—bespeaks his interest not just naturally in the human experience to which *fine amour* relates but also in its serviceability to the literary artist, and probably also in its relation to actuality, observed experience.

The lack of definition in Chaucer's understanding of *fine amour* is not surprising. First, total ambiguity, pretence, was a feature of the phenomenon from the outset. Second, acknowledgement of that ambiguity, explicit in the work of the last generation of troubadours who wrote in the *langue d'oc*, resulted in a profound change of attitudes in the poet-speaker to the lady he addressed. Then presently the conventions were subjected to successive modifications, whether actual or by selection and redistributed emphasis, by the French and Anglo-Norman *trouvères*, by Chrétien de Troyes and his successors,[9] by the Italian poets, by Guillaume de Lorris, and ultimately by Guillaume de Machaut and Jean Froissart.

It is not impossible—one should go no farther—that Chaucer saw poetry from all these phases. Collections of Provençal poetry, *chansonniers*, existed by his time.[10] He would have learned to read the language, *A maner Latyn corrupt*, easily enough, and Anglo-Norman imitators of the toubadours left texts about.[11] He knew the *Roman* (both parts, evidently) well enough, had read about Beatrice in the *Divina Commedia*, had seen at least one sonnet of Petrarch's.[12] The more extensive his reading, the greater his sense of a confused situation is likely to have been. Today, even with the advantage of historical perspective, students of medieval love poetry find the variety, the apparent inconsistency, the chronological and regional diversities of fine amour disconcerting (witness Boase's uncritical omnibus definition) and long for clear, positive factuality: there ought to be a code, something definitive to get one's teeth into.

Of course, there was never anything of the kind. The most striking feature of Provençal love poetry is the deliberately cultivated, flamboyant individualism of its composers, self-conscious performers striking attitudes, one of which was to pretend to entire sincerity, making their own rules, and essentially serious only about their virtuosity, of poetic technique, of linguistic and conceptual resource, and of music.

To coterie audiences such poets represented themselves personally and exceptionally as in a state of sexual tension, deliberately stimulated and carefully maintained, expressed in wittily extravagant language to a woman whose identity they made a show of concealing. She was 'the best'; to be desiring her was preferable to actually possessing some other woman: *Mais vuolh de vos lo deman/Que autra tener baisan.*[13] At the same time in the classic period of Provençal composition there was little if any spiritualization of her: whether directly or indirectly the poetic speaker registers his eroticism. The one I quoted has just said of the same woman, *par a la veguda/La fassa bo tener nuda* ('it's easy to see what a pleasure it would be to have hold of her naked') (lines 49–50). *Saber ben domnejar*, being an adept at expressing that class of specialized arousal and uncomfortable euphoria, called for technical expertise but, even more, for facility in witty novelty of concept and expression, ingenuity in making one's own set of rules within the outside limits. The consequence is a greater diversity of attitudes in the poetry as a whole than the generalized themes of *fine amour* if abstracted (as, for instance, in *The Allegory of Love*) would lead one to expect.

To compound this variety, there is the circumstance that awareness of the preposterous and essentially self-contradictory nature of *fine amour* was registered by the poets from the earliest period. It is behind the calculatedly obscene verse of Guillaume de Poitiers, the first recorded troubadour.[14] It expresses itself in open moral criticism from his near contemporary, Marcabru. Moreover, common sense keeps creeping in. Here is Bernart de Ventadorn, most exquisite of the love poets: 'Whoever heard of doing penance before the sin? The more I beg her the harder she is to me.' *Mas si'n breu tems no·s melhura/vengut er al partimen* ('but if she does not soon become more agreeable it will have come to separation').[15] And in the early thirteenth century there is Peire Cardenal's scathing poem, *Ar me puesc ieu lauzar d'amors*, built of and ridiculing most of the clichés of the poetry of *fine amour*.[16]

The thirteenth century also saw an increase of sublimation in troubadour love poetry, the tendency which was to characterize its Italian derivatives. At the same time the deep cynicism inherent in Provençal *fine amour* from the outset became wholly explicit, as in this passage from a poem by Daude de Pradas:

> I have now some pleasure from all the benefits that there are in love. For I have set all my hope, my thought and my application upon loving a gracious and beautiful lady; and I am loved by a young girl; and when I find a lively whore I take my pleasure with her. And I am not the less considerate of love if I divide it in three.
>
> It is Love's wish that I should love my lady with appropriate fervour so as to become of greater worth. And I love the young girl so as to keep her loving me. And above that, for my pleasure, I arrange to sleep one or two nights from month to month with some girl who is good in bed, not jaded, and discreet, to pay my dues to love.
>
> The man who wishes to possess his lady entirely knows nothing at all about the service of love. It is not loving service (*dompneis*) when the desire for full possession is realized.

Non sap de dompnei pauc ni pro
qui del tot vol se donz aver.
Non es dompneis, pois torn'a ver.[17]

As I interpret this poem it is not an expression of the decadence of Provençal *fine amour* but rather one of total candour about it. The pretence inherent in the cult from the outset is exposed: devotion to the lady is of a very limited and special kind, calling for little self-denial: libido is satisifed elsewhere. Think of the possibilities of misrepresentation in quoting those last three lines.[18]

I turn my back on the temptation to speculate about any resemblance between Daude's three kinds of women and those in Saint
Bernard's sermon on Canticles 1.3, *Introduxit me rex in cellaria sua*,
namely, *regina*, *adolescentula* and *concubina*,[19] to look at subsequent
developments of *fine amour*, which, by the differences they exhibit,
would, on the one hand, intrigue and perplex Chaucer to the extent
that he saw them as discrepancies in a whole and, on the other, make
generalizations in our own time perilous.

The first development is one of transplantation. It is notably
instanced in France by the poetry of the *trouvères* of the twelfth and
thirteenth century[20] and in England, on the one hand, by a small
number of anonymous Anglo-Norman love lyrics[21] and, on the other,
by some Middle English verse of the late thirteenth or early fourteenth century.[22] The striking feature of this situation is that, in at
least one particular, their occasional open, even blasphemous
eroticism, the Middle English lyrics are closer to the Provençal than
are the French:

> He myhte sayen þat Crist hym seȝe
> þat myhte nyhtes neh hyre leȝe,
>   heuene he heuede here.

'The man who was able to spend the night with her could say that
Christ was looking on him with favour; it would be heaven in this
world.'[23] The imitations by the French *trouvères*, while sometimes
very close to specific Provençal lyrics, were selective. Most of the
trouvère lyrics we have seem more abstract, more melancholy and
'romantic' than the Provençal types to which they formally correspond.[24] There are too few Anglo-Norman lyrics to generalize
about them: they are mainly important in suggesting that there were
others. There is no doubt that Chaucer saw at least Anglo-Norman
and English representatives of this phase. But the attitudes they
represent, though restricted and therefore differentiated as a
compound of conventions, are commonplaces of *fine amour*.

The essential differences come with the adaptation of *fine amour* as
an ethos of narrative, in the twelfth- and thirteenth-century French
romances: these are the main Northern French contributions to the
phenomenon. The adaptations are so radical as to amount to a major
transformation.[25] The first has to do with the ennobling force of love.
In Provençal poetry such improvement did not extend to the

troubadour's military performance. In the romances, by contrast, a direct connection between excellence as a lover and performance in battle was posited; to quote Jean Frappier, their theme was *armes et amour, encore et toujours*.[26] The second is an assumption, taken for granted in the romances after Chrétien, that romantic, exalted love could exist between the partners of a marriage. This sentimentalization of marriage in literature set up a radical difference, and a complicated one. It was socially problematic because of the actual women's subjection to their husbands in the law; it differed from actuality to the extent that marriages of the landowning classes were arranged by parents from considerations of property rather than the feelings of the young persons concerned. And it was morally sensitive in terms of the doctrine *Omnis ardentior amator propriae uxoris adulter est*: excessive affection in marriage was sinful.[27] Speculation about the reasons for this development is intriguing. There is the social one that societies at certain stages tend to restabilize themselves, or anyway to react against tendencies of instability; that might apply to the extent that *fine amour* reflected actual sexual mores. Another is simply that the religiosity of Northern French poets and their audiences (many of the romance writters were clerks)[28] was greater than that of the southerners, who had a name for irreligion. The development then appears as a moral rectification.[29] Yet another might be that the fabliau, having preempted adultery as a principal theme, socially devalued it and made it seem unfashionable as a component of polite or idealized narrative.[30] The likeliest reason, to my mind, is no more than a matter of literary practicality raised by the adoption of *fine amour* as a narrative ethos. In that genre, in a love story, marriage affords the ideal terminal objective. A lyric can fix a moment in an emotional career: outcome is not of consequence. But in the account of a drawn-out illicit love affair, the two possible endings are the decay of love, and death. So the 'immortal' lovers Tristan and Lancelot are paradoxically immortal lovers because they die in constancy of affection, their stories meanwhile having dragged on. One recalls that Chrétien did not finish his *Lancelot*, and how subsequent writers felt the need to endow the end of the affair with dignity and moment by associating it with the downfall of a kingdom. By contrast, in *Cligés*, with a freer hand, Chrétien could, after the sexual intrigue had begun to wear out its interest, bring all to a close and sanction the lovers' union in an ideal marriage. There is a third difference, less obviously radical, in the treatment of love in the thirteenth-century French romances. A marked interest appears in the mentality of lovers, as if the analyses of their disturbances of personality vied in interest with the events they were involved in.[31]

The analytic tendency is pronounced in the *Roman de la Rose*, which marks the next phase in the development of *fine amour*. Guillaume's gracefully erudite first part extends the analysis of the male lover's psychology and develops a blueprint of this; magnifies Ovid's Amor into a cult figure, a lord of terrible aspect; formulates his commandments; and, unexpectedly, raises the consideration of how the lady should behave. As for Jean de Meun, by deferring his declaration of authorship for some 6000 lines after he has taken over,[32] he reaffirms in *fine amour* an ambiguity even more extreme than that of its Provençal phase. For by that deferment the ostensible sweet idyllic idealization of the first part is set in a situation of imperative contrast, exposed to critical assay, weighed against rational, cynical, satirical disillusionment. The elegant courtship turns without warning into a deliberately prurient burlesque of, meanwhile, unmistakable philosophic implication. Such paradigm of play and reality is thenceforward a feature of *fine amour*. Whether or not Jean designed his continuation to form a unity with Guillaume's beginning, the text in Chaucer's day will have been read as a whole, the discrepancies of tone and literal sense deeply registered before the twofold authorship is discovered. As if that were not enough the *Roman* reaffirms the incompatibility of love and marriage. This poem was in Chaucer's blood.

The Italian version of *fine amour* he encountered in its extreme form in the *Divina Commedia*, a spiritualization of the woman addressed, to the point where it might seem immaterial whether she had a flesh-and-blood existence. In the Provençal lyric, we recall, she was for looks and manners and sometimes disposition 'the best,' but also a physical object; the poet wanted to touch her, and to have, in his language, *lo plus* ('the rest'). The Italian situation implied an unmistakable dichotomy, between a poetry professedly about love, characterized by great abstraction and intellectal toughness, and one of simple eroticism. A good instance is from Cavalcanti: in one poem he writes how love *Ven da veduta forma che s'intende* ('derives from a form seen and understood, which assumes, in the intelligence competent to receive it, a location and a place of stay as in a subject country')—a far cry from the heart-piercing *lanza* of love in

Provençal—and in another poem, *In un boschetto trova' pasturella*, represents (albeit exquisitely) the most elementary sexual fantasy.[33] He and the other Florentines who wrote in this manner were not court poets playing a game before a coterie but highly cerebral artists writing to satisfy themselves and to impress other poets of corresponding ability and cultivation. If Chaucer saw any of their work, as was chronologically and geographically possible, he may well have found it difficult through unfamiliarity with many of its concepts and references. Petrarch's love poetry might have seemed by comparison easier and, albeit spiritualized, much closer to his other experience of love poetry.

One more phase of *fine amour* relevant to Chaucer's love poetry, and at a further remove from the Provençal, is its manifestation in fourteenth-century France, most notably in the verse of Machaut, who was poetically active from the 1320s to 1377. Machaut's *fine amour* derives not from the imitators of the troubadours[34] but from Guillaume de Lorris.[35] What distinguishes it is Machaut's own involvement through his phenomenal prominence as court poet, an entertainer writing superb music and technically polished, if to some tastes insipid, verse for great magnates, a King of Bohemia, a King of Navarre, a Duc de Berry. The function of his poetry in that role, however disguised, would be to compliment the patron and his court, above all the ladies. There is an implication of subservience in his situation[36] which might be obscured by Machaut's eminence as a composer of music, and the urbanity of tone in much of his verse suggests that he was not embarrassed to make capital of his position. But one feature of it evidently struck Chaucer: a court poet had to appear knowledgeable about love, and only a man with experience of love could write truthfully about it: *Qui de sentement ne fait/Son dit & son chant contrefait*.[37] The court poet had necessarily to be himself in love. A good half at least of Machaut's considerable output purports to be about his emotional experiences, fanciful or actual, whether represented in lyrics, in allegorical narrative, or, in his last work, *Le Voir Dit*, the true story, as avowed autobiography. Moreover, Machaut was a cleric: at one time he held three canonries and a perpetual chaplaincy. That may for his French public have added spice to the interpretation of his allegorically recorded emotional life; it will certainly have endowed his account of the affair between the aging and decrepit priestly poet and a girl of under twenty with a certain sort of interest.[38] The story is further remarkable as a work of fine amour, where the secrecy of the affair and the good name of the mistress are paramount, and having regard to the degree of intimacy it reports, in that it gives the girl's name, in an anagram to be sure, but an easy one accompanied by directions for its solution.

Those various phases of *fine amour*, which we can see as historically related extensions of a single cultural phenomenon, would not have been discernible as such to Chaucer for all their greater proximity in time. He would see individual pieces, and might interpret evident differences of convention between them as discrepancies, any way of poetic practice. But by their differences they would promote eclecticism, a practical and pragmatic treatment; so his selective use of *fine amour* concepts and terminology and his identification of its more broadly interesting themes appear. He could certainly write most effectively in the high mode, as in Antigone's love hymn in *Troilus* II327, or in the lines of Prologue F to *The Legend of Good Women* beginning *She is the clernesse and the verray lyght*, which read like a personal love poem. But I nowhere find him appearing committed to the cult. He is mocking it already in *The House of Fame*; *The Parliament of Fowls* exposes it to cold philosophical and realistic examination; *Troilus* studies it in opposed terms of sexually generated illusion and moral actuality; above all it is represented in the Prologue to the *Legend* as a pretty game to be discreetly played. Alcestis, it will be recalled, is commended by the God of Love for having taught not merely *al the craft of fyn lovynge* but also 'in particular how a wife should conduct herself,' *namely of wyfhod the lyvynge*, and in a line which tends not to be noticed or quoted, *al the boundes that she oghte kepe*[39] 'all the limits which she ought to observe'.

His detachment invites speculation, and it is not enough merely to assert what is obvious—that *fine amour* was not something an intelligent person, even if a court poet, could take seriously in the second half of the fourteenth century in England. Detachment would develop for more particular reasons.

One such might be an increasingly critical view of his own situation as a court poet, expected to write for the diversion of patrons of inferior intelligence and cultivation. Striking the pose of devotee of the God of Love and servant of his servants had been part of his initial undertaking to import and naturalize contemporary French poetic modes. But with the ease of his mastery of these and the experience of Italian culture, the pose would become increasingly irksome. And if, as is possible, he came upon Machaut's *Le Voir Dit*, he is as likely as not to have read it as a crass exhibition of sexual boasting and indiscretion or as a paradigm of the ludicrous figure *senex amans*: it is only recently, after all, that Romance scholars have attempted to interpret the work as designed by Machaut to be ironically critical of *fine amour*.[40] What is not in doubt is that the mature Chaucer, in contrast to his earlier readiness to borrow from or imitate Machaut, pointedly adopts attitudes directly opposed to those of Machaut in *Le Voir Dit*.[41] He will not write any more love poetry like a court poet.

The conventions of *fine amour* were a main shaping influence on Chaucer's love poetry because of their intrinsic serviceability to him as a developing poet, because of their social vogue, and because, characterizing his first models, they equipped him with radical propositions that provoked examination of a primary human circumstance in terms of common sense and observed experience. But there was also an abundance of love poetry in the three languages Chaucer early commanded which had little to do with *fine amour* or which flouted it. This extended the range of masculine sensibility. For instance, into bitterness: a woman has kept her lover waiting too long before relenting; now she is no longer desirable, and he tells her so.[42] Or into fantasy: the poet meets a golden girl whose father is the nightingale and whose mother the siren, or he meets the daughter of the king of legendarily splendid Tudela; may God give him happiness, for he will never get her out of his head and heart.[43] In the pastorale Chaucer would find moral and social criticism of sexual selfishness and arrogance and pretence, or ridicule of the condescension of the gentleman who fancies he is conferring a favour on a shepherdess by propositioning her and is seen off by her peasant lover or her brothers or her dog. There he would be shown the woman's point of view in poetry.[44] This is dominant in the strain of French poetry that goes back (whether directly or by archaization) beyond the Provençal ascendancy to the popular lyric common to the romance cultures. These poems are about women, mainly unhappy in love: elegant ladies with antique names swooning for lovers who have been long away and then ride past their window,[45] young girls married to ill-natured or repulsive husbands,[46] girls whose lovers are away at or about to go on the crusade,[47] even a girl not yet fifteen, and lovely too, who feel sexual stirrings, *Je sens les doz maus desoz ma ceinturete*, and curses those who made her a nun.[48] It is because of necessarily assumed loss not possible to judge to what extent the variety of feeling suggested in such poetry was reproduced in Middle English counterparts. But Middle English poets do seem to have extended the range in one particular: there is a lyric representing the foolish infatuation of a girl with the priest who seduced her, and there are others in which the speaker is a girl seduced and then left pregnant.[49]

To what extent Chaucer was aware of how Ovid's multifaceted representation of the relation of the sexes underlay the European love poetry of his experience seems indeterminable. Two things, however, seem not in doubt. One is its presence: Ovid the profligate is behind *fine amour*: Ovid the student of his own and others' sexual psychology informs the *Roman de la Rose*; Ovid the mythographer furnishes always sensational, variously pathetic or ludicrous instances of the consequences of overpowering love; Ovid the man sensitive to the feminine predicament demonstrates a poetic register in *Heroides*. The other is that to the extent that Chaucer actually discerned Ovid's protean influence his awareness would have compounded confusion, if only because of the insistent moralization of his work by the French and Latin exegetes.[50]

Even an imperfect and ill-proportioned sketch of the multiplicity and variety of poetic concepts and matrices, of forms of thought, language and feeling for the composition of love poetry available to Chaucer must show how little likelihood there is of finding him in any unqualified alignment toward them. It is as if almost every intellectually or artistically attractive position in respect of this subject were matched by an equally attractive opposed or contradictory one. That literary situation alone must have amounted for Chaucer to an imperative to the exercise of judgment.

The shaping force of Chaucer's constantly enlarging poetic experience was, in the second and ultimately decisive instance, the accumulated and interactive structures of the philosophical and the pragmatically satirical and the canonical moral thinking of his time about the emotional and physical relationship of men and women. Elements of those structures are what the student of Chaucer encounters piecemeal in Robinson's notes or as selections in compilations of 'sources and backgrounds.' They stand there prominent and isolated, as often as not in apparent conflict. And indeed in the historically accidental sum of the fourteenth-century cultural fabric they were no more likely to have been harmonized than are the many discrepant concepts and attitudes in a modern person's world. As unresolved elements in an individual awareness they might qualify one another, interact and express the complexity of situations. In the fourteenth century, however, if the interaction went beyond that stage, it would likely end not in a harmonization but in the dominance of one element.

There is a case in point in *Troilus and Criseyde* (Book 1.232ff), where the narrator addresses the wise, proud, and eminent among his audience in a cautionary commendation of love. Love, he tells them, can quickly reduce their liberty of heart to serfdom; love will in all times and places turn out to be that which *alle thing may bynde*, love which has the power (and here the dictionary offers a wide choice) to join securely or fetter or ensnare or make subservient or unite harmoniously[51] all things, *For may no man fordon the lawe of kynde*, no man has the power to frustrate or annul the law of—does *kynde* mean just 'nature'? There is nothing in books, he goes on, about there being anyone more intelligent than those who were captured by love, or stronger or braver or more exalted. And this is as it should be, for the wisest of all have been gratified by love. In the dramatic situation the argument appears strong: that the law of nature cannot be frustrated seems incontrovertible, and no one in the audience is likely to think himself secure from love because more intelligent than Socrates or Aristotle or stronger than Samson or wiser than Solomon and so on. The point of interest is that, while in this context of sexually induced irrationality[52] Love must obviously mean Eros, in conjunction with *bynde* it signifies another order of love, that conceived of in neoplatonic thinking as the governing principle of the universe: *al this accordaunce of thynges is bounde with love, that governeth erthe and see, and hath also comandement to the hevene.*[53] And transcendingly *love* can mean the principle of the Great Commandment, the Pauline *caritas*. So the polysemy of *bynde* is unmistakable and necessarily significant. As for the rhyme word *kynde*, its usual meanings in the expression *lawe of kynde*, either 'law of nature' or 'natural moral law,'[54] are not at once evidently appropriate, and we look for others. If for instance *kynde* here means *natura naturans*, the creative principle,[55] then the law which no man can annul or frustrate is the sexual impulse with which species were endowed to ensure their continuation. And of course since 1370 or thereabouts *kynde*, from Langland's use of it, could also mean God the Creator.[56] As for the most intelligent and strongest and wisest men having been unable to resist love, the argument is a clerical commonplace: it evokes Socrates ruefully drying his head, or the 700 wives and 300 concubines who turned Solomon's heart from the Lord, or Aristotle, saddled and cavorting about the garden, ridden *De cheli que il voloit a ami,/Qui en le fin couvent ne li tint mie*,[57] by the girl he wanted, who in the end broke her word to him; that is, it recalls antifeminism.[58]

In that passage Chaucer has made fine capital of a number of conceptual schemes of greater or lesser order available in his cultural situation: as we identify them, they both invite and appear to defy resolution. We have recourse to the now quasi-formulaic explanation that he is writing ironically here; that is correct but inadequate. For irony, whether as a figure or as a mode of meaning, is also a symptom, and so here. The lines I look at begin the preparation for the re-ordering of love with which *Troilus and Criseyde* ends.

But I find more than just the reordering of love in Chaucer's poetry about the relation of sexes, and I wonder—to go further is not safe—whether there was not some circumstance in his own time and country which led to concern about sexual morality. Certainly the good Bishop Brinton was so concerned: of Luxury he said, 'This sin has reigned so scandalously among the magnates that I can invoke from the Psalms, as an applicable quotation, *contaminata est terra in operibus eorum*. As for adultery (he goes on, and these exact words he has used elsewhere) there is not a nation under heaven so disgraced by adultery as the English nation.'[59]

One knows the need to discount the repetitiousness and over-statement of the zealous preacher. Chaucer's concern I find expressed not in the strident tone of an anxious director of pastoral care but in studies large and small of the effects of sexuality. An obvious one which he examines extensively and intensively is the capacity of sexual selfishness to injure, to cause unhappiness: the first study is of Dido in *The House of Fame*, where significantly he adopts the pathetic Ovidian presentation. He reveals two sharp but contrasting insights into sex as a violation, an indignity, in the accounts of Constance's wedding night (MLT B 709–14) and January's apology to May, *Allas! I moot trespace/To yow, my spouse and yow greetly offende* (*MerT* E 1828–9), as if reading Peter Lombard's *foeda est et poena peccati* in those two radically different contexts. He conducts two set-piece studies of the extreme opposite of libertinism, namely virginity, one in a pagan ethos of the utmost rigor,[60] the other in the strictest Christian terms, where what a court poet would call *love paramours* is seen as love *in vileynye*, and sexuality is expressly *vileynye*.[61] He recognizes in Emelye the feeling of unawakened girls not ready for marriage (*KnT* A 2295ff). He inserts a remarkably gratuitous injunction of moral responsibility to those who have the care of young girls in *The Physician's Tale* (C 72ff.). How selfish and inconsiderate sexuality both deludes and destroys human dignity he represents in Sir January of *The Merchant's Tale*, one of the cruellest miniatures of satire in English literature; it is not impossible that he meant us to see the Wife of Bath—welcome the sixth!—in something like the same light. Then there is the Manciple's assertion of the humbug of *fine amour*: there is no difference between a gentlewoman and a maidservant who are unchaste except that in the one instance we use ameliorative language (*ManT* H 212–22). As to the effect of sexual selfishness upon integrity, *trouthe* in his language, he offers you May's histrionic, high-pitched speech just before she goes up the tree to her lover (*Mer T* E 2187–202), or the totally cynical monk and wife in *The Shipman's Tale*.

What conclusions a full and systematic examination of the kind I have just sketched might produce it is hazardous to forecast. One approaches studies like this with a presumption that they relate to soluble problems, but that may be a false presumption. It comprises too many others to feel secure, such as that an artist's career will develop along a uniform course; that if he accepts the absolute validity of the moral code in force in his time, he will always conform to it; that the literary works he produces will always perfectly represent his intellectual and moral position, to name only the obvious ones. But it is not easy to keep the implied cautions always in mind.

4
The Liberating Truth:
The Concept of
Integrity in
Chaucer's Writings

There seems nowadays to be some agreement in principle that we ought to try to understand Chaucer as a man of his time, that is, rather to define a historical Chaucer than to create our personal Chaucers. The Chaucer who anticipated the post-Darwinian 'enlightenment', who in all but the actuality was a graduate of Harvard not long before Child and Kittredge, an agnostic or anyway a sceptic genially tolerant of human frailty and just as genially observing the forms of Christianity, whose more pious works had to be 'early', has receded into the shadows of romantic criticism, giving place to the poet of an age of crisis,[1] or in another conception, the poet in whom moralist and artist were at odds.[2] For me this represents an advancement of understanding: I cannot conceive how an intelligent and sensitive man living in a world subject to pressures like those registered in *Piers Plowman* could have been unaffected by them. But I think a refinement of understanding is still possible. The historical dimension, the factor of the state of England, the Church and the world in the concern and thus the art of 'our sage and serious poet'—the term fits Chaucer pretty well—which will have been peculiar to his particular temperament and experience, can be more exactly defined. What appear to have been the concerns of the time which oppressed him most, or most often? These should be discernible in his selection and presentation of subject matter, from emphasis and frequency of occurrence in the first instance. If what then seems to stand out relates easily to late fourteenth-century values, forms of thought and linguistic matrices, the logic of the identification will be strengthened. And if finally it is possible to read the concerns, without critical violence, as part of the meanings of his works, that may seem to verify their relevance.

I have given away my own view of the subject in the title of this lecture. I do not find evidence in Chaucer's writings that he was drawn to the concept of apocalypticism or was preoccupied with the issue of theodicy, though he must have been aware of those grave contemporary preoccupations if only from their prominence in *Piers Plowman*. As to his having been an adept at spiritual exegesis, although he undoubtedly applied the procedure from time to time, his sustained application of it has not, in my view, been proved. I believe that Chaucer was primarily concerned with morality, the matter of the goodness or badness of human behaviour. That proposition seems so obvious to me that I feel it must be old-fashioned. Nevertheless many scholars and critics of my acquaintance who are called 'eminent', or 'distinguished' Chaucerians generally resist it, accusing me of 'pressing it too hard', or 'taking it too far'. That is my excuse for addressing you on the subject today.[3]

Chaucer's specific concern was, in my opinion, with those qualities which we nowadays sum up in the term 'integrity', 'the character of uncorrupted virtue, esp. in relation to truth and fair dealing; uprightness, honesty, sincerity'.[4] I find in the behaviour of his people, that is the personages he elected to represent or actually created, two salient appearances. One is the capacity of sexual selfishness, involving or leading to betrayal, to cause unhappiness, first repre-sented in the Dido story of *The House of Fame*. In that and similar successive representations it is almost always the breach of faith, the dishonesty, not the sexuality, that seems designed by Chaucer to appal. The other appearance is mere crass dishonesty, practised for material gain. The common factor of deceit, the violation of what Chaucer called *trouthe*, I find related to a larger conception of human behaviour in which moral and æsthetic considerations become hard to distinguish, one which might even imply a Chaucerian or a fourteenth-century poetic.

The beginning of my demonstration is necessarily affective: the feeling of being directed by authorial emphasis. The sum of the philandering lies of Arcite in *Anelida and Arcite*, of Aeneas whose desertion is twice related, of Jason twice fugitive from obligations of sexual loyalty, of Theseus and Demophoon, inconstant father and inconstant son, seems too large to be judged in the mere ethos of *fine amour*. The adulteries of Phoebus's nameless wife, and of Alison in *The Miller's Tale*, and of the nameless wife of the merchant of St

Denys, and of Lady May in *The Merchant's Tale* amount to an
augmentation of squalid deceit that silences in the end the laughter
generic in the fabliau. In the material dishonesty of Manciple and
Miller and Reeve and Shipman and Merchant there appears a scale:
they assume an order of criminalty as peculating housekeeper and
dishonest craftsman and crooked estate manager and pirate and
international speculator. At two extremes of law the Serjeant and the
Sumnour exploit human weakness. The alchemist Canon exploits
covetousness, the Physician preys on fear of the plague, Friar and
Pardoner on religious fears: frauds and charlatans and criminals and
confidence tricksters.

Considerations of genre have only limited force in softening these
impressions. For from the personages being so effectively, con-
vincingly represented, they acquire a second aspect, have as it were
two modes of existence. The one is indeed within the literary
convention where they occur, with its own scheme of 'morality' or
abeyance of morality, as in *fine amour* or fabliau. But the other is in
the general actuality of the fourteenth century where Chaucer conceived and his public received them. This latter aspect the reader with
historical awareness can never turn away from altogether. By the fact
of invoking the convention of the mode or genre in extenuation of a
personage's behaviour or as Chaucer's apparent condonation of this,
he is acknowledging the paramountcy of the other, of the actual
moral considerations. And those apply *a fortiori* if he scans, across
the artificial generic boundaries, the whole population of Chaucer's
oeuvre.

My reading proposes a development from court poet to moralist,
and in particular to moralist preoccupied with *trouthe*, integrity. This
is not radical. The moral orientation would be predictable in a serious
and intelligent person in later fourteenth-century England from the
pressure of social, religious and political conditions. As to the special
concern, that is first of all implicit in Chaucer's situation as a court
poet, having to write for the diversion of others probably of inferior
education and culture, of having to adopt postures of little dignity
such as that of the perennial lover,[5] of having to address a superior
intellect and talent to trivialities. There will no doubt have been
personalities then as now to whom such activity was not uncongenial:
being very close to the great, having their material favour, would
compensate for having always to agree with them, never to oppose
their wish or judgement. That for Chaucer this seemed degrading
appears from his Placebo of *The Merchant's Tale* (*I have now been a*

court-man al my lyf) represented as actually believing that the great do know better: *Nay, lordes ben no fooles, by my fay*,[6] a paradigm of successful self-deception compounding abject flattery. Chaucer's moment of realization will have been that in which he became aware of his strength, realized that he had learned from Machaut, court poet *par excellence*, all there was to learn there about poetry, and outstripped him. That is not a cynical observation: this was the moment of maturity when judgement became confident. And now fully self-aware, Chaucer would see in his own situation an implication of truth and falsehood, a concept of his own identity to which deceit and time-serving were repugnant. That concept will have extended to his art no later than his experience of reading Dante and presently Langland, experience of a wholly meaningful, uncompromising and valid poetry of truth.

By contrast he was discovering that some poets lie: this is registered in *The House of Fame*. One or the other version of that Dido story, whether Vergil's or Ovid's, had to be false. Here was an issue not merely of truth but of justice of report, and we must not patronizingly think the disagreement trivial. Those poets were *auctoritees*, Vergil as divinely favoured with the grace of messianic vision, Ovid if not actually a Christian saint at any rate an allegorical repository of truth.[7] Further, Chaucer may well have known, as Langland evidently did,[8] the friar John Ridevall's demonstration on grounds of chronology that it was impossible for Dido and Aeneas actually to have met:[9] that made both great poets great liars.

With the issue of literal truth of report there was associatively and conceptually linked that of truth of interpretation, of whatever class of text, scriptural, or otherwise sacred, or profane. The canonical limitation upon exegesis was lax in setting no requirement of intelligent relation between the literal and a higher sense: if the latter conformed to Christian doctrine it was acceptable.[10] The limit otherwise was the ingenuity of the exegete; this did not escape popular notice.[11] The unprincipled application of spiritual exegesis (called glozing in Langland and Chaucer) by the friars to their material advantage seems to have been a scandal.[12] Chaucer did not miss that this was a matter of intellectual as well as spiritual dishonesty: his friar in *The Sumnour's Tale*, undertaking to prove that the first Beatitude refers to the fraternal orders says, 'I don't think I have a scriptural text to prove that, but I'm bound to find it in some sort of gloss.[13]

In the moral thinking of Chaucer's time the related issues of truth of report and truth of interpretation, which Chaucer may himself have faced in composing his earliest surviving poem, when he represented the courtship of the Black Knight whose topical referent was John of Gaunt as that of an innocent youth,[14] were comprised in the enveloping conception of personal morality which we denote by 'integrity'. That actual word Chaucer almost certainly did not use; indeed if it was current in his English—the indications are not clear—it did not have the sense we give it. For that sense the word Chaucer used was *trouthe*.

Trouthe appears with a comprehensive moral meaning in the first version of *Piers Plowman*, that is, earlier than the first acceptable *O.E.D.* citation, from a Wyclif text dated 1382.[15] Without counting his personifications Langland uses the word in at least a dozen distinct senses. Three in particular concern my argument. One is 'honesty, honest practice, fair dealing', specifically in money relationships,[16] which *O.E.D.* does not isolate. A second is the one *O.E.D.* glosses 'Honesty, uprightness, righteousness, virtue, integrity',[17] represented in *Piers Plowman* in the sensational context of the salvation of the righteous heathen as a moral condition valuable without reference to religious doctrine. The third is 'Conduct in accordance with the divine standard; spirituality of life and behaviour';[18] again the *Piers Plowman* use is earlier than the Wyclif citation in the *Dictionary*. Those meanings, two of which together constitute what we today denote by 'integrity', are clearly established by their contexts. A fourteenth-century reader of the poem would have been directed to analyse them by the unmistakable complexity and possible novelty of Langland's generally polysemous use of the term: he also appears in *O.E.D.* (for what that is worth) as the first to have used the word to mean 'true statement or account, that which is in accordance with the fact',[19] and to mean 'true religious belief or doctrine',[20] and to have personified it as the Deity.[21] As the occurrences of this word multiplied there would necessarily develop in Langland's reader a sense of the extent of its implications of meaning.

What seems indicated by such lexicographical evidence—my brief demonstration could be extended,[22] and it is not material whether Langland was the innovator—is that in the 60s and 70s of the fourteenth century, Chaucer's artistically formative years, there was semantic development of a vernacular term for expressing a correspondingly developing moral and philosophical conception, that of the quality of a person's moral character seen as a whole rather than with respect to some particular sin, a conception of integral personality as we today understand the term.[23]

Something like that conception had appeared, severely formulated, in the Thomist scheme, where indeed the term *integritas* is used to signify a condition in man of being without inclination to sin; that condition was lost with the fall of Adam. 'In the state of innocence man's soul was adapted to perfecting and controlling the body, as it is now. . . . But then it had this life in all its wholeness (*hujus vitae integritatem habebat*) in that the body was completely subordinated to the soul, hampering it not at all.'[24] Original sin, which we have inherited genetically from our first parents, 'is a disordered disposition growing from the dissolution of that harmony in which original justice' (that is man's primal innocence) 'consisted, . . . a *sickness of nature*'.[25] This is effectively the misery of the human condition feverishly described in the treatise by Innocent III that Chaucer in the mid-1390s claimed to have translated.[26]

There is no need to be concerned about whether Chaucer read the *Summa Theologiœ:* the arguments assembled by Aquinas in his formulation of *integritas*, wholeness, were commonplaces of sermon and scriptural commentary, some from the time of Augustine onwards. They are implicit in Romans vii: 'I delight in the law of God after the inward man; but I see a different law in my members, warring against the law of my mind, and bringing me into captivity under the law of sin which is in my members. . . . Who shall deliver me out of the body of this death?[27] The relation between the two concepts of man's moral deficiency and his aspiration to an ideal moral condition evoke the third, of the return to a state of moral stability: liberation shall be from death, corruption, mutability. The liberating agency is truth,[28] *veritas per quam homines in presenti efficiuntur de regno Christi, . . . quedam impressio et participatio veritatis divine*, that 'truth by which men in this present life become of the kingdom of Christ, a certain imprint and sharing of the divine truth'.[29] Truth is a property of the *imago Dei*: everything is by so much of the more true *quanto imaginem Dei fidelius exprimit*, 'as it expresses the more faithfully the divine likeness'.[30] Through these and many similar commonplaces of later medieval theology the idea of truth came to embrace general moral excellence, ideal conduct.

It acquired extensions of meaning and emotional values well beyond the Aquinan formulation of integrity. A gloss on Pilate's question, *quid est veritas?* Chaucer's *what is trouthe or sothfastnesse?*[31] proposes that the Roman saw it as a fundamental principle of humanity, *quoddam principium hominum.*[32] Truth may well, said Bishop Brinton in his last sermon at St Paul's, preached on the text *Veritas liberabit*, Chaucer's *trouthe thee shal delivere*, be likened to the light of the sun, enabling sight, constant and indistinguishable.[33] The most analytical and particularizing medieval examinations of behaviour, the penitentials, find the opposite of truth to be an element of every capital sin. The proud will sin by hypocrisy, the envious by malicious detraction, as will the wrathful. Moreover wrath *stryveth alday again trouthe*: it takes away the quiet of a man's heart and subverts his soul. Avarice promotes every kind of deceit, lies, thefts, dishonest trading, perjury. As to lechery, a consequence of that sin is *brekynge of feith; and certes, in feith is the keye of Cristendom. . . . This synne is eek a thefte, . . . the gretteste thefte that may be, for it is thefte of body and of soule.* Truth concerns even sloth, the sin of inertia: against that sin the remedy is constancy, stability of mind, *stedefast feith.*[34]

In the Aquinan conception the primal innocence, man's *integritas*, was a state of harmony.[35] Commentators extended that notion to the present life: evil or sin is nothing else but a deficiency of natural harmony, melody and rhythmic proportion (*defectus naturalis harmoniœ, modi & commensurationis*).[36] In a very popular secular treatise, the *Moralium Dogma Philosophorum*, where the ideal life is one of tranquil integrity according to the norm of reason (*in tranquillo honestatis uiuere et ad normam rationis uitam reducere*) the author substitutes for the figure of harmony one of perfectly tuned musical instruments.[37] Sin is not merely contrary to positive divine law: it is against reason, for man's proper motion is *secundum rectam rationem*, in accordance with right reason.[38] The light of the mind and the subject of reason (*materia rationis*) is truth.[39] Integrity constitutes its own imperative, and would so even were it possible to conceal one's actions from God.[40] The idea of the wholeness of excellence, with truth as its central principle, acquired aesthetic and philosophical extensions in consequence of which it could appear admirable from other considerations than those of moral theology. The imperfect realization of that ideal of human behaviour became, in my view, the principal formative concern of Chaucer's mature writing. His attitude to and expression of it are as complex as the interpretations of experience at his disposal were various. At one extreme stood Innocent's *De Miseria*: 'there are nowhere rest and tranquility, nowhere peace and safety, but everywhere fear and trembling, everywhere grief and distress.'[41] At the other stood Boethius's *Consolation*, no less morally rigorous, but unremittingly serene and comforting. Somewhere between moved Seneca whom in *The Parson's Tale* Chaucer quotes in the company of Peter, Ezechiel, Augustine and Solomon,[42] who mocked the epistemologists, the only ancient philosopher much interested in individual personality, concerned to help men live in a sad, bad world.[43] Always there were the pulpit preachers who ensured there was no mistaking the sadness and badness: let Bishop Brinton, Richard II's confessor, speak for them from his last sermon: 'Whereas Truth once had three mansions, in that she dwelt in the heart without duplicity, in the mouth without faintheartedness, in the deed without shadiness (*Quia omnis qui facit veritatem venit ad lucem*: John iii), today she does not find a place to lay her head.'[44]

That dismal judgement is matched in Chaucer's moral balade *Lak of Stedfastnesse*: integrity is devalued, reason accounted idle talk, moral excellence no longer prevails, compassion is in exile, greed for profit blinds moral discernment.[45] If his command of the language of the moralist were in question it could be further shown by his descriptions of Parson and Plowman,[46] by the prologue to *The Man of Law's Tale*,[47] or the curtain lecture on the benefits of poverty in *The Wife of Bath's Tale*,[48] or by the startling outburst of injunction to those with charge of young persons in *The Physician's Tale*.[49] The question is rather, first, whether his moral concern was sustained, and in particular whether, as I believe, it centred on integrity, *trouthe*, and second, whether his work is the product of 'a struggle between the moralist who calls for judgement and the artist who refuses to judge, a struggle in which the artist usually prevails'.[50]

The two questions can be answered together by the proposition that the notion of a conflict between artist and moralist in later fourteenth-century England is both fallacious from its implicit assumption that the only kind of judgement is overt judgement and anachronistic in that the concept of amorality necessary for any 'victory' of artist over moralist did not then exist. Withholding overt judgement implies neither commendation nor condonation. At the same time the process of selection from observed or literary experience during artistic creation is a critical activity; the object of representation, whether a personage or its action, has come into being through acts of considered judgement by the artist.

In Chaucer's case the judgement will inevitably have been in terms of criteria accepted by his world as of absolute authority, those constituting Christian morality. That can be simply illustrated: the attributes, attitudes and behaviour of many of the Canterbury pilgrims correspond extensively to centuries-old formulations of estates satire.[51] Every such correspondence is the product of a decision by Chaucer, implies a moral judgement on his part, and will have evoked one from his public. Such judgements will, moreover, have been uniform, unlike our modern induced-stimulus reactions which differ with individual experience and environmental history. Whatever doctrinally fissile tendencies may have existed in the last decades of Chaucer's century, there was practically uniform acceptance of the moral system to which estates satire relates.

In that situation, for instance, the *Prologue* Narrator's approval of the Monk's contempt for the rule of his order[52] would necessarily appear preposterous rather than suggest authorial understanding and sympathy. It would raise the question why the actual poet had made the Monk's expression of contempt so strong. And Chaucer's audience would not fail to remark how many of the pilgrims belonged to estates notoriously vulnerable to satire, more properly to moral criticism, as if they had been selected for representation by the poet on that basis.[53] In modern critical terms, then, there is an implication that those pilgrims at any rate were not created for us to enjoy as charmingly quaint genre representations but are intensely dramatic realizations of various kinds of moral deficiency, of inharmonious personalities, exposed the more sharply to criticism by the vividness of their realization. And the implication extends to other Chaucerian personages which by their actions or attitudes invite moral criticism.

In identifying that implication I do not wish to suggest that Chaucer, whether he ever considered the question or not, was anything but first and foremost an artist, or that he was less concerned with poetic achievement than other poets of comparable stature, or indifferent to technical excellence, or lacking in emulation, or not passionate to meet his own standards as they mounted. My general proposition is that Chaucer's poetic had a peculiarly fourteenth-century character in which refinements of moral criticism and of literary effect are distinguishable only arbitrarily. I believe that in his historical circumstances considerations of morality were integrally a component of the truth of representation of a personality or an action: there could be a challenge to him as an artist to refine that representation, and even refraining from the moral stance which we look for might become a part of the technique.

Indeed Chaucer can be observed studying techniques of indirect moral representation. For instance, there had by his time developed out of confession formulæ a literary convention of moral criticism by self-revelation.[54] A personification such as Anger or Sloth in *Piers Plowman*[55] would describe at length a variety of hamartiologically associated sins which he had committed or to which he was subject. Such a confession would be packed with individually convincing detail, but from such disparate situations as to imply changes of identity precluding the realization of the speaker as a dramatic personality.[56] Chaucer develops that convention in the *Pardoner's Prologue* by restricting the class of moral offence to what would be conceivable within a single identity. In the Pardoner's case, however, the dramatic improbability of such total self-exposure survives. Chaucer refines the convention to the point of transcending it in the *Wife of Bath's Prologue*. By coherency of circumstantial detail, a connotative imagery establishing her personality through its setting in a realizable world, and by a consummately devised, quint-essentially loquacious manner of speech he makes her self-exposure wholly credible.[57] Beyond that still he uses the technique as it were casually within a story, for instance with the friar of *The Sumnour's Tale* who unconsciously reveals his cynicism about preaching and exegesis. The occasions of the developing technique are moral ones, and as the technique advances it continues to serve moral ends. To be sure the development can be called essentially artistic, from a preacher's demonstration to dramatic representation. But from its use the two purposes are not separable: it is not possible to speak of either as in ascendancy. The circumstance that the poet is likely to have experienced the gratification of a sense of success at his achievement is not immediately relevant.

Another probably self-gratifying device which Chaucer used extensively with varying subtlety is allusion evocative of moral criticism. In representations of estates satire types there is, for example, direct quotation as when the Monk of the *Prologue* sets no store by the comparison of religious who break the claustral rule to fish out of water.[58] But further, when the same Monk asks, *How shall the world be served?* there is at least a double allusion, in *world* to the moral maxim, *Si quis amat Cristum mundum non diligit istum*,[59] and in *served* to the servitude implied in *Quis liberabit?* Mention of food in connection with Friar or Sumnour or Pardoner recalls a current condemnatory quotation, *Vos qui peccata hominum comeditis*, 'You whose food comes from the sins of men, unless you pour out tears and prayers for them you shall vomit up in torment that which you consumed with delight.'[60] The Friar in the Canterbury *Prologue* and the Wife of Bath in hers are substantially direct quotations from the *Roman de la Rose*.[61] That professedly reformed libertine, the knight of *The Merchant's Tale*, was born in Pavia where traditionally not even a Hippolytus would be able to preserve his virtue overnight.[62] When Alison in *The Miller's Tale* had sworn to be Nicholas's mistress, 'Then as it happened', the story goes on, 'she went to the parish church' *Cristes owene werkes for to werche*; in due course their lovemaking was punctuated by church bells and the sound of choral singing.[63] The monk of *The Shipman's Tale*, propositioning the merchant's wife, swears his love for her by his *professioun*, his monastic vows.[64] Such quotations or allusions, too frequent to be accidental—and Chaucer's contemporary audience would be more fully attuned to them than we are—would by their nature operate as moral directives through their discordancy. They would imply some falseness, a lack of integrity in the object of representation. At the same time from their variety, subtlety and abundance Chaucer's pleasure in their use seems unmistakable.

In such devices the common element of discrepancy, disharmony, the ironic component, is effective only in terms of the morality which it recalls. In another kind of situation, as for instance when the *Prologue* Narrator calls the Monk 'supremely handsome', *a fair for the maistrie*,[65] and presently describes a grotesque figure bald as a coot, sweating profusely, grossly fat and with bulging eyes, a choice is put to the audience between accepting critical direction and acquiescing in the preposterous. In the allusions the choice lies between the moral reminder being deliberate and fortuitous. In the namelessness of the adulterous wife of *The Shipman's Tale* it is between seeing her essential moral nonentity and presuming over-sight by the poet. In the association of the love affairs of lovely Alison and Lady May with excremental functions it is between an intention of the poet to degrade them as sexual adventures and his tasteless-ness.[66] In the fine high style of Lady May's protestations of virtue just before she couples with Damyan[67] it is between an intention to signify the outrageousness of her lie and the poet's tone-deafness.

In all such instances, as in Chaucer's larger ironies like the commendation of the Monk I earlier mentioned, the appearance of discrepancy, or implication of falsehood, or possibility of mis-conception, of false reading, reflects an authorial judgement and directs the reader to repeat it, awakens a responsibility for evaluation in him. Moral judgement is between good and evil: Chaucer's directives may suggest that the decision is between integrity, a moral wholeness, and its opposite, the harmonious and the discordant, or the admirable and the ugly, falsehood being essentially ugly.

What Chaucer will seldom do is attach a moral label. I think this is from his having sensed that to do so with many of his subjects would falsify by oversimplification the representation of the unremittingly difficult choice which in his time shaped the human condition, that represented in Romans vii: 'I delight in the law of God after the inward man: but I see a different law in my members warring against the law of my mind and bringing me into captivity under the law of sin.' *Imfelix ego homo: quis me liberabit?*[68] 'I wish I had died the moment I was christened', says Langland's Everyman, Hawkin, 'it is so hard to live and be a sinner'.[69] Chaucer's poetic truth, the union of artist and moralist in him, is accuracy in representing that condition of conflict between the absolute excellence of the ideal and the power of the urge away from it. For total accuracy the difficulty of making what is known to be the right choice, or of identifying the right choice, or even of discerning or recalling that a choice exists, must be part of the representation. This Chaucer achieves by laying judge-ment upon the reader.

How variously he does this appears from, for example, the dilemma of Arveragus, the failure of Sir January in *The Merchant's Tale* to perceive the right alternative to his dissolute life, and the absence of a sense of sin in the adulterous couple of *The Shipman's Tale*. The first is the most complex: the direction lodges in the apparent paradox of Dorigen having to be untrue in order to be true. The story is an exemplary fable: the reader of Seneca and translator of Boethius did not work it over merely to produce a latter-day Breton lay. It illustrates a moral choice made in blindness: there is actually no dilemma. For, from the action being set in a pagan world[70] its characters by fourteenth-century thinking have imperfect spiritual understanding. Arveragus's difficulty of choice comes from not knowing that an oath given in jest or under misapprehension is not binding, that an oath to commit sin is not binding, even that Aurelius's recourse to magic would release Dorigen. A meaning of the story then is the importance of a real, that is a Christian understanding of truth, even in its contextually limited sense of 'faith or loyalty as pledged in a promise or agreement'.[71] The reader's difficulty, beyond that of Arveragus, comes from that meaning being qualified by the story representing the compelling power of truth, even in the pagan setting. This touches the contemporary interest in the absolute worth of virtuous conduct; we recall how Langland used the term *trouthe* innovatively to describe the behaviour of Trajan, the righteous heathen. *Ne wolde neuere trewe god but trewe trupe were allowed*, 'God in his truth would wish nothing else but that real integrity, even in a pagan, should be rewarded.'[72] The qualification then is that truth even imperfectly understood and sought in error has intrinsic excellence. In the case of the old reprobate, Sir January, the question forced on the reader, how it was possible for him to be so ignorant of the moral teaching about matrimony (*A man may do no synne with his wyf, Ne hurte hymselven with his owene knyf*)[73] would raise a contemporary issue, beyond his spiritual condition, of the gravest concern: the failure of the priesthood in their duty of religious instruction, particularly as confessors. The suggestion is that January's spiritual advisors during and especially at the end of his libidinous career had been like Sir Penetrans Domos at the close of *Piers Plowman*, a succession of what Brinton called *infideles confessores*, 'who do not speak solid truths to their penitents and thereby convert them from their most evil ways',[74] but who, hearing confession *ful swetely* and giving *plesaunt* absolution, told him only what he wanted to hear. As to the couple in *The Shipman's Tale*, the most striking feature of their representation is that they appear wholly without sense of guilt or moral offence. This effect Chaucer ensures by two means. First he gives the action a clear moral reference by making the adulterer a monk, and maintains that reference by a striking number of pious oaths and invocations during the arrangement of the assignation,[75] by the gratuitous detail that a young girl in the woman's care (whether her own child or not) is present while the monk and woman come to terms and he handles and kisses her,[76] and by references to religious observance: the monk is reading his breviary when they meet, he says a mass before dinner. Second, by details of style he suggests the attitudes of the personages: the monk's devotions are *his thynges*; the mass is said *hastily*, the first of a crescendo of adverbs mounting to his dining *richely*, splendidly.[77] If the moral direction of the apparently toneless and detached but deeply ironic representation is accepted, then the circumstance that the adulterers not only lack a sense of guilt but are pleased with what they have brought off is to be seen as not merely spiritual blindness, but *elacio inobedience*, exultation in their offence, a spiritual condition, Brinton observes, 'to be detested'.[78]

The extremes of attitude, unnatural sense of obligation shown in Arveragus of *The Franklin's Tale* and effortlessly fluent deceit in the tales of Merchant and Shipman, suggest three features of Chaucer's situation. One is that the various concepts denoted by the word *trouthe* constituted for him an ideal of morality, *the hyeste thyng that man may kepe*,[79] and its extremes of disappointment: *Trouthe is a thyng that I wol evere kepe Unto that day in which that I shal crepe Into my grave, and ellis God forbede*, says the charlatan alchemist in *The Canon's Yeoman's Tale* as part of his patter.[80] A second is that Chaucer found it possible to realize the larger ideal of integrity through narrative action only in special settings. Of this there are two striking instances. It is the unreality of the Franklin's Breton fairytale world that authenticates the infectious excellence of its personages, whereby in their behaviour the initially limited expression of *trouthe*, 'fidelity to a pledge',[81] growing by evocation of fine sensibility in Aurelius and generosity in the *philosophre*, comes to seem to have the dimensions of integrity, 'the character of uncorrupted virtue, esp. in relation to truth and fair dealing'.[82] And the exalted religiosity of *The Second Nun's Tale*, the legendary undiminished virtue of the early Church, exhibited in Cecilie's fervour, lends credit to her remarkable conversion of her husband, and his of his brother, this other set of infectiously excellent actions realizing a *trouthe* with the embracing sense 'True religious belief or doctrine'.[83] A third feature is that in Chaucer's representations of an actual world the ideal of integrity is generally realized in specific and limited forms of truth, as keeping the pledged word, the marriage vow, the religious profession, being honest in material things, and in terms of the commandments rather than any high philosophical principle. And to judge by his choice of subjects he saw even that limited truth as most often unfulfilled. At any rate among his lay personages, especially men, there are not many to whom, as to the Knight, he attributes devotion to integrity, *trouthe*, in any large, unqualified sense.[84] Even the wise and chivalrous Theseus of *The Knight's Tale* has, we recall, a past of *grete untrouthe of love*.[85]

In that situation Chaucer developed the art of representing human behaviour to the point where, apparently, giving it the label 'wicked' seemed to him an inferior artistic procedure. In representations from actual life he praises more often than he condemns, and his con- ferments of approval made from a moral stance are positive and clear. Clergy and church officials are a case in point. There is no shading in the descriptions of Parson and Plowman. Those two figures instance unmistakably, and are commended for, the virtues opposed to the traditionally formulated vices of their estates, the Parson in that respect a foil of perfection for Langland's delinquent pastoral clergy. In the case of other clerics and the minor officials of the ecclesiastical system his technique is indirect, to build into representations of their persons and activities, taken ostensibly at their own valuation, a variety of more or less subtle indices of their inadequacies as personalities, symptoms of disharmony in their lives, the traits revealing of moral deficiency, the false elements.[86] The effect is to devalue the whole character: whatever excellent attributes it might possess, the energy of the Monk, the persuasiveness of the Friar, the compassion of the Prioress are made, as falsely applied, to seem of little account from the implicit failure of *trouthe*, to a vow, a purpose of order, a right conduct. The method functions, with lay folk as with clerics, through the constant relevance, pervasiveness of the moral considerations which were determinants in the fourteenth- century understanding of personality, as a part of the individual's self-awareness and of other people's awareness of him. That is the circumstance which determines that in the Chaucerian poetic con- siderations of art and morality become indistinguishable.

Having refined this poetic excellently Chaucer nevertheless composed the prayer for forgiveness that appears at the end of *The Parson's Tale*, that *myrie tale in prose* designed to conclude his unfinished Canterbury scheme, *To knytte up al this feeste, and make an ende.*[87] Why, if Chaucer's art is essentially moral by his design, did he think to need such abasement, such debasement we might think, of his own creation?[88] My answer lies in the prevalent eschatological obsession of his time. I venture the historical opinion that the cruel logic of Christian morality was not often in the English Middle Ages as rigorously applied as toward the end of the fourteenth century, to oppress the thinking Christian with a sense of general moral deficiency (*I leue fewe ben goode*)[89] to the point where he might have no reasonable or confident hope of being saved.[90] And if he threw himself upon divine love and mercy he was risking delusion: 'Let no man flatter himself', Innocent had written, 'by saying, "God will in the end relent; He will not be wrathful for eternity". *O spes inanis, o falsa presumptio.*'[91] Given the constant awareness of moral issues evident in Chaucer's writings there is no ground at all for thinking him unconcerned about the state and fate of his own soul.

I have proposed that in his later works art and morality are inseparable, but he wrote of *translacions and enditynges of worldly vanitees*, and tales *that sownen into synne*, and prayed for intercession and forgiveness. There is a standard doctrinal explanation for that earnest prayer. The works in question could for the spiritually less developed reader be 'dangerous' in that their external worldliness, the magnificently represented beauty of the false good, or what Langland would have called the *harlotry*, the low comedy in them, might distract him from their essential morality. They were artistically too advanced; their morality was buried too deep, and in this Chaucer had placed his reader in proximate spiritual danger to his faith or morals.

Moreover, the poet was in moral danger himself simply in the execution of his art, the entertainment of the multiplicity of pleasurable technical considerations which in sum constitute literary activity. Its self-gratifying nature, the enjoyable sense of achievement, carried a risk of the sin of pride, and if persisted in with increased accomplishment, amounted to an *elacio inobediencie* of the artist; we recall Langland representing his Dreamer as rebuked for mere intellectual excitement: 'You are morally imperfect, *oon of Prides knyȝtes*, a companion of the standard-bearer of Antichrist.'[92] Worse still, in any gratification experienced at the pointing of moral offence the poet could fail in compassion, in charity. He could sin by motive in the course of representing man's sinfulness, the representation becoming an end in itself, pursued in vanity, or by designing the representation to give pleasure to others for his own credit, making capital of human weakness: *vos qui peccata hominum comeditis. . . .*[93] We must credit him with the moral sophistication implied by awareness of those possibilities. And there was the overriding question whether the composition of poetry on profane subjects was morally justifiable at all: the discussion, from early Christian times to Chaucer's own day had not produced a generally accepted affirmative answer.[94] Best, if one had been unable to leave meddling with poetry alone, not to rely on high-flown justifications of the activity[95] but to stand at the back of the temple with the publican, or to confess with Langland's Dreamer, *ich haue tynt tyme and tyme mysspended.*[96]

For in the danger of sin there was fear—whatever historical effort it may take we must remember that—such as reduced, even negated any artistic ascendancy, indeed devalued the very practice of his art, diverting his concern from any broad philosophical ideal of essential truth to personality he might have developed and cherished, to his own spiritual condition, by representing the need to be saved. That fear would turn him to a truth more instant in his need, the one proclaimed in the refrain of his balade *Truth*,[97] *a veritas . . . que Christus est*, liberating from death, corruption, the mortal body, servitude to sin and the devil[98] *tanquam causa efficiens, gratiam influens*, as an efficient cause, infusing grace.[99] In his sense of need for that grace and liberation Chaucer was a creature of his time.[100]

5
Philosophical Chaucer

Some of Chaucer's poetry expresses an unmistakable philosophical point of view. The dense texture of what we call the 'Boethian' lyrics, *The Former Age*, *Fortune*, *Gentillesse*, *Lak of Stedfastness*, is largely woven of topoi that were originally philosophical predicates. In that sense Chaucer, even while instancing the theme of Eliot's essay on Shakespeare and the stoicism of Seneca, that a poet's business is not to think but to make poetry out of other people's thinking, could be called 'philosophical', and of course there are the poems containing passages lifted out of Boethius. But using the term on those grounds would not much further our understanding of Chaucer, and so would have little point. It seems to me that we can call him 'philosophical' for a better reason, and I shall try to make a case for my opinion.

The situation in which a questioning intelligence of the fourteenth century would find itself was a closed system.[1] It had not always been felt to be so. For Anselm Augustine's 'Faith is to believe what thou seest not, truth is to see what thou hast believed', was not inhibiting. He moved on from there to assert not merely that faith is aided by philosophical enquiries, but that the Christian thinker, if he is not to be negligent, must strive to advance from faith to intelligible faith. The constricting change occurred in the thirteenth century when it became unmistakably evident that the newly available works of Aristotle would, to say the least, not make religious doctrine intelligible or show it to be reasonable: *non enim regnat spiritus Christi ubi dominatur spiritus Aristotelis*. The opposition of the entrenched theologians to speculative philosophy expressed in the Parisian prohibitions of 1210 and 1215, repeated more comprehensively in 1270 and 1277, *non legantur libri Aristotelis de methafisica et de naturali philosophia*, was absolute. The question *utrum sit possibile intellectui viatoris habere notitiam evidentem de veritatibus theologicis?* was officially closed with a negative.[2] The truth of a dogmatic system was asserted on the ground of its unintelligibility or, conversely, the inadequacy of human intelligence was postulated as evidence of the necessary truth of dogma.

It can require a major effort of the historical imagination, especially in younger people, to conceive of a situation in which intelligence of a higher order is willing to acquiesce in an absolute prohibition of its activity in specified fields: to us the restriction, 'You must not speculate in certain ways about these dogmas', would be odious and offensive. But it was widely accepted and observed, and the scepticism of the best thirteenth- and fourteenth-century minds was not mainly about doctrine, but about epistemology, about the limited capacity of the human intelligence to comprehend or account for doctrine.[3]

There are various explanations, which are not exclusive. One is that no intelligent alternative to belief was yet available: dogma was psychologically indispensable. Only Christianity afforded the concept of an organized universe, the primary intelligent concept of purposefulness, of a will acting to an end; that is, it stilled the horror of the random. Another explanation was the ultimate force of the doctrine that pride is sinful, of which the effect must have been to deny to, or to reduce for, an intellectually honest person, the psychological protection and reassurance afforded by a sense of achievement: he had to turn elsewhere for comfort in the loneliness of his personal human condition.[4] Another is that the Christian doctrines were then absolutely authoritative in a way scarcely conceivable today, when it is possible, as I have observed in amazement at close range, for professors of divinity in Anglican orders to express jointly in print their disbelief in the divinity of Christ; and when, in the Roman communion, personal interpretations in matters of belief and morals which not many years ago would have been roundly condemned as sophistical, are tacitly accepted.[5] It is for reasons like these that the speculative activity, when it outgrew the impulse to develop rational arguments in support of dogma, did not turn to radical questioning of the actual concept of dogma. 'Deviations' in medieval thinking took the form of believing differently about the same things as opposed to holding a different belief.[6] Wyclif's fundamentalism and predestinarian views illustrate this. No fourteenth-century philosopher of standing, in England at any rate, seems to have expressed rationalist opinions like those that began to be proclaimed in the eighteenth century. Irreligion, and with it scepticism about particular dogmas such as the benevolence of the deity, the immortality of the soul, or the virgin birth, seem—if contemporary reports deploring them are to be trusted—to have been of psychotic rather than intellectual origin, prompted by depressed, even desperate, misery among the peasantry, or by the selfish cynicism of ecclesiasts. All complexions of genuinely advanced thought assumed, or anyway professed, the Christian theology of Catholicism.

The dogmatic reduction of metaphysics implied the ascendancy of epistemology which characterizes the later thirteenth and the fourteenth centuries. Genuine speculation gave place to apologetics; these generally tended to subside into redefinitions of terms. One reads that there was lively philosophical activity in later fourteenth-century Oxford, but I can't find that any real development of understanding of the human condition was achieved there. The good intelligence of speculative bent was forced into a limited choice among those few subjects, such as grammar and mathematics, that did not encroach on higher doctrine.

No part of that sketch is new or original. Nevertheless I make no apology for presenting it. There is a quality in Chaucer which blurs the distinctions of time, and it is salutary to begin any study of him with the historical exercise. What I have sketched was Chaucer's intellectual milieu, seen in one aspect, and he did take—let us not forget—Innocent's *Wretched Engendering of Mankind* seriously enough to translate it.[7] His exceptional intelligence[8] was confined within the closed system of medieval Christianity which by its predicates both mounted a conflict between two sets of values, and characterized the conflict as unreal by asserting the immeasurable superiority of one of the sets.

At the outset of his career Chaucer may not have had much sense of that constriction, and as an amateur and layman he may not have thought of it as affecting him directly: the plight was in the first instance that of the professionals.[9] He did concern himself at some length with the lively contemporary issue that touched every man of his time, the tripartite crux of divine foreknowledge, predestination and free will, by undertaking to translate Boethius, but his translation mirrors its insolubility,[10] and not inconceivably the Nun's Priest's *I wol nat han to do of swich mateere* represents a final opinion of the profitlessness of discussing it.

The real effect will have been indirect and gradual as his

remarkable self-education proceeded: a developing awareness that two worlds existed, one imposed, patterned by inherited dogmatic structures, authoritarian and absolute, the other within his mind, permitting or even prompting question and speculation. Almost every feature of the former will have been calculated, in his particular time, to deepen his sense of anomaly, beginning with the moral shortcomings of the divinely sanctioned custodians of its dogma from the top down.[11] Chaucer was confined in the one world by what psychologists of religion have called the 'need to be saved' and drawn to the other by almost every element in his cultural experience.

Thus even while Boethius's *Consolation* seems to have been redirecting him to simple faith by its failure to enlighten him on its inilluminable main topic, it was taking him, as has been said, 'on a sophisticated journey through four great philosophical systems'.[12] It was illustrating, if not the effectiveness, certainly the elegance of human intelligence in its higher orders, acting out the right of speculative search, and extendedly demonstrating the existence of an undogmatic intellectual tradition.

What other profane philosophy Chaucer read we can only surmise. He mentions Seneca more than 30 times, and certainly the *Moral Epistles*, *De Beneficiis* and *De Clementia* were available and being read in his time. But the presence of so much stoic doctrine in Christian teaching makes it hazardous to argue for any direct obligation of Chaucer to Seneca from resemblances. As to Macrobius—and whether or not one calls him a 'philosopher', he was a notable transmitter of philosophical ideas—there is no real reason beyond the availability of compendia to question Chaucer's having read his *Commentary* as well as the actual *Somnium*. Then there is Cicero's *De Officiis*, that other text written in adversity, possibly Boethius's actual model, where in Petrarch's view Cicero sounds like a Christian apostle. We have no census of the manuscripts of the work, but they were evidently numerous, were still being produced in the fourteenth century, and on the showing of medieval English library catalogues, were well distributed. The work was also extensively quoted, for instance by John of Salisbury, figures largely in florilegia, and, without acknowledgement, in the *Moralium Dogma Philosophorum*.[13] But what matters is less which profane philosophers Chaucer read than that in the ideas attributed to them he will have seen anticipations of proclaimed Christian truths, some of them very important to a thoughtful man's conception of himself, affirmations in effect of the value of human intelligence, that *sapientia huius mundi* is not invariably *stultitia apud deum*.

So the Senecan elements in the *Consolation*, which work—as Chaucer cannot fail to have remarked—never invokes scripturally revealed truth or dogma, will have illustrated the possibility of a purely intellectual defence against the malignancy of circumstances. As for the *Somnium*, we know from *The Parliament of Fowls* that Chaucer saw enough of this to single out that same stoic advocacy of disregard for the world in its pagan form, but here as an act of courage and resolution rather than of rejection. Here, also, was the ideal of devotion to *comune profit*, that is of the moral value of service, along with a concept of a reward of joy without end for such service, and another ideal, that there would be an end to the punishment of the wicked. This was a heady combination, one represented, moreover, in the cosmic setting that Chaucer had learned of and come to admire in Dante. And in *De Officiis* as indeed also in Macrobius's *Commentary* he will have found what he knew as the cardinal virtues, with their formulation credited to Plato; and will have found Cicero writing of the man who possesses them, *formam ipsam . . . et tamquam faciem honesti vides*, 'You see the very model and as it were the countenance of integrity'.[14] This is a concept that Chaucer came to value in itself.

Such intellectual experiences were necessarily both exhilarating and enlarging. *Beati pauperes spiritu* is a predicate that goes against the human grain. Here, by contrast, was sketched a world of the intelligence, untouched by any imputation of degeneracy, of the physical and spiritual degradation that is implicit in the doctrine of original sin,[15] one where the existence of freedom of rational choice was taken for granted, where good conduct was held to be absolutely valuable, where it was possible to conceive of a man behaving virtuously on rational grounds alone. Out of this, I find and offer as my proposition today, Chaucer developed as a moral philosopher in a real sense of the expression. I mean that he came to use his intelligence in the analytical manner we understand philosophical thinking to imply, on questions of ethics, moral values and choice, with the consequence that in at least some of his poetry he is more a moral philosopher than a moralist.

There is nothing remarkable in his having been concerned with morality: so were all the good poets in England in his time. In perspective we can see their concern not just as reflecting an ethical crisis, but as variously signalling a point of major social change, an intuition of an evolutionary moment. The direction to intellectual interest in ethics came from various quarters, among them poetic theory.[16] The poetic activity was a branch of ethics, its function, observable even in Ovid, *maxime delectare et delectando tamen mores instruere, quia omnes auctores fere ad ethicam tendunt.*[17] Concern with morality, if charitably expressed, was itself morally commendable.[18] Moreover this was the field of philosophy with unqualified theological sanction. No other was as rewarding to cultivate: *nullus feracior in ea locus est nec uberior.*[19] And its lines of thought were recommended from being known to reach back to the classical past: there lay an implication that those pagan philosophers who had in their teaching anticipated Christian morality (that is, we would say, whose teachings had been absorbed by the early Church) had been the objects of very special grace.[20]

What is remarkable is the deliberative element in Chaucer's consideration of morality. Much of what passed for moral 'philosophy' in the Middle Ages we would call moral 'instruction'. The subject of *ethica, que moralis dicitur,*[21] the moral branch of philosophy, was the cardinal virtues; *ethica* treats of right and wrong conduct, its function not to speculate but to teach: *nobis morum informat doctrinam.*[22] Good and bad conduct, what was moral or immoral, had been canonically defined, and the definitions were for the most part represented as based upon dogma. In effect the distinction emphasized by modern moral philosophers like Rawls and Williams, between making moral judgement and analysing their nature or the nature of moral choice, between ethics and meta-ethics,[23] seems not to have appeared as a philosophical issue to medieval thinkers, who saw moral choice in terms of the doctrine of original sin. By contrast, if I read Chaucer correctly, there are signs in his works of preoccupation not primarily with conduct—he does not question the value or quality of the Christian prescriptions—but with issues of values and choice in the behaviour of individuals. In that preoccupation I see the moral philosopher.

There is a variety of reasons, likely to have been interactive rather than discrete, why Chaucer should have been impelled to speculate about moral questions. As a man of excellent intelligence he will have been, as I earlier suggested, highly sensitive to anomaly, that is to the unreasonable, the discrepant element in human situations. There are innumerable indications of that sensitivity in his work; it is obviously one source of his irony. But when his representation touches issues of values and choice in the report of personage or narrative action it will also have been a powerful stimulus to moral speculation. The great anomaly lay in one question. Why should there be conflicts of values, a predicament of choice? What are the grounds on which people make choices between conflicting values? Do dilemmas of choice really exist? If there are absolute grounds on which moral choices can reasonably be made, therefore indeed must be made, why do people choose wrongly?

Such thinking would in the closed system inevitably lead back to the absolutist answer, to the resolution of the conflict of values by recourse to a transcendent set of values, in terms of which it must appear that no real conflict existed. That the conflict which by such recourse was held not to exist nevertheless appeared to persist would identify the point of return as original sin, and the return would not be a happy one, for the Pelagian dream, like the dream of universalism, dies hard. And their deaths would amount to yet another reduction of human intelligence, in the directive to put aside those questions which persist in the mind and terrify the spirit (they are recurrent in *Piers Plowman*): why are judgements that would be monstrous in a man to be accepted as necessarily benevolent in the deity; why is *potentia absoluta* such a wonderful mystery in God when it would be tyranny in a human sovereign? Such abhorrent specula-tions, which Langland made his characters express or condemn, Chaucer addressed obliquely.[24]

He evidently found consolation in the exercise of purely philo-sophical consideration of moral conduct. Here was an area in which the speculative intelligence could be indulged without reproach. Glaucon's challenge had attraction even for medieval canonical moralists; it turns up attributed to Seneca, without the name and as an affirmation, not a question, in *The Parson's Tale* by whatever unascertainable stages of transmission from Plato's *Republic*: we see it in *De Officiis*, and in the *Moralium Dogma Philosophorum*.[25] The answer to the challenge, by implying the existence of an intellectually ascertainable moral absolute, and by postulating reason, intelligence *per se*, as a ground for good conduct, would incidentally restore to that faculty some of the status denied it by theological reduction.

There would, moreover, be excitement in entertaining the concept of value, expressed in personality and behaviour, as an intellectually conceived absolute. There is no mistaking the implication of that excitement for Chaucer the dramatic poet from *Troilus and Criseyde* onward. In the details by which Chaucer effects his magnificently Bradleian illusions of character we can observe his insight into how immoral behaviour carries a value cost, even to the extent that when the personage does not feel that cost, does not care about value, his not feeling or not caring is part of the price he pays, an element in the diminution of his value.[26] In the detail of Chaucer's representation of personages and—outside narrative—in the pasts their albeit Bradleian existences imply, we can observe another insight: that, in the scale of values philosophically established, self-gratification takes a lower place than any activity which benefits others, and that even as between self-gratifying activities there is gradation; near the top are the grades of vanity—twenty volumes of Aristotle and Aristotelian commentary on your shelves—and at the absolute bottom the cynically selfish satisfaction of appetite.[27] Moreover we can in such situations see Chaucer the speculative moralist scrutinizing the predicament of choice: every sane person wishes the best for himself, and the best in himself, and many or most misconceive the best.[28]

A concomitant of those insights is Chaucer's enhanced understanding of the aesthetic aspect of morality. That was, of course, not a novel conception. A typically medieval expression of it is the hamartiologists' and pulpit preachers' representations of sin as hideous, or—in another form—in the concept of the harmonious personality being reflected in appearance as well as conduct, so that defects of personality show themselves in revealing details of expression or movement.[29] Chaucer's understanding of the principle was apparently more penetrating and profound, namely that the ugliness of immoral behaviour can be indicated without necessary recourse to grotesque exaggeration like Langland's in the Confession of the Sins—though Chaucer does make use of this.[30] A set of actions involving, let's say, three personages, in which none suffers, indeed from which all emerge to their own gratification, a situation which thus by pragmatic standards cannot be faulted, when he represents it in even the most dispassionate tone, acquires the quality of a paradigm of the squalor of selfishness.[31]

Another exciting feature of the analytical thinking of lay moral philosophy will have been its affording a further area of free intellectual exercise by admitting the theoretical possibility of conflict of values. In respect of that possibility the Christian morality of the Middle Ages differed absolutely from modern moral philosophy. It is a tenable proposition that the human condition itself implies inherent conflicts of value which cannot be resolved without loss of value.[32] Such a proposition would have been inconceivable in the fourteenth century simply from the accepted transcendency of divine values. What might appear a conflict was necessarily a failure of perception in the agent of choice.[33] There was no genuine, substantive disagreement about individual moral conduct.[34] I am not suggesting that Chaucer was in any way in advace of, or superior to, that situation. And I do not for a moment suppose that he wished by intellectual rather than doctrinal considerations of behaviour to reach any other conclusions than those of his religion about morality. If he actually ever formulated an objective, it may have been to examine the arguments for those conclusions by the means of narrative representation. Seen in another aspect he was asserting the liberty, the independence of his critical intelligence, in one of the few ways available in his day, a self-gratificatory activity to be sure, but nearer the top than the bottom of the scale of such activities. Chaucer may well have understood this of himself: one recalls the Clerk, cherishing his books and scholarship as a kind of hallmark of the respectability of intelligence, unconcerned to get a benefice—his kinsfolk were, after all, supporting him—notwithstanding the crying need for educated parochial and diocesan clergy.[35]

Chaucer's entry into moral philosophy was by way of the method of the problematic situation where a moral choice is implied. That is usual: the moral philosophers, however rarified their speculative thinking about good and evil in the abstract, end up analytical thinkers, referring to a historical situation, or inventing a situation, or representing a personage in a situation, where, either, choice is called for within the model, or a moral definition is required from without. Generalizations about morality must be actualized as problems of moral choice. There is a virtual folklore of such problems; Cicero in *De Officiis* III refers to an apparently well-known compendium of them.[36] Modern moral philosophers sometimes illustrate from historical situations where a moral issue has already been identified: for instance, to what extent were the generals in the plot against Hitler bound by their oaths as officers, and so on, but they also invent: what is the moral responsibility of a house-burglar on the job if he finds the owner of the house in process of murdering his wife?

With hindsight Chaucer's development of narrative as an instrument to perform this function seems easy, inevitable. The circumstances were favourable. The primary one will have been the reiterated connection of poetry and morals: poetry was classed under ethics, was *moralis* because *de moribus tractat*: the end cause of poetry is *ad virtutes inducere et a viciis removere*.[37] Given the absence of clear distinction between moral philosophy and moral instruction such formulae of classification are bound to have been suggestive. Another important circumstance must have been the traditionally exemplary function of narrative: any sequence of reported action sufficiently formed to have a recognizable beginning and end, having enough shape to be called a story, was conceived of as possessing inherent meaning, that is, essentially paradigmatic. From the constant use of fiction in terms of that conception by preachers for moral instruction, it will have been deeply imprinted. Chaucer's innovation, the building of a moral issue, a moral question, into the narrative structure in such a way that there was no need to make it explicit, that what medieval literary theory would have called the rhetoric would convey it, has implications for the superior quality of his art which I may only mention here. What suggested it we shall never know: it could even have been such a trivial model as the frivolous convention of the *demande d'amour*.

What is important is less where the suggestion came from than its effect: this established the difference between some of Chaucer's writings and exempla as vehicles of moral instruction. His works challenge, only rarely do they exhort or condemn. It is a question of attitude and intention. The preacher in the exemplary tradition uses the models, the stories, to promote canonically sanctioned modes of conduct or to illustrate the effects of failure to observe them. The student of ethics, our poet as moral philosopher, develops the inherent meaning of his stories as diagrams of moral choice.

It is the excursion into intellectual as distinct from canonical ethics, the pretence that there could be genuine difficulty in distinguishing right and wrong, as opposed to difficulty in following the known right course of action, that makes this possible. At its simplest, when the exercise is conducted outside the Christian perimeter, the effect is crudely powerful, and at the same time remote. So *The Franklin's Tale*: is a husband ever right in advising his wife to be unfaithful to him? And *The Physician's Tale*: is there any conceivable situation in which it could be moral for, that is, morally incumbent on, a father to kill his daughter? Those questions are loaded with issues of choice, with conflicts of values in the abstract; they could stand as classic problems of moral philosophy until Christian considerations are admitted; then they lose, if not their drama, certainly their significance in the moral sense.

When the setting of the story, or the milieu of the personages whose implied history contains the moral predicament is Christian, Chaucer's combination of philosophical insight and dexterity in preserving its independent exercise is especially apparent. An illustration is his studies of 'success', of the commonplace that people want both to be the best kind of person and to have the best kind of life.[38] A friar is *the beste beggere in his hous*, a lawyer is a uniquely successful *purchasour*, that is, accumulator of landed property. The question whether they are in error in their conception of best-ness Chaucer does not even raise. But with the imputation of success he implies the existence of whole value systems by which, in each case, their success is measurable. So the systems themselves are severally and jointly exposed to scrutiny: we are led to consider their orientations, and why they should have any force.

That brings out a significant particular, namely that the *Prologue* Friar's success implies a disregard which is immediately and unmistakably unadmirable. When he says of association with the wretched and the destitute, *It is nat honest, it may nat avaunce For to deelen with no swich poraille* (246, 247), his disregard of a notable value, a primal ideal of his order, is part of the reduction of his own value, of our opinion of him. So Chaucer is seen identifying a theorem of moral philosophy about selfishness: what it looks like in a man not merely to have misconceived the 'best kind of life' but deliberately to have chosen what is evidently not a good life, its ultimate index of success the ability to get a farthing out of a destitute and barefoot widow. So too in the Prologue Monk's contempt for study and the rules of his order, or in the Pardoner's 'Why should I live meanly when I can make money by preaching humbug like this?'. One can generalize, 'cynicism is unadmirable', but in so doing one acknowledges that without recourse to canonical morality Chaucer has identified a moral value and communicated it in a way calculated to arouse emotion, exploiting the feature of moral values that they are not matters of easy opinion; *de gustibus non est disputandum* does not apply to them.

Chaucer's application of this circumstance, the capacity of moral issues to generate emotion, as an instrument of moral philosophy, is one of the principal distinctions of his later poetry. An instance is *The Merchant's Tale.* By canonical standards there is precious little morality in it; by the conventions of the fabliau there would be excuse for the adultery in the discrepancy of age between wife and husband. But the adultery does not occur within a perspective of Christian morality: the presence of the god and goddess sets January's garden in another world. Nor is it told as a fabliau: there are certain elements of tone and style inappropriate to this. The stylistic register in which Chaucer creates lovely May, appropriate to high romance (1743–7), differs radically from that in which he creates lovely Alison of *The Miller's Tale* (3233–70). And May's response to Damyan is explained in what pass for terms of *fine amour*: *Lo, pitee renneth soone in gentil herte! Heere may ye se how excellent franchise In wommen is whan they hem narwe avyse* (1986–8). One would not call Alison Carpenter a *wench*, but, as the Manciple observed in his tale, '*Men leyn that oon as lowe as lith that oother*' (222).

The Merchant's Tale is among other things an invitation to consider the nature of deceit and its effects. The question whether there are circumstances which could extenuate the immorality of deceit, which seems to be suggested elsewhere, as in the descriptions of Manciple and Reeve,[39] is not material here, where Chaucer is examining the essential nature, the quality of deceit. The index of the moral philosopher's understanding of the essential nature of falsehood is finally the distance, in May's self-righteous speech of protest, between her words and her actual intention, which he indicates by literary contrivance, by style.

In *The Shipman's Tale* the moral philosopher examines the bearing of injury to others or the absence of such injury on the morality of actions. To do injury to others is axiomatically immoral; Chaucer is examining the converse, that if no one is materially injured by a set of actions the issue of morality is not raised. In material terms none of the three principals in this tale is the worse for what transpires; it could even be argued that all gain some advantage. In fact Chaucer's manner of proceeding makes it clear that material terms do not apply. The highly contrived tonelessness of the representation rules out any engagement with the personages, such as one can experience in warm fabliaux like *The Reeve's Tale*; the effect is to throw the lying and the money trick into greater prominence than the joylessly cold adultery. By that means of mirthlessly representing a fabliau story Chaucer creates a paradigm of the ugliness of deceit; seen with a cold eye the behaviour of the monk and the woman is totally unadmirable. From its so appearing they have lost value, and have thus been harmed by the action, and their presumed lack of concern about this would constitute still further loss. The implication, in the philosophical sense of that word, is that it is not possible to conceive of any immoral action that does not in some way do harm.[40]

Not all Chaucer's narratives, obviously, are readable as studies in moral philosophy; in some the morality is plainly Christian, in others it is not evidently to the fore. But to think in terms of moral considerations can become habitual, and it is advisable to be alert to that possibility in Chaucer's instance. Not that this always rewards: it can produce puzzles. Why did Chaucer, having among other excellences attributed three of the cardinal virtues to his righteous heathen, Cambyuscan of *The Squire's Tale*, withhold from him the fourth, namely temperance? It is hard to believe that this was an oversight.

More seriously, there is enough philosophical consideration of moral issues in Chaucer's writings to reveal one of his deepest and most preoccupying concerns, and to show him, given his religious conditioning, as amazingly perceptive. The concern is with the problem of moral choice. Why do people knowing what is the right choice make the wrong one; or, if the difference between right and wrong is absolute, why should it be difficult to identify the right choice; and above all, why are some people able to make right choices in such a way that out of a succession of right choices there develop personalities with the quality of integrity, a pronounced tendency to make the right choice? Conversely, how did the Summoner and Pardoner get to be as they are?

Chaucer did not formulate the predicament in those deliberately stark terms of the modern moral philosopher. In his time it was addressed in two great patterns of thought, the half-theological, half-metaphysical one occupied with determinism and predestination, and the exclusively theological one invoking the doctrine of grace. By translating Boethius, Chaucer registered an inmistakably serious interest, at least for a time, in the former. His exertion, and it must have been *a greet penaunce*, brought him great gains as a poet, whatever it may have failed to bring him in the way of enlightenment. As to the doctrines of grace, I do not find him actively involved with them as Langland was, though doubtless he took from them such personal comfort as, in the rigorous eschatology of the later fourteenth century, they could afford an intellectually honest man.

Meanwhile experience forced the issue upon him in the shape of the observed divergence between appetite, or appetite expressed as self-interest, and morality, and the accompanying consideration that the divergence was greater, or much greater, in the case of some people than of others. He will have been forced to think how, ideally, the capacity for moral action would be available to any reasonable person to whom the question of morality could even present itself; that such a man would arrange his values in a hierarchy by which the divergence would be reduced or abolished.[41] And he could not miss seeing, he evidently did see, that the actuality was most often otherwise, but also—this is the point—that whether that capacity for moral action and right choice was present or not had an accidental look. He will have known the theological doctrine that passed for an explanation, that the operation of divine grace was mysterious, and no doubt he accepted this.[42] But writing as a layman and thinking as a moral philosopher Chaucer seems to have seen the individual disposition and the motives for which moral choice is made as a matter of chance, of the *yiftes of Fortune and of Nature*—a concept he could have got from *De Officiis*.[43]

If I am right Chaucer here anticipated the modern moral philosopher's distinction between constitutive luck, by which a man has the qualities which enable him to live as a moral, or reasonably moral person, and incident luck, which determines the circumstances in which he will move.[44] The conception so put would of course have been abhorrent doctrinally in his time, and it is there that Chaucer's activity as a moral philosopher would have been checked by the bounds of the closed system. Why some men responded to grace and some did not might be a mystery, but the explanation of randomness would not do at all. And there Chaucer's excursions into moral philosophy would always have to end.

6

Music 'Neither Unpleasant nor Monotonous'

The study of Langland's versification begins with the question why he chose to write in the alliterative long line, to which the answer must lie in his insight into the unsuitability of the 'octosyllabic' measure, the *lyght and lewed* four-stress rising rhythm with couplet rhyme, for his subject as he conceived it. From the indications of education and intellectual sophistication in his poem the choice was almost certainly deliberate and critically based rather than a matter of regional sentiment or cultural pressure. He discerned that of the two non-stanzaic verse systems available in the 1360s this was the one better suited to extended treatment of a grave and complex topic. A corresponding perception distinguishes his attitude to the alliterative tradition itself. This also appears judicious and critical: he employs very few of its distinctive mannerisms. Half a dozen synonyms for 'man' and one verb-formula are all that can be confidently related to the historical tradition.[1] Certain terms of Scandinavian origin with a dialect flavour, for instance *cairen*, *gate*, *silynge*, and *tyne*, are not in that category and the presumption is that he used them for alliterative convenience, as he evidently did the dialect alternatives *ayein/ageyn*, *chirche/kirk*, *ȝyue/gyue* and the pronoun *heo*.[2] He took from the tradition, as from the resource of dialect variety, what was conveniently serviceable, in that eclecticism instancing the same independence and originality which characterize the style and content of his poem.

Langland used the alliterative long line with remarkable virtuosity. It is paradoxical, in view of the consensus about his stature as a poet, and the progressive demonstration of modern *Piers Plowman* scholarship how careful and studied is his art, that the technical excellence of his versification is not appreciated. The old notion that his metre is 'uncouth', that he 'was not very particular' about it and 'frequently neglects to observe the strict rules',[3] that he had 'small regard for grammar',[4] and the misconception that because a fourteenth-century Englishman was educated primarily in Latin and French he would not be concerned about the spelling of English or understand its grammatical structure[5] still appear to influence critical attitudes: Langland's versification is unpolished, careless, and perfunctory.[6]

Poets generally have been more interested in the craft of versifying than their readers, and there is an a priori unlikelihood of a great poet being a careless technician. Langland was alive to the difference between good and bad performance: *is noon of pise newe clerkes*, says his text, *That kan versifie faire* (xv.373, 374). He left no sign that he might be unsure of his own ability. His Dreamer-poet is never made to invoke the modesty-topos, or to express concern about the possible technical shortcomings of his verse.[7] To write in verse about a topic is *To reden it in Retorik* (xi.102), hardly a modest expression. The hazard in verse-making is not doing it badly, but taking sinful pride in it, indulging in it to the neglect of spiritually more rewarding activity. Under rebuke of this the Dreamer makes a perfunctory excuse, as if for all the charge being well founded he does not take it seriously and means to continue in his way (xii.16 ff). These attitudes are sketched by a poet in command of his style[8] who will, as a writer in English at that literary moment, have been not merely conscious of the form of his art but self-conscious about it. In terms of that appreciation the chance of his having been casual about his versification appears slight. Either he was unaware of his limitations or we have misconceived his purpose. The latter is undoubtedly the case. Two further reasons for the misconception must be added to the legacy of misdirection.

One is failure to value correctly in Langland's case the relation of a successful poet to his verse system. To conceive of it in terms of the remembered misery of schoolboy exercises, of how he 'manages to fulfil the requirements of the metre', is obfuscating. It is to himself that the mature poet is answerable for his management of the verse medium he adopts or adapts and uses. Some of the gratification he derives from his poetic activity will come from awareness of having said to his satisfaction what he was impelled to say within the self-imposed prescriptions.[9] These are truisms which should not have to be affirmed. A result of the poet's success is that his versification exists as part of the meaning of his poetic statements, not merely because the verse is effective in making that meaning more emphatic, clearer, more evidently interrelated, but also because it will engage the reader's auditory interest and confer the combination of physical and intellectual pleasure experienced when pattern and meaning are simultaneously apprehended. A kind of 'fallacy of rules' which over-emphasizes the need for the poet's regularity is possible. Certainly by writing in verse he undertakes a formal responsibility. But in his success it becomes a pleasurable one, a means of achievement, and he will cultivate it, not behave in respect of it like someone who cheats at patience. There will be an immeasurable difference of quality between his performance and that of a barely competent versifier such as Lydgate; this puts another set of standards into effect.

The second reason is misappreciation of the fourteenth-century alliterative long line as a verse medium. From the number of its syllables not being regulated, and its rhythm being indeterminately rising or falling, it has been judged incapable of modulation.[10] The systematicians who have tried to establish its nature by 'scanning' quantities of lines have been handicapped by inadequate means of notation which either obscure or fail to register the auditory interest of the alliterative long line in good use.[11] Moreover because they have in general neglected to make enough allowance for scribal damage, especially in texts uniquely preserved, the norms they propose are necessarily to some extent false. The indifferent quality of most alliterative 'poetry', however notable the exceptions, can make the long line seem a crude instrument.

If this were true of the alliterative long line as Langland uses it there would be slight regard for his poem and little pleasure to be derived from reading it. The greatness of a poem implies technical excellence: its metre, as a component of style and meaning and feeling, must be commensurate with its other features. What distinguishes Langland's use of the line is his evident perception that alliteration can have a substantive phonetic existence independent of the metrical accents[12] of a line, that the recurrence in a certain proximity of the same initial phoneme or conventionally associated initial phoneme sets up a pattern of a different character from the rhythmic pattern of the line,[13] one established in the first instance by auditory experience of the recurrence, without necessary relation to the variations of tone, pitch and volume by which the rhythmic pattern is sensed.[14] The two patterns might coincide; lines where this occurred in the first three of four metrical accents would be normative. To make the patterns coincide only partially was to modulate the line. In such cases the pattern of metrical accents would be established and maintained by semantic stress;[15] the more or less different disposition of the alliterative pattern (still fulfilling its initial or historical function of 'genre specification')[16] would both create auditory interest by disappointment of conventional expectation and generate poetic energy by provoking consideration of possible reasons for the departure from the norm. How strikingly Langland operates this principle has been variously noticed.[17]

The norm upon which he modulates his verses is a line containing four semantically determined metrical accents, divisible two and two at a grammatically tolerable point of pause, of which the first three accents fall upon syllables which alliterate, that is, begin with identical or conventionally associated consonant phonemes or with vowel phonemes. The rhythm of this norm is indeterminately rising or falling; the number of its unstressed or more lightly stressed syllables is not fixed. The immediately obvious possibilities of modulation are in the number of metrical accents, the extent and exactness of coincidence between the two patterns, accentual and phonemic, the presence of hypernormative alliteration or of a second alliteration differing from the normative, and the position of the pause. From a presumption set up by the character of the poem the dominant pattern in a line is the semantically determined one of metrical accents: the rhythm of the line will be a performance-rhythm. The alliteration, the generically distinctive formal feature of the line, will contribute to its intellectual and emotional meaning as a second pattern.

The brilliance of Langland's versification begins with those lines of *Piers Plowman* which exemplify that norm and are therefore by definition not modulated. They illustrate how well he understood and exploited the potential of the option of rising or falling rhythm and the freedom of syllabic number. A few typical illustrations will have to suffice. There are lines of 'average'[18] length with rising rhythm: *Ac loue and lowenesse and leautee togideres* (III.291), *For his luþer lif þat he lyued hadde* (V.380). There are lines of similar length with falling rhythm: *Lurkynge þoruʒ lanes, tolugged of manye* (II.219), *Drede at þe dore stood and þe doom herde* (II.208). There are markedly long lines with rising rhythm: *For no cause to cacche siluer þerby, ne to be called a maister* (XI.174), *And dide hym assaie his surgenrie or hem þat sike were* (XVI.106); and lines as long with a falling one: *Lentestow euere lordes for loue of hire mayntenaunce?* (v.250), *Coueitise comþ of þat wynd and crepeþ among þe leues* (xvi.28). There are lines which give an effect of being appreciably shorter: with rising rhythm, *I shal seken truþe er I se Rome* (v.460), *In dolful deþ deyeden for hir faith* (xv.522); and with falling rhythm, *Adam and Eue he egged to ille* (i.65), *Falsnesse I fynde in þi faire speche* (xvi.154). There are lines with adjacent metrical accents in the first half: *For þat is þe book blissed of blisse and of ioye* (xi.168); and in the second half: *And is as glad of a gowne of a gray russet* (xv.167); and across the caesura: *Er I wedde swich a wif wo me betide* (iii.121). It is not easy to find two lines which one would confidently 'scan' the same: the variety is huge.[19] Its first effect is constant auditory interest.

The interest, tension, generated by modulation is at least as much intellectual as it is sensory. Expert modulation implies for the reader/hearer the question why the poet undertook it, which directs him to the meaning of the line.

That appears even from the simplest kind of modulation to be found in *Piers Plowman*. This is represented in lines differentiated from the norm by the presence of a fifth (in a few cases even a sixth) semantically established metrical accent on an unalliterating syllable. Such accents, which necessarily alter the whole rhythm of the line,[20] surprise by their presence outside the norm, disappoint by not alliterating, and represent the contextual necessity or importance of the words where they fall as vindication of the modulated rhythm. Lines so modulated are quite common: discounting those where strong disagreement between good readers about relative grades of stress is possible, the type is well established.[21]

The additional metrical accent occurs at the beginning of the first half-line: *For béttre is a litel los þan a long sorwe* (Prol. 191), *The kýng haþ mede of his men to make pees in londe* (iii.221), *And lásse he dredeþ deeþ and in derke to ben yrobbed* (xi.268), *And for góddes loue leueþ al and lyueþ as a beggere* (xiv.264), *How énglisshe clerkes a coluere fede þat coueitise hiȝte* (xv.415). Less often it occurs between the two alliterated metrical accents in the first half-line: *And riden fáste for Reson sholde rede hem þe beste* (iv.30), *Amonges crístene men þis myldenesse sholde laste* (xv.258), *And assoille men of álle synnes saue of dette one* (xix.190). In a few lines it comes after both alliterated metrical accents in the first half-line: *Why sholde we þat nów ben for þe werkes of Adam* (x.115). It occurs before the alliterating accent in the second half-line: *And haue power to punysshe hem*; *þánne put forþ þi reson* (ii.49), *And what meschief and maleese críst for man þolede* (xiii.77), *Til it bifel on a friday, a lítel bifore Pasqe* (xvi.139), *Which is lif þat oure lord in álle lawes acurseþ* (xviii.107), *Conscience criede, 'hélp, Clergie or I falle* (xx.228). Very occasionally a line will have two additional metrical accents on un-alliterating syllables unmistakably imposed by the sense in the context: *Ioye þat néuere ioye hadde of rí3tful Iugge he askeþ* (xiv.111).

A more intricate modulation occurs when semantic emphasis appears to compete for attention with the alliterative pointing: a syllable, most often a monosyllabic word, adjacent to one of the three normative alliterating syllables, has as much as or more semantic importance than this. Here the rhythm is not supplemented or extended but complicated by ambiguity. Depending on the meaning of the line in the context, the adjacency of the two kinds of distinction, phonetic emphasis and alliteration, either results in level stress (itself a kind of modulation) or raises doubt about which is dominant. Disappointment of expectation of the coincidence of patterns becomes auditory experience of their distinct effects.

Such words occur before the first alliterating syllable: *Yé, lord, quod þat lady, lord forbede ellis!* (iii.112), *And keép som til soper tyme and sitte no3t to longe* (vi.263), *And whát man he my3te be of many man I asked* (viii.5), *If fáls latyn be in þat lettre þe lawe it impugneþ* (xi.304), *The chíef seed þat Piers sew, ysaued worstow neuere* (xix.406). They also occur before the second: *I wolde þat éch wight were my knaue* (v.117), *And breþeren as of óo blood, as wel beggeres as Erles* (xi.200), *Boþe to riche and to nó3t riche þat rewfulliche libbeþ* (xiv.152), *Dos ecclesie þís day haþ ydronke venym* (xv.560), *So nede at grét nede may nymen as for his owene* (xx.20). And they occur before the third: *And in fastynge dayes to frete ér ful tyme were* (ii.96), *And blody breþeren we bicome þere of ó body ywonne* (xi.202), *Willynge þat men wende hís wit were þe beste* (xiii.291), *It is lighter to leeue in þré louely persones* (xvii.46), *Alarm! alarme! quod þat lord, éch lif kepe his owene!* (xx.92). They occur before two of the alliterating syllables: *Forþi lakke nó lif ooþer þou3 he moóre latyn knowe* (*XI*.214), *Goód hope, þat helpe sholde, to wánhope torneþ* (xvii.315); and even before three: *Thré leodes in oón lyth, noón lenger þan ooþer* (xvi.181). In at least one instance two occur before the third alliterating syllable: *And seide to Sathan, ló! here mý soule to amendes* (xviii.327). Occasionally they follow the alliterating syllable: *And lawefulle men to lifhóly men liflode brynge* (xv.308), *And suwed þat Samaritan þat was so fúl of pite* (xvii.87).

There are, further, lines which, combining these two modulations, have both an unmistakable independent additional metrical accent and one that appears to compete with a normatively alliterating syllable for prominence. Examples are: *Wit and frée wil, to eúery wiȝt a porcion* (VIII.53), *And be we nóȝt vnkynde of oure catel, ne of oure konnyng neiþer* (XI.212), *Leneþ hé nó lif lasse ne moore* (XIII.17), *Confortour of creatures; of hým comeþ álle blisse* (XVI.190).

The sense of competition for prominence between the two patterns of metrical accent and alliteration in lines modulated like the last two kinds relates to the distinctive function of the alliterative long line in expert use. The dominant pattern will always be the pattern of metrical accents corresponding to the semantic content of the line. This is because the intonation it implies is indispensable to effective communication. And in works where most lines are unmodulated the alliteration can become so associated with metrical accentuation that it comes to seem merely the generic mark of the verse form, unreflectively identified with tonal emphasis, or an aid to reading, or the ear can (in self-protection against monotony) become insensitive to it as an auditory experience.[22] In the modulated lines of *Piers Plowman*, which are numerous, the distinctiveness of alliteration as an indicator of prominence is clearer. The alliteration in modulated lines which does not coincide with or become lost in vocal emphasis appears in a role not so much secondary as functionally independent, makes its point less insistently and with subtler suggestion than, by its nature, does the energetic distinction of pitch, length and volume.

The kind of modulation which exhibits most clearly Langland's understanding that the two patterns exist independently and are separable occurs in lines where at some point metrical accent and alliteration must be differently located because the alliterating syllable is (less commonly occurs in) a 'grammatical' as opposed to a 'lexical' word, one which would not normally bear stress in connected speech[23] and upon which the context does not confer relative importance.

In the following lines the word is a monosyllabic preposition: *It is noȝt by þe bisshop þat þe boy precheþ* (Prol. 80), *Ye shul abiggen boþe, by god þat me made!* (II.128), *I dar not for fere of hym fiȝte ne chide* (IV.52), *Boþe afyngred and afurst, and for chele quake* (X.60), *And from fendes þat in hem was and false bileue* (XIX.47), *And flapten on wiþ flailes fro morwe til euen* (VI.184), *Tel me to whom þat tresour appendeþ* (I.45), *Treuþe herde telle herof, and to Piers sente* (VII.1), *And wommen wiþ childe þat werche ne mowe* (VII.101), *That þeiȝ we*

wynne worship and with *Mede haue victorie* (III.352). The alliterating
preposition and its metrically stressed object are not always adjacent
syllables: *And a title, a tale of noʒt,* to *his liflode at meschief* (XI.300),
The bisshop shal be blamed bi*fore god, as I leue* (XI.311). The
alliterating word may be a form of the verb *to be* without evident
special contextual stress: *And as a Brocour brouʒte hire to* be *wiþ fals
enioyned* (II.66), *That is baptiʒed* beþ *saaf, be he riche or pouere*
(X.351), *And beden hire be bliþe*: for *we* beþ *þyne owene* (III.27),
Ooþerwise þan he was *warned of þe prophete* (III.275), *I waitede
wisloker and þanne* was *it soilled* (XIII.342), *Raþer þan to baptiʒe
barnes þat* ben *Catecumelynges* (XI.77), *Ac wisdom and wit* were
aboute faste (IV.81). It may be a negative particle: *He þat neuere* ne
dyued ne noʒt kan of swymmyng (XII.165), *Noght of þe nounpower of
god, þat he* ne *is myghtful* (XVII.316). It may be a possessive adjective:
And þe myddel of myn *hand wiþoute maleese* (XVII.195).

If Langland's understanding of the separability and distinct modes
of function of alliteration and metrical accent and his capacity to
apply this were not otherwise evident there might be warrant for
judging lines like those just quoted to be 'irregular' or 'incorrectly
versified' or else to instance a perfunctory fulfilment of the generic
requirement. But the *a priori* likelihood that the lines are
purposefully modulated directs to scrutiny of the relation between
the alliterative and metrically accented words. This proves to be
closely phrasal: of preposition and object, linking verb and
complement, quasi-preclitic adverb of negation and verb, possessive
adjective and noun. The modulation disappoints expectation of
alliteration on the accented syllable of the phrase, the centre of its
'pitch contour', but in compensation by separating the patterns
divides and sets off its components and implies the government or
modification which unites them. In such an understanding, which if
Langland did not achieve himself he could find in his Priscian,[24] the
modulation appears a function of meaning, calling for sensitive
reading to be sure, but no more wayward or careless a distinction of
an unstressable syllable than is the use in generic alliteration of
grammatical words with special contextual importance, as for instance
So bi hise werkes þei wisten þat he wás Iesus (XI.238) or *And ek, haue
god my soule, ánd þow wilt it craue* (XIII.164).[25]

One extreme of sophisticated modulation in *Piers Plowman* is
found in the poet's use of alliteration beyond the requirement of the
generic norm. Such alliteration has been misconceived as 'not

functional, but decorative'.[26] It is of course impossible for any element of a poem which has power of engagement to be inert ornament, 'not functional'.[27] In fact the modes of function of hypernormative alliteration in *Piers Plowman* correspond approximately to those recognized in classical times, that is the imitative and the associative.[28] The difference is that Langland's practice transcends the one and refines the other.

The transcendence consists in understanding the particular applicability to alliteration of a principle that modern criticism accepts but finds hard to express definitively, namely that the patterns of sound experienced in reading verse are determinants of the effect of poetic statement beyond simply giving pleasure.[29] Our emotional and intellectual response to a passage, respectively particularized by denotation and connotation, is intensified by auditory experience of pattern in its language; in the simultaneous apprehension of the whole we impute to the semantically empty constituents of the pattern, here to the initial sounds organized as pattern by their recurrence, the meaningfulnesses of the expressions where they occur, so that their a-logicality is not merely subsumed into, but greatly enhances, the entire significance.[30]

So, when the Dreamer expresses the criticism that *pilgrymes konne wel lye*,

> I seiȝ somme þat seiden þei hadde ysouȝt Seintes;
> To ech a tale þat þei tolde hire tonge was tempred to lye
> Moore þan to seye sooþ, it semed bi hire speche.

> (Prol. 50–2)

the additional alliteration is not 'senseless and tasteless stuffings of the line with five or even six alliterated words'[31] but a factor in our reaction to the speaker's disillusionment at the abuse of a pious institution. Even a fourth alliterating syllable, of whatever grade of stress, draws the three generically formal ones into prominence: the alliterative pattern seems momentarily to dominate, and in the impression of effortless fluency of alliteration we hear the glib fabrications and are drawn to the Dreamer's attitude.[32] So at the trial of Wrong in IV we hear multiple alliteration as the smooth persuasiveness of his defenders which might pervert justice;[33] it figures also in the speeches of the temptresses by the Mirror of Middle Earth.[34] But its function is not specialized: it can equally well lend persuasiveness to the explanation of a mystery or force to a rebuke, seem to imply the extreme gravity of an offence, suggest a state of moral confusion, or simply give an impression of increase of pace.[35] It can be used to rhetorical effect. Which of two men thrown into the Thames is in more peril, goes the question, the one who cannot swim

> Or þe swymmere þat is saaf by so hymself like
> Ther his felawe fleteþ forþ as þe flood likeþ?

> (xii.166, 167)

The sensory contrast between the even distribution of alliteration in 166 and its imbalance in 167 is an auditory inducement to compare their content. The two hypernormative alliterations, *so* in 166b and *forþ* in 167a, thrown into contrast by their respective prominence as a grammatical word and as the third in the half-line, further set off the adjacent opposites of choice and helplessness. We sense the point of the exemplum as a physical, an auditory experience; in the daring near-rhyme alliterating with itself and differentiated only by modal inflexion, however, the boundaries of physical and intellectual or emotional experience are less clearly definable.

In that respect lines with vocalic alliteration are a special case. This is because the actual constituents of their alliterative pattern, the initial vowel phonemes, whether or not preceded by *h*, can be uttered with variable frequency (heard as pitch) and variable length. That is, the alliterating sounds themselves are capable of bearing stress and metrical accent. So the alliterating vowels play a larger part in the dramatic fabric of the line than is possible for alliterating consonants. In normative vocalically alliterating lines there can be exceptional force in the direction of the coinciding patterns to semantic importance: for instance in *Coueiteþ hé noon erþely good, but heueneriche blisse* (xv.175) to the exceptional identity in the pronoun, or in *For Antecrist and híse al þe world shul greue* (xix.219) to the appalling implications in the possessive. In lines with hypernormative vocalic alliteration, because the differentiations between the extremes of heaviest and most lightly stressed alliterating syllables can be so fine, there are special effects. The vocalic beginnings of words not metrically accented are assumed into the pattern formed where alliteration coincides with the metrical accents: the gradations of stress developed by the contextual meaning and feeling set up a kind of tune. For instance, in *To hem þat hengen hym heiʒ and his herte þirled* (ɪ.174) the pronouns and possessive adjective are coloured by the emotion arising from the relation of their referents; in *For if heuene be on þis erþe, and ese to any soule* (x.305) *if*, *on* and *any* by their function in the 'contrary-to-fact' speculation acquire metrical importance as subtle exponents of the meaning; in *For hem þat haten vs is oure merite to louye* (xɪ.183) from the paradox in the doctrine the grammatical words which express it have very subtle graduations of stress. Such instances could be multiplied.[36]

Langland's refinement of the associative or 'grouping' function of alliteration[37] appears in a variety of highly sophisticated modulations. A simple but extreme illustration of its operation is afforded by a number of lines where the phrasing or syntax compels deferment of the medial pause,[38] as in *Pardon wiþ Piers Plowman truþe haþ ygraunted* (vɪɪ.8) or *Lere hem litlum and litlum et in Iesum Christum filium* (xv.610). The effect is refined when, in lines already so modulated, he introduces secondary, extrageneric alliteration. This functions primarily as an intellectual rather than a sensory and emotional device, a figure of thought. We hear words with similar beginnings as a group: words so grouped by an alliteration other than the generic one are also by that feature set apart, and this directs us to consider how their meanings might be related. Then even the perception that the secondary alliteration is explicable as an accident of the vocabulary of the topic can enhance understanding. The range of application is considerable. Sometimes the secondary grouping appears merely for emphasis: *And flour to fede folk wiþ as* best be *for þe soule* (xɪv.30). But often it is more subtly directive: for instance in *And gan wexe wroþ with lawe for* Mede *al*moost *hadde shent it* (ɪv.174) by setting off *almoost* it indicates that the King's anger is specifically at how close Mede came to destroying the legal system. And in *And somme seruen as seruauntʒ* lordes *and* ladies (Prol. 95) the secondary grouping points to the menial nature of the activity, not merely improper for a theologian, as is looking after the royal revenue, but also degrading.[39]

Similar functions are observable where, as is not uncommon, secondary alliteration occurs in otherwise normative lines. It is seldom safe to explain this as accidental. For instance in *Ac for þe beste ben* som *riche and* some *beggeres and pouere* (xɪ.198) Langland could have written *opere* for *some*;[40] or in *And inobedient to ben vndernome of any* lif lyuynge (xɪɪɪ.281) used any number of combinations such as *man lyuynge*, *lyues creature* and so on. And it is not material whether he consciously chose the alliterative combination; by virtue of existing it is functional: the two conditions of life are formally separated, the category is the broadest conceivable. The secondary alliteration occurs in various positions.[41] A refinement is to make it cross the generic one, as in *Suffraunce is a souerayn* vertue, *and a swift* vengeaunce (XI.379). The device generates engagement by auditory suggestion of a significant relation between the concepts linked and set apart by the secondary alliteration and their joint bearing on the rest of the statement: in *Forþi* ech *a wis wiȝt* I *warne*, *wite wel* his owene (Prol. 208), where there is already from the hypernormative generic alliteration a portentous quality about the mouse's wisdom after the event, the vocalic secondary alliteration, gradually forced on our notice, sets off the selfish triviality of the actual advice.[42]

There are lines with two possible generic alliterative patterns. In some the effect is merely formal: distributive, for instance in *Somme in Eyr*, *somme in erþe*, *somme in helle depe* (I.125). But often the patterns correspond to relations of meaning, as in *For I wol go wiþ þis gome*, *if god wol yeue me grace* (XIII.181). Here one significance is Conscience's rejection of the friar's evaluation of Patience implicit in his decision to accompany the latter as a pilgrim, the other his acknowledgement that he needs divine help in the enterprise. Each alliteration sets off both meanings, but in different proportion. The implication is of the paramountcy of the second.[43] There are even a few lines with two possible generic alliterations and a secondary one to boot, like *Sire Se-wel*, *and Sey-well*, *and* here-*wel þe* hende (IX.20).

Langland's concept of language as *a game of heuene* (IX.104), 'a celestial diversion', and the abundant wit in his style confirm the suggestion of effective playfulness here and in other places. For instance in *I haue an Aunte to Nonne and an Abbesse boþe* (V.153) there is a choice between a vocalic alliteration and one produced by colloquial misdivision. In

> *Presul* and *Pontifex* and *Metropolitanus*,
> And oþere names an heep, *Episcopus* and *Pastor*
>
> (XV.42,43)

the contrast between grand Latin and homely English, the modulation in the separateness of alliteration and metrical accent in

Episcopus, and the secondary alliteration of its tonic and post-tonic syllables with *Pastor* are elements in our impression of the Dreamer's misguided elation. In *Thyn euenecristene eueremoore eueneforþ with þiselue* (xvii.137) the near-*annominatio* is not accidental.

The extensions of this dimension of Langland's verse technique into style and meaning which signal the end of my demonstration are a study in themselves, too large for consideration here, but they must be noticed. They can be briefly illustrated from the names of his personages which alliterate. There the pattern can have several functions. It will always constitute qualitative progression: call True-Tongue Tom and the name is apt and right for him (iv.18).[44] It can generate meaning: calling Abstinence an aunt (v.383) implies strict and uncomfortable but ultimately beneficial correction. It can create dramatic humour, as with the names of the two lawyers in the trial of Wrong in Passus iv. First they are Warren Wisdom and his companion Witty (27), next Wisdom and Sir Warren the Witty (67), then Wisdom and Wit (76, 81), and finally there is Warren Wisdom again (154).[45] Their variable names suggest shiftiness, unreliability, the bewilderment of the layman in a court of law.

There has been some welcome awareness of the stylistic intricacy of *Piers Plowman*.[46] Analysis of its metre would demonstrate a corresponding quality there. The technical excellence of Langland's verse has been repeatedly sensed through the barrier of amateurish misconceptions: even Saintsbury's mistaken notions could not put down his sensibility: 'There *is* music in this *un*metre; and, what is more, the music is neither unpleasant nor monotonous.'[47] Understanding will come with correct evaluation of differences. One is between the alliterative long line and the Chaucerian: no good purpose is served by looking for the qualities of the one in the other, since they simply function in different ways. The second is between Langland's alliterative long line and those of its other versifiers. In that dispersed and undocumented tradition there would be no consensus about a norm, or rules: the individual poet's conception of the verse form would be the accidental product of his special experience of it rather than a least common denominator. Some wrote wooden and regular verses, easy to scan, whether because they were conforming to what they conceived of as rules or through lack of ear and understanding. As for Langland, his alliterative long line works, and its effective operation is explicable in terms of modern criticism. This is unlikely to be an accident. More probably it reflects the quality of his sensibility, artistic insight, and control.[48]

7
Poetry and Lexicography in the Translation of *Piers Plowman*

That a poem is essentially not translatable will be evident to literary critics simply from consideration of the inseparability of form and content in poetry. The abstractions by which we define those concepts appear as intellectual exercises or critical expediencies when we attempt translation. The translator immediately discovers how the external form of his poem as a complex of linguistic norms implies classes of meaning both beyond the lexicographical and totally peculiar to the language in which it was composed: namely the physical effect of significant form, that is of organized sound expressing organized sense; and the emotional experience insofar as this is developed by connotation. Neither of those classes of meaning is authentically transferable into another language; the translation will either lack them or, more probably, offer substitutes. Its form in that other language will create more or less appreciable new meanings of those classes.

Theoretical discussion of translation by linguisticians reaches the same conclusions more laboriously. One reads, for instance, 'the greater the significance of the form for the comprehension and appreciation of the message, the more difficult it is to find appropriate formal equivalences in the receptor language,'[1] or, 'the degree of difficulty in approximating the content of the original increases with the relative importance that connotative meaning properties possess in the text to be translated.'[2] The implication of the expressions 'more difficult' and 'degree of difficulty' in those quotations, that there is a possibility of full success, appears not intended; the almost invariable conclusion of any theoretical discussion is that wholly satisfactory translation of anything but purely utilitarian prose is impossible. Any translation describable as a 'self-contained literary work of art' must to the extent of the justice of that description differ existentially from and imperfectly represent its original.[5] By axiom, moreover, no translation is wholly satisfactory to anyone competent in the language of its original. What does in theory appear to be reproducible in translation is the form of event and thought in a poem, its abstractable prose meaning.[4] Even this can be difficult in practice.[5]

The nature of the problem makes theoretical discussion of translation, especially by linguisticians with evidently little experience of the activity or of poetry, unenlightening. It is also repetitive; the approaches to the predictable negative conclusion tend to differ mainly in the variety of jargon employed. Even in the liveliest discussion, things seem new which have been forgotten: Steiner in *After Babel*,[6] dismissing, without naming him, Dryden's division of translation into variously 'metaphrase, paraphrase and imitation'[7] as 'the sterile triadic model,' the 'perennial distinction between literalism, paraphrase and free imitation,' because it is 'wholly contingent,' without 'precision or philosophic basis,' offers as if something novel, 'the key fact that a fourfold *hermeneia*, Aristotle's term for discourse which signifies because it interprets, is conceptually and practically inherent in even the rudiments of translation.'[8] But that is not new: without the gratuitous multiplication of categories it will be old hat to anyone who has ever had to translate an English author into Latin, and it was expressed forty years ago, in language endearingly free of jargon, as 'that thinking things out again which is the foundation of translation as a fine art.'[9]

What matters in Steiner's sentence is the statement that the three-fold classification 'has no precision or philosophic basis,' in other words is arbitrary. That is true of any categorization of translation, never mind how manifold. For any translation is at best a second-best, not a liberation from 'the need for learning a language'[10] but a makeshift to supply a deficiency of linguistic knowledge. And the management of detail in any translation will be governed by the unique relation between the character of the text being attempted and that of the recipient language and culture at the moment of translation. From both these considerations every translation worth taking seriously is an event of wholly casual origin and a pragmatic solution of a particular problem.[11]

This applies *a fortiori* to translating *Piers Plowman*, by which I understand producing an authentic modern English version of the work. The added force comes from the poem being itself in a form of English, differentiated only historically and only partly so differentiated. The English of 1978, directly descended from that of 1378, has changed and continues to change in many particulars of grammar and lexicography but not uniformly or systematically and not always (to the untrained eye) visibly. So the Jakobson definition of what he calls 'intralingual translation or *rewording*,' as 'an inter-pretation of verbal signs by means of other signs of the same language,'[12] applies only if one adds the qualifier 'where necessary.'

For both psychological and linguistic reasons intralingual transla-tion is very difficult.[13] The historical identity of the two forms of the language, evident to anyone from their extensive similarity of appearance, introduces an emotional element, subconscious resent-ment of the need for translation, such as expresses itself in the indestructible illusion that Chaucer's English, if its spelling is modernized, is pretty directly accessible. A word which looks the same in modern as in early English ought, after all, to mean the same. In fact there is a double semantic variable: of contextual aptness, as in an ordinary lexicographical situation; and of historical aptness: is there evidence that the word was actually used in a particular sense at a particular period? So in theory a fourteenth-century word and its twentieth-century descendant identifiable visually as such can have totally different sets of semantic values, or approximately identical sets, or some approximately identical and some chronologically differentiated values. Elementary generalizations, of course, for any reader of Middle English, but if he is honest he will agree that while the first and second possibilities give him little trouble, the third, by far the most often instanced, is easy to overlook. It bedevils the interpretative, the analytic function of translation from Middle English (as of course also from other early languages into their descendants).[14] And it haunts the expert translator from the early to the modern form of his language, who can find himself in a state of mind analogous to that of the genuine bilingual, who finds it difficult to translate at all closely from one of his languages into the other.

Here then is our predicament: in the first instance poetry is not susceptible of perfect translation; in the second, the greater a poem the less chance there is of a translation doing it even poor justice—and then, in the third, translating from early to modern English involves special, initially lexicographical hazards. In that situation what is the best pragmatic solution? What compromise is right, when some effects cannot be transferred, between what can be sacrificed and what must be preserved? The answer may emerge from consideration of the extent to which some of the various formal elements of the poem can genuinely be rendered accessible today. The essential beginning must be interpretation. Then, on the presumption that the desideratum is to create not a modern approximation to *Piers Plowman*[15] but the most accurate possible representation of those features of it which are realizable in modern English, the translation acquires the character of an open act of historical cognition in which, prima facie at least, the form of event and thought, the 'conceptual framework' of the poem will be a factor. How correct that presumption may be will now be my concern.

The first and most important single element of external form to be lost in producing the kind of translation I have just described is the verse. Reasons for translating *Piers Plowman* into prose could be multiplied,[16] beginning with the fact that no verse system equivalent to the alliterative long line is in use today, but the main reason must be the impossibility of reproducing together in modern English even a remote correspondence to the intricate and subtle music of Langland's verse and the intricate and subtle argument of his sense. That is a categorical assertion, but much of the rest of this essay will incidentally demonstrate its correctness.

It goes without saying that the loss by translation into prose is immense. Its scale can be gauged from the critical proposition that there are in the poem many passages of doctrinal or homiletic substance now largely destitute of any but historical interest which still read enjoyably in the original because of the technical brilliance of the verse that expresses them, a brilliance in which Langland's often highly ingenious satisfaction of the formal requirements of the alliterative long line can seem the least remarkable element. Ironically, with the loss comes a hazard: the translator into prose will often want to reduce alliteration with lexicographically unnecessary synonyms, or redistribute alliterating terms, in order to avoid uncomfortable effects like those in Malory's transprosing of *The Alliterative Morte Arthur*.

Another salient quality of external form lost in translation of *Piers Plowman* is concision and with concision poetic energy. That loss could, for what it is worth, be measured: the Penguin translation of the B version runs to 1,000 lines more than its original. What actually matters, of course, is the greater diffuseness of individual statements. There are various linguistic reasons for this.

One is loss of meaning in the modal verbs *shall*, *will* and *may*. We today use the first two pretty indiscriminately as future auxiliaries. But in Middle English *shall*, among other senses, signified certainty of outcome:[17] *no dynt shal hym dere as in deitate patris* (xviii.26),[18] 'it is certain that no blow will injure him in his godhead' (the reason why Christ jousts with Death in his human nature); or else necessity, compulsion:[19] a master who holds back the pay of his servants says *Ruþe is to here rekenyng whan we shul rede acountes*, 'it is pathetic to hear what I owe when we are obliged to make up the accounts' (v.427); or else imposed obligation:[20] *Thow shalt seye I am þi Suster*, says a whore to a pardoner (v.642). And *will* in *Piers Plowman* more often than otherwise signifies some aspect of volition. Such meaning is, for example, evident in *if þow wilt be gracious to god do as þe gospel techeþ* (vi.227),[21] or where Avarice lends money to *folk þat lese wol*, 'people who are willing to lose'[22] a clipping from every coin (v.247); and Envy expresses his change of heart, *I wole amende þis if I may*, 'I am resolved to correct this if I am able' (v.134).[23] As for *may*, which along with its preterite *might* we generally use to express possibility, permission or sanction, in Middle English its primary sense was 'having the ability or power to carry out an action,'[24] as in the last example, or in Envy's description of the effect of his gastric ulcer, *I myȝte noȝt ete many yeres as a man ouȝte*, 'I have been unable to eat normally for many years' (v.121). These verbs are very common; their Middle English meanings are seldom clearly conveyed by the modern forms and often call for more extended paraphrase.

Another reason is the disuse of subjunctive forms in modern English. Where Middle English can by the subjunctive express, for instance, uncertainty: *What man of þis world þat hire were leuest*, 'the man who might be dearest to her' (iii.6); or hypothesis: *This were a wikkede weye*, 'This would be a cruel road' (vi.1); or condition: *founde I þat his pardoun Miȝte lechen a man*, 'if I found that his pardon was able to cure a person' (xiii.252,253), almost invariably modern English needs several words to transmit the full meaning.

Similarly the obscuring of the dative function adds to the prolixity of translation. To give just one instance: *This were a wikkede weye*, the converted people of the field complain, except if one had a guide *That myȝte folwen vs ech foot*, 'who would be able to trace each foot (of the road) for us' (vi.2). Subjective and objective genitive uses are frequent in Middle English. It is said to the man who makes ostentatious benefactions, *god knoweþ . . . þi cost and þi coueitise*, 'your disposition and how avaricious you are in fact' (III.67,68). They can seldom be translated without expansion.

A feature of Middle English syntax and particularly of Langland's usage is the infinitive construction where now a finite clause is customary. There are, for instance, infinitives of purpose with un-signalled change of subject. Avarice lends money *to legge a wed and lese it*, 'on such terms that the borrower puts down collateral and forfeits it' (v.241); or of prescription in a legal document: *And þei to haue and to holde . . . a dwellynge*, 'And it is further specified that they shall own and retain ownership of' (II.102,103); or of injunction: *Preestes and persons wiþ Placebo to hunte*, 'Parish clergy are not to hunt, but to recite prayers such as the Office of the Dead' (III.311). In every such instance an accurate translation will be longer than its original.

That will also be the case where, as is common Middle English usage, personal and relative pronouns are unexpressed and modern English requires them. It will be the case where the style is paratactic and the logical relation of the parts of sentences is not indicated. That is a characteristic of Langlandian style: I give one notable instance which has tricked editor[25] and translator. In the third line of the poem the Dreamer tells how he dressed himself in sheep's clothing, *In habite as an heremite, vnholy of workes*, literally, 'in a hermit's habit, unsanctified of conduct.' This appears in a current translation as "in the garb of an easy-living hermit," as if there were a distinctive dress for the less pious hermits.[26] But the whole point of the statement is the Dreamer's admission of the discrepancy between his appearance of pious living and actual unregeneracy, possibly to be read as a kind of act of humility by the poet, and this must be made explicit in translation at whatever cost of compression. The need becomes extreme where the text instances a stylistic mannerism that goes beyond parataxis to the point of illogical ellipsis. A small illustration: a speaker says of a woman under accusation, 'I shall put her to the test myself, and *soopliche appose*' (III.5); the last two words, literally 'question truthfully' or 'truly', can mean only 'question in such a way as to get a true answer.'[27] There are larger ones. The personification Sloth resolves to attend church regularly: *Shal noon ale after mete holde me þennes Til I haue euensong herd* (v.453,454), literally, 'Drinking after dinner will certainly not keep me from church until I have heard vespers,' which is meaningless unless we supply 'I shall not drink' before *Til*.[28] And to illustrate another grade of ellipsis, a speaker tells how Jesus Christ allowed himself to be betrayed *to se þe sorwe of deying*, 'to experience what mankind suffers in death'; then she goes on, *The which vnknytteþ alle care and comsynge is of reste*, 'which casts off all grief and is the beginning of repose' (xviii.214,215). That rider seems to diminish the divine benevolence[29] and translation must properly supply the doctrinal connection.[30]

The qualities of concision and diffuseness of style can appear as characteristics of the external form of a poem, but because they are determinants of the intensity of its effect they are also necessarily factors in its feeling. An analogous generalization, of somewhat greater complexity, applies to the classifiable figures of Langland's style in their relation to the emotional meaning of *Piers Plowman*. To the extent that this is abstractable, the emotional meaning, the feeling of *Piers Plowman*, exists also as form. That form varies serially to constitute an incremental whole from situations of particular emotional quality. In diversity of stylistic effects it corresponds to the mixed style of religious writing, varying with pastoral admonition, high doctrinal explication, simple spiritual movements like penitence, religious exaltation, estates criticism, or apocalyptic anxiety. As we read we sense the changes of effect in large emotional movements, as if particular passages were definable units with integral capacity to evoke special responses. But in fact those movements relate to often gradual variation of texture, specifically to the classes of figures combined in a passage and their ordinal collocation, the figures existing by intellectual definition, but effective as language charged with feeling.[31] The possibility of reproducing their effects in translation is then at the outset a matter of the extent to which both the individual figures and their effectiveness in combination survive or can be reproduced in modern English. Let us look at some.

I begin with allegory, the most immediately striking, although actually by no means most distinctive, element in Langland's style. The more elementary uses readily survive translation thanks to their establishment in the modern English tradition in the seventeenth and eighteenth centuries. More special uses are harder to preserve. There is for instance momentary personification, sometimes accompanied by lexicographical difficulty. For instance, a prayer for the king runs, 'May God grant you to govern your country *so leaute þe louye*' (Prol. 126). The verb *louye*, 'may love,' establishes *leaute*, the fourteenth-century form equivalent to modern English *loyalty*, as a personifica-

tion. But precisely as a personification it is untranslatable by
'Loyalty'; it seems to mean either 'your loyal subjects' or, in my view
more probably, 'law-abiding people.'[32] Whichever meaning one opts
for, some of the tension of the original is lost along with the
personification. Local personification can generate considerable
meaning. For instance, goes a homily, it is easier for a poor man than
a rich one to avoid the capital sins. If he wrestles with Anger he is
bound to lose; against Gluttony his indigence protects him; his bed is
too cold and uncomfortable to encourage him in Sloth. As for
Avarice, and here the figure of wrestling recurs, but this time the
poor man is allegorized as Poverty, the latter is *but a petit þyng,
apereþ noʒt to his nauele*, 'only a tiny creature, doesn't even come up
to Avarice's navel, and it was never much of a bout between a big and
a small opponent' (xiv.243,244). The abrupt personification is not
casual. It evidently enables the homely index of height, and appears
pointed by the gallicism *petit*, which may be a Langlandian first use,
and if so suggests affectation. These features between them draw
attention to the assumed tone of sardonic humour in the passage—it
is, after all, preposterous to commend poverty—and as for a poor
man being free of the desire for possessions, his innocence is likely to
be only relative, a matter of scale. So we are forced to consider the
real, the spiritual reasons for the commendation of poverty. How
much of that will come over in translation? Then there is double
allezorization: '*Now repente*,' *quod Repentance*, "Now repent!" said
Repentance' to Anger (v.182); if a starving man steals a loaf or a
naked man a shirt, *Nede anoon righte nymeþ hym vnder maynprise*,
'Necessity straightaway stands surety for him,' says Necessity himself
to the Dreamer (xx.17); in the collapse of the Church at the end of
the poem Contrition abandons contrition because of the 'comfortable words' of his confessor (xx.369–71). The double allegorization
looks like a demand by the poet for thoughtful attention; this is not
likely to survive translation. Allegorization is not constant. In one
place Patience is a guest at a dinner (xiii.29), in another a garment
(xviii.168); the gold coins called florins are variously retainers of a
powerful woman so crowding the streets as to obstruct the free
movement of personified integrity (iii.157)[33] and an illness with which
a clever lawyer is afflicted, which makes him speak hypocritically
(iv.156).[34] In these and many similar, more complex instances[35]
allegory has become a figure of thought, simultaneously a
personification and a metaphor.

The texture is even more intricate when the allegory occurs in a macaronic context. Not that macaronic verse is itself necessarily hard to translate. For instance to use '*Contra!*' in a scholastic dispute (x.349), or to qualify a statement with 'That is *in extremis*' (x.352), or even to make a bilingual pun, *Fy on faitours and in fautores suos*, 'Shame on those who beg needlessly and those who support them' (xv.215) are transmittable professional mannerisms. And when the Dreamer reports, *I drow me in þat derknesse to descendit ad inferna*, 'I made my way in that darkness . . .' (xviii.111), the Latin is the poet's invocation of the Creed for authority in an apocryphal matter. The right course would seem to be to keep the Latin here. But other macaronic puns are more dynamic. For instance a cynical friar, able from the proceeds of the confessional to eat well, nevertheless gets a very sour sauce unwholesomely ground *In a morter, Post mortem* (xiii.44); the pun in collocation with the verb confers a minatory tone. And there is another grade of difficulty in, for instance, a reference to the parable of the wedding feast: *Multi to a mangerie and to þe mete were sompned* goes the text, 'Many were summoned to a feast and a meal'; when they had all arrived the porter unlocked the gate *And plukked in Pauci pryueliche*, 'snatched in a few without giving a reason for his choice' (xi.112,114). Here *Multi* and *Pauci* give the scriptural reference;[36] the complicating elements are *mangerie*, a pretentious or ceremonious term, and *plukked*, used for sharp, abrupt, or violent action, instead of the ordinary words *feste* and *nom*; they signify the special nature of the occasion and the apparent arbitrariness of the selection, and charge the passage with the Dreamer's anxiety about predestination at this point.

How serviceable Langland found the macaronic device, especially in combination with allegory, appears from his use of it at two high climaxes of the poem, meticulously prepared occasions of intense religious as well as poetic emotion. The first is the moment of spiritual transformation of the people of the field after the confession of the sins and Repentance's prayer:

Thanne hente hope an horn of *Deus tu conversus viuificabis nos*
And blew it with *Beati quorum remisse sunt iniquitates*.

(v.506,507)

The second comes after the defeat of Death and the devil, when Mercy, Truth, Righteousness, and Peace are brought into accord by Love and there has been, in Christ's speech of victory, implication of his ultimate mercy to all mankind:

> Truþe trumpede þo and song *Te deum laudamus*,
> And þanne lutede loue in a loud note,
> *Ecce quam bonum & quam iocundum.* (xviii.422–3)

In both passages the effective elements are: satisfaction of the yearning for freedom from guilt and for assurance of salvation, figured in the reconciliation of the opposed abstractions of divine justice and divine mercy; physical realization of the abstractions through the archetypally moving activity of music; and then the expression of these in the resonant Latin of the Psalms and the great hymn, evocative from a lifetime of religious observance. Each element is bound to lose some effect in translation, the combinations much more.

The problem set the translator by such striking, complex uses of relatively simple figures, whereby rhetorical form generates feeling that enters the abstractable meaning as an assertion of its force, must be evident. That of producing the finer texture of Langland's style, the detailed economy of language by which he controls response, is just as severe.

A markedly distinctive feature of his style is wit. One of his means of creating wit is incongruity, through use of a term of a grade one would not, prima facie, have expected in the context. It is possible that in some instances the device may be merely self-gratifying, playful, or else a generation of stylistic energy to sustain attention: the poet once refers to language as *a game of heuene* (ix.104) a celestial diversion, so to speak. Sometimes the incongruous terms, commonly in alliterating positions and often finite verbs, have a look of being intellectual replications to the auditory form. So Lady Meed (here personifying the expectation of loot) claims that in the French campaigns she *batred* the King's soldiers on the back and made them *hoppe for hope* of having her at will (iii.199,200); Christ made Lazarus *rise and rome* before the Jews (xv.595); he *knokked on* the moneychangers in the temple with a cord (xvi.128). And verbs denoting physical actions by personifications, as when Repentance *ran* to give out the theme of the sermon (v.60: for the theme see 182), or Do Better *is ronne*, 'has run' to the religious life (viii.91) or where Truth sees Righteousness 'come running' (xviii.165) may be primarily inducements to acceptance of the personifications by imputing to them visualizable physical activity.

But elsewhere similarly incongruous verbs develop ultralexical meaning, which cannot be translated succinctly and moreover may need explication. Intelligence nowadays is ineffectual unless it *be carded* by Covetousness (x.18), dragged out slowly and laboriously into a usable state like matted wool with a carding comb. Scripture *skipte an heiȝ*, 'skipped aloft' (hardly appropriate of a preacher), into a pulpit and preached on the uncomfortable text 'many are called but few are chosen' (xi.107); the unexpected verb can suggest how readily and easily the concept of predestination might become an anxious preoccupation. Not all the learning in Christendom could *cracche*, 'scratch, scrape, grab' the just, pagan Trajan from hell (xi. 144): the difference of grade between subject and predicate has adverbial force. Lazarus is *Lollynge* in Abraham's bosom (xvi.269); his posture of helplessness, as of a baby too young to hold its head up, suggests the condition of dependency of 'our forefathers in darkness' upon divine grace. Hope *cam hippynge*, that is 'followed hopping along,' after Abraham and the Samaritan (xvii.62), carefree (for the moment) as a child at play. Covetousness *logged*, 'trotted un-hurriedly,' to a judge and 'jousted' in his ear, thus suborning him (xx.134); the leisurely verb implies that no great effort such as getting into a gallop was needed.[37]

When this ironic use is of other parts of speech than the finite verb it can extend meaning even farther. In an ideal world *Bisshopes Bayardes* will be *beggeris Chaumbres* (iv.124): literally the fine mounts which bishops ride (but for a few notable journeys Christ travelled on foot, we recall) will be accommodation for paupers; the meaning extends to all prelates who live in the style of lords temporal. Corrupt parochial clergy are blind buzzards (x.272); the criticism— the context is of the beam in one's own eye—is pointed by the nature of the buzzard (in British English the hawk *buteo buteo*), despised as useless for falconry,[38] and remarkable only for its keen vision. In his first epiphany, as a peasant farmer, Piers Plowman speaks of the fall of Adam and Eve as eating *apples unrosted*, that is raw, or unbaked apples (v.603). He is talking in the language of his class at this point, a part of establishing his initial character. Baked apples were a main item of peasant diet in the poor season of a bad year, namely late summer before new grain came to market (vi.292–9); at that time they would be windfalls or still green on the tree, and pain would come to those who ill-advisedly ate them raw. The great command-ment of love is described as a 'charm' (xvii.20,23). The unusual application of that term directly and extensively evokes contrast between the efficacy of a central doctrine of Christianity and the delusion of belief in magic like that of Hawkin earlier in the poem:

> goddes word ne grace gaf me neuere boote,
> But þoruȝ a charme hadde I chaunce and my chief heele.
>
> (xiii.340,341)

'God's word and his grace were never any good to me; I had luck and my main success from a charm.' In those examples the irony, an index of the discrepancy between, variously, actual and right conduct, or Piers's character early and later in the poem, or of the scale of difference between temporal and eternal values, is implicit in the incongruity of language. It is easily enough explained, but what does the translator use to render Bayard and buzzard and 'unrosted' apples? There are many such instances. The problem is as hard when the device of irony consists in using concrete terms for abstract, particularly doctrinal and spiritual concepts. Hell is the *poukes pondfold*, the devil's 'pen' or 'pound' (xvi.264); the Dreamer has *þouȝtes a þreve*, 'twelve sheaves' or 'two stooks'[39] of thoughts about the Trinity (xvi.55). In the Middle English such expressions make us think of errant man as like a strayed farm animal, and of how perplexing to the plain man is the most immense doctrine of Christianity; in translation they will merely appear eccentric.

Another practically untranslatable feature of Langland's style is the pun,[40] whether homeophonic or perfectly ambiguous. As the reader will know, in the Middle Ages as in classical times the pun was neither a social misdemeanor nor a device for amusing theatre audiences with sexual innuendo, but a valued and commended figure of thought.[41] For an instance of the echoic kind: it is said of a sinful man, *Moore to good þan to god þe gome his loue caste* (xiii.356), 'The man loved property more than God.' The echo, differentiated only in the vowel, evokes the doctrine of the true and false good, which condemns him. A mismatched couple married for money have *no children but cheeste*, 'strife' (ix.172), again differentiated only in the vowel from *cheste*, a 'strongbox.' And Glutton, once he was got home from the tavern, *after all þis excesse he had an Accidie* (v.359), 'after all this excess succumbed to sloth'; here the pun operates by *excesse* and *Accidie* in collocation evoking *accesse*, 'a seizure, an onset of fever,'[42] and the sloth consequent on his sin appears a sickness of the

soul. In a trial for robbery with violence a clever defending lawyer
argues,

> Bettre is þat boote bale adoun brynge
> Than bale be ybet and boote neuer þe bettre. (ɪv.93,94)

'It is better that injury should be made good by compensation than
that wrongdoing be punished and no compensation paid.' His
glibness, to the impression of which the puns (incidentally also
personifications) contribute, suggests how legal brilliance can
obscure issues and obstruct the right course of law.

And puns by ambiguity: on Judgement Day a bishop will be
accountable, the preacher tells a sinner, for

> What he lerned yow in lente . . .
> And what he lente yow of oure lordes good to lette yow fro
> synne,
>
> (v.294,295)

that is, for 'What he taught you in Lent and what he gave to you from
our Lord's treasure to hinder you from sin.' The exact rhyme of *lente*,
'gave, bestowed on' with the name of the penitential season suggests
that the gift of our Lord's treasure might be comfort and guidance in
the longer penitential exercise of preparing for another life. A
wealthy man concerned for the state of his soul should be entertained
not by minstrels but by the poor and sick; these will at his death
comfort the man who in his lifetime *liþed hem* (xɪɪɪ, 451), that is either
'listened to them' as minstrels, or 'improved their condition' as
objects of charity.[43] At a dinner party the Dreamer is infuriated by
the conduct of an important guest, a friar theologian, and says 'I shall
dispute with this *Iurdan wiþ his Iuste wombe*' (xɪɪɪ.84). *Iurdan* was the
name of a contemporary theological controversialist;[44] it also means
'chamber pot' or 'glass vessel with a bulb-like body;'[45] and *Iuste* can
mean 'just, righteous,' or 'vessel with a narrow, long neck and a large
bottom.'[46] In those cruel puns the poet has made the Dreamer
express the bitterness and anger of simple Christians at what they saw
as the cynicism and failure of dedication of the friars. They are
untranslatable.

Poetic form, concision and along with this force of statement, the energy expressed through feeling generated in a highly figurative style, and extensive ultralexical meaning: a dismal list of probable loss in the translation of *Piers Plowman*, and it is by no means complete, for my demonstration was restricted to a few differences between the early and present language and some figures characteristic variously of religious dream visions or of Langland's personal style.

There will also be loss of tonal effect, the quality of utterance which, as of an historical voice, is part of the experience of any significant poem. The tone of this one is simply not reproducible in today's English. There is space to illustrate this only in respect of some altered usage; the matter of the Dreamer's tone of voice as an individual, a main factor in our impression of him as a dramatic personality,[47] is too large a subject for this occasion. As to the historical authenticity, our language has no longer any usage corresponding to the pious oaths that lard the speech of even the most innocent characters, or to violent but unobscene terms of abuse like *sherewe* or *feloun* or *lorel* or *losel* or *ribaud* or *harlot*[48] or *boie*.[49] For the imaginative numeral usages of Middle English we substitute colorless adverbs: *hewe fir at a flynt foure hundred wynter*, 'strike fire from a flint four hundred winters' says the poem of an unavailing activity (xvii.248); 'for ever' is the translator's attempt.[50] Our criteria of value are less vivid: we no longer gauge worthlessness by a sop or a pea or a piecrust[51] or a rush or a stalk of cress. Our food habits have changed: the expensive dishes relished by Friar Jordan (xiii.41) we would think of as sloppy messes, and the bacon rejected by the peasants when times are good (vi.309) has become dear. A poor man in those days dressed in *russet* (viii.1) the tweed that we buy when we can afford it. As for money, supposing it were possible to assess the value in 1378 of *a pound of nobles*, 'a pound weight of gold coins of a particular kind first minted by Edward III' (x.295), still the visual effect of the original correlative would be unreproducible. And how can we equate *two pens*, evidently more than enough, which the Samaritan gave for the keep of the man set upon by thieves (xvii.79)?

The questions multiply. Why, for instance, is a priest called Sir Piers *of Pridie* (v.312)? How can breaking wind be a form of entertainment (xiii.231)? Why does Friar Jordan use the name *dido* to dismiss a statement as fanciful nonsense (xiii.172)? What were Folville's laws (xix.247)? Countless such details of information which Langland and his creation the Dreamer and their contemporary

audience took for granted have had laboriously to be recovered or
await recovery. The expressions embodying them require annota-
tion, not translation. To that extent again the character of the
translation as a source of literary and dramatic experience is
diminished.

The conclusion is in sight that an authentic poetic equivalent to
Piers Plowman is not reproducible in modern English: the
particular instance substantiates the generalization. And so
lexicography can appear the least of the translator's problems. The
impossibility has to do with feeling, from the nature of the external
form, and because language changes make the modern lexical
equivalent more diffuse than the original; or with the inseparable
compound of feeling and ultralexical meaning generated in figures of
speech and thought, to describe which, let alone reproduce it, would
need a sustained commentary; or with tone, if only because of the
linguistic and cultural remoteness of the poem. It should, however,
also have become evident that there is compensation for the loss of
the poetry in the understanding of the reasons which impose the loss.
That is how *Piers Plowman* is available as an act of historical
cognition. And also, once we acquiesce in the sacrifice of its poetry
(to possess which we need, after all, only to learn Middle English) it is
available as a form of event and thought.

But the availability depends on a translation which accurately
reproduces the abstractable prose content of the poem, and so
lexicography regains its true appearance of primary importance.
Such a translation is theoretically feasible; the dictionaries available
are, in general, good or adequate. It is also practically difficult. The
translator will be well advised to adopt as a working principle that
historical differentiation of meaning between a fourteenth-century
word and its twentieth-century descendant is as likely as not, and
never guess.[52] So for instance in the fable of belling the cat he will
translate *venyson* (Prol.190) unspecifically as 'game' in its primary
historical sense, and avoid the absurd suggestion of a domestic cat
pulling down a deer.[53] He will not be misled by *yonge men* (III.214)
when the expression means 'yeomen, personal attendants,'[54] or by
stokkes (v.576) where it means 'idols, graven images,'[55] or by
vnderstonde (XIV.279) where it means 'be receptive to instruction,
pay attention.'[56] The dictionary is there to protect him against
mistaking historical descent, so that where the text says of the slothful
ways of a reprehensible couple that they *breden as Burgh swyn* (II.98)

his translation will read not 'breed like' but 'get fat like town pigs.'[57]
He must believe that his poet is intelligent and that accordingly where
his translation makes poor sense it is probably wrong. If then he uses
the dictionary intelligently he will not write of eminent lawyers with
an eye out for lucrative cases (Prol.211) that they 'stood swaying
from side to side' when the verb in question also affords the contextually appropriate sense 'wait in readiness or expectation.'[58] And
when a sinful man confesses that he is generous in charitable gifts
losse pere-by to cacche,[59] apparently 'in order to incur loss by that
means,' the nonsense must direct him to the lexicography of *losse*,
which, he will find, can mean 'praise, admiration.'[60]

He must read his text with vigilant understanding. Then, where it
says that Charity is not found *at Ancres pere a box hangep* (xv.214),
remembering that anchorites were walled up in their cells and
unlikely to 'carry almsboxes'[61] around like modern charity workers,
he will understand that *pere* means 'outside whose cells.' And when
Christ proclaims after his descent into hell, *lede I wole fro hennes Tho
ledes pat I loue, and leued in my comynge* (xviii.400,401), he will
recognize the violence of the occasion and not translate *I wole* by "I
shall."[62]

His respect for his poet's language and its meaning ought to check
him from setting up, so to speak, his own meaning. So where the text
says of the lawyers profiting from the crime of Wrong, *Tho wan
Wisdom and sire waryn pe witty* (iv.67) the fact that he finds *wan*
difficult[63] will not induce him to leave it out of his translation.[64] And
similarly he will not suppress the Dreamer's challenge to his
audience, *ye men pat ben murye* (Prol.209), 'you people who are
laughing,' at the fable, of course, because he does not perceive how
the poet is signalling the important bivalent analogy between
ludicrous and serious in his immediate subject.[65]

There will be a wide variety of instances of what theorists call
'emic' concepts, 'culture specific'[66] in the historical sense, which he
will find it not just impossible to translate perfectly but even difficult
to annotate; one such is *curteisie* with its adjective *curteis* used in
religious connections.[67] He will find some distinctively Langlandian
uses awaiting their lexicographer: for instance *bidders and beggeres*,
which looks like a doublet but may have a complicated sense relating
to the immorality of begging, or the opposites *winner* and *wastour*,
apparently relating to a combination of notions of morality and
economics with no modern equivalent. He will need to be continually

vigilant in translating the general term *clergie*, with a range of meanings between 'the second estate' and 'learning,'[68] not to mention its particular, *clerk*, with a comparable variety. The prima facie easy terms *truth* and *loue* and *charite* will test his theology.

Prose translation notwithstanding, he will need a sensitive ear. If the connotation of an original term survives, he must keep the term. In the catastrophe at the end, where the text tells how in a wild attack Death *to duste passhed* (xx.100), 'beat into dust' kings, knights, emperors, and so on, he must know better than to substitute 'powder' for 'dust' because the dust–mortality association is still strong.[69] Correspondingly he must command the tonal values of modern English and not represent the words of a proud woman forswearing her besetting sin who says in effect, 'I shall never again succumb to pride, but keep myself humble' (v.67), as 'Here's an end to all my swaggering airs.'[70]

With all these cautions his translations will at best be jejune, a melancholy event.[71] His concern must be that, by working as knowledgeably, seriously and respectfully as he is able, and giving himself no airs, he will keep the inevitable disparagement of his poet to the unavoidable minimum.

8
The Perplexities of William Langland

There are situations for which, at their height, it is impossible to achieve durable and intelligent explanations because the forms of thinking available at that moment are inadequate. *Piers Plowman* constitutes the response of a poet with an organizing intelligence of a considerable order to such a situation, that of eschatology in fourteenth-century England. Its paradigm is the variety of appearances the poem can present: of a statement of recourse to doctrinal reassurances realized in powerfully imaginative expression; or of a succession of compulsive recurrences to the ultimate incomprehensibility of the relation of God and man as the age conceived this historically; or of a reaction of indignation at men's failure to respond to divine love; or of an immense concern about the consequences of that failure.

Those appearances are contrived. They can all be related, but they are not all complementary. Some, indeed, imply major anomalies and contradictions; these the poem, read as a whole, does not resolve. Its ultimate expression of helplessness, the real feeling of its end, must derive from Langland's perception of the impossibility of resolution. We cannot safely impute to him the attitudes of the Dreamer, which are in the first instance only immediate dramatic registers of that sense of impossibility. The poet may well have actually refrained from defining his own attitudes. In any event his own perplexities will necessarily have been of another order of insight than those of his creation, the hasty, headlong Dreamer. The evidence for this is the poem, whether seen as a distancing of a predicament to the last point short of dismissal or as a sustained expression of optimism, an act of faith.

Langland's experience of intense spiritual unease, far from being remarkable, was part of a *prise de la conscience* of an entire society for which the existing forms, social, intellectual, and religious, were no longer adequate.' That condition arose 'from the very heart of Christendom'; its preoccupation was the state of the Church, reform the focus of attention.[1] In those particulars Langland is typical.

To judge from the texts of his poem, he conceived of himself as essentially orthodox and would likely have been appalled by the imputation to himself of heterodoxy, let alone heresy. The poem clearly and repeatedly affirms the great articles of the faith: the existence of an omnipotent, personal, trinitarian God, the immortality of the soul, the original sin of Adam, the essentially necessary benevolence of the Deity towards mankind, the redemption, the divine origin and authority of scripture. Some of its most vehement writing registers that certain of those major doctrines were being questioned: a striking instance is the coarse violence in the speech of Dame Study in Passus X.[2] In the case of lesser doctrines such as that of indulgences the text allows that doubt might arise, and even harmlessly if followed by the act of faith: *This is a leef of oure bileue, as lettred men vs techeþ*: . . . *And so I leue leelly, lord forbede ellis* (B.7.181,182).

It is not possible to establish whether Langland was acquainted with Wyclif's most radical works, but many Wycliffite notions were common talk in the 1370s, and Langland shows acquaintance with a fair number of them. For some he clearly has no time. He accepts the need for an episcopal hierarchy, which Wyclif questioned; he insists on the value of annual, even frequent, communion and of oral confession, which Wyclif decried; and as for the latter's finespun arguments about transubstantiation, he simply scouts these: the host contains the flesh and blood of the Child that was born to the Virgin: *Here is breed yblessed, and goddes body þervnder* (B.19.385,17.100). In such and similar matters his text shows him as a good son of the Church in bad times.

About the badness of the times Langland was in no doubt. Some of the particulars of his anxiety are commonplaces in the history books: the always imminent plague, poor harvest and famines, the difficulties and discontents of working men, concern about the government of the realm with the prospect or fact of young Richard's succession: '*vae terrae vbi puer rex est!*' (B Prologue 196). There was also a less ponderable but very real condition of the times, the insecurity which comes from an intuition of change, of the decay of institutions, or simply from these being challenged. Hatred and envy—so the sermons ran, apparently with some accuracy—were causing men to reject the divinely appointed order. Social pressure was mounting from below. With the shortage of labor, serfs could become free tenants; shopkeepers and skilled artisans showed intense hostility to their betters; soap manufacturers bought knighthoods for themselves and their sons after them.[3] One recalls in this connection the Man of Law's accumulation of a landed estate with a view to a title, the Franklin's social aspirations, the curtain lecture in *The Wife of Bath's Tale* on how *gentilesse* has nothing to do with blood descent, a subversive way of thinking that was widely current. 'The order of these various ranks in the community,' which in the words of John Bromyard 'ought to be like the position of the strings upon the harp,' was being disarranged and the instrument no longer gave forth 'a sweet melody.'[4] Authority both lay and clerical was being challenged on two distinct counts.

Paradoxically the challenge, in both forms, originated in the Church and specifically in the sermons of the preaching friars expressing the perennial movement of moral reform. The most formidable challenge to the doctrine and system of social gradation or *degree* originated in the dogma that men are equal in the sight of God, which was not taught with any revolutionary intention, but to restrain those less fortunately born from the sin of envy. Bishops of excellent virtue like Brunton of Rochester preached that the rich and the poor, in their common religious privileges and many other things, 'are alike and equal,' not for any purpose of subversion but to apply 'a powerful spiritual and moral corrective.' Nevertheless, from that doctrinally unassailable position it was no great distance to Bromyard's 'True glory does not depend on the origin or beginning from which anything proceeds but upon its own condition,'[5] which in modern terms means that a man's worth, in the true sense of the word, depends on the state of his soul. At this point there could appear a perplexing conflict with the originally complementary doctrine that the existing social order was divinely appointed for the assignment of responsibility in the community: *ther is degree above degree as resoun is; and skile is that men do hir devoir ther as it is due* (*Pars T*.763).[6] For it could not fail to strike a thinking person in later fourteenth-century England that many of the magnates of the land, both lay and clerical, were honouring their obligations of care and stewardship only poorly if at all. What was *their* 'true glory,' their moral worth? So preaching and teaching, designed to hold envy and unrest in check, could seem to be questioning the justice of the existing order. Our thinking person of the fourteenth century would not have had the kind of information to know that Christianity has essentially nothing to do with social orders except by historical accidents. His concern would be with the interrelation of authority, social order, and morality.

The second form of the challenge was bluntly moral: those in authority were not worthy of their authority and status. Applied to the worldly great this criticism carried a brief and simple implication: they were not just likely but almost certain to be damned. Why should those who, in Langland's words, *delit in wyn and wildefowel and wite any in defaute* (B.10.367), who relish roast wild duck and burgundy and know of anyone about who is destitute, have heaven both in their enjoyable sojourn on earth and hereafter (B.14.141)?

The consequence of the moral deficiency of such men, the sin of Dives, was limited to themselves; indeed it could be held to benefit the poor, since poverty endured in patience was conceived of as *pure spiritual helpe* (B.14.285), affording opportunity to acquire merit. Lazarus, after all, ended up in Abraham's bosom. But the immorality of the great in the clerical estate, and indeed of all worldly clergy, was another matter, for this must have a direct and calamitous effect upon the whole community of Christian souls. To be sure the episcopate contained some excellent administrators such as William Courtenay, incumbent of three successive sees, and John Thoresby of York, author of the Catechism, as well as the scholar bishops Thomas Cobham and Roger Mortival, not to mention the saintly Brunton. But it appears that they were generally thought too few to provide even the little leaven that leaveneth the whole.

Of the clergy in fourteenth-century England the common criticism was that by their evil, or at any rate their worldly living, they vitiated the effect of good doctrine, instancing the unsoundness of the presumption that knowledge of right action is necessarily accompanied by the ethical sense to put it into effect. Langland's Friar Jordan of Passus XIII exemplifies this. His definition of the Three Lives is, as far as it goes, as valid as any other in the poem, but he does not live in accordance with it: *þis goddes gloton*, complains the Dreamer, *wiþ his grete chekes Haþ no pite on vs pouere; he parfourneþ yuele That he precheþ and preueþ noȝt compacience* (B.13.78–80). The self-indulgence of the clergy discredited their moral teaching; to restore its effectiveness they should exemplify it themselves: *Lyue as ye leren vs*, urges the reforming voice of Reason; *we shul leue yow þe bettre* (B.5.44).

Of the criticisms of the clergy which figure in the poem, both as their shortcomings injured the laity and with respect to their own salvation, most are commonplaces of estates satire and contemporary preaching. Langland was far from the first in his time to censure the grand living of the higher clergy, the illiteracy and neglectful incompetence of parish priests, the venality of the ecclesiastical courts, the deaf ear turned by the bishops to complaints about connivance between parish priests and pardoners, the uncharity between friars and the beneficed clergy, the diversion of educated priests—sadly needed for pastoral care—to lay occupations, the decay of monasticism, intellectually with the ascendancy in theology of the friars and morally through sloth and irregular living. But this circumstance does not appear to have diminished his concern. In the last version of his poem he gives to Piers, now by his career in the B version become a wholly authoritative spokesman, a particularly violent address of accusation to bishops: 'You are asleep, if such a shocking thing can be said! The wolves have broken into your sheepfolds and your watchdogs are either blind or terrified (*'canes non valentes latrare'*) while the wolves gorge themselves': *'lupus lanam cacat eg grex incustoditus dilaceratur eo* . . . I leue by þi lachesse þow lesest many wederes' (c.10.265,266,269); those lost sheep are layfolk damned through the negligence of their pastors and bishops. Here is the imputation of hireling shepherd to the successors of the apostles.

Of most ecclesiastical institutions the criticism in *Piers Plowman* is somehow qualified: for instance there are *Bysshopes yblessed* who,

> *if þei ben as þei sholde*
> *Legistres of boþe lawes þe lewed þerwiþ to preche,*
> *And in as muche as þei mowe amenden alle synfulle,*
> *Arn peres wiþ þe Apostles;*

(B.7.13–16)

and the criticisms of the monastic clergy—proposals for disestablishment, Abbot of Abingdon and all—appear tempered with nostalgia: *if heuene be on þis erþe, and ese to any soule, It is in cloistre or in scole*.[7] But of friars almost the only good Langland can find to say is that there was once a time when Charity wore a friar's habit, but that was many years ago in St. Francis's day: *In þat secte siþþe to selde haþ he ben knowe* (B.15.232). He saw the friars as the greatest single source of peril to the contemporary Church; each of the three versions proclaims this: *But holy chirche and hij holde bettre togidres The mooste meschief on Molde is mountynge vp faste.*[8]

The details of his criticism of friars do not seem novel. Some may actually have originated in the early disputes among the Franciscans themselves, others in the thirteenth-century rivalry between friars and the monastic orders.[9] Many echo remarkably a complaint against the friars laid at a Convocation in Canterbury in 1356.[10] Langland's treatment of friars is sometimes cruel as well as severe, for instance when he elaborately supports the punning misapplication of the Pauline *periculum est in falsis fratribus* (B.13.70,73). The Dreamer's failure of charity here stems from fear. For him the friars were followers of Antichrist *for he gaf hem copes*; they propagated error, *made fals sprynge and sprede* (B.20.55,58). Their admitted brilliance as theologians made them the worst instances of discrepancy between teaching and conduct, between the principles of their foundation and their immense wealth. In them had lain the hope of Christendom for the renewal of the Church and they were disappointing it. Where other religious were at fault for sloth or the sins of the flesh, their offence of cynicism and lack of principle was against truth itself. To cap it all they were brazenly insolent. That point is worth a moment's attention. In the year 1371, when Jean de Meung's *Fals Semblant*, the archetype of wicked friars, had been current for almost a century, two Austin friars were not embarrassed to lay before Parliament a petition 'asking for the disendowment of the monasteries for the common good'.[11] Whether Langland knew of that event is not determinable, but he expresses a lively sense of such insolence by some of his deepest irony in B VIII when the Dreamer asks two Friars Minor *where þat dowel dwelleþ* and they reply *amonges vs he dwelleþ, and euere haþ as I hope, and euere shal herafter.*[12] The Dreamer's answer is 'But even the *just* man sins seven times a day!' The friars were betraying the Church—it is a friar with licence to hear confessions who, in Passus XX, contrives to delude Conscience, the moral judgment which decides between right and wrong, for a moment, gets access to Contrition and drugs him, and thus achieves what the direct assaults of Antichrist could not bring about, the fall of Unity Holy Church. It seems that Langland considered the friars' exploitation of the confessional for financial profit their worst offence, for it interrupted and corrupted man's relation with God.

Had the corruption of the clergy been Langland's only concern he would not have been exceptional; that situation undoubtedly represented itself with equal force to many of his contemporaries. What is exceptional is the penetration of his insight into its implications. In this, particularly, he appears the highly intelligent poet I have called him. The prophetic quality of his poem, which recommended it so strongly to the mid-sixteenth century, was not an accident. He sensed the indivisibility of the hard-won human concept of ethics, specifically that the religious and the lay estates—as his age described them—were functionally interlocked. Of course he would not have used that expression. His text speaks of a Christendom, which ought to be united, and of mankind as God's errant creation, not of a social structure within which a self-aware species had to learn to live with and continue to respect itself. But what he unmistakably and extensively represented in his poem was man's innate tendency to sacrifice ethical principles to material advantage—*radix malorum est cupiditas*—and the consequence as a progressive and damaging devaluation of the concept of integrity in all its aspects. One recalls the values, literal and allegorical, which Langland assigned to the word Truth.[13] The Dreamer's bitter assertion in the last version of the poem, that the situation is either self-destructive or explosive—*Lyfholynesse and loue han ben longe hennes, And wole, til hit be wered out or oþerwise ychaunged* (c.6.80,81)—has more than just local dramatic force. *Piers Plowman* is in part a consideration of available explanations for that state of affairs.

There is the elementary theodicy of the pulpit preacher: the state of the world is evil because God is punishing men for their wickedness. This theme runs through the poem in all versions. The pestilences were sent purely for our sins, says Reason; the destructive gale of 1362 was a punishment for pride (b.5.13–15); famine will come to chastise idle and recalcitrant workmen (b.6.322–4); pride has now grown so rife among all classes of men that prayer has no power to hold off the pestilence (b.10.76–80); through the sinfulness of man the physical world is running down (b.15.347 ff); the present wars and wrtechednesses are the consequences of avarice (b.15.542,543); the corruption of the clergy, runs an addition in the C version, is what has made God turn away from man and from His creation (c.18.78 ff).

But here there is a plight of logic, for a part of the wickedness of the world is the sinfulness of man. Correspondingly, out of the admonition that if we did our duty there would be endless abundance and peace (c.18.92,93) the next question arises: why then do we fail to do so? Is God permitting this by withholding grace, as if to reject us? Moreover, why is it that the innocent are so often punished with the sinful (B.10.80; C.12.62)?

The corruption of the clergy could appear the most prominent feature of that vicious spiral of reasoning. They were failing, the most exalted conspicuously so, to perform the high function of spiritual care entrusted to them. Thus the pope in Avignon seems to simple Hawkyn to lack concern for the welfare of Christendom (B.13.244–9), and the professional theologian Friar Jordan thinks the situation of the papacy beyond remedy: not all the intelligence in the world, he says, joined to the powers of valiant men, can accomplish a peace between the pope and his enemies (B.13.173–6). An ignorant country parson mocks the papal claim to precedence over the king as protector of Christian people (B.19.442–6). Extremes of simple prejudice and cynicism typify the various attitudes of Englishmen in the second half of the fourteenth century.

Criticism of how the pope exercised his authority led necessarily to discussion of its right nature and extent, culminating in Wyclif's *De Potestate Papae*. Whether or not Langland saw that work, which appeared in 1379 or 1380, *Piers Plowman* shows acquaintance with many of its propositions, some of which go back to Ockham or to Marsilius of Padua: denial of the apostolic succession; denial of an apostolic foundation for the papal claim of legal jurisdiction; assertion of papal fallibility; the question of procedure in papal election; identification of a bad pope as Antichrist. The text of the poem does not, however, support Wyclif's extreme abolitionist views. To be sure, allegorized Grace in Passus XIX warns Piers that when Antichrist comes, *Pride shal be Pope, Prynce of holy chirche*, his escort the cardinals Covetousness and Unnatural Conduct (B.19.223,224). But the *lewed vicory*, the unlettered country parson whose criticisms of the papacy later in that passus are after Reason's plea to the pope to *haue pite on holy chirche* (B.5.50) the sharpest in the poem, prays for the reform of the pope, not the abolition of the papacy (B.19.442). As to the right of election, that lies in *loue and lettrure*, in charity and erudition. '*Therefore*,' says the Dreamer in the B version '*I kan & kan nauȝt of court speke moore*': 'There is more to be said about this but the obligation of charity restrains me from saying it' (B Prologue 110, 111). In the C version that faintly sanctimonious line has gone. Instead Langland introduces Conscience, Moral Judgement, whom he had developed in B as one of the

heroes of the poem: 'Do not dispute the election,' he enjoins the
Dreamer, 'for the sake of holy church' (c.1.138). That is
unmistakably an act of faith by the poet; it also has immense
prophetic implications.

Controversy engendered arguments to diminish hierarchical
authority. Wyclif was presently maintaining that 'Whereas the king's
power was fashioned in the image of Christ as God, that of the priest
was to be compared with Christ's humanity.'[14] The relationship he
envisaged is evident. Nothing in *Piers Plowman* seems to reflect that
remarkable argument, but the poem chimes with Wyclif and earlier
thinkers in representing kings as correctors. The monastic orders are
threatened: *þer shal come a kyng and confesse yow Religiouses, And
bete yow, as þe bible telleþ, for brekynge of youre rule* (B.10.322,323).
Allegorized Scripture, Sacred Writing, quoting Isaiah's *Quomodo
cessavit exactor?* (B.10.333), represents the lay estates as responsible
for the good conduct of the religious orders, for checking their
rapacity and lordly living. In Passus XV the tenor of a long criticism
of clerical delinquency appears in these lines:

> If knyghthod and kynde wit and þe commune and conscience
> Togideres loue leely, leueþ it wel, ye bisshopes,
> The lordshipe of londes lese ye shul for euere.
>
> (B.15.553–5)

That is to say, the end of prelatical temporal power is bound to come
if the knightly estate and the common people, living together in
harmony, exercise their intelligence in the discernment of moral
issues. It would, indeed, be a charitable act to disendow the Church,
to reverse the donation of Constantine by which those who inherited
the authority of Peter were poisoned. The C version is most specific
here in an added passage:

> Were preest-hod more parfyt, þat is, þe pope formest
> That wiþ moneye menteyneþ men to werren vpon cristine, . . .
> Hus prayers with hus pacience to pees sholde brynge
> Alle londes to loue, and þat in a lytel tyme.
>
> (C.18.233–6)

The corruption and worldliness of the clergy at all levels, from the
princes of the Church down to ignorant parson and simoniac friar,

seemed calamitous. The terrible notion was actually expressed, that pastoral delinquency of any sort increased the number of souls lost to God and against the bravely confident hope expressed by misquotation in *Piers Plowman* that *sola fides sufficit to saue wiþ lewed peple* (B.15.389) there was the view of some, including presently Wyclif, that a sinful priest could not efficaciously administer the sacraments. In either event the words attributed to John Chrysostom in *Piers* XV would seem to apply: *Si sacerdocium integrum fuerit tota floret ecclesia; Si autem corruptum fuerit omnium fides marcida est* (B.15.118). By occasioning a general falling off of piety, and by threatening the efficacy of the sacraments, especially that of penance, the sinful clergy was seen to endanger the operation of that grace which appeared to constitute the only hope of mankind burdened with Adam's sin and its own.

And there is the centre of the medieval perplexity: the burden of sin. 'If only,' says Everyman Hawkyn, 'I had died immediately I was christened, in a state of grace! It is so hard to live as a sinner; we can never escape sin' (B.14.323–5). The immensity of an evolved concept of absolute excellence contains within it the individual sense of inadequacy according to its terms. Sin had come into the world by divine forbearance; why would God have seen fit to exercise this, having foreknowledge of the consequence?

> Why wolde oure Saueour suffre swich a worm in his blisse
> That biwiled þ womman and þe wye after,
> Thoruȝ which werk and wil þei wente to helle,
> And al hir seed for hir synne þe same wo suffrede?
>
> (B.10.108–11)

And further, is it just for God to punish present man for Adam's old sin?

> Why sholde we þat now ben for þe werkes of Adam
> Roten and torende? Reson wolde it neuere!
>
> (B.10.115–16)

In these passages at the actual centre of the poem, the questions of divine benevolence and justice are openly raised by Dame Study; she dismisses them with a remarkable mixture of coarse abuse of the doubters and a deeply pious act of submission to the divine will: *Al was as he wolde*, she prays,

lorde, yworshiped be þow,
And al worþ as þow wolt, whatso we dispute.

(B.10.132–3)

The poet knew the other answers: the concept *O felix calpa*, to judge
from the poetry it evoked, seems to have been satisfying to him for
the way its paradox conveyed a sense of the infinitude of divine love
(B.5.480 ff). And there was that intriguing notion that God had
permitted man to sin because otherwise man could not have understood the meaning of joy (B.18.218–21). Both were more comforting
than the bald Ockhamist assertion that God is subject to no law, but
acts at his own good pleasure (B.12.216), for this seemed to put man's
soul at total risk. There was little warmth, moreover, in the implication which presently follows, that God made his ways mysterious so
that man might gain merit by his faith (B.10.256).

Nevertheless, from their conduct many men are to be damned: *I
leue fewe ben goode* (B.10.444). Works are essential to salvation: *qui
bona egerunt ibunt in vitam eternam* (B.7.113), and in another place,
reddit unicuique iuxta opera sua (B.12.213). Yet it is because of
Adam's sin that salutary works are lacking in man. The sense of divine
arbitrariness extends: grace of repentance was given to one of the two
thieves beside Christ on the cross; why was he in particular chosen?
The Dreamer is authoritatively enjoined not to ask, for this is a
mystery:

Alle þe clerkes vnder crist ne kouþe þe skile asoille.
Quare placuit? quia voluit.

(B.12.214–16)

But in that case what man knows whether he is to be saved? The
Dreamer is shown as concerned for his own salvation; he wonders
whether his name was entered in the 'legend of life' or not written
there for some particular offence (B.10.380–2). The theme of election
recurs. The parable of the wedding feast,

Multi to a mangerie and to þe mete were sompned,
And whan þe peple was plener comen þe porter
    vnpynned þe yate
And plukked in *Pauci* pryueliche and leet þe remenaunt go
    rome,

(B.11.112–14)

many are called but few are chosen, makes the trembling Dreamer agonize about whether he himself might or might not be one of the elect. Langland was evidently more than just aware of contemporary interest in the related questions of predestination, grace and works, divine foreknowledge and free will.

The comfort given to the Dreamer in this anxiety is of another scripture text with contrary implication, a significant register of Langland's awareness that in this as in other matters scripture could be used to support opposed doctrinal positions. Theology, says Dame Study, has vexed her a thousand times. Indeed, once, as if to demonstrate his insight, Langland makes Ymaginatif, the allegorized reflective faculty, outrageously apply 1 Pet. 4.18, *Saluabitur vix justus in die iudicii* to a totally alien context (B.12.281,282).

The attribution of bad logic to the reflective faculty registers both a deep-seated need in the poet to believe in the salvation of mankind, and contemporary suspicion of the intellect, which could not proffer both rationally acceptable and spiritually reassuring explanations of the ways of God to man. For such failure, and for even suggesting the implication that the bases of belief might be rationally questionable, the intellect, which could apparently only destroy, not reassure and make secure, was suspect. It was their passion for knowledge which had thrust Adam and Eve out of paradise, says the poem (B.15.62,63), and the sinful man would be better engaged in considering the state of his soul than the wonders of creation: *melius est scrutari scelera nostra quam naturas rerum* (B.11.231). Both patristic teaching, in that quotation making its triumph over pagan philosophy by the echo derogatory of Lucretius, and the hierarchy of the later thirteenth century in its turn, had depreciated the value of human intelligence as an instrument for attaining spiritual truth. But the fullest expression of anti-intellectualism came with Ockham and his teaching of the inaccessibility of God to the human intellect: God's *potentia absoluta* lay outside revealed truth. The concept was pervasive because it gave a kind of relief to fourteenth-century perplexity. *Leue we vre disputisoun*, wrote an anonymous but considerable poet of the 1380s,

> And leue we on him þat al haþ wroȝt;
> We mowe not preue by no resoun
> Hou he was born þat vs al boȝt.[15]

That Langland did not easily commit himself to anti-intellectualism is evidenced simply by the existence of his poem, and more intricately by the role of personified Reason and his close association with Conscience, the personified ethical sense. Langland is likely to have accepted that natural knowledge is unavailing to salvation—*sapiencia huius mundi stultitia est apud deum* (b.12.138)—and that only God can have perfect knowledge (b.15.52,53), but he dramatically, and I think not inadvertently, reveals his sense of pleasure in the possession of knowledge and the effective use of intelligence in his unsuppressable Dreamer's exclamation, *Alle þe sciences vnder sonne and alle þe sotile craftes I wolde I knew and kouþe kyndely in myn herte!* (b.15.48,49). That is of course a sinful aspiration, as he was roundly told.[16]

Piers Plowman is made up of perplexities created in Langland's world and time by oppositions: between perfection intellectually conceived and the imperfect actuality; knowledge of right conduct and failure in those who possess that knowledge to act righteously; the *imago dei* and man's tendency to besmirch it with sin; the God of Justice and the God of Love; divine and worldly wisdom. Heresy has been called 'the outlet of a society with no outlets.' In such a situation Langland's outlet was his poem. It embodies and is to a large extent shaped by a number of the reactions of his world to those perplexities.

The first reaction was one of over-compensation. Where the poem reads like pulpit moralizing the harshness and condemnatory tone are generated, I have no doubt, not by self-righteous zeal but by anxiety. That Langland had no great view of his own moral condition can be seen from the acts of humility set in various parts of his poem. But where the matter was one of questioned moral values—the expression *'How shal the world be served?'* comes to mind—his self-reassuring reaction seems to have been to assert those values all the more strenuously.[17] Where Langland's anxiety seems to have been deepest, about the failure of duty in those who have care of souls, his tone is harshest and most cruel.

Another reaction was to entertain, as an explanation of the state of affairs, the apocalyptic or cyclical view of history. Apocalypticism seems to reflect a socio-psychological state, generated in both individual and group mentalities which, from a highly developed ethical sense and subconscious awareness of what can be called the processes of post-type evolution, detect the imminence of major social change, which is then interpreted in terms of the concepts and language available at the time; it is of course not limited to the Middle Ages. The late medieval expression of this mentality was the cyclical view of history which Morton Bloomfield has shown to be a principal determinant of the shape of *Piers Plowman*.[18] An element in that view is Antichrist, the arch-enemy of Passus XX, a perennial figure of eschatology who materializes out of man's subconscious manichaeanism at critical phases of human history and whose coming, so the thinking goes, will precipitate an apocalyptic crisis. Him Langland represents as an amalgam of the capital sins, emblematic of their corruptive and destructive force. His standard bearer is Pride; his main agents are the friars, whom he has bought with presents; it is one of these who infiltrates and is responsible for the downfall of the citadel of right.

With the onslaught of Antichrist the Dreamer withdraws from the world and from all activities but charity. Here Langland is representing a reaction like that of the Franciscan Spirituals, who put their faith in quietism and humility, suffering and patience in the name of Christ, and in the hope for the future. Such withdrawal from the world is an element in the apocalyptic view that change 'was for God, not for man to achieve. . . . The very imminence of change made in an incentive to patience, not action.'[19] Their position implied an abnegation of responsibility, nostalgia for more primitive levels of experience, and the negation of growth and coherence.[20] I do not impute such a state of mind to Langland, having regard to the energy implied in his poetic activity: his poem exists, after all, by virtue of its being a major response to the world in his time. But his representation of the flight from the world seems lovingly executed. The fools whom the Dreamer imitates have not merely chosen the better part; they are heroic (B.20.61–7).

A reaction of a very different sort was towards apocatastasis or universalism, the belief that it is God's purpose, through the grace revealed in Christ, to save all men. One basis of this belief is 1 Tim. 2 where Paul writes of Christ that he 'wants all men to be saved and to come to the knowledge of the truth' and that he 'gave himself as a redemption for all.'[21] It has a history of emergence and rejection from Origen on, and was several times condemned.[22] Its persistence as a great hope was possibly encouraged in the later Middle Ages by the concept of the absoluteness of divine will: 'He did all things that he wanted: therefore he saves all,'[23] expressed very specifically in the Ockhamist teaching of the ascendancy of God's *potentia absoluta*: 'Righteousness consists in what he wills, and that is wholly rational which he decrees.'[24] This belief, the essential attempt to reconcile divine love and divine justice, constitutes an intensely dramatic theme of Passus XVIII where, in the dream of redemption, Christ proclaims that at the final judgement he will come as a crowned king with an angelic escort *And haue out of helle alle mennes poules* (B.18.372,373). I do not suggest that Langland embraced the heresy, and I judge that had he done so he would have ended his poem with Passus XVIII. Christ speaks, after all, in a dream, and what he says can be read as no more than expression of a deep hope for which theology affords no warrant, *quia in inferno nulla est redemptio.*[25] That hope brings little comfort in XIX and XX.

In Passus XVIII the scale of the drama and the stature of its protagonist make to seem trivial the confusingly various and apparently discordant evidences of the fathers and doctors—and if one dares to say it, those of scripture—from which the perplexities represented in the poem derived. But the effect is local and temporary: the perplexities survive as what informs the poem. Langland was not writing as a professional theologian but as a highly intelligent and tolerably well-informed poet making poetry for his own comfort out of the thought and feeling of his time. The tension of his poetry exists largely by virtue of his reserve, the selectivity of his representation, its arrangement by series of associations. These are indices of an intellect too fine to be tranquillized by the available, simple formulations of complicated issues, but with nothing to put in their place.

It must be said that he is no defiant rebel. He is always ready to renew the act of faith. What is significant of him is the recurrence of the need for renewal. For his concern is profound; he senses unmistakably that he is living within and writing about a major crisis of ethics, the outcome of which will affect the future of his world. It is in the end Conscience, the allegorization of moral judgment, the ethical sense that can appear the supreme achievement of human evolution after the development of self-awareness, who awakens the Dreamer. But Langland has no solution and proposes none: he must simply believe that in the end all will be well because the alternative is inconceivable. This appears from the major addition to the C version in which he represents the Dreamer admitting to being an inveterate

speculator, a gambler hoping with a fool's optimism, against Reason
and Conscience, for the change of luck that will turn all his misspent
and wasted days to advantage, for a little bit of that same divine grace
which Conscience invokes for Langland's world at the end of the
poem.

9
Langland and Chaucer: An Obligatory Conjunction

It ought to seem remarkable that Langland and Chaucer, side by side so to speak in the later fourteenth-century English scene, appear, until just the other day,[1] so rarely studied or discussed together as in that situation. The extent to which critics of either poet are able to ignore the existence of the other is striking. Not even the obvious alternative considerations are generally raised: *either* how the same component historical factors, given some secondary variables (Chaucer's *yiftes of Fortune and of Nature*)[2] could produce such radically different poetries, *or else*, how two poetic oeuvres with such immense appearances of dissimilarity can have so much in common. Yet on clear consideration the near-contemporaneity and adjacency of the two poets is bound to contain a challenge. Maybe it is from absence of reflection that there has been failure to discern or respond to this. For prima facie the one poet can appear historically more remote than the other; with the other we sense closer kinship; he seems more accessible, which means in effect more easily modernizable. From such appearance of an extreme difference between Langland and Chaucer a generalization that study of the two in association would not be rewarding can easily take shape.

The real logic of the situation is the reverse. For it is actually in cases of difference like this one that comparison is especially illuminating. Where the similarity of two poets is immediately or easily evident comparison will only particularize it, and is therefore less imperative. In the instance of our two poets, comparison will first promote accurate identification of the differences between them and direct to explanations of such differences; but it will also, in the course of those operations, bring out unsuspected similarities. Thus the work of both figures will necessarily be illuminated. Langland and Chaucer may seem (though they are not so) as different as chalk and cheese. Well, if our understanding of chalk and cheese were as imperfect and debatable as our understanding of the two poets, it would be imperative to compare chalk and cheese, to study them in conjunction.

Thus the first effect of so studying Langland and Chaucer is likely to be an adjustment of attitudes. Some Langland scholarship seems too recondite, suggesting (if not intentionally) that the significant communication of *Piers Plowman* is accessible only to special kinds of erudition not primarily literary in our modern sense of that term. Juxtaposition of the two poets may improve such an attitude by representing *Piers Plowman* as a literary work of art, and Langland as aware of other creative activity than spiritual exegetics.[3] And some literary discussion of *Piers Plowman* is amateurish, exhibiting deficiencies of critical training, not to mention imperfect understanding of the modes of function of verse and poetry. In wider competition such stuff might less easily get into print. As for Chaucer criticism, it will, from the poet being more emphatically located in his time, receive the correction of its dominant tendency to solipsistic indulgence in the Bradleian fallacy[4] and the redirection back to a historical approach which it seems constantly to be in need of. Already by such adjustments enhancement of understanding promises to be rich.

Systematic study of the two poets in conjunction might begin with the historical consideration—what shared and what distinctive elements in their education can be presumed or identified. Some common ground of instruction can be predicated: in grammar, in the rhetoric of Donatus's *Ars Maior* and Everard's *Graecismus*— rhetoric including instruction *in modo versificandi et prosandi* and in letter writing—and in reading Latin poetry.[5] Distinct from such lower school subjects we can presume rigorous inculcation of Christian doctrine (it is the Chaucerians who may need to be reminded of this) and experience, whether systematic or casual, of the allegorizing activities of the classicizing friars. Then, predictably of Langland and as a caution to Chaucerians, the comparison will throw into sharper relief the directive power of that, by their time, already more than three centuries old system of moral categorizing, estates satire, how it shaped Chaucer's attitudes to personality as much as it did Langland's (one reason, obviously, for the many resemblances between their attitudes) and moreover provided Chaucer, for the account of his pilgrim parson, with the explicit language of clerical reform.

Beyond such relative certainty study of our poets in conjunction may well, in adjacent areas of relative indeterminacy, establish some probabilities. These may have to do, for instance, with how much knowledge of profane rhetoric Langland had beyond that in the school grammars or comprised in the *artes predicandi*, with whether Chaucer knew about other of those French religious allegories so determinative of *Piers Plowman*[6] than de Deguileville's *Pelerinage de vie humaine*, the first version of which might have suggested the trick of the dreamer falling asleep over a book,[7] whether he was versed in anti-fraternal literature or whether his friars descend exclusively from Fals-Semblant, whether there is any real evidence that he was an adept in what its medieval practitioners called tropology.[8] As to Langland, given the conspicuous absence of the Roman poets, and notwithstanding Deguileville's direction to it, of the *Roman de la Rose*,[9] and of Machaut and of the Boccaccian proto-renaissance from *Piers Plowman*, can I trust my ear when it seems to hear in the poem echoes of Peire Vidal or Chrétien or *Amis and Amiloun* or *The Seven Sages* or Arthurian knight-errantry?[10] And would it be possible to establish from 'evidence' the a priori likelihood that Chaucer had by 1382 read *Piers Plowman*?

Comparison beginning from the common basis of their education in Latin grammar shows both poets aware, and similarly, of poetic composition as a technical activity requiring special skill. Composing verse about a subject is *to reden it in Retorik*, that is, to present it in language rhetorically organized.[11] It is the *rethor excellent*, knowledgeable in *his colours longynge for that art*, who can do justice to an exceptional subject in verse.[12] When the activity is well conducted the result is beautiful; the adverb of praise applied to both *versifien*, the composition of verse, and *enditen*, the organization of the language of a poem, is *faire*. Another adverb used to modify *enditen*, 'to compose,' is *formaliche*, 'in due or proper form, correctly,' this by Langland, considered by some to have been care-less about his own metrics and to have written something hardly distinguishable from alliterating prose. None of these 'newe clerkes,' if you look closely, *kan versifie faire ne formaliche enditen*: so says an authoritative speaker in *Piers Plowman*. Their education in languages is defective. The reason may be a wrong turning taken in the study of grammar, *þe ground of al*, namely towards interpreting it exegetically rather than textually; in consequence it *bigileþ now children*, is now confusing young minds.[13] What should be called

'Saintsbury's error,' his proposition that, because Chaucer (and *a fortiori* Langland) were taught not English grammar but Latin grammar in French, they would be less than fully sensitive to precise use of English and careful versification,[14] would here appear to be corrected, if Chaucer's insight into the variety of English dialects and orthography in his time, expressed for instance in anxiety about the mismetering or miswriting of *Troilus*, did not already confute it.[15]

When we look at the two poets' conceptions of themselves as artists, complex and revealing patterns of similarities and differences take shape. Both are self-conscious about their art. Both invoke the modesty *topos*, in each case indirectly. In *Piers Plowman* Ymaginatif, the reflective faculty, represents the triviality of his preoccupation to the Dreamer-as-poet: *þow medlest þee wiþ makynges*, you busy yourself with composing poetry,[16] where the expression *medlest þee wiþ* and the belittling generic plural *makynges* can seem to imply derogation. In *The House of Fame* the preceptorial eagle scants Dreamer-called-Geoffrey's actual intelligence and patronizingly allows that he does the best with the little of it that there is in his head.[17] In *The Parliament of Fowls* the guide Africanus, undertaking to show the Dreamer *mater of to wryte*, adds the derogatory qualification, 'if you had any skill at putting words together'.[18] In *The Canterbury Tales* the Man of Law implies, as in Chaucer's absence, his ignorance of *meters*, versification, lack of skill in managing rhymes, and indifferent verbal resource.[19]

In fact neither poet appears to suffer from the artistic handicap of modesty. The concern expressed in *Piers Plowman* relates not at all to the poet's actual artistic capabilities; if anything it suggests awareness that his expression of them might not be the activity most needful to his salvation. As to the poetic medium, language (Langland cannot have been unaware of his command of it), this he once exalts by the voice of Wit, intelligence, as *spire . . . of grace, And goddes gleman and a game of heuene*, 'the beginning of Grace, and God's entertainer and a celestial delight,' incidentally embodying three direct puns in the dynamic figurative exaltation.[20] As for Chaucer, his Dreamer in *The House of Fame* has scarcely taken leave of the patronizing eagle when, behind a screen of appeals to the Muses and Apollo, he is made to register Chaucer's conviction of the validity of his artistic percpetion and gift of expressing this, its strength assessable from the cento of Dantean language by which it is signified.[21]

Comparing the two gives significance to a self-confidence approaching arrogance discernible in both poets: from its being twice diversely manifested in comparable degree it incidentally bespeaks a new condition of poetry in postconquest England.

In *Piers Plowman* the principal indication is the short passage of ironic allegorical comedy near the beginning of B 12, where the Dreamer tells how he saw the truth of Ymaginatif's *þow medlest þee wiþ makynges and myȝtest go seye þi sauter*, and to produce some sort of excuse maintained that his poeticizing was a recreational activity, adding a tag from Dionysius Cato, *Interpone tuis interdum gaudia curis*, 'give yourself an occasional break'.[22] The designedly pre-posterous nature of that excuse first appears on recollection that some 350 lines back it was the legitimacy of using poetry to criticize public scandals such as the venality of the friars that the Dreamer was concerned about, and that here Ymaginatif had seen the Dreamer's purpose as teaching people right conduct, *what dowel is, dobet and dobest boþe*, and that the embracing subjects of the whole poem, divine justice, divine grace, and salvation, were of absolute seriousness. The immediate meaning of the irony seems then that the poetic activity so employed is valid, that the writer is competent to conduct it, and generally that, as it seems to him, the question of excuse or justification is absurd.

Chaucer's arrogance, also indirectly revealed, but by a different sort of correlatives, is of comparable intensity. In his case its source is, first, his successful emulation as an Englishman of the con-temporary French mode of poetry and, second, the gratification experienced while actualizing in his own career the enlarged conception of the status of poets and the nature of poetry learned from the Italians. There seems little doubt that Chaucer was now trying to match their achievement in its turn—and there is con-ventional precedent for such an attitude towards literature even of manifestly superior excellence—although he left no verbal evidence of this comparable with Dante's *Taccia Lucano, taccia . . . Ovidio*, or Claudian's *Taceat superata vetustas*;[23] we might, however, take it that by suppressing Boccaccio's name altogether Chaucer effectively imposed silence on him. Moreover, his injunction to the book of Troilus not to vie with other works but to be submissive to all poetry and to kiss the footprints of Virgil, Ovid, Homer, Lucan, and Statius, by its clear echo of Statius,

> *nec tu divinam Aeneida tempta,*
>   *Sed longe sequere et vestigia semper adora,*[24]

is Chaucer's equation of himself with that poet. Moreover the collocation of poets here, with Statius significantly replacing Horace, is the one in the *Inferno* of which Dante wrote:

> *mi fecer de la loro schiera,*
> *si ch'io fui sesto*

'they took me into their band as the sixth member'.[25]

From those passages, keeping in mind that a poet writes all the parts and manipulates all the puppets, and on a reasonable presumption that both Langland and Chaucer were compulsive writers, a pattern of characterizing difference emerges. The arrogance of Chaucer was, to some degree consciously, shaped by an artist's ambition; by contrast, for Langland the circumstance that he experienced self-gratification and fulfilment from his poetry may have been for the main part and for long obscured by the obsessive concern his topic aroused in him.

That difference draws attention to how their topics broadly differentiate the two poets. In Chaucer one senses a search for matter of substance; one can read *The House of Fame* as allegorizing a stage in that search. It even contains a suggestion that the notion of translating the *Aeneid* had passed through his head: *I wol now singen, yif I kan,/The armes and also the man.* There is another suggestion of the search at the end of *The Parliament of Fowls.*[26] Such an impulse to *some work of noble note* may have been spontaneous; more likely it was generated by the Italian experience. I see the unsuccessful search registered in his ability to echo Dante's high style and his inability, for want of a warranting subject, to sustain it. Maybe reading *Piers Plowman* intensified the search. It can have been that poem which turned him to the ephemeral splendours and self-inflicted miseries of sinful man as Chaucer represents him in *The Canterbury Prologue* and *Tales.* By contrast, in *Piers Plowman*, for all its quest motif, there is no real search, but rather an irresistible pressure of movement from the consideration of sinful man (with little of splendour about him here) to the ostensible first cause, God's forbearance of Satan in the Garden, thence on to the question of the indispensable grace and the immensity of man's need for it, and at length, turning from open considerations of theodicy as impious, to the absolute act of faith by means of which alone in late fourteenth-century England could be sustained from despair the Christianity of an intellectually honest, intelligent, and sensitive man.[27]

A major consideration relating to our poets' conceptions of themselves and their art is how they register in their poems their personal problem of art and morality, the concern for the state of his soul to which each was brought by the inexorable eschatology of fourteenth-century English Christianity. In Langland's case the point of indication—aside from his poem as a whole—is the dramatic allegory he set into the C version before the Confession of the Sins, a colloquy between the Dreamer-as-Poet, Reason, and Conscience, that is the ethical sense. With Chaucer it is of course what he calls his *retracciouns*. An immediate difference is that Chaucer's prayer for pardon and act of contrition are unmmistakably spoken in his own person, whereas the passage in *Piers Plowman* can be related to Langland himself only hazardously, by reading its allegory auto-biographically. So Chaucer's position, from which he singles out some of his writing as *enditynges of worldly vanitees*, that is, frivolous compositions, and others as positively immoral, can seem the more abject.

The situation is not so simple. Superficially the profane topics of the one poet, especially what Langland would have called his *tales of harlotry*, would seem morally indefensible. By contrast Langland's sacred theme must appear unreservedly commendable. But the difference goes beyond topics to the essential poetic of the two writers. In the one instance, Chaucer's, we have an art that represents behaviour immoral by the accepted standards of its time without explicit disapprobation but on many evidences, from a standpoint of deep moral awareness, the accuracy of the rep-resentation, its truth, made complete by including in it the attractiveness of the wrong course of action. There would be spiritual danger here, however, in the self-gratifying nature of the poetic activity, by which it could assume the character of an end in itself rather than an act of moral judgment and so, by making capital of the sins of others, be a failure in charity. But this was also a situation that would allow Chaucer to identify some of his writing as spiritually meritorious and take comfort from this. What had to be excused was not the practice of poetry but its misapplication.[28]

Langland's poetic has a totally different appearance, which seems to put the spiritual postures of the two in sharp contrast. In one of the exchanges about writing poetry that I have referred to, made to seem to arise naturally out of a blaze of the Dreamer's anger against friars, the issue, by implication one of failure in charitable behaviour, is explicitly whether it is morally lawful to write poetry in rebuke of sinful conduct. The affirmative answer is legalistically arrived at: *It is licitum . . . ech a lawe it grauntep*; the speaker does not take the question of charity into account.[29] In the second, not much farther on, the allegorized reflective faculty, Ymaginatif, reminds the Dreamer how for years he has been admonishing him without avail to take thought for the condition of his soul, and there he is, *Always scribble scribble, Eh!*, busy with his writings when he ought to be at his penitential and devotional exercises or praying for his patrons. Anyway there are plenty of books on his subject. Here is raised the question of the absolute moral validity of the activity: 'I saw clearly that what he said was true,' the Dreamer admits, and then tells how he made a sophistical and obstinate answer and, by the convention of the genre, went on writing his visions down.[30]

These two passages appear to be registers of the poet's concern; they do not seem intended to be either self-assertive or self-justificatory. But they contain no act of contrition. Langland was apparently not satisfied with them, for the second disappears in the C revision. In C there is a new passage relating to the Dreamer's activity, and this one puts Chaucer's *retracciouns* in a different relation. It stands very prominently just before the sermon by Reason that brings about the Confession of the Sins and has the look of a carefully staged piece of drama.[31] The Dreamer, mentioning that he is a writer early on as if by the way, tells how, in lazy enjoyment of his prime of life, he comes by—which can mean 'acquires'—Conscience, that is, the allegorized ethical sense, and as his memory idly ranges over his past, Reason confronts him with the brutal question, 'What can you do, what good, what use are you?' The degree of implied uselessness appears from the kinds of work Reason enumerates in his question, mainly farming activities (here we remember Piers) symbolic of contributions to the community, positive work of charity '*Hem pat bedreden be bylyve to fynde*. The Dreamer is a *wastour*, not a *wynnere*. In reply he puts forward a welter of excuses which on analysis are seen to constitute a meticulously constructed fabric of grievances: at loss of support and patronage; at failure to hit upon an agreeable occupation other than the one under criticism; at how the distinctiveness of the clerical estate ought to shield its members (even the idle ones) from the degradation of certain kinds of labour; at the preferment in the Church of the servile and the illegitimately born; at the social thrusting of the commercial class; at how the wars have impoverished the aristocracy; at how the children of poor gentry are passed over; at the prevalence of simony; at how the world is going to the bad—a brilliant representation of an embittered failure finding reasons for his condition everywhere but in himself: his argument, that he is doing the best he can. But Conscience will have none of this, and at length the Dreamer breaks down.

The prominence of this passage just before the Great Confession, the character of the Dreamer's excuses, and the specific terms of his admission of fault suggest that its function, already from the circumstance of revision evidently calculated and important, is more than simply to fill out the personality of the Dreamer. He does, to be sure, have a private encounter with the Preacher and so becomes the first of the penitents; in that sense we can see the passage allegorizing an act of humility by the poet just before what already by the time of the C revision may have become one of his most popular pieces. But the Dreamer's specific admission to having wasted and misspent time recalls the exchange in the earlier version between Ymaginatif and the Dreamer: *þow . . . myȝtest go seye þi sauter.* Any activity not specifically directed to attainment of salvation is misspent, even the composition of poetry on improving and spiritual themes.[32] But that is not all, for in the Dreamer's spate of excuses, represented as attempts to distract from his own shortcomings by reciting his grievances and the evils of his time, the poet can seem to be registering an insight of awful clarity into the nature of his own zealous anger against the abuses of religion: this not merely is irrelevant to his salvation but relates to his own moral inadequacy. We recall how in the earlier version Langland represented the justification of using poetry for moral criticism, *to arate dedly synne*, in terms of legitimacy.[33] So here the implication is of a failure of charity, which Langland makes evident in Conscience's mockery of the Dreamer's excuses and of his defensive implication that he offers the *Preyers of a parfyt man*: he is told, 'I can't see that this applies in your case!'

This is the point on which the Dreamer's succession of defences finally breaks up. Their quality was never great. He says, first, 'I was trained for a particular life, and I never found any other that I liked except that one, and if I have to live by my own effort I ought to do the work that I know best' (lines 35–43). That is, for one thing, wilful, and for another poorly based because of the nature of his 'work', which presently appears in the second excuse: 'I earn my subsistence by praying for the souls of those who maintain me' (45–52). But that places the Dreamer, along with the *Bidderes and beggeres* who protest, *We haue no lymes to laboure with, . . . Ac we preie for yow* (B VI.124, 125), in a reprehensible way of life. The third excuse is no excuse: 'Anyway it is wrong to make a cleric do manual labour, and the world is going to the dogs because the principle of degree is being abused, so don't rebuke me' (53–81). The fourth excuse, finally, has a hypocritical flavour: 'My sense of right and wrong tells me what Christ would have me do; the prayers of a man in the state of grace, and a prudently conducted penitential life constitute the labour that pleases our Lord most dearly' (83–8). Reason's dismissal of this last argument as inapplicable because the Dreamer, in effect a beggar, a *faitour*, is not even in a state of grace, finally reduces him.

We translate the Dreamer's bitterness and envy into the poet's conception of himself as writing not from high principle but from what we would call his aggressions. The poet sees, if only momentarily, the act of composition as self-gratifying and therefore, to the extent that it fails in charity, sinful notwithstanding its ostensible pious objectives of spiritual understanding and moral reform.

Here is the real abjectness, in that self-condemnatory drama; by contrast Chaucer's *retracciouns* seem serene, almost confident. The comparison has refigured our images of the two poets in this particular. Now Chaucer appears as possessing the greater moral simplicity, that is, innocence, the morality of his situation as poet clearly defined in his sight. Meanwhile Langland appears with a cruel gift of self-perception, insight into his own damning arrogance and pride,[35] in atonement of which, he senses, no coda of contrition is adequate.

That the Dreamer's apologia and Chaucer's *retracciouns* register their first experiences of insight into their individual problems of art and morality seems improbable. More likely the insight came gradually to each as he acquired full awareness of the exceptional quality of the poetic gift that exerted compulsion over him, and along with that recognized his inability to refrain from exercising it, his addiction to the fulfilment it conferred. Whether apologia or *retraccioun* marks the terminal points of either of the two careers is less material than the evidence of concern with the morality of the poetic activity that they register.

In terms of that concern Langland and Chaucer are in the same historical perspective. Both were impelled to write about behaviour in their bad times, their almost exclusive concern with people evincing a new sensibility. The one poet spoke openly in admonition and correction, the other seldom so because it had become an element in his poetic to represent, by withholding the moral label, the attraction of the false good, the difficulty of taking the course known to be right, or of identifying it, or even of realizing that a choice existed. Both, as poets, were driven to attempt to organize and account for their observed experience in terms of a system of explaining human existence rigorously prescribed and not conceivably adjustable by sophistries such as are available in modern religions. Within that system, moreover, their very success as artists carried the risk of moral offence: pleasure in the exercise of their skills, possession of a sense of achievement, of self-respect, could touch the sin of pride.

That historical perspective shows the two, finally, in positions other than those commonly assigned to them. Chaucer, whose expression of religious submission has embarrassed some critics to the extent of making them want to deny its authenticity or else its sincerity,[36] appears in the spiritually easier situation. His access and inclination to a palliative philosophy and to the absorbing culture of antiquity afforded him terms and forms of thought, Ovidian or Stoic or Boethian, to express his sense of the world in decay and so to distance it, as in the Boethian lyrics. The rights and wrongs of his poetic career are clear in his mind, the wrongs easily acknowledged. By contrast the poet of moral and spiritual topics, writing in entire orthodoxy, whom we commonly think of as more securely religious, appears vastly less serene, his acceptance hard and thrawn. Denied, whether by circumstance or temperament (those *yiftes of Fortune and of Nature*), the illusory comfort of the classical, he turned his early-realized mastery of the skills of language and poetry to represent cheerless schemes of apocalyptic and chiliastic organization. The forms and matrices these afforded him conferred on Langland in their implication of the imminence of change a kind of prophetic vision, but they can have brought him little comfort or assurance of the sort to be felt in Chaucer's elementary prayer for forgiveness and intercession.

10
Langland and Chaucer II

Langland and Chaucer belong together. The existence of such a both complementary and contrasting pair in a single generation is a remarkable phenomenon. In some respects they differ extremely, but the features in which they are similar are as notable as those which differentiate them. They resemble each other more than either resembles any other of his contemporaries, and they differ more substantially from those contemporaries than from each other.[1] To study them together illuminates understanding, and enhances appreciation of both.

There you have a parcel of my impressions, formed in occasional and desultory consideration over the years. It is not put to you in provocation, as a challenge, but to suggest what prompts me to more systematic literary comparison of the two, such as I shall sketch for you today.

The beginning is to look at Langland and Chaucer as craftsmen, the particular in which they may appear to differ most, simply because poets attach more importance to the technical details of what they write than do their readers, for many of whom the warm but unformed surge of response, or else concern with the poem as a clinical subject on which they can show themselves to advantage, can be prior considerations.

A poet's technical undertaking will be shaped by the verse system he elects to use. It is likely that both Langland and Chaucer made educated choices in that respect, primarily informed by the same school training in grammar, elementary rhetoric, the reading of Latin poetry, and the *modus versificandi et prosandi*, this latter comprising discussion of both accentual verse and cursus rhythms as well as quantitative measures.[2] The limiting factor will have been not their understanding of critical issues, but the range of choice available in their vernacular.[3] So—setting aside speculation about lost juvenilia[4]—

we picture, at the outset, the one poet intending a longish religious allegory, and the other a *consolatio* in the French mode for a powerful patron. For serious undertakings like these there were available, in English, aside from stanzaic systems initially developed for lyric and song, the relentless septenary measure of *Ormulum*, the shapeless and ill-defined strophic line of Robert of Gloucester's *Chronicle* and the *South English Legendary*, the prevalent, almost two-century-old adaptation of the French octosyllabic couplet, and the regionally preserved and distinguished varieties of the alliterative long line.

The immediate models of both poets, Guillaume de Deguileville's *Pelerinage de Vie Humaine*, and the *dits* of Machaut and Froissart, were in or mainly in the French octosyllabic. Langland's reason for rejecting its English equivalent appears from the degree to which the texture of *Piers Plowman* is denser than that of the *Pelerinage*; he will have sensed that his poetic conception, what was in his *hed ymarked*, could not be realized in a metre so *lyght and lewed* (Chaucer's terms, of course).[5] With Chaucer the difference lay in his actually wanting to reproduce in English the effects of his models: to use an approximation of their metre was a part of his replication. After completion of *The Book of the Duchess*, the naturalization of French vogue art triumphantly accomplished, Chaucer used the octosyllabic only once more, this time explicitly critical of its lack of strength, that is of its inadequacy for expression of complicated syntax, and of its unstylish associations in English. But Langland, if, as it appears, he spent his poetic career attempting to realize his idea of a single work, was committed—short of throwing all away and beginning afresh—to the metre of his original choice. Out of those different situations the technical development was natural, given the stature of the poets: in Langland's case to perfect his use of the alliterative long line, in Chaucer's to experiment until he developed a verse system apt, in his hands, for both *ernest* and *game*.

It is not surprising that Chaucer's performance as a verse technician should have received the more notice. His identification of a narrative vehicle in the Middle French lyric stanza that we call rhyme royal, and his subsequent introduction of the five-stress rhyming couplet,[6] are landmarks in the history of English poetry. By contrast Langland gets less than his due. One reason why is that whereas the text from which opinions of Chaucer's metrical skill are formed has had most of the scribal damage to its metre silently removed (not many people have, until recently, seen Chaucer texts in the raw), Langland, to his disadvantage, has generally been read in a text metrically debased by scribal miscomprehension of his meaning or his metre, and indeed the opinions persist that he was an indifferent versifier, or careless about his metre, or that this metre was, in any event, little removed from prose.

Such opinions need correction. As to Langland's originality, because we do not know in what form he received the tradition of alliterative verse composition we cannot gauge his innovations. But there is one historical fact: he is the Middle English poet using this metre who gives most evidence of awareness that stress and alliteration are distinct, and not necessarily related, phonetic features, and that because of their distinctness they can be used to achieve, in complementary or counterpointed patterns, an exquisite modulation.[7] Either he learned this from great poetry that has been lost without trace, or he saw into the potential of the medium. In what he can be shown to have read, indeed in what survives, there is nothing that approaches, let alone matches, his use of this metre in versatility, subtlety and music.

As to the musical effects the two achieved, I would describe them as different kinds of magnificence. Chaucer's, totally efficient, minutely inventive, unfailingly sensitive and melodious, occasionally witty, versification will not be disputed: it is to be recognized as a main formative element in the English poetic tradition. But for me Langland's versification is musically the more complex and interesting. Even more than Chaucer's, or because of its ancient origin necessarily more, it is a performance metre.[8] And its music is essentially subliminal (the difficulties of the critics attest to this), enabling, as Langland may have designed, the reading of matter already in his own time hard or unappealing or distressing, and in part, today, of interest mainly to literary historians and amateurs of the psychology of religion. You can dispute the comparative evaluations; what seems not debatable is that the technical excellence of both poets is what Petronius, writing of Horace, called *curiosa felicitas*, the result of great taking of pains over detail.

The character of the verse systems of our two poets is reflected in the development of their styles. In both styles one prominent feature is syntax.

Chaucer's poetry illustrates an advancing relation. In the octosyllabic lines of *The Book of the Duchess* and *The House of Fame* (I judge these his earliest surviving works) the brevity of the intervals between the rhyme markers evidently created a sense of urgency that discouraged complex syntactical formations in favour of elongated, quasi-paratactic ones. This could only be a handicap in the treatments of subjects of any intricacy. In the rhyme royal stanza, apart from the need for extended anticipation of rhyme, which could not fail to affect at least the rate of semantic development, there was the regulatory pressure exerted by the formal auditory structure upon the natural tendency to variety of length of semantic structure, to what in prose one would call paragraph length. Both accommodation and resistance to the pressure are elements in the style of Chaucer's rhyme royal narratives. As to the five-stress couplet, that might have exerted its tendency to end-stop. We take for granted the sweet natural flow of Chaucer's narrative discourse; it would be nearer the truth to recognize that this effect, the fluency, the almost always appropriately controlled pace, were attained only by considerable effort. The verse systems Chaucer successively adopted or adapted or developed were in the first instances hard disciplines rather than the assets he makes them seem from his successful use.[9]

Langland's achievement consists in identifying and actually exploiting the dominant, if not domineering, feature of his verse system, its powerful caesural pause. That caesura, in the hands of indifferent users, could evidently impose wooden regularity: line after line in the same rhythmic shape, syntactic and semantic patterns. Some Middle English alliterative verse reads as if its writers actually worked for such an effect. Langland identified the caesural pause, in its essentially grammatical character, as a function of meaning. He counterpoints line-end, caesura and syntactical termini. His syntax will impose a strong logical break at the caesura of an end-stopped line; or a syntactical unit beginning at the caesura will overrun the line end and finish at the next caesura, or at the next line after that, or even at some other point arbitrarily set by his arrangement of meaning. He uses the caesura to punctuate, or as a point to insert a parenthetic statement or a resumptive subject or object, to enable parataxis, or to suggest the informal grammar of conversational give and take. Sometimes he develops the caesural suggestion of a two-part line rhetorically by parallelism or chiasmus. So the caesura becomes a component of style. To describe the effect of his line subjectively, it is less often of a melodiously fluent progression than of constantly demanding nervous interest.[10]

Still in the critical area where versification and style are hardly distinguishable, there is alliteration. In medieval poetry at least, when that feature of language, which can occur naturally through accident of the vocabulary of a topic, or through subconscious impulsion to an alliterating synonym, attracts notice, occurs so prominently as to seem deliberate, it is a figure of speech, homoeoprophoron or parhomoeon.[11] Chaucer used it so, occasionally, for evidently special effects, such as to describe a tournament or a naval battle: in such cases it operates by phonetic suggestion, a function early identified by the rhetoricians. We are made strongly aware of the stylistic distinctiveness of such passages.[12] In Langland's verse system it is genre-specific. Here Chaucer's deliberately distinguished line, *There shiveren shaftes upon sheeldes thikke* would be normative and unexceptional. In *Piers Plowman* alliteration as a feature of style beyond genre-specification has a radically different mode of existence.[13]

It is for a start an element in the modulation of the line according, for example, to its coincidence or non-coincidence with rhetorical stress, to there being more than the normative three similar initial phonemes in the line, or to the generic alliteration being ambiguous, that is double, or to the line having secondary, non-generic alliteration. But further, because the essential character of the alliterative long lines creates in a responsive reader an enhanced sensitivity to initial phonemes, just as Chaucer's verse system creates expectancy of rhyme, all alliteration beyond the normatively generic will have certainly a musical but also a semantic suggestion, and so a stylistic effect. Alliteration, metrical considerations aside, is thus a powerful determinative element in Langland's style. This suggests that after impressionistic comparisons between his style and Chaucer's there remains a task of difficult analytical criticism still to be attempted.

The extreme distinctiveness of effect of the two men's styles is unlikely to have originated in differences of early education, for they were almost certainly taught from the same grammar book. And if the one was further schooled in *ars poetica* and the others in *ars predicandi*, that also would not account for the distinctiveness, since the two rhetorics differ mainly in the ends to which they apply the same principles. Most probably, it was determined first by the texture, the 'grain' of the verse medium each chose, and at the larger end by the intrinsically different prescriptions of representational narrative and moral allegory. It is these latter, also, which turned one poet to the manner of proto-humanism and the other to pre-established forms of admonition and moral complaint. The common beginning and the divergence of purpose are the determinants of difference.

Both poets were evidently well founded in *grammar, the ground of al*,[14] and exhibit understanding of syntax as a prime determinant of style. One sign of their efficiency at applying this is how they variously either exploit the characteristic looseness of its character in Middle English or else, for special effect, replace this with complex and compressed arrangements. Langland by those means achieves an expository manner interesting in its actual, syntactical, that is logical form, which, so to speak, confers intelligence upon the subject matter.[15] In Chaucer's case, his greater variety of topics makes it hard to give a single, really typical illustration, so I will propose that a considerable element in the impression of the deviousness of Pandarus's character is the syntax of the statements Chaucer puts in his mouth.[16] From such considerations the good artificiality of the writing of both is apparent, the *cura* by which the *felicitas* was achieved. But because their topics have in general such different appearances the superb craftsmanship of the two is variously rather than equally apparent in the subjective aspects of style.

Langland's control of pace, for instance, may seem more striking than Chaucer's, that is, the capacity of his text to increase or reduce our rate of apprehension and so confer a sense of varying rate of progression in the discourse. But that appearance is almost certainly not related to any superiority of technique.[17] For merely to be reading at a single long text like *Piers Plowman* makes one necessarily more sensitive to the rate of apprehension, of progress. And moreover that poem has no governing time scheme to which its reader can imaginatively commit himself. And there are no personages with whom he can, so to speak, keep time. Most of them merely come and go; as for the Dreamer-Narrator, his life chronology is carefully disturbed. So the reader who is critically alert becomes aware of how the style is governing his sense of pace. By contrast, in Chaucer's writings after the octosyllabic period we are mainly in a world peopled like our own, one with similar days and nights. We commit ourselves to its time-schemes easily, and may not notice how Chaucer controls these, notably in *The Knight's Tale* and *Troilus and Criseyde*, just as rigorously as Langland controls that of his shadow world.[18] Yet the stylistic means of control are the same, allowing for difference of context: the character of the vocabulary, especially with respect to the incidence of polysyllables, the nature and arrangement of the syntax, the complexity of communication related to both those circumstances, and the distribution of rhythmic intervals set up by the semantic groups.[19]

In command of vocabulary both poets were evidently exceptional. At first sight Chaucer looks like having a statistical advantage. The entries in the Chaucer concordance are reported to number between 8000 and 9000, while the vocabulary of the three versions of *Piers* is between 5000 and 6000 words.[20] But because of the component of technical terms from *The Astrolabe* and *The Manciple's Tale*, not to mention *Boece* where there will certainly have been coinages and importations, the disparity was not in itself necessarily a disadvantage to Langland. In any event, however much the achievement of the two is differentiated by the forms, subjects and ostensible purposes of their writing, both evince altogether exceptional control over tonal effects, and with that, the capacity to elicit emotional responses to their topics, or acceptance of topics across historical divides.

There is one notable difference here. In a comparison Langland's modes can seem provincial, up-country, and Chaucer's polished, urbane, international. But meanwhile Langland is translatable: all texts of his poem, as variously preserved in dialects of the Southwest Midlands, or Northumberland, or London, have equal force. By contrast an integral element in the Chaucerian effect is his localized language: *Troilus and Criseyde* in the dialect of Shropshire would be another poem.

This difference, and the circumstances that produced it, can cloud the comparison. It is easy to take for granted the sense Chaucer confers of being in a literary milieu, as proper to the mainstream of the English poetic tradition, forgetting that this tradition is his own unprecedented creation. Correspondingly Langland's performance can seem remarkable.

We observe how into fifty-odd lines, for instance from B XIV 29 onwards, Langland can cram effects successively conversational, hymnodic, loftily proclamatory of solemn doctrine, and prosily homiletic. Everywhere in his poem we find passages of nervously flexible expository writing, but within these, markedly varied tones: the apocalyptic excitement at the end of B III followed quickly by the brisk business of the lawsuit in IV, the compulsive urgency of Hawkyn's self-exposure in XIII, the exaltation of the canticle praising Charity and the remarkably sustained indignation at ecclesiastical corruption in XV.[21] As readers for whom many of Langland's topics and issues have no intrinsic validity we can be surprised at the readiness and strength of our response.[22]

Meanwhile it is possible to take control of style for granted of Chaucer, and so undervalue him. We expect everything from him: the thin clear streams of language in the French mode of *The Book of the Duchess*, the sugared or the ornamental Boccaccian style in the *Parliament*, the high resonance of philosophical utterance after *Boece*, the exalted tone of the Dantean echoes, the hard dry sharpness of the moral reformer's language as in the description of the *Prologue* Parson and Ploughman; nothing can have been hard for him. But of course we have here the product of taking infinite pains.

So in the comparison we might undervalue Chaucer's power to evoke the quality of the spoken word: garrulousness, learned or colloquial, the rough give-and-take of the fabliaux, the polished conversation of aristocrats, the expression of emotion verging on despair.[23] The situations in which Chaucer the dramatic poet represents his personages are by and large timeless and thus readily accessible: so we fail to appreciate the ear that caught the quality of speech in them and the control that created and communicated this effect to us.

In *Piers Plowman* there is nothing like Chaucer's range and versatility in this particular. When, occasionally, Langland's subject afforded him scope for snatches of dialogue or for spoken diatribe this can be lively enough.[24] But that subject seen as a whole implies another kind of drama, and whether he could have matched Chaucer's performance as a dramatic poet in the usual sense is as academic a consideration as whether Chaucer in other circumstances could have constructed stage-plays.

What Langland distinctively exhibits is a quite phenomenal ability to vitalize allegorical personifications. His choice of topic committed him to attempt this, and without effective models. The personifications in Part I of the *Roman de la Rose* are realized—as far as that can be said of them—by pictorial typification, and the impression of their movement is stilted; those in the second part exist imaginatively by virtue of the interest their arguments and opinions excite. In Deguileville's *Pelerinage* the personifications are scarcely alive. What school Langland learned in if he was not self-taught we do not yet know, but already his earliest personifications are represented easily, without self-consciousness; they are experienced as imaginative realities. Their mode of imaginative existence awaits detailed study, but some elements of Langland's method stand out. There is the attribution of characterizing emotional language: *þou dotide daffe*, says Holy Church, *dulle arn þine wittes* (A 1.129); linguistic wit in report of physical movement: *Scripture skipte an heiʒe*, 'skipped aloft and preached' (B xi.107); Hope came 'hopping along after' (B xviii.62); linguistic wit in characterization: as of *abstinence myn aunte* (A v.211); or of the two wide-set eyes of Book, Holy Scripture (B xviii.230); or symbolic orientation: Truth comes out of the East (B xviii.117–9). By such and similar means, and by the sense of energy that originates in his metre, Langland induces us to accept, across historical, cultural and conceptual chasms, the incongruous, the preposterous and the, to some, intellectually repugnant. His *tour de force* is the creation of lively and engaging allegorical drama, as at the dinner party in B XIII where the host, his servant who waits at table, and three of the five guests are personifications, and the best dishes are moral precepts. Chaucer wrote nothing like this and may not have wished to: his *Tale of Melibee*, given the circumstances of its narrator and introduction, is not to be adduced in comparison.

The truism that style is a principal mode of meaning in the work of writers of the first order is useful to invoke at this point because of the considerable difference of its applicability to Langland and Chaucer, especially in the latter's narrative poems. There it relates to the several kinds of engagement requisite in experiencing *Piers Plowman* and, say, *Troilus and Criseyde*. In this and Chaucer's other narrative poems meaning lodges in the actions of the personages. Its fully effective communication requires inducement of the reader's imaginative realization of those personages. The exigency of style lies, then, in representing them and their milieu; the registers of style will in general be prescribed by the latter. In such a situation, because of the nature of the illusion, the greater the author's success the harder it will be to analyse his style. So Chaucer makes us will an actual existence of the world he has built and peopled in our consciousness, to the point where we prefer to stop short with interpreting its events in terms of the actuality it resembles, rather than as an effect of the complex of linguistic norms from which the impressions derive. The success in Chaucer's choice and management of these, that is of his language, and the unobtrusiveness of the process, can make us overlook that every effect of engagement, every direction of response down to our slightest sense of innuendo, exists by virtue of Chaucer's command of style.

By contrast Langland's style functions as a mode of meaning obtrusively, by intellectual engagement rather than imaginative suggestion. For instance the figure of *adnominatio*, which when Chaucer uses it otherwise than in rhymes stands out as unusual, as with Troy being destroyed and Calchas calculating, is very common in *Piers Plowman*, and can almost invariably be construed to augment meaning; there are even macaronic instances of it. No awkward-seeming expression in *Piers Plowman* can safely be imputed to its poet's resourcelessness. In the very second line of the poem the stilted circumlocution *I shop me into a shroud as I a shep were* (A Pr2) signifies not Langland's inability to put the plain prose *I dide on shepes clopyng* into metre, but the hypocritical pretence to a sanctified way of life which the Dreamer attributes to himself at the outset: thus periphrasis and elaboration of grammar figure a sham. So of the priest called *Sir Piers of Pridie* sitting with the Flemish prostitute in Betoun's Bar, the quotation of his name from the canon of the mass just before the consecration, *Qui pridie quam patuit*, signifies the profanation of the life of a man whose fingers daily touch the flesh and blood of Christ. The at first sight incongruous, or alliteratively expedient, or merely playful term invariably proves to be meaningful. It is a friar, in the tradition of John Ridevall, who uses the name Dido to signify a story of no account. The country parsons consigned, in the apocalyptic spiritual regeneration at the end of B III to *dyngen vpon Dauid*, must literally 'flail away' at their Psalter—*dyngen* being a verb appropriate to the threshing-floor—with the energy they have been applying to farming the glebe of their benefices.[25] Adam and Eve eating unroasted apples is not a piece of waggishness on the poet's part, but a suggestion that in their sin they were a little like impatient hungry peasants stuffing themselves with half-ripe windfalls in the lean season before Lammas, and suffering for it.[26] The childish sing-song of Piers's account of his services to Truth in his first epiphany at the end of the Great Confession is not a gratuitous little indulgence in verbal music, the poet showing us he can make a tune, but a figure of the commendable simplicity—unless you become like unto little children—of Piers's submission to the divine will: *I do what he hotep.*

The genre in which both masters of versification and style first appear, their juvenilia suppressed, or unidentified among fourteenth-century anonyma, or simply lost, is the dream-vision. Their choice of this reflects the immediate historical situation: What literary kinds, genres, were available in the middle bracket of the century to match their projected requirements? Their choice was, at the same time, sophisticated.

Each poet at the outset registered that his use of the genre is ironic. To the *Piers Plowman* Dreamer his experience seemed a *ferly of fairie*, 'a marvel from the otherworld of the fays.' In describing his incurably deep love-melancholy the Dreamer of *The Book of the Duchess* pointedly reproduced a long passage from an un-distinguished contemporary French poem familiar to his audience. Both poets evidently understood the dream vision to be a mode of meaning, its generic features not prescriptions but serviceable devices to that end. There was a lesson to that effect, if either needed it, at the conclusion of Deguileville's *Pelerinage*: 'If I have not dreamed this dream well, I pray that it be put to rights by those who know better how to dream, or who can improve it.'[27] Neither poet treats dream-realism simply as a device of significant form: Langland occasionally intrudes the preacher's voice; Chaucer divides the dream of *The House of Fame* into books. Both use the conventional implications of the season and setting of dreams positively and negatively, spring or December, *plesaunce* or desert. They multiply or dispense with guides: two in *The House of Fame*, none in the *Prologue to the Legend of Good Women*, many in *Piers Plowman*. Both poets, however, promote the implication of the supraliteral meaning of their dream-visions. The status of Langland's first guide, Lady Holy Church, according to contemporary dream theory, signified that at least this part of *Piers Plowman* was to be an *oraculum*, in which she will reveal 'what will or will not transpire, and what actions to take or avoid'.[28] It is a matter of course to the *Book of the Duchess* Dreamer that his dream will require interpretation; the Dreamer of *The House of Fame* prefaces his report with a summary of the theory of dream significance and a curse upon mis-interpreters.

Both poets develop the potential of the genre. In this particular Chaucer's achievement, no doubt because he presently abandoned the dream-vision, can seem the less radical. It begins early, however, and registered the insight which one comes, from his later work, to take for granted. He found the device of the Dreamer reading before he falls asleep in Deguileville. There the book in question, *Le biaus roumans de la Rose*, is hard to relate meaningfully to the dream that follows, unless there is significance in the extreme difference of the two dream visions. But the reference may well mean no more than that it was reading that unlikely poem which prompted Deguileville to write his own dream allegory.[29] By contrast, In *The Book of the Duchess* Chaucer uses the device to signify an additional dimension, a logical one of ratio and proportion, in the dream which follows: Seys and Alcyone are to the Knight in Black and the Lady White as the Knight in Black and Lady White are to John of Gaunt and Blanche of Lancaster. In *The Parliament* the character of the Dreamer's bed-time book, namely Cicero's *De Republica*, shows that it must relate to the content of the dream which follows: it sets the scale of meaning and proclaims the values to be applied to this. The first form of *The Prologue to the Legend of Good Women* looks like an experiment in the use of the dream-vision as a story frame. If that appearance is true the revision, whatever its other significances, registers Chaucer's self-corrective perception of the impracticability of such use. For in this second version he awakens his Dreamer before setting him to write. Hereabouts, also, is the point where one sees the dream-vision ceasing to be serviceable to Chaucer; he had developed needs which it could not meet.

Langland meanwhile put the greatest load upon the genre that it was ever made to bear in its history: his needs, it appears, intensified rather than changed as he wrote. So any statement in his poem as it progresses may be subject to the presiding qualification of the genre, that it was spoken in a dream. Even Christ's assertion during the raid on hell in B XVIII that he will, without fail, come in divine glory to save all men, has precisely the authority of a wish (however deep-seated) that figures itself in the mind during sleep, its truth, whatever else, not a truth of doctrine. Langland's formal innovations are at least as striking. The first is the—as far as I know—unparalleled development of the simple dream-vision into a kind of career of dreams, bounded formally by recurrence of the initial theme and setting at the end, within which the Dreamer develops a personality and acquires a biography. Langland's ultimate refinement, twice instanced, is to set dream-vision within dream-vision. This must, so to speak, at least double the generic implications, impute special meaning to the content of the inner dream. In the one case that content turns out to contain a syllogism about salvation: if the pagan

Trajan can be saved for his *pure troupe*, his integrity and nothing else, then there is a power in works to merit grace which, for the Christian with his added advantage of baptism, holds out hope of salvation on a reasonable basis.[30] In the other, which the Dreamer calls a love-dream, an ecstasy,[31] it signals the return of Piers the Plowman after long absence, now transformed to symbolize at least the realization of the *imago dei* in mankind, the effectiveness of grace against evil, and at one point the human nature of Christ.

The gauge of the emotional importance of this passage is the represented effect of Piers on the Dreamer: at the mention of Piers's name he swoons, *al for pure Ioye*, and immediately experiences the inner dream, which is illuminated by his excitement. Within the dream, which consists essentially of a recondite tropological figure and a swift review of Christ's life on earth to the redemption, the Dreamer experiences encouragement and hope, but at the moment of Christ's victorious death he awakens, desolate for the loss of Piers, and sets out in distraction, 'like an idiot', in search of him, and of reassurance anew. Langland uses the Dreamer thus as an instrument of feeling, which here is meaning, and of momentum.

Langland's and Chaucer's developments of their dreamers as functions of meaning, and Chaucer's extension of that function into waking narrative, are not matched in the medieval literature of Europe. The process begins with the insight of both poets into the potential of the invitation implicit in the genre to identify dreamer and poet as a means of engagement. It continues in their creation of highly sympathetic narrative personalities, not alternating between moral arrogance and ostentatious humility like the Dante of the *Commedia*, nor tediously self-important like Machaut's projection of Machaut in his poetry, but engagingly obtuse, impulsive, anxious, repeatedly depreciated personalities, ready with response but often mistaken, slow in perception, above all constantly interesting for the evident intelligence of their conception and presentation. They stumble on vital issues and unwittingly reveal predicaments of spiritual understanding and morality; their incapacity to cope with these forces the reader to examine the nature of the concern of the actual poets with those issues and predicaments.

As to the relation between these figures as personalities and the actual poets, in Chaucer's case it is demonstrably remote. Not one of the attributes of Chaucer's dreamers or of his pilgrim-narrator appears in the man evidenced in the records of Chaucer's career, one of proven ability, proven integrity and presence, discreet, dependable, a custodian of the royal interest. With only Chaucer's writings to go by we would have little notion of the actual man. That indicates a presumption of corresponding distance between William Langland, about whom we have no information except his birthplace and his father's name, and Will the Dreamer of his poem. In Chaucer's situation there is implied a caution that the picture of Langland formed from Will's reports of his life and ways might be imperfect, even quite false. But because we will see the poet on the page rather than holding the pen the romantic fallacy dies hard. The attempt to recreate a historical Langland from the attributes of his dreamer still goes on.[32]

On grounds of both literary convention and the substance of his poem, which is unmistakably for an educated audience, the likelihood is that Langland exploited the illusion of the authorial personality as much as Chaucer did. He was clearly writing for readers united in the concerns registered in his poem, probably educated clergy anxious for ecclesiastical reform, and I would guess that he wrote from within that group. There is little chance that his audience, recognizing how the author writes all the parts and manipulates all the puppets, would unthinkingly impute to him the Dreamer Will's recurrent spiral of anxieties about grace and works, predestination, original sin and divine justice to the poet in any simple way, or read the poem as a record of the poet's own search for salvation, as a *Bildungsroman*. They would see it as a representation of the almost intolerable situation to which fourteenth-century theological and eschatological thinking had come, a generally applicable predicament of faith and hope. The irony of the Dreamer's represented helplessness in that predicament, where the best counsel appears to have failed him, would also generally apply.

The composition of Chaucer's audience was by contrast mixed, and within the broadest range: from the totally arrogant aristocrats of the blood and their elegant ladies, literate and with some taste and cultivation in French poetry, to savants like Ralph Strode, logician, philosopher, learned jurist and himself a poet. The princes will to the extent of their capacity have admired without much understanding; one thinks of the ladies as making a pet of the poet, and some at least of his writing will have been at their bidding, for their diversion.[33] His more learned friends[34] will have responded to the rich texture of erudition in his work. Any serious person of whatever estate will have recognized its moral implication, but there may not have been the uniformly deep commitment, such as Langland could presumably count on, to match the poet's own. The potential for irony in the whole situation was huge, but most so in this last particular. There would lie the inducement to write in the first instance for himself, to live out to his own satisfaction that idea of the poet he had found abroad in Italy and nurtured at home in England behind the posture of excessive bookishness, of unaptness for love, of alienation, of being *elvish*.[35]

With Chaucer's abandonment of the dream-vision comparison of our poets changes proportion: Langland's further development appears as an intensification, Chaucer's an extreme extension of what, on historical presumption, they shared at the outset. Langland exploits the dream vision to the point where for quality of art or power of effect he has no equal in its use; Chaucer, after his schooling in the genre, experiments with an appearance of system in almost every available literary kind.

The distinctively acute moral awareness of their generation equipped both with remarkable insight into human behaviour, from which they drew the capacity to represent the grotesque with ultimate compassion and to show the appealing with cautious reserve. But at that point their poetics create divergences which prescribe very different models for representation of the subject they share. Langland's are generally schematic, boldly drawn translations of the hamartiologically generalizable into visualized action; they are effects, not portraits. Chaucer achieves the impression of particularized individuals in a credible setting from accumulations of significant minutiae, with implications corresponding to the ambiguities and ambivalences of actuality. Langland's man is immediately measured by the peril of his soul, an oath Piers often uses. The poet sees and exhibits his Everyman, Hawkyn, in a predicament both wretched and immense, caught in the cruel dynamism of a divine scheme apparently out of control.[36] Set against him is the ploughman he names Peter, whom he makes the archetypal focus of hope. Chaucer's created personages are not archetypal, but they have enough of both particular and universal to take their places as the first figures in the notable gallery of personages of the English literary tradition. In such ways what Chaucer called *the yiftes of fortune and of nature*, accidents of particular environment and of heredity, operate to differentiate our poets extremely in the common historical situation.

Of the two Chaucer appears cosmopolitan, international, a time-spanner. By contrast Langland's focus may seem narrow: no classical furniture or Roman ruins or hillsides in Lombardy here, but a bristling complex of theological and moral and spiritual cruces. Seen another way he spans the history of creation: he is one of the poets who wrote about the rebellion of Satan and his fall. A French prince, Charles of Orléans, imitates in English Chaucer's minor lyrics; in Bohemia a movement of religion which bids fair to change the direction of history is strengthened by the ploughman figure whom Langland celebrated.[37] There is nothing like these two poets in Europe in their time, and for nearly two centuries after that.

I bring them finally together in their failure to complete their life's work: an unfinished revision of *Piers*, and an incomplete *Canterbury Tales* symbolize the condition of English poetry in their time.

11

Conjectural Emendation[1]

Conjectural emendation as an editorial practice has a bad name in English studies. What A. J. Wyatt once called indulgence 'in the luxury of personal emendations'[2] has seemed to imply a kind of capriciously irresponsible selfishness inappropriate to a discipline dedicated to the preservation of a tradition, and for all the time that has passed since he wrote thus in 1894 there is still a feeling that such self-indulgence is, if not 'the greatest', certainly a grave 'disqualification for discharging duly the functions of an editor'.[3] Further, the suspicion of presumptuousness that attaches to all emendation falls most heavily upon the kind called conjectural, which, as I understand the term, is practised when an editor rejects the evidence afforded by his manuscripts and in defiance of this proposes as the lost original a reading for which no manuscript evidence exists. The situation that has generated this attitude (which I do not think I have misrepresented) is of some complexity: while the unsatisfactory character of received texts is generally acknowledged, and the need for good editions is manifest, the fairly extensive, but not very well-co-ordinated discussions of the theory and practice of editing have fallen short of agreement.

One principal objection to conjectural emendation—it has also been laid against less venturesome kinds of editing—is that it includes an element of uncontrollable subjectivity. The popular conception of that subjectivity is excellently illustrated in Vinaver's introduction to his edition of Malory: he is there writing about his own situation when confronted with the necessity of evaluating conflicting evidence from two sources, the Winchester manuscript, and Caxton's print of a lost manuscript.

> The traditional method consists in selecting from each of the two texts or groups of texts the 'best' readings they can offer so

as to produce what is often inappropriately called a 'critical' text
. . . the value of such a text depends on the clear understanding
that what is 'best' is not what seems best to the critic, but what is
attributable to the author. And it so happens that it is not
humanly possible for any critic, however cautious and competent, to maintain this distinction. For the more he is bent on
his task, the less he can conceive of himself and the author as
two distinct individuals whose ways of thinking and writing are
inevitably unlike, who are both liable to err, each in his own
unaccountable way, just as they are capable of choosing two
equally 'good', but conflicting, forms of expression. There may
be various degrees of skill in the handling of the situation, and
various degrees of accuracy in the results; but the procedure
proves in the end . . . . disastrous; . . . the fault lies . . . with
certain habits of mind inseparable from any practical application of the method, habits which broadly speaking amount to
the belief that whatever satisfies one's taste and judgement
must be 'good', and that whatever is 'good' belongs to the
author.[4]

For anyone who agrees with him Vinaver's objection must apply *a
fortiori* to the conjecturing editor, who rejects as 'bad' an actual,
received, often unanimously attested reading, and prefers, would set
in its place a hypothetical reading, one which he himself has invented.
What wild fancies must we expect of him when even editors soberly
regarding a choice of manuscript readings are incapable of sustained
intellectual discipline?

For such anxieties there are undoubtedly grounds in the history of
textual criticism. The capricious, or inept or misguided conjectural
emendation is one of its recurrent themes. Of Bentley, for instance,
'impatient, . . . tyrannical, . . . too sure of himself', A. E. Housman
wrote

he corrupts sound verses which he will not wait to understand,
alters what offends his taste without staying to ask about the
taste of Manilius, plies his desperate hook upon corruptions
which do not yield at once to gentler measures, and treats the
MSS. much as if they were fellows of Trinity.[5]

Bentley was not, Housman also implies, altogether intellectually honest or wholly secure against self-delusion: 'many a time when he feigned and half fancied that he was correcting the scribe, he knew in his heart . . . that he was revising the author'.[6] In the century following Bentley's, less brilliant but equally wayward, irrational and arbitrary conjecture appears to have been a common practice of editors of classical texts.[7] Two extreme attitudes can be observed: Bentley's seemingly arrogant *Nobis et ratio et res ipsa centum codicum potiores sunt*[8] and the more romantic one expressed by Dr. Johnson:

> The allurements of emendation are scarcely resistible. Conjecture has all the joy and all the pride of invention, and he that has once started a happy change, is much too delighted to consider what objections may rise against it.[9]

Excessive subjectivity, an identification with the author leading to the assumption that the editor perfectly commanded his style, or a supersession of author by editor, were bound to discredit both conjectural emendation and, by association, to some extent at least the whole practice of editing. Whether this effect was altogether just has not seemed to matter; and the brilliance of many conjectures, especially in the texts of the Greek and Roman poets, some so intrinsically excellent that for most readers they own the status of received readings, has not sufficed to check it. The demonstration of the fallibility of editorial judgement had been too extreme.

If therefore a modern editor, especially of a vernacular text, professed to identify corruption when his manuscripts did not necessarily indicate this (that is when the archetypal reading of the manuscripts was not in doubt), and further professed confidence in his ability to restore the actual words of his author, he was behaving at best ill-advisedly, at worst with unbecoming conceit of himself. The current scepticism about conjecture extended, as it may still do, to the whole editorial process, and one form of the flight from judgement has been 'to condemn any critical treatment of manuscript material beyond a mere reproduction of the extant tradition or of one of its representatives'.[10] 'One should' (I quote a student of Bédier reporting the master's view) 'select a manuscript which is of the poet's own dialect, which is relatively old, which does not have many mechanical defects and one should reproduce this text without attempting correction unless there is a proved slip of the pen . . . versification should not be corrected.'[11] This appeared the judicious, the laudable scholarly course: 'möglichst die lesungen der handschrift zu wahren'.[12] Housman, however, drew attention to another aspect of the conservative editor's mentality: 'an editor who wishes to be praised . . . must defend the MS. tradition not only where it appears to be right but also where it appears to be wrong';[13] and again, 'assuredly there is no trade on earth, excepting textual criticism, in which the name of prudence would be given to that habit of mind which in ordinary human life is called credulity'.[14] We have, I hope, laid aside the caustic address of Housman's generation of editors, but perhaps in textual criticism our world is still as topsy-turvy; at any rate it might seem so when an eminent contemporary editor asserts in all seriousness that 'The line of least resistance in textual studies is to declare a reading corrupt and substitute one's own.'[15]

That statement, however plausible it may *prima facie* seem, does not accurately represent the situation. It must mean, in its context, that emending conjecturally is in general easier than accounting for a received reading. But that proposition is manifestly false because, if conjectural emendation is correctly practised, it must begin with and embrace accounting for the received reading; it is thus, as the more comprehensive operation, obviously a more difficult one than any which it comprises.

Moreover the statement does not reflect general opinion. This, as I see it, has two main attitudes: one that the excesses to which conjectural emendation has been carried have made it disreputable; the other that since it is very often possible to conjecture alternative readings for a crux, none of which can be validated, the more disciplined scholarship is to refrain from the activity.

These attitudes, on the face of it, seem reasonable; moreover they should, one might think, serve to moderate speculation, to control the operation of judgement, to safeguard the desirable principle of restraint. If, however, the arguments behind them are examined they appear with less credit. For instance: conjectural emendation is an activity which has been, and thus can be, badly conducted; because of this possibility it ought to be avoided. Or, conjectural emendation is an activity at which one can make mistakes; it is thus dangerous to an editor's reputation and he should therefore avoid it. Or, conjectural emendation cannot produce results of absolute certainty; it is therefore unprofitable and should be avoided. The first and second of these lines of thinking condemn themselves as mean-spirited; the third loses force from the indisputable consideration that there are very few results of literary scholarship in general for which the claim of absolute certainty can be made. In view of this the presumptive character of the results of textual criticism, and specifically of conjectural emendation, cannot cogently be invoked as a special, arbitrarily applicable objection to these particular forms of the activity. Such arguments lack force and we dismiss them easily; but there still survives a deep-seated objection to conjectural emendation, arising from a very natural human state of mind, the instinct for security.

That instinct would be best satisfied if the texts of ancient authors were generally sound.[16] Since that is not the case the next best reassurance would be to have available a system of editing which would eliminate or at least reduce the possibility of error in that unfortunately necessary process by removing the element of judgement from the operation or minimizing it; there should be a formula whose answers would replace the irresponsible, subjective decisions of erratic editors. It was to perform this function that the system called recension was devised. The twin considerations that it seldom if ever works (because stemmata turn out to be bifid, thus affording no casting vote, or because the evidence permits no stemma to be constructed), and that some impudent critics have presumed to discredit its logic as well as its practicability, have failed to dismiss the *fata Morgana* of a mechanistic system of editing. That continues both to exert its attraction and to obscure the real nature of the situation.

To this last the great modern theorists of textual criticism (I think particularly of Maas, Pasquali and Greg) have not been blind. They recognized and proclaimed the indispensability of judgement in editing. Above all Maas, and there is irony here, for he is nowadays often invoked as the modern exponent of recensionism, emphasized the editor's obligation to the ultimate exercise of judgement, the conjectural emendation which is my subject: 'Erweist sich die Überlieferung als verdorben, so muss versucht werden, sie durch divinatio zu heilen.'[17] The eclectic treatment of his theories is like that suffered by those of Alphonse Dain, now most often followed in a relatively unimportant objection to unduly minute collation, but in fact a merciless critic of erroneous notions about editing. Dain too pronounces on conjectural emendation, in terms strikingly similar to those first of Maas, then of Housman:

'Si le texte transmis est mauvais, on n'a pas le droit de ne pas essayer de l'amender. . . . Ce qui est détestable, de toute façon, c'est de garder un texte mauvais par sourci de s'écarter le moins possible des leçons du manuscrit.'[18]

These uncompromising statements were made by critics with wide experience, not just of the early literature of one vernacular, but of the long history of textual transmission in two classical languages, men thus well apprised of the hazards and difficulties of conjectural emendation. They might seem to restore the matter to its correct proportions. The 'line of least resistance' is not unbridled emendation (which would in any event be quickly subjected to ridicule) but the attitude of total scepticism about the capabilities of editing which, abrogating decision, shifts responsibility to a manuscript and prints this—on the argument which I have heard 'that one would at least have an authentic medieval form of the poem, as opposed to one incorporating the dubious hypotheses of a modern editor'. A harder course is to accept the principle that 'the duty of an editor is to edit', and to use available manuscript evidence for reconstructing an archetypal text. But the hardest course of all is to recognize the axiomatic corruption of such an archetype, and to face the implications of this condition. Each of these stages must be a more anxious, exacting, and challenging operation; but the second and third cannot fail to protect the study of literature against the postulate implied in the first: that its data are false to an indeterminate but certainly large extent. And they avoid the unhistorical corollary of the doctrine of passive 'editing': that the ancient or the medieval public did not care about the quality of its texts.

If nevertheless what Maas has called the 'reprehensible fear' of admitting that textual criticism is an operation which may not attain completely satisfying results[19] prevails, there is a harder argument still, which seems to create an intellectual obligation to conjectural emendation. This was first (as far as I know) formulated by Maas: 'In the nature of things it is much more harmful when a corruption remains unidentified than when a sound text is unjustly attacked . . . the unsignalled corruption vitiates the general stylistic impression.'[20] It has been more explicitly stated by Dr Sisam:

> To support a bad manuscript reading is in no way more meritorious than to support a bad conjecture, and so far from being safer, it is more insidious as a source of error. For, in good practice, a conjecture is printed with some distinguishing mark which attracts doubt; but a bad manuscript reading, if it is

defended, looks like solid ground for the defence of other readings. So intensive study with a strong bias towards the manuscript reading blunts the sense of style, and works in a vicious circle of debasement.[21]

Old and Middle English scholars will know how large this circle can be; the lexicography, the grammatical study, the notions about metre, our critical judgements and the literary history of the periods are embraced in it.

This concurrence of Maas and Sisam extends to a further conception of the function of conjecture: for Maas it is an essential part of what he calls *Examinatio*, 'Prüfung' of the quality of the received text;[23] Sisam correspondingly believes that 'there would be a real gain if conjecture, instead of being reserved for the useful but disheartening task of dealing with obvious or desperate faults, were restored to its true functions, which include probing as well as healing.'[23]

These considerations, which from their nature are not lightly to be dismissed, seem to define the true, ancillary function of textual criticism: an activity designed not to afford it practitioners either an outlet for self-expression or a secure and comfortable occupation, but to contribute to the right understanding and evaluation of older literature. They express the means by which that function will be exercised: through restoring, or attempting to restore, or indicating the damage suffered by texts in transmission, not in order to 'improve' these but to recover their historical truth, in itself and as a basis for other knowledge. Thus active editing, whether positive in establishing originality of readings, or negative in merely identifying corruption, or conjectural, in proposing hypothetical original readings which would account for putative corruptions, appears an intellectual responsibility, and one which from its character it would be wrong to abdicate or to restrict because its problems are not often or always conclusively soluble. In these terms conjectural emendation loses any character of unbridled self-indulgence and seems, rather, a valuable activity, hazardous indeed to the reputations of those who undertake it, but if correctly practised more likely to promote knowledge than to mislead.

Supposing the force of such arguments to be accepted it might seem desirable to look again at the theory and practice of conjectural emendation. In such a reconsideration the question is bound to come up how the results of the practice can be validated; to this the answer is that a conjecture can be validated conclusively only by the emergence of new textual evidence which supports it; otherwise it can appear as only more or less probably correct. That is a part of the nature of textual criticism, to which I shall recur. There is a second, related question: how the danger of 'improving the poet's work by brilliant conjecture' is to be avoided. This must be answered in terms of the degree of danger, which will depend on the nature of the text, and the quality of its author. There are, to be sure, some Middle English writers whose works invite improvement; I am not concerned with them. In the case of a major poet the danger must seem small from several considerations: first there is the intrinsic unlikelihood of any editor possessing such a capability; second, there is the extreme probability (demonstrable as such beyond reasonable doubt) that a bad reading in a great poem is scribal, not authorial, which must limit the number of occasions where the danger is real; third, the observation of a rationale in conjecture can restrain the creative impulses of an editor. There remains a further question: is the twentieth-century editor as good a judge of the originality of readings as, say, a Middle English scribe copying a near-contemporary poem? Has he any grounds for challenging a reading which, from its unanimous attestation, was evidently acceptable to many such scribes? At the risk of arrogance my answer must, with respect to a competent editor, be affirmative. He has a purpose, to recover what his author actually wrote; from all indications scribes, if they had any purpose of a comparable order, had a different one in which the concept of originality of readings was not included. And his equipment is, except in some notable cases of isolated detail, superior to that of the scribes: he has the comparative evidence of his collations, which they lacked; with the advantage of print he has a better general and particular knowledge of the text than theirs; and he has access to information about the history of lexis, grammar and dialect which no scribe (at least in medieval England) could have possessed.[24]

Of the above questions the fundamental one is the first. Various opinions about the means of assessing the probable truth of a conjectural emendation are to be found in the literature of textual criticism. For instance Housman specified 'fitness to the context and propriety to the genius of the author' as 'the indispensable things'.[25] Hall in his *Companion to Classical Texts* required that a conjecture must satisfy both the two tests of 'Transcriptional Probability' and 'Intrinsic Probability', that is the conjecture and corruption must be in a paleographically explicable relation, and the conjecture must 'suit the context, the author's style and vocabulary, and any general laws which have been proved to apply to his works'.[26] Maas formulated two criteria, a primary one of the appropriate quality of the style and substance of the conjectural reading, and a secondary one of its likelihood to have given rise to the suspect or impossible received reading.[27] These and similar generalizatons, whether satisfactory in themselves or not, might well fail, however, to allay the doubts of the sceptic, for all, ultimately, operate by the subjective judgement which he distrusts.

But if, as seems to be the case, subjective judgement is an invariable element of all editing except the most elementary, and since editing seems an indispensable activity, it is necessary to ask two questions: what justification is there for our sceptic's deep-seated distrust, and how can the dangers of subjectivity be minimized? I find the answer to both questions in the nature of the study of literature. This comprises very few activities where subjectivity in some form or other does not play a major part; we accept its presence in many cases; can we reasonably balk at it in others? Where we take the presence and function of subjectivity for granted we know how to test it. We study not the particular attractiveness of any of its conclusions, but the quality of the processes by which this was attained. We do not discard the practice of literary or interpretative criticism because bad criticism has been written; we scrutinize its assumptions, measure its affective constituents against our own responses, apply the tests of logic to its inferences, repeat its processes to better effect, thus incidentally advancing knowledge. To me it seems that the conclusions of textual criticism, and particularly of conjectural emendation, can be similarly tested, and the subjective element in them thus controlled.

As I understand editing an edited text has no absolute authority: it is as sound or unsound as the case the competent editor can make out for it. An edition constitutes an attempt to account for available phenomena in terms of what is known about the circumstances which generated them. To that extent it has the character of a scientific activity. It operates by advancing hypotheses to explain data, and tests such hypotheses in terms of their efficiency as explanations. Those which pass the test it accepts as presumptively, not absolutely true; they remain subject to revision or rejection if new data come to light or more efficient hypotheses are devised. Its character implies an editorial obligation to expose its procedures and the precise extent to which their results are speculative for scrutiny.[28] In such a process conjectural emendation can represent itself as not merely legitimate, but even on particular occasions strongly indicated, and it will be directed less by Maas's *Fingerspitzengefühl*, though that must play its part, than by deductive and inductive thought. Thus viewed it resumes the character of a respectable activity, one meriting a better name than *divinatio*. We can, admittedly, seldom if ever estimate the absolute truth of its conclusions, but correspondingly we can never know absolutely of any ancient texts except autographs that their words are the words of the authors. All textual criticism except the most elementary is an assessment of relative probabilities, and the authority of ancient texts must always vary—in the last analysis indeterminably—from line to line. 'Wer sich fürchtet', wrote Maas, 'einen unsicheren Text zu geben [and one might add 'oder zu bearbeiten'], wird besser tun, sich nur mit Autographa zu beschäftigen.'[29]

I suppose that the feature of conjectural emendation logically rather than psychologically hardest to accept is its rejection of unanimous manuscript testimony. In Housman's words

> The MSS. are the material upon which we base our rule, and then, when we have got our rule, we turn round upon the MSS. and say that the rule, based upon them, convicts them of error. We are thus working in a circle, that is a fact which there is no denying.[30]

In other words, we reject certain evidence on the grounds of other evidence from the same source; this strikes at the principle of authority. But may it perhaps not be that the force of the principle of authority in textual criticism has been misconceived? Let us look on the preceding situation from another aspect. The editor of a major poet must begin with a presumption of the excellence of his author; he is also governed by an axiom that texts, including archetypal texts, are corrupt. The excellence of his author is a matter of consensus of critical judgement; the axiom is a matter of manifest fact. Further, that excellence has survived notwithstanding the axiomatic deterioration of his texts, and must thus once have been even greater than the received texts now represent it to be. Is it then such bad thinking for his editor, where the text seems inferior in particulars although unanimously attested, to impute the falling off to archetypal scribal corruption? Such an inference, as the logic of literary studies goes, might seem good rather than suspect.

It is, of course, subjective, speculative and hazardous. The subjectivity enters when, in a situation where manuscripts offer no choice of readings, the editor carries out a comparison between the received text and his *idea* of the uncorrupted poem, of how the poet would and would not write. Assessing the quality of the received text he concludes that it exhibits characteristics which, in situations where manuscript evidence was divided, were produced by scribal variation. It is speculative because the editor goes on to propose what the poet actually did write, if he did not write the words unanimously attested by the manuscripts, having regard to his performance elsewhere. It is hazardous, although more to the editor's reputation than the poet's, because of the possibilities of error. The editor may mistake in identifying archetypal corruption, from a misconception of his author's *usus scribendi*, in which I include matters of language and literary form; or from a misunderstanding of his meaning, local and general. And he may conjecture badly, either through failure to identify the causes and processes of corruption which should guide him back to the original reading, or through lack of flair, *Fingerspitzengefühl*, which is an indispensable part of his equipment. But taking full account of this situation I will assert that the editor has not so much a right as an intellectual obligation to attempt the recovery of truth. The risk is to himself; however inept he may be he will not—I invoke Maas and Sisam—injure the poet.

Assuming that an editor who accepts this obligation is competent, are there any means by which he can protect himself against the dangers of his undertaking? The answer may lie with Maas, who describes the theoretical situation in which ideal conditions for conjecture would exist. In this situation evidence would be such as to permit a classification of errors specifically likely in particular periods of history, literary kinds, and types of transcription, either from manuscripts with surviving exemplars or from manuscripts whose exemplar can be reconstructed by recension. By this means the probable incidence of any specific type of error in given circumstances could be established. In addition it would be possible to ascertain the quality of the archetype, and this could happen where such an archetype was reduced to the status of a variant text (*Variantenträger*) or even of a derivative text (*codex descriptus*) through earlier branching of the tradition, or where it appeared as a quotation (*Zitat*). In such a situation the demonstrable classes of error would also, Maas asserts, be presumable in those areas of the text where no control is available, and no means of checking the archetypal quality exists. In other words a knowledge of the incidence of the typical corruption to which any given work was exposed or susceptible, and the possibility of assessing the quality of its archetypal text, that is the exclusive common ancestor of the surviving copies, would be the ideal determinants first of the need for conjecture and second of its accuracy.[31]

The tone in which Maas describes this situation suggests some doubt on his part about the likelihood of its actually ever occurring. In fact it is instanced in *Piers Plowman*. Each version of this poem survives in many copies, and its archetypal text can generally be recovered without difficulty; thus Maas's ideal classification of typical error is abundantly possible. For long passages two, or even all three versions, correspond: where unrevised B corresponds to A the B archetype has the character of a *codex descriptus*; where B corresponds to unrevised C it appears in C as a *Zitat*; where the three versions correspond B has both characters. Each revision was carried out on a copy of the immediately preceding version antecedent to the archetypal copy of that version; thus the quality of the archetypal texts can be assessed by comparing them where they correspond.

The editing of *Piers Plowman* will then afford an ideal occasion for re-examining the relation between the theory of conjectural emendation and its practice. From the re-examination it will appear that the distance between the rationale and its confident application must vary from crux to crux and can be immense. Instances of demonstrable archetypal corruption will range from those where the original can be conjectured with some assurance of acclamation to others where, while the received reading is manifestly corrupt, neither text nor context affords any indication of the words of the lost original. This situation is in the nature of the activity. The logical respectability of conjectural emendation is unassailable: the material question in any given editorial situation must be whether it was worth attempting, and this will be answered in terms of the competence of the particular editor. Criticism of conjectural emendation, as of all active editing, must bear not on the legitimacy of the operation but on the quality of its execution.

12
The Text of *The Legend of Good Women* in *CUL* MS Gg.4.27

Some differences between the text of the Prologue to *The Legend of Good Women* in Cambridge University Library MS Gg. 4.27 (henceforth called G) and that preserved in the other manuscripts of the poem are of such character or extent or both as to be most easily explicable by a hypothesis of authorial revision. But acceptance of that hypothesis implies a need to examine all differences between the two texts in its terms. At the same time, from the axiom of the necessary corruptness of texts, not all differences can be authorial. The problem of distinguishing between revision, that is, authorial variation, and the scribal variation inevitable in manuscript transmission is probably the most delicate operation in all textual criticism.

It is here complicated by the question which version is antecedent. To my knowledge that question has never been resolved in terms of absolute proof. There seems just now a tacit consensus that the G version is the revision. But the consensus seems to rest more on dissatisfaction with the subjectivity of the arguments for the antecedence of G than on the quality of those for G being the revision. Ideally, then, identification of scribal damage in both versions of the *Prologue* would be effected without reference to the direction of revision.

This essay gives the results of such an attempt. The method of obtaining them has been to examine the unique unoriginal variants of G in that part of the poem where revision is not presumed, namely the *Legend*; from that examination to form a 'profile' of the immediate scribes or scribe of G; and to set that profile against differences of a comparable scale between the two versions of the *Prologue*. The exercise was conducted in full awareness of its limitations, which are those that qualify all applications of the theory of textual criticism. Here, specifically, the decisions about direction of variation in all interesting or significant cases are subjective; the arguments on which they are based—that is the explanations of individual variations—are speculative; the result is 'only another hypothesis'. What is in question is not absolute proof but a plausible explanation of a class of phenomena, the essential object of all literary study.

The position of G among the manuscripts of *The Legend of Good Women* is obscure. Since in the *Legend* all manuscripts are copies of the same poem they necessarily have an exclusive common ancestor, if nothing else the author's copy. Beyond that, classification of the manuscripts by variation from a text formed upon full collation[1] places all the manuscripts except G in two large families. One of these, $\{ < [T(FB)]TH > \}A^3 \}$, is solid for the whole poem. The second comprises the remaining manuscripts except G as and when these are represented: before line 800 as $< [P(TrA^1)]S >$, and soon after that point, at its fullest, as $< [S(TrA^1)][PR] >$, then later in the poem with fluctuating subgroups. It is not possible to relate G confidently to either main group on the basis of agreement in unoriginal readings. It figures in more than 100 random agreements with single manuscripts, unrelated manuscripts, or subgroups, but shares no considerable number of unoriginal readings with either main group. In other words, most of its unoriginal readings were accumulated in the most recent stages of its tradition.

Classification of the manuscripts also reveals that in those recent stages of transmission the text of *The Legend of Good Women* in G was much corrupted. For this poem at least G is in no sense a 'superior' manuscript.[2] By the most conservative estimate the text of G in the *Legend* has more than 200 individual unoriginal variant readings of a substantive nature. In another more than 200 it forms 92 random groups by coincident variation: 10 groups of 2 manuscripts based on a total of 54 variants; 19 groups of 3 (44 variants); 24 groups of 4 (42 variants); 7 groups of 5 (17 variants); 15 groups of 6 (27 variants); 7 groups of 7 (7 variants); 9 groups of 8 (13 variants); and one group of 9 manuscripts based on a single variant. It shares another 30 odd unoriginal variants in a pair or with two to four other manuscripts, so clustered as to suggest contamination rather than coincident variation.[3] There is an identifiable scribal variation for every seven lines of G's text of the *Legend*.

Among the individual unoriginal readings of G unmistakably mechanical variations are the more numerous. The most frequent source of such variation seems to be inducement of the preceding copy. its effect is identifiable in the following instances:4 603 nothyng to hym] to hy*m* nothyng (*position of* Hym *at head of line*); 840 slow] slayn (slayn 837); 880 leef] lyf (sle *preceding*; 903 yfere] that (That *prec.*); 920 to] for (For *prec.*); 1082 She] And (And 1066–71, 1074, 1075, 1079, 1080); 1102 And] Of (Of . . . of . . . of 1101) (*so Robinson*); 1138 his yonge] this blysful (blysful 1137); 1189 hire] oure (am-orou-s *prec.*); 1240 this whan] whil (whil that 1239); 1259 they] ʒe (ye 1257, 1259); 1263 may2] may it (may . . . it *prec.*); 1267 so pryuy] so trewe (so trewe 1266); 1387 ful] wol (wel 1386); 1486 hem] hy*m* (his *prec.*); 1489 For] Or (Or 1488); 1526 That half so] That so (That to 1525); 1568 his] hire (hire 1567); 1591 of al] I clepid (cleped 1590); 1608 with] *and* (And 1604, 1605, 1606 (2), 1607); 1734 she let hyre eyen] h. e. l. s. (of hire werk she tok: *object in first position* 1733); 1752 was] is (h-is w-i-t *prec.*); 1756 His] This (Th-e 1755); 1924 And] But (But 1918, 1921); 1964 Mynos] Thesi*us* (Theseus 1960); 2000 To] And (and . . . and 1999); 2056 As] So (So-ne . . . knyght 2055, As/So myghte 2056); 2088 yow] the (ye-ve *prec.*); 2182 for] with (with *prec.*); 2187 I] that I (*so Rob.*) (that *prec.*); 2314 Of] For (*so Rob.*) (Or 2313), agros] aros (reste 2313); 2358 can] coude (coude 2357); 2487 him] she (she *prec.*); 2500 as] that (That *prec.*); 2501 which] that (That 2500); 2521 so] to (*so Rob.*) (to *prec.*); 2598 deyen] turne (turne 2596, Sa-turne 2597); 2658 dremes it is] d. is it (drem-es it *prec.*); 2686 That] And (And 2685).

Anticipation of following copy is another frequent source of mechanical variation in G's text of the *Legend*. Its effect is identifiable in the following instances: 810 drery] dredy (dredful 811); 881 am] al (c-al-leth *following*); 897 departe] depare (t-rewely *fol.*); 1000 she] he (he *fol.*); 1003 sholde] schule (la-, lo-, -le *fol.*); 1058 biknew] he knew (he *fol.*); 1115 the] to (to *fol.*); 1149 thanked] thankyth (*present tense fol.*); 1202 fair] bright (bryghte *fol.*); 1213 go bet] bobet; 1242 upros] a ros (a-nd . . . a-non *fol.*); 1264 Tak] Thak (Tak hede . . . th-is *fol.*); 1352 But] But ʒit (yit *fol.*); 1425 yle] ylde (called *fol.*); 1437 boles] bole (dragoun *sg. fol.*); 1643 hereupon] here vp (upward 1645); 1660 wedded] weddyth (th-e th-ridde *fol*); 1685 to] to me (memorye *fol.*); 1717 yate] ʒote (p-o-rter . . . n-o-n *fol.*); 1726 walles] wal (fallen] fal G *fol.*); 1729 it stingeth] me thy*n*kyth (I thynke 1730); 1766 That] ʒit (Yit 1767); 1826 he] this (this *fol.*); 1986 any] *om* (m-an fol.); 2007 whan] what (that *fol.*); 2044 no man] non (con-ne *fol.*); 2094 is] nys (no *fol.*); 2101 final] fenal (en-de *fol.*); 2215 come] cone (contre/cuntre 2216); 2267 preyde] preyeth (th-at *fol.*); he] ho (wo-lde *fol.*); 2275 but] myghte (s-yghte *fol.*); 2484 recorde] recordith (deth . . . corde 2485); 2613 flour] flourys (lef is *fol.*); 2660 which] wit (noot *fol.*).

Occasionally substitution of an unoriginal reading appears to have been induced by features of the text both before and after the point of variation: 1251 at] of (oo-n . . . an-o-thers w-o); 1330 hath he] he hath (he let 1326, he gan 1328, he lafte 1332, he . . . stal 1333); 1496 oure] hire (hire 1493, pleye . . . hire 1497, 1498; 1543 on] in (this-i-s . . . n-y-ght); 1786 this] the (he 1785, she 1786, 1787); 1933 com aboute] fil a. (caste lot 1933 *and* On riche or pore 1934 *suggest the collocation* 'lot fell'); 2072 As] And (And 2070, 2073).

Grammatical attraction, this is, subconscious scribal interest in the completion of an anticipated grammatical relationship, in consequence of which a delaying element of text is omitted, was probably responsible for the following accordingly mechanical variations: 933 a] *om. (adj ~ noun)*; 999 with him] *om. (verb ~ adv.)*; 1032 for to] *om. (adv. ~ verb)*; 1173 For] *om.* (so 1172 *~ that 1173); 1174 ek so] om. (conjunction ~ complement)*; 1341 allas] *om. (demonstrative adv. ~ referent)*; 1398 which] *om. (noun ~ modif. clause)*; 1566 grete] *om. (prep. ~ object)*; 1567 him] *om. (verb ~ direct object)*; 1599 which] *om. (noun~modif. clause)*; 1741 of him] *om. (subj.~ pred.)*; 1809 swich] *om. (prep. ~ obj.)*; 2038 that[1]] *om. (conjunction ~ referent clause)*; 2356 eek] *om. (modal verb~ infinitive)*; 2554 is] *om. (comparative conj. ~ referent)*. Grammatical attraction can induce variation of word order, as at 1640 *shulde hir neuer] s. n. h.* (so Rob.) where the attraction drew together the modal verb and its intensifying adverb, and at 2137 *Theseus of hire hath leve take] T. hath of hire . . .*, where subject and predicate were drawn together. And it can produce an overlay of two constructions, as at 2053 *Oon of the gretteste men] On of the gretteste man*.

Inducement of a common collocation is the probable explanation of a further number of mechanical variations. That common collocations existed in Middle English is unlikely to be debated, and an experienced ear will recognize a store of them. The difficulty is that a particular word could figure in several common collocations. Nevertheless the following individual variants of G in the *Legend* seem explicable in this way: 642 he[2]] sche (he and she); 647 be] to be (bidden to); 87 noyse or] ony (withouten any, *and note* o-n-y/n-o-y) 944 olde] owene (his owene); 1003 to] the (the longe while); 1018 than] thus (thus hath); 1133 thise noble] *om.* (alle thyng(es)); 1203 folk] men (sike men); 1457 rede] ryde (gon or ride); 1934 on] or (*so Rob.*) (riche or pore); 1948 lad] gon (gon forth); 1996 this] the (*so Rob.*) (the fend); 1999 roum eek and space] bothe r. and s. (both . . . and); 2266 to] with (wende with); 2449 olde] owene (*cf.* 944); 2539 folk] men (men may).

The scribe of G was evidently also prone to error through distraction by a variety of less easily classifiable features of his exemplar. In 773 *whan*] *that* looks like the product of uncertainty about how the grammar of the sentence would develop. In 784 *sholde*] *wolde* he was probably thinking '*they wolde meten*'. In 1737 his difficulty with *Embelished*, for which he substituted *Emblemyschid*, to the contrary effect, is the probable cause of his omission of *eek* from 1736 and the dislocation of 1738 and 1739.[5] Omission of *But* from 1770 probably was induced by the difficulty of the distinction being made, which arises from a special use of *delit* with moral colour, as in *fol delit*, 'sexual misconduct'. In 1977 *Than*] *This* (so Rob.) is the byproduct of an unconscious confusion of numbers registered in *suster*] *systeryn* at the end of the line (see next page). In 2008 *on*] *as* the substitution probably anticipates unconsciously 2009 *or*] *as* where the scribe did not see the meaning of *or*. In 2216 *to*] *to to* the dittography probably occurred through hesitation about the sense of 2215: surely her worse fate would be for no ship at all to come. In 2267 *preyde*] *preyeth* the distraction need have been no more than the length of the line. In 2345 *hir*] *his* relates to the scribe's difficulty with *fond*, sc. 'upon his arrival'. In 2508 *strem*] *storm* the distraction will have been the proper name; no manuscript reads Robinson's *Sytho*: the variants are *Sitonie*, *Scython*, *Sitoy(e)*, *Sitoio*, *Cyteys*.

A number of the G scribe's unoriginal variants are elementary scribal aberrations. Misreading of *kk* is all that there is to 756 *wikkede*] *welkede*. Mistaking *t* for *c*, followed by subconscious misdivision, produced 1160 *to the*] *comyth*. Initial *s* of following *smerte* caused 1597 *sorwes*] *sorwe*. Suspension trouble produced 1581 *devourer*] *deuoure* and 2125 *manere*] *mane*. There are omissions by homoeoarchy at 800 *woman wolde*] *wolde*, 904 *to this*] *to his*, 1246 *hadde hir*] *hadde*, 2210 *she speketh*] *speketh*; by homoeoteleuton at 951 *forth with*] *forth*, 1429 *nowher was þer*] *nower was* (so Rob.), 1733 *werk she tok*] *werk tok*, 2396 *that it*] *that*, and 2579 *sholde be*] *shal be*. Eyeskip caused 1177 *him telle his*] *his* and 1536 *Hym*[6] *had leuer hymself*] *Hymselue*. And the omission of lines 2506, 2507 is as pretty an instance of homoeoarchy (*But tymes foure* 2504, *And foure tymes* 2506) as any textual critic could wish for. At 913 *as swythe*] *a swythe*, 1313 *leste degre*] *leste gre*, 1813 *At thilke*] *At Ilke* and 2525 *trusted I*] *truste I* (a corrector erased the pronoun) there are unmistakable auditory errors. Another class of auditory error resulting from the phonetic situation where [v] and [$] are heard identically as instanced in 1473 *blyue*] *blythe* (so Rob.) rhyming with *aryve*, and 2176 *blyve*] *swythe* rhyming with *dryve*. The same idiosyncrasy[7] explains 1977 *syster fre*] *systeryn fre*, the adjective having been heard as the numeral.

Variation arising from the scribe's response to and participation in the meaning of the text naturally occurs, but is limited in variety and amount. A number of substitutions make the text more explicit: 815 that] that þat; 941 he] *and* he; 1055 whan] whan that; 1454 With] And with; 1482 to²] for to; 1571 preyede] preyede to; 1702 that] *and* that; 1813 the] here; 1950 in] into; 2027 Whan] And whan; 2064 ther] than; 2293 it go] he do; 2324 a] that (*so Rob.*); 2372 tolde] hire tolde; 2480 dighte] let . . . dighte; 2683 As] And.

A number of his sustitutions make the text easier in other ways, grammatical, lexicographical, or somehow contextual: 718 estward in the world was tho dwellinge] tho was in that lond Estward dwellynge (*so Rob.*) *making the reference of* estward *clearer*; 737 which that] that which *establishing the somewhat remote reference to the wall* (718); 870 now] tho *in resistance to the present aspect of preceding* hath; 916 ago] Igo (*so Rob.*); 928 In thyn Eneyde and Naso] *In Naso and* Eneydos (*so Rob.*); 1163 hir] his *in resistance to the literary gender*; 1171 drem] slep *no dream having been mentioned*; *1247 to²*] as; 1283 land] landys *because the generic singular is difficult*; 1339 unbynd me] brynge it *dismissing the figure*; 1351 rof hyre to the herte] rof hyre hert; 1423 Now] Tho; 1439 bethoughte] bethoute hym; 1541 swich] whiche; 1753 wel thoghte he] he woste wel; 1812 Romayns] Romeyn (*so Rob.*); 1826 is falle] be falle *eliminating a change of construction*; 2248 hire] that; 2345 fond] say; 2396 fynde] wete; 2469 doth] don (*cf.* 1826); 2570 called was] was callid *to prose order*.

A small number of substitutions makes the text more emphatic: 603, 741, 1749 was] nas (*so Rob.*); 1099 his] al hese; 1367 Rede] Rede he; 1684 telle] ne telle; 1728 to] sore; 1821 verray] worthi; 2176 blyve] swythe; 2188 torente] al . . . torent; 2293 that] euere; 2294 kneled and so] he so fayre hire; 2590 raft] beraft; 2714 ferre] forth (fer *Rob.*)

Ideally it would be determinable whether these variations of G to a more explicit or otherwise easier or to a more emphatic reading were deliberate. But the question has no general or simple answer. Such variations can have occurred as a consequence of imperfect attention to detail, the scribe picking up a block of lines or even as little as a couplet and modifying it at the moment of registration or during its retention in his memory. In theory the stronger his interest and response, the greater the likelihood that a substitution to—say—a more emphatic reading would be deliberate. In practice one has only the variants from which to gauge the strength and nature of response. In this instance they have proved disappointing, but it may be that their very drabness is significant.

The same principle applies to his more elaborate variations, or sophistications. Here, however, there may be a greater possibility of assessing deliberate alteration, of identifying the point at which the explanation of unconscious variation is acceptable. The remaining individual variations of G in the *Legend* can be arranged in terms of that possibility.

Thus 1175 *therwithal*] *ek thereto* is probably not an expression of stylistic preference but a subconscious compensatory substitution following accidental omission of *ek so* from 1174. And 1352 *yit*] *right* is unconscious smoothing after *But*] *But ʒit* variation at the beginning of the line, the scribe's disconcertment registered by his omission of *seith*. In 1730 G's line *It styngith me whan I thynke on that place* may well be from its poor sense an unconscious adjustment after the unconscious anticipation of copy, *it stingeth*] *me thynkyth* in 1729. By contrast in 2525 the sophistication is visibly deliberate: after *trusted*] *truste* substitution *I²* is erased so as to turn *truste* into a substantive object of *may I pleyne*.

In another group of variants that look like sophistications it is not possible to rule out unconscious substitution. Thus at 1143 *noble*] *holy* it seems not impossible for the radical substitution to have been subconsciously induced by 1140 *god*, 1141 *moder hye above*, 1142 *liknesse of the child*, 1144 *scripture*. At 1932 the absence of *yeer* from G might register a momentary misconception that the choice of victim would fall on every third man, or might be part of the variation through distraction that shows itself in 1933 (above, p. 165). At 2009 *To slen hym or*] *And slen hym as* could be a subconscious mis-conception of how the fight would go or a deliberate 'correction'. At 2215 *come*] *ne cone* the negative, of which the *m n* error is a subconscious reflex, could be a thoughtless reaction to the text immediately preceding or a deliberate change based on the scribe's failure to identify the worst feature of Ariadne's predicament. At 2430 *And*] *That* (so Rob.) the scribe may equally well have unconsciously misread the line as a result clause or deliberately rejected its character as the resumptive assessment of Demophoon's whole situation.

A small group of sophistications have an unmistakable look of being deliberate. The relation of the variants at 785 *grave under*] *graue out of* and 788 *this grave*] *there graue* is too complex for an unconscious substitution. At 1131 *clothes broches and ek rynges*] *clothis and ek brochis ryngis* the variation looks very like a conscious move toward parallelism with 1132 *Some for to were and some for to presente*. At 1166 *waketh walweth*] *waileth and sche* is designed to reduce the undignified element in Dido's behaviour. *In 1217 wilde hertes*] *bestys wilde* (so Rob.) the substitution was designed to elevate the action, the scribe having missed the poet's intention of anticlimax. At 1370 *gentil*[1]] *tendere* he again mistook Chaucer's tone. *In 1468 whylom*] om. he misunderstood the modification of the adverb and excluded it as inappropriate. In 1737 *Embelished*] *Emblemyschid* he could not accept that tears might be an adornment. In 1815 *bothe at ones*] *bothe atonys bothe* he corrected his initial error to another order than that of his exemplar by cancelling *bothe*[1]. In 1994 *That*] om. is the result of his failure to see that the conjunction introduces the whole process specified in 1994–6.

Another group of variations comprises sophistications of the metre: 587 *at*] *vnto* (*obeysaunce being read as tetrasyllabic*); 725 *Tisbe*] *And Tysbe* (*so Rob.*) ('*correcting' a 'headless' line*); 759 *but*] *but if* (*after loss of final e from* herte); 1246 *loved*] *I louyd* (*after omission of* hire); 1337 *ful*] *and ful* (*loss of final e:* ofte); 1391 *payed*] *hath payed* (*loss of final e:* goode); 1433 *moche*] *meche othir* (*loss of final e:* moche *pl.*); 1482 *to*] *for to* (*loss of final e:* take); 1718 *abyde*] *gan abyde* (*loss of final e:* dore); 2027 *Whan*] *And whan* (*Orignally a headless line*); 2134 *oughte us herof*] o. *herof vs* (*so Rob.*) (*smoothing the rhythm of a heavily modulated line*); 2184 *hath*] *hath now* (*so Rob.*) (*loss of final e:* herte); 2324 *hath*] *hat he* (*loss of final e:* force); 2328 *loude*] *loude a* (*loss of final e:* loude); 2419 *brende*] *it brende* (*loss of final e:* force); 2328 *loude*] *loude a* (*loss of final e:* loude); 2419 *brende*] *it brende* (*loss of final e:* torche) (*so Rob.*); 2554 *harder*] *hardyere* (*after omission of* is); 2593 *houses*] *howses that* (*after omission of* his).

There is a pattern discernible in the independent variation of G in

the *Legend*.[8] The amount of elementary mechanical error induced by
misreading of letters, difficulty with suspensions, homoeoarchy or
homoeoteleuton, and auditory confusion is small. At that level
copying appears to have been pretty attentive.[9] There is a somewhat
larger number of variations attributable to the subconscious effect of
linguistic conditions, that is grammatical attraction and inducement
of common collocations. The largest class of variation derives from
preoccupation with meaning. While the scribe is copying he has in
mind as well as in memory the context of the words immediate to his
pen and thus is subject to a variety of unconscious error induced by
preceding or following or surrounding copy. He also, unconsciously
or deliberately, substitutes more explicit or otherwise easier
readings; these make up about a fifth of G's independent variation in
the *Legend*. The suggestion of indifferent intelligence in such variation is confirmed by the proportion of his sophistications, in themselves not numerous, based on misreading or misunderstanding. His
metrical sophistication is elementary, mainly a register of objection
to headless lines or of providing syllabic surrogate for phonetically
devalued historical or grammatical final *e*. The slightness or, just
possibly, restraint of his emotional response to the stories appears
from the relatively small number of more emphatic substitutions he
makes. But of course he may have been puzzled or put off by the
singular tone of the *Legend*. The impression is of a relatively careful,
dull man, whose dullness actually increased his susceptibility to
error.

That impression is strengthened by analysis of the several hundred
unoriginal variant readings in which G agrees coincidentally with
other manuscripts or groups of manuscripts. The most appropriate
illustration of this will be from the instances where such variation has
been admitted to Robinson's text of the *Legend*. From the excellence
of his editorial flair they are not very numerous, and of course the
more elementary errors are absent. The following are examples:

Variation induced by preceding copy: 794 likyng] hast PFfG (faste
790, laste 791); 815 forgladde] so glad TFBSTrThA¹G (so sore 814);
1139 tellith thus] telleth vs RG (th-th); 1263 I] ye TFBTrThG (ye
1257, 1259, 1260, 1263); 1269 dau*n*ce] daunces TrSPA¹RG (festes
prec.); 1547 entent] assent TrA¹G (inn-ocent 1546); 1659 And . . . a
. . . traytour] As . . . (a) . . . t. A³A¹A²G (as a traytour 1656); 1777
(than) he hath] (than) hath he FBSTrA²G (tha ~ ath, *with further
variation by omission of* than); 2239 this] his SAG (his 2237); 2421

had] hath FBSThA³G (possith *pres.* 2420); 2453 lyked] lyketh FBSTrThA³A²G (doth *pres.* 2452).

Variation induced by attraction to following copy: 1202 is fair as] as fair/bright as STrPA¹RG; 1357 I make] make I STrA¹G (I ~ my *fol.*); 2063 to] to SA²G (swtch *fol.*).

Variation induced by surrounding copy: 1285 thus] so SPRG (yn-o-gh, w-o-le, m-o-re 1284, ysw-o-re 1285; 1780 vnto] into A²SG (in *prec.*, in 1781); 1967 ther] *om.* TFBSThA³A²G (happede ~ per cas); 1981 this] his TFBThG (he his 1980, he is *fol.*).

Substitution induced by a common collocation: 1241 yeden] came/comyn TFBSThPRG (comen out); 1639 ne] or ThG (lef or loth); 2102 on] vpon TFBTrThG (hereupon).

Variation to a more explicit reading: 968 the] his TFBThG; 1150 the] this TFBThA¹G; 1194 Vnto] Into STrA¹G; 1235 chaunge] c. her PRG; 1316 lat] and l. PRG; 1583 to] into TrSA¹G; 1784 Wheþer] Were it STrA³A¹A²G; 1795 swerd] poynt STrA³A¹A²G; 2168 seyde] s. that GSTrThA²; 2676 Danaos sone] lyno TFBThA³A²G.

Variation to an otherwise easier reading. (i) *smoothing the tense:* 1114 nys] nas/ne was/was TFBTrThPA¹RG; 1163 hath] hadde SThPRG; 1273 wol] woldes FBSThPRG; 1409 hath] had TrA¹G; 1835 may] myght A¹SG. (ii) *to prose order:* 1626 am I] I am A³G; 2477 agayn he wolde] he w. a. SA³A²G. (iii) *to fuller grammatical expression:* 2329 helpe] and h. SA³A²G; 2592 What] That what TrA²G; 2637 Ne nolde] Ne I nolde GS. (iv) *to lexicographically easier readings:* 925 Bere] Be to TFBSTrThA¹G; 973 knytte] cutted TSTrThPA³A¹G; 1472 lay the ship that Iasoun] that the ship of J. STrA¹G; 2332 Foreferde] For fere TrThA³G.

Sophistication: 866 wax] was TFPA³FfG *eliminating* box . . . wax *echo*; 2092 your gentilesse] giltles yow *misconceiving the argument* TrA²G; 2255 full²] eke SA²G *eliminating repetition*; 2553 or] and TFBThG *objecting to Chaucer's alternative offerings for* intumulata (*Heroides* ii. 136).

Variation to smooth metre: (i) *supplying a syllable after devaluation of final* e: 907 euer] evyr yet A¹TrG; 1041 trouthe] and t. TFBSPA³G (womanhede); 1063 hadde] she h./h. she STrPA¹RG (herte); 1649 name] a name TThA³G, as] ryght as TrSA²G (name); 1754 he] that he TrSA¹A²G (more). (ii) *supplying a syllable after other loss:* 1015 to] vnto TFBSThG (comen] com); 1971 compleynt] compleynyng STrA¹A²G (stoden] stode). (iii) *regularizing stress pattern:* 1776 he forth rit] forth h. r. SA³A²G; 2684 streyneth her] hire streyneth

TrA²G. (iv) *adjusting because the hiatus is not valued:* 1024 Had ben in this temple] Hadden in this temple ben TFBSTrThA³G. (v) *adjusting because elision is not valued:* 2337 to his²] to SG.

There is no difference of character or quality between these readings, where G agrees with other manuscripts, and those in which it varies alone. The likelihood is that they were admitted to the text of the *Legend* not for their quality but because its editor's ignorance of the frequency of coincident variation led him to be impressed by the mere fact of G being in agreement with other manuscripts. They reflect the distractions and preoccupations of the same dull and limited mentality exhibited in G's unoriginal solo variation.

The demonstrated character of G's scribal variation has an immediate bearing on the question of revision in the *Legend*. The whole pattern of that variation is such as to establish a primary unlikelihood that any differences between the *Legend* text of G and that of the large family are authorial. Those differences which have been discussed are the results of scribal variation in G or its immediate tradition. Where the text of G is superior the explanation is scribal variation in the tradition of the large family. There was no revision of the *Legend*.

There is further bearing on the two texts of the *Prologue*. Decision whether any given difference between those texts is authorial has hitherto had to be based on simple judgements of literary criticism. Is the difference of a kind one can imagine Chaucer wanting to make? That question now has a complement. Is the difference one within or beyond the demonstrated limits of the G scribe's capacity to effect? And if within those limits, is it, from conforming to his habits of variation, better interpeted as not the product of authorial revision? The position is thus altered. Axiomatically the G text of the *Prologue* contains scribal errors. Because we now know the characteristics of its immediate scribe's variation, we can identify them by editorial techniques rather than by arbitrary critical judgements. Knowledge of his *usus scribendi* has introduced an element of system into the procedure.

So, immediately, it is clear that the larger differences which distinguish the two texts would have been quite beyond his conception and execution. His incapacity to grasp the larger sense of his exemplar is indicated in the *Legend* when his copy shows no sign of disconcertment at the break of sense on ff. 417ᵛ–19ᵛ (449ᵛ–50ᵛ), where he copies lines 394–429 before 358–93[10] without registering that he noticed the inconsequence. We can be confident that any substantial difference between the two prologue texts is not by G and therefore presumably authorial.

As to the smaller differences, the indication is that any which relate intelligently to the meaning or feeling of their context, or show any command of expression, or answer to the better hypotheses of revision, are not to be attributed to him.

There is, however, a substantial residue of differences where G's readings do not answer to such description but can be related to the character of its scribe. The text of G in the *Prologue* contains more than 40 unique variant readings of the kinds identified as scribal in its text of the *Legend*, and in about the same density (one in about 12 lines as opposed to one in about 11). It also contains 40 variants of such kinds in which it agrees with one or more manuscripts of the larger family.[11] The similarity of the G readings in those situations to G's individual variations in the *Legend* suggests that they are scribal. If that suggestion is correct, Robinson's texts of the prologues can be improved at a number of points.

Where G's lines are unique Robinson did identify and correct 10 scribal errors.[12] G's tendency to metrical smoothing points to an eleventh in 225, where the 'and' in *Vp on the softe* and *sote grene gras* looks like an attempt to repair the rhythm after phonetic devaluation of the weak adjective inflexion, and incidentally suggests that the whole form of the line is scribal, the original being as in F118. There is more interesting meaning to *smale gras* than to *grene*.

Where there are corresponding lines in the two prologues Robinson admitted to his text of G, where they will inevitably be read as revisions, a number of readings which on the showing of the present analysis should be attributed to the G scribe. He did, to be sure, express awareness of the difficulty of decision, but then invoked the 'peculiar authority' of G[13] in support of their adoption.

It will be recalled that in the *Legend* many G variants were explicable as induced by the preceding context. That explanation will account for two differences between the texts of the *Prologue:* 4 *yet*] *this* (*that* 3) and 48 *this flour*] *these flo*uris (*floures* 38, 41, 42, *dayesyes* 43). Difficulty with local meaning of the kinds instanced in G's *Legend* variants appears also in its *Prologue* text. In 377/357 *tiraunt ne crewel*] *tyraunt* and *crewel* the scribe took *tiraunt* in its more general abusive sense (*OED* s.v. 6 and 3, 4) or else did not know the sense 'despotic'. In 490/480 *the lyke*] *the lestyth* he mistook the finesse of Alcestis's 'even though it may not please you', and substituted a word implying the subsidence of desire in the Dreamer, and uncharacteristic of her general attitude to him. Two G *Prologue* readings are more explicit: 305/231 *estaat*] *degre*[14] and *413/398 in*] *with*. Four readings in the G *Prologue* are easier: 78/66 *thogh*] *If* where *thogh* has the less immediate meaning 'supposing that' (*OED* s.v. *Though* 2); 123/111 *surmounteth*] *surmountede* and 128/115 *hath*] *hadde* smoothing the tense; 217/149 *flourouns smale*] *manye flourys* (other manuscripts agree with G in this variation at 220/152 and 529/517). Three G readings look like metrical smoothing: 5 *dwellyng*] *that dwellyth* regularizes the rhythm; 127/115 *sore*] *sore hadde* compensates for devaluation of the adverbial inflexion on *sore*;[15] and 447/437 *If that*] *That If that* puts a head to a headless line. Here the scribe may seem to have been caught in the act: the capitalization *That If that* very possibly reflects an exemplar in which the line began *If that*. The resemblances between these readings of G and the individual G variants in the *Legend* makes them look very like scribal products. They are to be sure not very numerous, the few in fact that eluded Robinson's flair and good taste. But they have a serious bearing on the nature of Chaucer's revision here and in other works.

So does a passage with somewhat larger and more serious differences between the texts of the two prologues which, in the light of the demonstrated variational habits of the G scribe, are more likely to be his work than Chaucer's. This is 139/127–152/138. G's text here reads as follows.

Some songyn on the brau*n*chis clere	127
Of loue *and* that Ioye It was to here	
In worschepe *and* in preysyng of hire make	
And of the newe blysful somerys sake	130
That su*n*gyn blyssede be seynt volentyn	
At his day I ches ʒow to be myn	
with oute repenty*n*ge myn herte swete	
And therwithal here bekys gu*n*ne mete	
The honour *and* the humble obeysau*n*ce	135
And aft*er* dedyn othere obseruau*n*cys	
Ryht on to loue *and* to natures	
So eche of hem to cryaturys	138

Merely from its sense and metre this passage cannot be authorial in form, and editors have recognized its necessary corruption.[16] The question is whether the passage also owes some of its present form to revision, or whether it is simply a much debased form of the text represented in F 139–52. The answer is critical because of the adjacency of a major difference between the texts with an unmistakable look of revision. It can, however, now be considered without concern for any 'peculiar authority' of G.

Straightaway, then, the form of G 127, 128 is seen to derive from unconscious omission of *And al his craft* through *And–And* eyeskip, possibly encouraged by the run-on grammar of the original (F 138, 139). Then, deliberately or unconsciously, the now too short line is filled out with *on the braunchis* from (original) F 143. Next, by inducement of the common collocation *song(en) of loue*, there is omission of *layes* from 127 with metrical padding by supply of *and that*. After G 130 there is omission of two lines like F 143, 144, probably unconscious, the inducements being homoeoarchy (compare F 141, 144 *In*, 142, 145 *And*) or a subconscious feeling of having already copied F 143 (*on the braunchis* G 127), or both in conjunction; even the difficulty of F 144, which calls for observation of the restlessness of small birds, might have contributed. G 131's evidently unoriginal *That* attempts to smooth the sense after the loss, and G 132 *For on his*] *At* actually echoes *That* and registers preoccupation with whether the smoothing will do.

It is not quite so easy to account for the just as manifestly corrupt form of G 135–8. *Yelding*] *The* in 135 resists explanation. But 136 *To love*] *And after* may again be the product of resistance to a run-on line; 137 *That longeth*] om.] *Ryht* can have occurred through attraction between *observauncys* and (*on*) *to* with subsequent padding; the desperate form of 138 might be prudish censorship of a naughty original like F 152.

The differences between the two texts of the *Prologue* in 139/127–149/135 were clearly not produced by revision. Whether revision has anything to do with the differences in the rest of the passage seems not finally determinable. But the whole passage can be seen as a sum of the sort of corruptions the G scribe was capable of, and if G's text here is seen as a scribally corrupted reflex of that of F, the level of quality in the sophistications is just about right for him. Why there should be so much corruption in such a short passage can only be guessed at. In any event it does not seem good editorial practice to attempt to restore a revised text here.

What has been shown about the quality of G's *Legend* text has also relevance to about forty variant readings in G's *Prologue* at points where the two versions have corresponding lines, in which G agrees with one or more manuscripts of the larger family. Of those readings Robinson adopted thirteen in his text of F, presumably as the originals of both versions. Another six he did not adopt for F but let stand in G, presumably as revisions. The quality of the readings in both groups fails to support his judgement. They conform to the types of G's characteristic individual variation in the *Legend* and might better be interpreted as the products of coincident variation by G and another manuscript or subgroup.[17]

Of the G readings Robinson adopted for F one is explicable as produced by attraction to preceding copy: 449/439 *as*] *what* PSA¹G (*with* prec.). Three register misreading of the original: 11 *men hath*] *men han* TFBThG taking the impersonal pronoun for the plural noun; 403/389 *And it so be*] *And if so be* STrA¹G missing *And* = 'If'; 404/390 *dredeful*] *sorouful* STrA¹G substituting an attitude of Christian penitence for the abject submission of a disarmed rebel after defeat, *in his bare sherte*. Two are substitutions of easier readings: 131/119 *of*] *from* STrA¹G, 261/215 *of*] *for* STrA¹G. The rest sophisticate the metre. Two smooth the stress pattern, that is eliminate modulation: 1 *I haue*]*haue I* STrA¹G, and 141/129 *In worshipynge*] *In worshyp and* TrA¹G. One, 480/470 *vnderstonde*] *and u.* SG 'normalizes' a headless line, at cost of the dramatic effect of the caesura. And four supply compensatory syllables: 121/109 *gomme*] *gomme or* TFBG and 502/490 *soore*] *sorer* A¹STrG after devaluation of final *e*; 435/425 *blyve*] *as blyve* STrA¹G after loss of the infinitive inflexion of *sweren*; 508/496 *and*] *and that* STrG in failure to appreciate or from objection to the punctuational hiatus *Love and*.

The six cases where Robinson lets G's reading stand, presumably as authorial revisions, are of similar quality, conforming to G's characteristic variations. One is explicable as induced by preceding copy: 313/239 *it*] *hym* PG (*his* prec.). Another is a more explicit reading: 306/232 *the*] *that* TrA¹G. Another is easier: 529/517 *florouns*] *flouris* TBSTrPA³A¹G. And three sophisticate the metre: 221/153 *fyn*] *fyne and* A¹G where *perle* has become a monosyllable; 238/170 *se*] *wel Ise* SG compensating for loss of the end syllable in *myghte*; and 317/243 *It*] *For it* SG putting a head to a headless line.

Robinson had flair, *Fingerspitzengefühl*, but why the readings in the first group seemed to him like the originals of both versions and those in the second like revisions it is hard to conceive—unless he was merely influenced by sigils. Both groups belong to the same classes: readings within the capacity of the G scribe and therefore not necessarily either original or authorial revisions; of kinds explicable by the processes of scribal error; and of kinds to which, where G's individual variation is exposable to analysis, he showed himself prone.

Accordingly, even in the *Prologue* G has in a strict sense no 'peculiar authority'. More correctly the manuscript is remarkable in respect of *The Legend of Good Women* only because of the paradoxical situation where it uniquely preserves an authorial version of the *Prologue* copied by an immediate scribe notably subject to error.

Two considerations emerge. One is that G's text of any other work by Chaucer does not merit automatic respect; it is as good as G's particular exemplar of that work, subject to the damage done by its immediate scribe, can be shown to be.[18] A manuscript is as good as its readings. The other is that G's variation in *The Legend of Good Women* affords a remarkable demonstration of classes of changes which here, specifically, Chaucer did not make in his revisions, and which should not readily be imputed to him in other situations.

13
John M. Manly (1865–1940) and Edith Rickert (1871–1938)

Because John M. Manly and Edith Rickert's edition of Chaucer came out in 1940, not long before America's entry into the Second World War, it received less notice than its size and pretensions merited. There seem to have been few reviews, and those generally muted from consideration of Manly's recent death.[1] The work was evidently important. No Chaucer edition before it had been supported by such an elaborate apparatus: six volumes to accompany less than two of text. The appearance of authority from this was bound to be immense.

That appearance, the difficulty of the subject, and, it must be said, the opacity of the presentation, have protected the authority from challenge for more than a generation. Its import has been, principally, to question the originality, even respectability, of the texts of other editions of the *Tales*, to devalue the previously esteemed Ellesmere manuscript (El) and to give currency to the proposition that the main difficulty with the textual criticism of the poem is the result of the combined effects of authorial revision and what these editors call 'editing'.

To question the originality of existing texts is healthy, and not just as an antidote to complacency or sloth. It is part of a gradual process by which the damage done to literary works of art in the course of manual transmission is repaired. It took about five centuries of the process to attain such consensus as now exists about the texts of Greek and Roman antiquity.[2] In that perspective we in Middle English have only just begun to edit,[3] and the Manly–Rickert results accordingly represent an early rather than a late or final stage in the establishment of the text of *The Canterbury Tales*. That reduction of its authority can be held to apply particularly to the discrediting of the text of the Ellesmere manuscript, for the proposition that Ellesmere's occasional superior readings should be excluded from the text of the tales because 'it is very clear than an intelligent person, who was certainly not Chaucer, worked over the text' when the manuscript was copied[4] is a crucial one.

The postulate of authorial revision involves the most problematic factor in textual criticism. One way of knowing that authorial revision occurred is from external information, but none is available here. It can be fairly presumed to have occurred in certain classes of situation, such as will be allowed to exist in parts of *The Canterbury Tales*. But where there is no external information, and where such situations do not obtain, the only means by which authorial revision might be identified is editorial judgment. And once the likelihood of its occurrence in a textual tradition is admitted, it must figure in every comparison of variant readings. It is hardly possible to exaggerate the importance of assessing the likelihood of its occurrence correctly.

From these considerations, which bear ultimately on every detail of the text of *The Canterbury Tales*, the importance of a correct evaluation of the edition must be apparent. For instance, the text, without any punctuation, has a most authentic appearance; one would think it based on the ideal copy text; only by the way, and under other headings, does one discover that its form of language is synthetic (1.x.151). The editors tell us that their basis of collation was 'Skeat's 'Student's Edition' ' (2.5), but not whether they took into account the extent to which that is an edited text. There is frequent reference to variants 'of classificatory value' for establishing genetic relation, but no information about how the editors assessed that value. There is mention of Maas's *Textkritik* (2.20), but no account of whether or how Maas's general prescriptions were translated into a practical system for editing. We are not clearly informed what sorts of variants are excluded from the apparatus[5] or, for that matter, how the variants at the foot of the text in Volumes 3 and 4 were selected; I have not yet found out. From the theoretical information supplied it is impossible to establish what the editorial procedures were, and thus also how effectively they were applied.

The first determinant of the quality of any edition must be the method adopted by its editors and their understanding of that method. Here the method is recension (1.xii), a process originally devised to exclude subjective judgment from editing. In theory it applies information about the genetic relation of the manuscripts of a text to eliminate their scribal readings and by that means to recover the archetype, or exclusive common ancestor, of the manuscripts.

The effectiveness of recension as a control of editorial judgment and a means of recovering the archetype is necessarily in absolute and direct relation to both the completeness and the correctness of the 'family tree', or stemma, of the manuscripts. Without a complete stemma, recension, in any meaningful sense of the term, is logically impossible.

The governing principle of the classification of manuscripts is that there is no other evidence for genetic relation than agreement in unoriginal, that is, scribal or 'wrong', readings. From this arises an immediate difficulty of distinguishing between agreements in original and agreements in unoriginal readings. To collate manuscripts a base is needed, a norm from which to record their divergences of reading. Obviously not all the groups formed by agreements in variation from such a base are necessarily genetic. Where the base has unoriginal readings the group-forming agreements may be in original, in right, readings and thus have no genetic significance. To distinguish the genetic groups it is necessary to identify originality in the base. That can be done only by prior editorial judgment, by establishing a hypothesis of direction of variation in as many as possible of the instances where variational groups founded on rival readings have taken shape. The edition does not refer to this operation.[6]

There is a second difficulty to compound the first, namely, that not all agreements in unoriginal readings are products of vertical transmission: some must have come about by lateral transmission, that is, contamination, whether deliberate and visual, or unconscious and memorial, and some by coincident variation. Thus, further, not all agreements in unoriginal readings are necessarily evidence of genetic relation. The editor is again thrown back upon his judgment: to classify the manuscripts he must somehow distinguish between genetic and random variational groups, identify the evidentially valid agreements.

Manly and Rickert were aware that agreement in original readings is 'non-classificatory' (2.24), but the edition does not show that they were troubled by the indeterminate originality of their base for collation, 'Skeat's 'Student's Edition' ' (2.5).[7] What seems to have preoccupied them was the second difficulty of classification, that created by convergent variation (2.20–7). To counter this they made an independent venture into the rationale of textual criticism with the postulate that 'The law of probability is so steady in its working that only groupings of classificatory value have the requisite persistence and consistency to be taken as genetic groups' (2.22). That postulate is a fallacy, for it assumes that manual transmission is uniformly erratic (all texts are equally corrupt), that there will always be relatively abundant agreement in error between genetically related manuscripts. Scribes copying Middle English manuscripts were not generating 'mass phenomena' in respect of which 'the regularity of the operations of chance' (2.23) can be invoked, but operating as highly specialized individuals in sets of highly individuated situations. Of course the editors knew that the assumption was baseless; they appear not to have seen how it affected their postulate.

The data to which, according to the account in Volume 2, such editorial thinking was applied were full of bewildering contradictory indications inherent in the textual situation; from the work being unfinished, the possibility of authorial revision, of arrangement by a literary executor or by stationers; from the divisibility of the work, from its status and evident popularity, the possibility of unauthorized copying; from 'correction' and sophistication. The editors show no awareness that in such a situation the genetic relation of the manuscripts might be irrecoverable. Indeed, they imply that they were successful by publishing their text as one 'established by the process of recension' (2.40), the text of the exclusive common ancestor of the surviving manuscripts, one determined by 'a scientific process' in which the role of individual judgment had been reduced to the minimum.

In fact it is the product of an immensely complex system of contingent hypotheses which seldom account for all the data and are sustainable only by the constant exercise of that editorial judgment which the editors set out to exclude. In the classification of the manuscripts editorial judgment is constantly applied to dismiss contradictory evidence. The classifications exist only by virtue, first, of the unremittingly expeditious, indeed opportunistic, agility of editorial distinctions between vertical and lateral transmission, and then by identifications of 'borrowing,' 'editing,' and authorial revision which by their frequency come in time to acquire an appearance of *petitio principii*.

The demonstration of the inadequacy of the classifications as instruments of recension is the complexity of the explanations in *Survey of the Classification* (2.41–4), and the struggles with discrepant evidence in the successive parts of that volume: twenty pages on the manuscript relations in *The General Prologue*, forty-one

for *The Knight's Tale*, twenty-seven for *The Wife of Bath's Prologue*
and *Tale*, almost never a clearly defined situation. In *The Merchant's
Tale* the classification invokes two changes of exemplar implying
revision (3.375); it proposes seven lines of descent for *The
Physician's Tale* (4.65) and eight for *The Shipman's Tale* (4.108), and
twelve for *The Franklin's Tale* (4.34). Occasionally what is presented
as a classification looks like an admission of defeat (3.39). The
classification repeatedly begs the question of its completeness by use
of the expression 'independent groups and MSS' (cf., for example,
4.83): within a stemma, by definition, no groups or manuscripts are in
any significant sense 'independent.' And the expression evidently
means 'unclassified and probably unclassifiable here.' Whenever one
examines the evidence for a group, it is unimpressive in its variants
being indistinguishable in kind from those dismissed as 'non-
classificatory.' How the editors differentiated between the two sorts
is obscure.[8]

It is hard to believe that they were unaware of the limitations of
their results, here and throughout. For every classification that
involved 'unplaced groups' or 'independent manuscripts and small
groups' or 'variable groups, loosely related' amounted to an
admission of failure to classify, and every new explanation of such
discrepancy would increase the scale of the *petitio principii*. That
fallacy stands out very clearly at one point in the Introduction (2.39,
40).[9] We read how, notwithstanding 'the fact that in many of the tales
the text is derived not from a single archetype but from texts which
sometimes represent different stages of composition,' the editors
'proceeded as if all MSS were from the same archetype, being on the
watch, however, for indications of separate origin and separate lines
of descent,' in the confident certainty that 'the ordinary processes of
classification would call attention to readings and MSS not derived
from [a single archetype] and would enable the textual critic to
distinguish such varied sources as had not become entirely unrecog-
nizable by the spread of vulgate readings.' By that fine language the
editors were effectively if not consciously announcing that in carrying
out 'the ordinary processes of classification' they would prejudge
their results. There is a warrant for critical interpretation of the
results of collation—which is what Manly was writing about here. But
where the textual situation is extraordinary, the 'ordinary processes
of classification' are inoperative.

It comes to this: that we do not have a complete, or even a reliable partial, stemma of the manuscripts of *The Canterbury Tales*. Even the one discernible family, $<a[b(cd/d^*)]>$, is, as Root (*SP*, pp. 6, 7) pointed out, imperfectly defined and unstable because of—other qualifications apart—the paucity of clear evidence for d. The editors must have understood that in the best circumstances, where the manuscript reading of this family could be confidently identified, its evidential weight was that of precisely one manuscript. But there is no sign in the edition that they faced the implication of this: that one single substitution at the group-ancestor stage would differentiate all members of that family from the 'unplaced, independent copies and small groups.' What is presented as an archetypal text is at best the text of the exclusive common ancestor $<a[b(cd/d^*) >$. Its dignification by the symbol 0^1, which is bound to suggest a text at one remove from the author's copy, has no warrant.

Such, however, is the opacity of the presentation that the classification has in effect gone untested. Manly expressed concern that the 'impression of complication and variability' made by it would raise the question of its correctness (2.41), and Root (*SP*, p. 7) discussed this. *Pace* Root, who thought it might take 'at least a year' to test that correctness, the manner of presentation makes it virtually impossible to test it from the information given in the edition.[10] Much of the work will have to be done again,[11] and if it is to produce results worth the name, the analysis of variant groups will have to be conducted by a better rationale than any discernible in the Manly-Rickert edition.[12]

The object of classifying the manuscripts was to enable recovery of the text of the *Tales* by recension, that is, in simplified terms, the elimination of scribal error through identification of the point in the manuscript tradition where it was introduced; the editors also call it the 'genealogical method' (1.xii; 2.12, 40, etc.). That both its logic as a rationale and its practical feasibility are open to question they nowhere recognized. Its operation is far from simple,[13] but one searches Volume 2 in vain for any account of how Manly and Rickert understood and carried out recension. Root suggested that 'the failure of the editors to explain the procedure adopted in constituting the text must . . . mean that they found it impossible to follow any uniform procedure' (*SP*, p. 10). Dempster, in a loyal attempt to interpret the edition, admitted that 'there is no short road to the understanding of Manly's choice of readings,'[14] and the way her attempts to find some principle tail off into lame discussions of particular instances suggests that there is no long road either. Sometimes the apparatus does not even list the manuscripts in support of the reading adopted.[15] The notes where one was led to expect discussion (2.40) are sometimes perfunctory or even noncommittal. But if there was no uniform procedure, what did the editors substitute for one?

They were not subject to the first fantasy of textual criticism, that all texts are sound.[16] As for the second, the fantasy of a 'safe' method, one affording reassurance, which would eliminate the need for 'unscientific' critical thinking, indeed for any critical thinking at the crucial final stage of *examinatio*,[17] there are unmistakable signs of this in Volume 2. But that volume as a whole and with it the critical notes to the text reveal that, far from fulfilling any hope of a 'scientific process' (2.20), the editors' 'system' grew into a monster both tyrannous and inefficient, which gradually forced them into the position of having to rationalize its discrepant or speculative results, to exercise 'judgment' constantly, in the determination of 'classificatory value,' of whether readings were 'errors,' that is, accidental, or 'editing,' that is, sophistication, of what was an inferior reading or an authorial variant. In short, the edition shows them carrying out editorial processes not in the determination of originality but in defence of a dubious stemma from which initially they had expected support and direction.

The arguments of their apologists must in justice here be set down. The edition was published under pressure. The editors did not receive the expected financial support. The edition does not fairly represent their intellectual quality or their command of textual criticism. Their failure to describe their procedures adequately should not be taken to imply that they had no rationale. The exposition in Volume 2 is 'so cryptic and confusing at times' because much was lost in the final revision: 'Lack of space forced [Manly], as nearly the last act of a sick man, to cut that account to the bone.' A main element in the original conception of the undertaking had been 'to test recension.' The published text of the *Tales* represents an earlier stage in editorial thinking that that of Volume 2.

Some of those considerations cannot fail to elicit sympathy from anyone with experience of large projects, and doubtless in sum they account for certain features of the edition. But the eight volumes loom massively in Chaucer scholarship, exercising effect and influence without qualification by the editors' biographies. Therefore, in the end, the edition must be assessed *per se*, to establish whether the influence it has exerted and might continue to exert was warranted.

The authority of any edition involving textual criticism, whatever its theoretical basis, necessarily relates largely to the quality of the editorial judgment applied to the individual textual situations. Such judgment develops with experience of scribes and their ways. The accumulated generalizations about scribal proclivities[18] become real through sustained observation of the behavior of particular scribes during the long labour of collation. It is forced upon the editor that because scribes did not copy by the word, but took into their memory blocks of text such as stanzas or paragraphs, many variations with an intrinsic appearance of deliberateness are likely to have been sub-consciously induced, especially if the scribe had previously copied the same text. The editor gets a sense of probable direction of variation, of scribal as well as authorial *usus scribendi*. He learns to distinguish the effects of carelessness and to predict variation. By observation of visible variation of individual manuscripts from a putative group reading, he acquires insight into the possibilities and likelihoods of variation at the level of subgroup and group. He develops the flair of the textual critic, Maas's *Fingerspitzengefühl*. The editorial judgment exhibited in this edition is not distinguished for that quality.

There are, for a start, occasions when the editors show no sign of awareness that there is an editorial problem. At 3.146: A 3592 *go god thee spede* there is variation *go/so*, and a strong likelihood that *so*] *go* variation occurred coincidentally through inducement of following *god* or of *Go*, line 3596, or of both, but there is no critical note or any sign of awareness that this is a minor crux. For 3.399: E 1909 *He is as wys discret and secree* with variants *and as secree/and eek secree* there is a critical note, 'Some such word as 'eek' or 'as' was omitted by 0^1 (3.476), but at 2.280 agreement of El and Cambridge University Gg.4.27 (Gg) in reading *as secree* is classified as 'patently by *acco*,' that is, by coincident variation. This is a weird logic which, having correctly identified direction of variation, i.e., that there was an omission, and recognized the likelihood of coincident variation in the alignment of agreements, stops short of the obvious interpretation of the evidence: that from there being two inducements (*a-nd a-s* and *a-s s-ecree*) to omission of *as*, it was likely present in the original. Then El and Gg agree not by coincident variation but in preservation of the original. If there was coincident variation, it was in omission of *as*, and possibly also in supply of *eek*. For 3.163, A 4020 *Iohn knew the wey hym neded no gyde* with *hym/hem* variation, the note (3.443) reads, 'The original reading seems to have been 'hym.' The alteration by (sc. to) "hem" by El and others is unnecessary.' How the editors formed their judgment of originality here is not clear. In the sense that the context accepts either number of the pronoun, the 'alteration' they assume would be unnecessary. But experience would have indicated that the likelier variation was *hem]hym* through inducement of singular *Iohn* and *he* 4021, and protected them against the question begging term 'alteration.' So too in 4.273: B 4438 *Though god forwoot it er that it was wroght* with a variant *I was wroght*: here it is allowed that 'The attractive reading 'I' may be original,' but laid down that 'the variation between 'I' and 'it' is intentional' (4.515). Here is a situation where unconscious variation either way would be easy: through inducement of the philosophical cliché, or of preceding *it* (4437, 4438). And, of course, with the strong inducement to substitution goes a corresponding likelihood of coincident substitution.

The editors misread various classes of typical evidence. For instance, at 3.251: D 368 *Ben ther noone othere resemblaunces* there are variants *other(e) manere, other(e) of thees, other(e) of thy, other(e) of youre*, described as 'four different attempts to emend' (3.458). But this is a clear case of loss of original *manere* by homoeoteleuton. A slightly more complex instance is 4.139: B 1883 *Til that oure hoost iapen to bigan* with variants *to iapen þo, to iapen, iapen tho, to iapen he, iapen he*. For the editors the original was 'obviously' *iapen tho* (4.499). But that original is unlikely to have generated the pattern of variation. The original likeliest to have produced that pattern is *to iapen tho* or *to iapen þo*, where simply the consideration whether to spell the last word *tho* or *þo* would be distraction enough to cause random variation. Of this a first stage might be *to iapen to*. From that, *to iapen he* is explicable as a sophistication, *iapen to* as a confused correction (the scribe having meant to omit the first *to*). At the next stage *iapen he* and *iapen tho* are sophistications of *iapen to*. This kind of pattern is not uncommon and becomes familiar with experience. So do accidental omissions like that of A 637, 638 (3.28) from Hg Bodley 686 (Bo[2]) occasioned by homoeo- and homoarchy: *And . . . drynke . . . wyn* line 635; *And . . . dronken . . . wyn* 637, *Thanne wolde he speke* 636, 638. The editor who can recognize them is in less danger of suggesting that the lines are 'a happy afterthought' of the poet (3.425); he will also appreciate the possibility that omission might occur coincidentally.

It is not clear that in their judgments the editors took account of the tendencies discernible in scribal variation, subconscious, indeterminate or conscious; they miss very obvious instances. At 3.313: D 1983 *And chiden heere this sely innocent* the critical note (3.467) is preoccupied with a variation of little difficulty, *sely*] *holy*, induced by the common collocation 'holy innocents,' and impossible in the context. They miss or ignore the good possibility that the original read *hir the, heere* having been caught up from line 1981, and *this* being a more explicit substitution. At 3.272: D 929 *Somme seyde that oure herte is moost esed* there is a variant *hertes be* which the critical note (3.460) describes as an 'intelligent emendation.' In fact it is a variation to an easier reading from the more difficult distributive singular, called a 'bad reading' by the editors.

At 3.44: A 974 *ther is namoore to telle* the predictable variation *is/nis* occurs, as also at, e.g., A 901, 1274, 2722, 2847. I find it hard to believe that the editors did not know how freely these expressions would replace each other, or to see the inducement here to *is*] *nis* by *n-amoore* or by the tendency to increase emphasis, or that to *nis*] *is* by the common collocation *ther is*. But they apparently did not: the critical note (3.427) solemnly treats this is a crux, even raising the question of 'archaizing.' At 3.304: D 1696 *And thurgh out helle swarmeden al aboute* a number of copies lack *al*, which is, however, taken to be the archetypal reading. There is no note to this line and no sign of awareness that *aboute*] *al aboute* is in this context a predictable variation to a more emphatic reading by an enthusiastically participating scribe. At 3.351: E 583 *And bad this sergeant that he pryuely/Sholde this child softe wynde and wrappe* there is variation *wel/ful softe*. The note (3.472) explains these variants as 'emendations by early scribes' because the line 'seems to have lacked a syllable.' Whether or not the line seemed so to the 'early scribes,' the adverbs are more likely to be variations, very possibly unconscious at that, to more emphatic readings. The same is true of 3.162: A 3977 *The person of the toun for she was feir / In purpos was to maken hir his heir* with variation *feir*] *so feir*, that is to a reading more emphatic and explicit both. Had the editors been more familiar with the *usus scribendi* of scribes, they would not have observed, after excluding *so* on manuscript evidence, that is, presumably by recension, that 'stylistically 'so fair' seems necessary' (3.443).

Familiarity with the ways of scribes should have enabled the editors to interpret slightly more complex situations like 3.383: E 1436 *And streight to the deuel whan I dye*, with variants *so streight, so*

go streight, go streight. Here they found the evidence 'on the whole
. . . to be in favor of a headless line lacking both 'go' and 'so''
(3.474). Actually it favours *so streight*. The variation *so] go* will have
been by unconscious misreading, probably of 8-shaped *s* for *g*, or by
inducement of the concept of motion in the line; *so] so go* will be a
separate variation to a more explicit reading; and *so streight] streight*
omission by homoarchy. At 3.47: A 1031, where the adopted text
reads *Dwellen this Palamon and eek Arcite*, there is a variant *This
Palamon and his felaw Arcite*. The critical note (3.427) seems to mean
that *Dwellen* was first accidentally omitted, and in a copy of the
manuscript so affected, *his felawe* later substituted for *eek* to fill out
the line ('it is obvious that this reading is an editorial emendation').
Actually the following considerations obtain. First, the line and its
immediate context do not seem to have any obvious features that
would have induced accidental omission of original *Dwellen*. Second,
if it had nevertheless been omitted, the likeliest sophistication would
have been supply of a verb, of *Lyueth* on the suggestion of line 1028,
or even, by felicitous restoration, of *Dwelleth*, of which the sense
'continue to be' stands out in the context. Third, the line without a
verb is vastly *durior lectio*. Either a verb must be understood, or else
Palamon and Arcite are by ironic syllepsis additional subjects of
lyueth in line 1028. Fourth, as between *eek* and *his felaw*, the former is
the likelier padding to the experienced eye. It is from this sort of
misinterpretation that the 'intelligent editor' of Ellesmere[19] derived
his existence.

There are situations where the editors react to the text like scribes.
An instance is 3.47: A 1038, 1039 *For with the rose colour stroof
hir hewe/I noot which was the fairer of hem two* with *fairer/finer*
variation. Of the alternatives the scribal one is almost certainly *fairer*,
either a thoughtless, more explicit substitution, or because scribes
misread line 1039 to be comparing the rose and Emelye, not the
colour of the rose and her complexion, for which *finer* is the
appropriate term (*MED* s.v. *fin* adj. 5). Our editors identify *fairer* as
original, presumably by recension, and explain *finer* as 'an emendation by the El group' (3.428). The possibility is not raised that *fairer*
might have been substituted coincidentally.

There are some indications of superficial reading of the text. At
3.300; D 1647 *After the text of Crist Poul and Iohn* with variants *text
crist of Poul*, *text of Poul*, and *text Crist Poul* the editors presume loss
of *and* between *Crist* and *Poul*, and find it strange that 'none of the

scribes supplied the obvious lack' (3.465). But *and* is not obviously lacking: the three names are not a set of equivalents. Just conceivably the line as the editors print it is original, meant to be read with a portentous pause after *Crist*, a kind of colon of silence to introduce the Scripture references. More likely it read *of Crist in Poul and Iohn*; the preposition written as *i* with a suspension would easily be lost without trace, or even obscured by a caesural punctuation. At 3.314: D 1993 *Be war from hire that in thy bosom slepeth* with *hire/ire* variation the editors rightly connect substitution of *hire* with the second half of the line, but their note (3.467) seems to suggest that *ire]hire* might be by deliberate substitution and indicates no awareness that the words were as good as identical phonetically, that Chaucer had made a pun and probably intended it.[20] Those considerations would have prevented them from taking manuscript alignment seriously, printing *hire* as the archetypal reading, and speculating why Chaucer failed to correct it. At 3.169: A 4171 *Lo swilk a couplyng is ymel hem alle* there is variation *complyn/complyng/copil/compen/company*. For the editors *complyn* is 'probably an emendation by a few scribes who independently sought for a better meaning than was suggested by the ancestral reading 'coupling' ' (3.445). That is to stand the concept of coincident variation on its head. They are proposing repeated independent scribal substitution of a reading which happens to be conveniently introduced by *melodye* 4168 and *sang* 4170 and ironically anticipates *the feend is on me falle* of 4288,[21] in fact a much harder reading. Had they borne in mind that the speaker is a clerk, they might have taken note of how the word is woven into the texture of the narrative. As for the actual coincidence, that will have been in variation from *complyn*, possibly spelled *complyng* (see *MED* s.v.); written with a suspended *m*, and given the expectation of the genre, this would inevitably be corrupted to *couplyng*, and coincidentally. There is little likelihood that *couplyng* was the archetypal reading.

Whether or not this is a fair representation, some editorial judgments suggest insufficient familiarity with Middle English. Everett noticed 'either carelessness or uncertainty in the handling of linguistic material.'[22] There is amateurishness in their treatment of problems involving language, as for instance, in two successive critical notes, where one reads that 'modern idiom, no doubt, prefers "out swarmen from," but Chaucer seems to have been influenced by 'out of,' ' and that 'the uses of prepositions are so different in early

and modern English that one is often surprised.'[23] Had the editors
turned to the articles on the prepositions *from* and *of* in *OED*,
they would not have written the nonsense about Chaucer being
'influenced by' *out of*.

The dictionary is an editor's primary instrument, but it is not often
cited in the critical notes, where there are some unmistakable indications that they underestimated the difficulties of Middle English
lexicography, to the detriment of their interpretation of the evidence.

At 3.103: A 2527 *Honoured weren into the paleys fet* there is
paleys/place variation. The critical note (3.433, 434) observes that 'by
making the place of assembly the courtyard of the "paleys" Chaucer
got a more definite picture.' This seems to mean that *paleys* is an
authorial revision of *place*; the suggestion implies that the editors did
not know that *paleys* and *place* have an area of synonymity (*OED* s.v.
Place sb. 5b). Actually *place* is *durior lectio* both from its polysemy
and because it must be given dissyllabic value for the metre. Either
reason could induce random substitution of *paleys*. At 3.18: A 383 *He
koude rooste and sethe and broille and frye* the variation *broille/boille*
is troublesome because it does not correspond to genetic preconceptions: this generates an elaborate note (3.424). They evidently
did not consult *OED*, where both words are shown to have only
recently come into use in Chaucer's time to denote cooking processes. With considerations of relative difficulty out of the way, they
might have noticed the contextual features likely to induce unconscious, therefore possibly coincident *broille*] *boille*: that is, the
presence of *boille* in lined 380 and of *sethe* later in line 383. For 3.334:
E 137 *That thurgh youre deeth youre lyne sholde slake*, with *lyne/
lynage* variation, the note reads: 'The change from "lynage" to
"lyne" was possibly made by Chaucer himself, for greater accuracy,
but it is confined almost entirely to the independent MSS of Group
IV, and may be a purposeless scribal substitution' (3.469). In fact,
lyne, as highly polysemous, is much the harder, and *lynage* the more
explicit and easier reading, therefore likely to have been substituted
independently. There is no basis at all for talk of revision. At 3.252: D
387 *I koude pleyne and I was in the gilt* the variation *and*] *and* ʒet,
whan, *thogh* is called 'scribal efforts to subject Chaucer's colloquial
construction to formal grammar' (3.458). This may seem hard to
credit, but the editors evidently did not know the senses 'If,
supposing that,' and 'Even if,' of *and* (*OED* s.v. *And* Conj. C 1, 2)
and were reading this construction as paratactic. At 4.259: B 4045 *By*

nature he knew ech ascensioun the significant variation is *knew/krew*. Again the editors had genetic problems: a factor in their choice of *knew* as archetypal was that *krew* 'seemed the more likely emendation' (3.514). Leaving aside the consideration that the one manuscript reading *krew* is Hg, distinguished by 'entire freedom from editorial variants' (1.276), the quasi-transitive use of *krew*, 'announced by crowing,' as in *There is no cock to crowe day* (*OED* s.v. *Crow* v. 1c), is a much harder reading and probably original here; the obvious and easily coincidental substitution is *knew*.

In all those instances consultation of the dictionary would have safeguarded the editors. It is ironic that when once (apparently) they did consult it, for 3.135: A 3265 *A broche she bar vpon hir loue coler*, it disappointed them by not giving *lou* as a variant spelling of the adjective *low*: 'No one seems to know the term "loue coler."'' They missed the help it afforded ('"Low coler" is equally unknown' (3.440)) in offering them the sense 'Situated not far above the ground or some other downward limit' (*OED* s.v. *Low* a. and sb. 2), for which the context would have made the 'downward limit' clear. Although *loue* here may not be a 'true form,' it unmistakably stands for the weak form of the adjective; one is surprised that they did not recognize it as such.

Where aids were less readily available, the editors' inexperience of the language shows even more. Of 3.348: E 508 *Ne I desire no thyng for to haue/Ne drede for to lese saue oonly ye* with variation *ye/þe* they comment, 'Chaucer undoubtedly wrote "ye" for the sake of the rhyme' (3.471). The confident 'undoubtedly' will have been evoked by the circumstance that Hg, El, and Gg read *þe*. But there is doubt. Chaucer's practice elsewhere, as in *Troilus and Criseyde* I 5, where he rhymes *Troye: joie:fro ye*, at least raises the question whether he would have used the reduced form of the objective case of the plural pronoun in a stressed position to rhyme with the [e:] of *me* and *be*. Moreover, Griseldis's use of the familiar singular pronoun here cannot be ruled out: the usage of singular and plural in address was far from systematic in Chaucer's time. Even in this tale where social distance is emphasized it fluctuates. At lines 127–40 the spokesman for his people, addressing the Marquis, uses a plural imperative in line 127 and singulars in lines 134 and 135; and for his part the Marquis occasionally uses the formal plural to Griseldis (e.g., at lines 350 ff., and—interspersed with singulars—in lines 477–97). Indeed, the circumstance that elsewhere she always addresses him with the

deferential plural makes the singular *durior lectio* here and so liable
to be corrupted. Above all the resemblance of þ and *y* in many
fifteenth-century hands would promote misreading, especially with
inducement from the sense of social difference between Griseldis and
Walter. Any one of those considerations should have given rise to
editorial doubt. Moreover, a very plausible dramatic reason can be
found for Griseldis lapsing into the singular at this moment of acute
stress. At 3.281: D 1189 *But he that noght hath ne coueiteth to haue* a
number of manuscripts do not read the infinitive sign. Their
genetically embarrassing agreement is explained as 'a bit of editing
done independently at least three times' (2.215). It is, however, more
likely that *to* was supplied independently in variation to a historically
easier reading. At 4.263: B 4174 *Oon of the gretteste auctor that men
rede* the note (4.514) shows no awareness that the line in this form
was produced by unconscious overlay of two constructions by a scribe
or scribes uncertain which to write down. At 4.265: B 4226 *A dong
carte wente as it were to donge lond*, where several manuscripts do not
have *wente*, the explanation offered for the line in the text is that
wente 'was a marginal correction for "were" and was misunderstood
by the scribe of O¹' (4.515); in other words, he added it instead of
substituting it for *were*. But *wente* is not a 'correction'; it is a variation
to a more explicit reading, and the probably original *as it were
to donge lond* is respectable Middle English for 'as if for the purpose
of manuring land.'²⁴ At 3.185: B 47–9 *I kan . . . no thrifty tale seyn
That Chaucer . . . Hath seyd hem* the grammar embarrasses the
editors: 'Chaucer is sometimes confused in sentences involving a
negation in a subordinate clause. We shall doubtless come nearest to
his intention if we read "that" in this line (47) and "nath" in 49'
(3.447). It is not impossible that Chaucer did write *Nath* and that this
was corrupted to *Hath* through misreading of the initial capital. But if
he wrote *Hath*, which seems likelier, the confusion is not with him,
for *That* in line 47 has the good Middle English meaning 'Because.'²⁵
Of 3.135: A 3285 *Wy lat be quod ich lat be Nicholas* with *ich/she*
variation, the critical note (3.440) classes *she* as 'an easy scribal error
caused by the resemblance of "ich" and "sche" (with long *s*),' the
whole of line 3285 being 'the exclamation of Alison.' But *quod ich* is
simply not Middle English for 'I said' in 'Stop it, I said! stop it!' It is an
unemphatic formula signifying report of direct speech. Middle
English equivalents of 'I said!' here would have subject-verb order
and be in the present tense.²⁶ The original was almost certainly *she*,

with substitution induced by *I, my* in line 3284 and *I* in line 3286. *N-ich-olas* following could have induced the spelling.

There is a strong suggestion in these instances, which are typical, that the editors did not sufficiently respect the difficulties of Middle English and were overconfident about their knowledge of the language. That circumstance, along with their inexperience of and misconceptions about the scribal mentality, accounts for the inability to read manuscript evidence which their edition exhibits time and again. It accounts, also, to some extent at least, for their having formed and insistently postulated the notion of the scribal 'editor' and his activities in the manuscript tradition of *The Canterbury Tales*.

It has not been the general practice to use the terms 'editing' and 'emendation' to denote scribal substitution. For scribal variation presumed deliberate the usual term is 'sophistication.' Knowledgeable editors use it cautiously, aware of the degree and variety of change that the scribal subconscious can effect in a text between its being taken through the scribe's eye into his memory and being set down, laboriously letter by letter, on the page. They know that between, at the one extreme, the wholly accidental error produced by a simple failure of signals between eye and hand, and at the other the calculated, purposeful alteration, there is a huge area of uncertainty. Here even the limited degree of scribal participation implied in the effort to comprehend could set up distractions. Distraction could originate in anything the scribe had ever copied before, including the text at hand, and produce memorial contamination, or in his own experience, or in his sense of grammar, in all the patterned forms of language he habitually used or avoided, in his response to what he had just copied or preoccupation with development to come. Almost every element of interest or response he was capable of was a potential source of distraction and of consequent variation without his being fully or even at all aware of what was happening.

Of course, sophistication did occur, and must be allowed as a factor in the restoration of texts. It can be identified in the visible effort of the scribe of the single manuscript or subgroup ancesor to improve a group reading corrupt in his exemplar, in additions that expand to the detriment of the formal or generic integrity of the text, in changes that have an appearance of being systematic, or changes of a scale or manifest intention beyond the conceivably subconscious, like the adaptations of the links in Hengwrt. Manly had at hand the opportunity of studying sophistication in the manuscript Harley 7334 (Ha⁴) which is extensively so affected.²⁷ He does not seem to have taken it.

The absence of any systematic thought about the nature of scribal variation, indeed, a general poverty of editorial insight, shows itself particularly in the treatment of the Ellesmere manuscript. This is of such a character as to suggest that it was emotionally based, as if the editors were under some compulsion to discredit the manuscript which clouded their judgment. Was it a need to produce a conclusion different from the current one? Robinson, it will be recalled, had in 1933 described Ellesmere as 'the best copy.'²⁸ Or did Ellesmere have to be put down because they could not classify it, because its existence outside their already dubious stemma was a potential dismissal of the whole hypothesis? For there will have come a stage of commitment when retreat, the admission of failure, became impossible and counterattack the only course. In whatever event, the Ellesmere variants are the subjects of a long succession of rationalizations and opportunistic explanations as discrepancies that do no credit to Manly and Rickert's editorial expertise. This will appear from scrutiny of a sample of the variations designated as 'emendations' in Volume 2 and the Critical Notes.

At 2.91 there is a list of seven instances of Ellesmere editing in the *Prologue*. Two are more likely to be scribal substitutions of more emphatic readings: 188 *his] his owne* and 824 *in] alle in*. At 234 *faire] yong* will be unconscious substitution on inducement of *y-euen* before it and *yonge* 213. At 421 *engendred] they engendred* is a more explicit variation. In 612 as between *coote* and *gowne* (also, incidentally, the reading of group *a*) one variant will be a substitution of a more habitual collocation: the question is, which? The scribe had read *coote and hood* in line 103 preceding, and the words were apparently connected in a proverb.²⁹ To anyone uncommitted to recension, *gowne* can thus seem the likelier original. Either way substitution will have been unconscious. So also at line 858, where *in this manere* (*a* reads it too) is 'editing'; in fact, it may easily have been the original, with *as ye may here* induced by *herkneth what I seye* 855 and *seyde* 858. That leaves 240 *euery/alle the*: originality here is indeterminable, since we do not know what was the friar's territory. But, then, neither did the scribes, and between the two readings *euery* is unmistakably the more emphatic, not to mention a practical impossibility.

In *The Knight's Tale* the editors identify thirteen 'unique readings in El showing a possible editorial intention' (2.127). Three of these are accidental: 1260 *thyng that*] om (by homoeoteleuton, *wh-at, th-at*); 1337 *somer*] *sonne* (by confusion over minims or an *er* suspension); 2828 *and folk*] *and eek* (by inducement of the common collocation). One variant is more explicit: 871 *yonge*] *faire*. One is an easier reading: 1560 *lynage*] *kynrede* (compare the same substitution by Gg at 1110). One is more emphatic: 2219 *and with*] *with ful*. In four instances the Ellesmere reading can have, to an unprejudiced judgment, the appearance of originality. At line 876 the original certainly contained *yow*, whatever its position. At 931 *waille/crie* the likelier substitution is *waille*, on inducement of the common collocation *wepe and waille*. In line 1156, Ellesmere's past tense, required for the meaning 'You did not know until just now,' is incidentally attested in other manuscripts. In line 2874 loss of original *hadde* will have been by homoarchy. In one instance, line 1933, the Ellesmere reading is to be classed with the other attempts to come to terms with an original necessarily difficult on the showing of the variation. Was this because of syllepsis in an original reading *Of loue that I rekned haue and shal?* The two readings that remain resist explanation. But at line 2220 variation between the formulas *as ye shal heere* and *in this manere* recalls that at line 858 preceding (see above). And at 2952 *fyr*]*place* is unmistakably variation to an inferior reading with a scribal quality about it.

In *The Miller's Tale* the editors identify three classes of Ellesmere variation relevant to this examination. In the first class there are eleven 'certain errors'; in the second, six which 'may have been deliberate changes' (2.149). All but one of these, however, are explicable as unconscious variations: 3575 *shaltow*] *shal I* induced by following *I*; 3599 *teche*] *preche* induced by *sermonyng* 3597; 3608 *dede*] *lost* induced by the common collocation; 3540 *gete*] *brynge* variation to an easier reading (*geten* in this sense was just coming into use in the fourteenth century). One Ellesmere reading, 3810 *amydde*, looks original; it would have been replaced on the inducement of the common collocation *smiten in*.

Then there is a group of variants where, we are advised, a change has been made 'for the purpose of correcting and regularizing the line' (2.149). The description does not stand up to scrutiny. At 3228 *men/man* is simply morphological: these are two forms of the indefinite pronoun. Two variations are mechanical: at 3624 *he* was

omitted through attraction between *hand* and *made*; at 3735 *were*]
was was induced by following *wa-r*. Four are substitutions of more
explicit readings: 3541 *had*] *had be*, 3621 *after*] *after that*, 3626 *Vnto*]
Into and 3778 *I*] *And I*. In 3576 the probable original was not *his* but
the, and Ellesmere's *hir* is simply another variation to a more explicit
reading.

Next there are four 'errors in which editing is clear' (2.150). One of
these, if not a substitution of an easier reading, is a misreading of a
difficult because unanticipated original: 3697 *cougheth*] *knocketh*
(compare *tougheth* Harley 7335 [Ha⁵], where the scribe's eye simply
refused the difficult original sense). In the other three instances it can
be argued that Ellesmere preserves a reading both archetypal and
original. At 3251, between *silk* and *grene*, it is possible to account for
grene] *silk* variation by the recurrent suggestion of *silk* 3235, 3240,
3243. But no scribe is likely to have had the leisure to hit on the
appropriately obscene suggestion of a leather purse with a 'green'
tassle. At 3362, as between *rewe* and *thinke*, *rewe* is too easy to have
been corrupted, whereas polysemous *thinke*, apt only in the sense
'remember, bear in mind' (*OED* s.v. *Think* v.²5) is likely to have
been ousted by the easier word. For 3810 *in/amydde*, which re-
appears here, see above.

The instances of 'editing' I have examined are typical of the
editors' evidence for the occurrence of that process, which they
represent as a deliberate and systematic undertaking to improve the
text: 'it is very clear that an intelligent person, who was certainly not
Chaucer, worked over the text when El was copied' (1.150). It is in
fact anything but clear. Ellesmere's status has still to be assessed, but
it is certainly not to be measured in terms of the editors' evidence for
'editing.'

Their evidence for authorial revision is no better. This can be
illustrated from *The Miller's Tale*, where they find nineteen lines in
Ellesmere with variants which are 'as readings just as acceptable as
those supported by the stronger authority,' a part of the evidence
which for them 'points perhaps to ultimate derivation of El from a
working copy containing about twenty alternative readings which
may have originated with Chaucer' (2.150, 151). These will now be
examined.

For a start, three of these variations are classical instances of
indeterminacy: 3620 *And/He*, 3654 *in/of* and 3819 *sette/sit*. These
are scribal variables with nothing to choose between them where the

substitution can as easily have gone either way. In four others Ellesmere probably reads an unconscious variation; in 3289 *hym*]*hire* can have been induced by *hir* 3291, 3293; in 3505 omission of *it* can have been caused by attraction between *telle* and *man*: in 363 *seten*] *sitten* can have been induced by *st-i-lle* following; in 3761 *clepen*] *cleped* can have been caused by following *d-aun*. Four Ellesmere variants are more explicit: 3333 *a*]*his*, 3443 *And*]*Til*, 3660 *With*]*With a*, and 3828 *lay*] *he lay*. Those at 3443 and 3660, notwithstanding their possible status, are excluded from the apparatus at the foot of the text. One Ellesmere variant, 3482 *on* (2)] *of*, is an easier reading. Two, at 3477 *loke*] *what loke* and 3828 *That*] *That yet*, are more emphatic. That leaves six which, because they could readily have generated the readings preferred in the text by very common processes of corruption, have the appearance of being original. In three the reading of the text looks like unconscious substitution: 3466 *heuest of*] *heuest vp* and 3470 *haf of*] *haf vp* by inducement of the common collocation *heuen vp*, and 3593 *folk*] *men* by inducement of surrounding *wh-en . . . be(e)n*. In 3519 *than an*] *than in an* will be variation to a more explicit reading; 3418 *thyng*] *nothyng* and 3510 *am*]*nam* variations to more emphatic readings.

These are typical instances of Ellesmere variants represented by the editors as products or possible products of authorial revision. Along with the others like them so classed at various points in Volume 2 and in the Critical Notes, they form part of the question-begging system, involving also 'editing' or 'emendation' and 'borrowing,' by which the discrepancies in their classification are excused. To examine them all will be a major study in itself. But there are two lists of presumed authorial revisions, at 2.38, 39 and 2.495–518. Manly offered the second list in part tentatively, as 'possible slight retouching of some of the tales' and in part apologetically as unfinished work by Rickert (2.501), but the first apparently had his backing and may fairly be here examined.

For a start there are the prologues and endlinks. Here simply the likelihood that Chaucer had not decided on any final order of tales when he stopped writing[30] carries with it a corresponding one of revision. Moreover, the passages in question are long enough to enable the unavoidable critical judgment, whether they are Chaucerian, to be attempted with some degree of confidence. Even so only some of the editors' instances are clear cases.

One is B 1163–90, the *Man of Law Endlink*; this, from the existence of D 1665–1708, which dispose of the Summoner otherwise, can be presumed to have no longer any function, though 'superseded' would be a better description than 'cancelled,' since the passage has survived. Here there is every warrant for inferring authorial change of intention or enlargement of conception. So also the longer form of *The Nun's Priest's Prologue*, B² 3961–80, very likely registers a heightening of Chaucer's dramatic conception by insight into the possibilities of contrasting responses by the Knight and the Host. But in the instance of the *Physician-Pardoner Link* at C 287–300 the situation is not as clear because of the undismissed possibility of split variation.

The Host's mockery of the Nun's Priest, B² 4637–52, is correctly describable as 'undeveloped' rather than as 'cancelled.' On indication of line 4652, Chaucer intended it to lead to another tale. The likelihood is that he never decided who was to tell this: nothing could be more characteristic of an unfinished work. The explanation of the absence of the passage from many manuscripts may be simply that there were arrangers of the tales who disliked its inconclusiveness more than they relished the Host's mockery.

A more problematic instance is E 1212a–g, spoken by the Host at the end of *The Clerk's Tale* and classified by the editors as 'Remnant of a cancelled link.' There is no actual evidence of the act of cancellation, only a disturbance of the editorial hypothesis of classification. When that consideration is set aside, *The Merchant's Prologue* follows on well enough from E 1212g across the change to couplets that was bound to come in any event. And actually E 1212a–g as a final stanza of rhyme royal appropriately fastens the Clerk's ironic lyric[31] to his tale and, far from breaking the continuity,[32] sets up another pair of contrasting responses like that to *The Monk's Tale* noted above.

A different situation exists at B² 3568 in the *tragedie* of Pedro of Castile. The editors explain the two forms of this line, *Thy bastard brother made the to flee* and *Out of they land thy brother made thee flee* as revision occasioned by the topicality of the subject: the reference to bastardy became impolitic when the claimants to the throne were reconciled. There is unquestionably that possibility. But there is another, that the line with *thy bastard brother* resulted from scribal variation to a more emphatic reading. Indeed the line without the sense 'into exile,' *out of thy land*, is not notably apt. There is enough doubt here to make the line poor evidence for inference about early and late forms, or about cancellation of the 'modern instances.'

Within the actual tales likelihood of revision is not so easily presumed, and does not show as clearly. The issue arises in the tales mainly from the presence or absence of material. There decision about revision will relate to how both presence and absence can be accounted for.

Critical opinion about the literary quality of the material confuses the issue in the case of Dorigen's list of instances of heroically chaste women, F 1426–56. It was evidently the editors' violently unfavourable opinion which directed their judgment that the archetype was at this point 'an unpolished working draft' (2.314,315). The oracular voice of the classification seems, however, to have been ambiguous, for earlier in the same volume (2.39) the passage was labeled 'Possibly not in early version.' They seem not to have allowed that a fourteenth-century response to the list might have differed from theirs, or even that the length of the list might be a Chaucerian correlative of Dorigen's hysterical state. Scribes had great difficulty with the spelling of the proper names here, and the absence of the passage from some copies may relate to this.

By contrast there should have been no problem for the editors with the five passages (D 44a–f, 575–84, 609–12, 619–26, 717–20) in *The Wife of Bath's Prologue* but not found in a good many copies. None of these passages could bring any discredit on Chaucer. All can be read as meaningful additions. And no reasons suggest themselves for the cancellation or accidental omission of any one. From those features they compel a hypothesis of authorial revision, but for the editors they constituted a predicament from the need to account for their presence or absence in terms of the classification. The extreme complexity of the resulting explanations is a further criticism of that hypothesis.

How plausible we find the classification will determine whether we accept the description of F 1493–8 as a 'late addition' (2.39). There is certainly an element of doubt. Why should the lines not come from an early version for reading aloud and be generally absent because the poet suppressed them when he took the tale into the Canterbury scheme? More seriously, because the passage breaks the narrative flow just before a climax, it was particularly liable to omission by oversight. And there are features, in effect homoeoarchy of this and the following paragraph, that could occasion accidental omission: *Parauenture* 1493, *Of aventure* 1501; *heep* 1493, *happed* 1501; *yow* 1493, *hir* 1501.

The recurrence of propositions about authorial revision that arise from genetic considerations is notable. There is the instance of A 3721, 3722, a 'late couplet, copied only by El and borrowed thence by other MSS' (2.38, 150–51).[33] This is the only Ellesmere variant in *The Miller's Tale* to be taken seriously as a possible revision. But the lines could have been accidentally omitted. They interrupt the action just before a climax and would be liable to omission simply from that feature; or they could have been lost by homoeoarchy: *Thanne . . . thee* 3720, *Now . . . thou* 3722. Accidental loss would explain the situation in Selden, where the couplet is at the foot of the page in the main hand with a direction to its right location (3.442); that is how scribes who caught themselves out in omission commonly put the matter right. Coincident omission is an easier explanation of this situation than revision and borrowing from Ellesmere. Other considerations apart, its pristine condition argues against Ellesmere having been available for general consultation; and as for that manuscript 'very close to it' (1.536), where are its progeny? All the while the absence of these lines from some manuscripts questions the classification.

At A 3155, 3156 similarly, the genetic hypothesis dictates: 'Obviously these lines were not in 0^1.' They were, variously, 'procured by the ancestor of El from some other Chaucerian copy' or 'may well have been composed by the intelligent editor of El' (3.439, 440), or they were, 'if by Chaucer, cancelled later' (2.38). It should by now have appeared that creating the delicious irony whereby the drunken Miller rebuking the Reeve echoes the God of Love rebuking the Dreamer is not in that intelligent editor's style. The lines were most likely omitted through eye skip: *goode . . . oon* 3154, 3155; *knowes-tow . . . thow* 3156, *ar-tow . . . now* 3157. Whether the omission was coincidental would be determinable only if an effective classification was available.

A similar bias of editorial judgment appears in the treatment of D2159–2294, the last episode of *The Summoner's Tale*, not found in the manuscripts of one group, d^{*1}. From that absence the editors infer that the lines were 'possibly not in the earliest draft' (2.38), that the group text 'represents an earlier and unfinished form' of the tale (2.229). But lack of the passage is the main evidence for the existence of the group here, which 'is held together primarily by [its] absence' (2.228). The editors know an easier explanation: loss of a folio with the very usual content of thirty-four lines per side. But they reject this in favor of a speculative preconception.

So also in the treatment of two adjacent instances, at E 1170–1212, where 1170–6 are taken to have been 'absent from the pre-CT version,' and 2101–12 to have preceded 1195 in the 'first draft for CT' (2.38). To judge by manuscript evidence, some manuscripts lack 1170–6 because of a physically defective exemplar. As for the presumption of transposition, the 'first draft' order, from the poor sequence of discourse it affords—*hem* 1201 lacks a grammatically plausible antecedent—is very likely scribal, and can have come to be by several of the processes in which text is disordered. In this category belong F 1001–6, described as 'not in the early draft and misplaced by the scribe of 0^1' (2.39). There was probably displacement here, but the likelihood is that the disordered lines were 999–1000, omitted from an original position as in the adopted text through attraction between 998 and 1001 and copied in at the next convenient point.[34] The extreme instance of prejudicial interpretation is D 829–56, 'Possibly not in the earliest draft of WBP' (2.38). The lines are absent from one single manuscript. To be sure, the proposal is only tentative (cf. 2.194, 195), but it should not have been made. We have here the loss of the content of a last leaf of a gathering.

In the instances so far examined, there was nothing about the quality of the alternatives to exclude the possibility of authorial revision. That is not the case with the rest of the proposed revisions. The instance of 3.81: A 1906, 'Left unrevised' (2.38) is simply an irrelevancy. It is clear from the apparatus that there was random variation here, and we have no assurance that the archetype read like the text. The speculation in the critical note (3.430, 431) does not merit taking seriously.

The remaining instances have to do with scribal variation. Thus 3.28: A 637, 638 are absent from two manuscripts by homoarchy (*And* 635, 637, *Thanne wolde be speke* 636, 638); the speculation about a happy authorial afterthought inserted in the margin of the text (3.425) is gratuitous. If Hg had not been one of the manuscripts concerned, the omission might well have passed unremarked. 3.12: A 252a, b, 'Preserved by Hg and borrowed thence by five other MSS' (2.38), were most probably lost for the very reason our editors think Chaucer might have cancelled them, 'as interrupting the flow of the narrative' (3.424). Intervening syntactical units are particularly liable to omission. An added source of distraction might have been the contextual difficulty of *vertuous* 251. The lines are actually necessary

to the sense, to make 256 intelligible. Another couplet so lost is
3.109; A 2681, 2682, 'If by Chaucer, cancelled later' (2.38). Here a
contributory circumstance might have been *And* 2680, 2683, which
could conduce to eye skip. At 4.238: B² 3616 *he spak right noght*] *he
saugh it noght*, 'Rewritten' (2.39), substitution for the undoubtedly
original *spak* (*Inferno* 33, *sanza far motto*) occurred because
preceding *herde* suggested the common collocation *herde and saugh*.
At 3.45: A 992 *freendes*] *housbondes, lordys* is variation to more
explicit readings. This instance occurs among the proposed authorial
revisions, but in the critical note (3.427) both variants are called
'emendations.' At 3.44: A 980 *wan*] *slough* is a scribal substitution of
an easier reading: *wan* with the object *penoun* and the special sense
'earned the right to display'[35] is difficult without close attention, and
substitution of *slough* on the inducement of *Mynotaur which that he*
preceding would be predictable. There is no critical note. At 4.53: F
1321 *Repenteth*] *Bithynke* is another scribal substitution of an easier
reading: the sense 'Think better of it' (*OED* s.v. *Repent* v.3) is not an
obvious one. This instance does not figure in the apparatus at the foot
of the page. Finally, at 3.108: A 2655–56 there is a confusion
symptomatic of the editorial predicament. As between *He cryde hoo
namoore for it is doon* / *Ne non shal lenger to his felawe gon* and *Vnto
the folk that foghten thus echon* / *He cryde hoo namoore for it is doon*,
the second couplet, from its flabbiness and lesser advancement of the
sense (whom, after all, could Theseus be shouting to?) is the scribal
one. It may have seemed the necessary archetypal reading because it
is in the manuscripts of standing, Hg, El, Gg—how can they be wrong
together, agreeing in error as if genetically related? So at 2.38 this
difference is by authorial revision, 'Couplet rewritten.' But in the
master apparatus one alternative is presented as accidental omission
made good by supply of a spurious line (5.258), and in the critical
note there is wavering between that explanation and 'Chaucer having
written a new couplet'; the expeditiously available 0² turns up here
(3.434). What we actually have is either subconscious recasting of a
difficult line in the scribal memory or sophistication. The reason for
the variation will have been the contextually difficult use of *felawe*,
'one of a pair of opponents' (*MED* s.v. *felau*(e n. 10).

All this is regrettable. There is, after all, a rationale for identifying
authorial revision. It is not foolproof, but it can protect thoughtful
editors. Identification of revision is necessarily subjective, for it
assumes the critic's or editor's capacity to identify a superior quality

in the author's writing, to distinguish between the *usus scribendi* of author and scribe. The subjectivity is, however, directed and controlled by experience of the extent to which scribes can deface a text and the characteristics of such defacement. Part of the act of judgment will be discernment of authorial intention, on a presumption that when the author made a change he had an object in view and that it has been attained. Scale is a factor: if the area of the text affected is large, there will be more information available for the critical act; in small instances the determinant will be more likely whether a direction of variation by characteristic scribal substitution suggests itself.

A further generalization arises from the unfinished state of *The Canterbury Tales*, but it must be correctly understood. Thus, because the parts are generally complete in themselves but the assemblage (*after the newe gise*, the compilation) was not completed, the likelihood of both revised and unrevised forms surviving is not uniform: it is obviously greater in passages with structural function. Where the text survives in both earlier and revised forms, there are, also obviously, at the points of revision two manuscript traditions. But in good logic these cannot be postulated until revision has been otherwise established; they cannot be argued from alignments of variational groups, since these become genetically significant only when the variants in which they agree are identified as unoriginal readings. The time has come to look at the structure of arguments that sustains this edition.

First, the editorial proposition that a classification of the manuscripts has been accomplished from which by recension an archetypal text of the poem can be recovered has no foundation. There is no such serviceable classification. At almost every stage, and making generous allowance for the possibility that different tales may have different manuscript traditions, the scheme of relationships leaves a greater or lesser residue of manuscripts unaccounted for. Thus, even supposing any proposed stemma to be locally accurate, what has been accomplished is only a partial classification, the identification of a family, or complex of groups, not the relation of all the manuscripts. That information can at best reach back only to the group ancestor: this must be understood to be the limit of its serviceability. The editors' 0^1 is no more than that—supposing their classifications to be correct.

Second, the proposition that explains the failure of the classification to account for all the manuscripts by postulating differentiation of archetypes has not been demonstrated. The evidence for the 'intelligent editor,' for 'borrowing,' and for widespread authorial revision does not bear examination. The Ellesmere variants proposed as evidence for editorial activity turn out to be the very commonplaces of scribal substitution—except those which appear as original and the probable sources of the other variants. The 'borrowing' depends on a *petitio principii* of genetic relation and on disregard of the frequency of coincident variation, and it further potulates a fifteenth-century clearing house for *Canterbury Tales* readings that is hard to believe in. As for authorial revision, with some striking exceptions the editorial proposals are not firmly based.

Third, the quality of judgment exhibited in all the editorial processes, the theorizing, the interpretation of detail, and the general conclusions, has an amateurish look. This can be masked by the very obfuscating codification of the data in many parts of the edition, but it shows, naked and unhappy, in the earlier part of Volume 2, and especially in those ultimate moments of editorial self-exposure, the Critical Notes. One can trace the growth of an increasingly severe predicament. The editors committed themselves to recension, in itself a logically questionable method. Then they discovered that their subject resisted it. They disregarded the basic principle of manuscript classification in favour of a romantic confidence in the uniform operation of the laws of probability in a situation composed of factors calculated to disturb such operation. What they call recension turns out to be a succession of adventitious accommodations to conflicting evidence. From the number of mistaken identifications of direction of variation in simple instances, let alone misinterpretations of more complex variation, they seem to have been grievously handicapped by inexperience of the process of scribal variation.

Whatever other limitations their edition may be judged to have, Manly and Rickert's troubles began with the procedures for classification that they adopted, apparently without adequate consideration or real understanding of the implications. There is an a priori unlikelihood of their results being sound. Either to dispose of their consequent propositions or to reinstate them, the classification will have to be attempted again: their results are untestable from the information given in the edition because of the virtually impenetrable system of symbols they employed in presenting their evidence. There is no telling what the result may be if the attempt is expertly carried out.[36]

Meanwhile, it will be judicious to abstain from using the propositions of this edition as bases for further argument, especially about the prehistory of the manuscript tradition of *The Canterbury Tales* or about the superiority of this or that manuscript.

14
'Good' and 'Bad' Manuscripts: Texts and Critics

The issue of 'good' and 'bad' manuscripts is lively just now, and there has been vociferous objection to the two terms, for various reasons some of which are mistaken. Thus: the terms have moral overtones; but do such overtones intrude in discussions of good or bad wine or cheese? They express value judgements; but so does the whole study of literature, for if all texts were equal the concept literature would be of another order, and editing an irrelevancy. The real objection to the terms is that they are inadequate to describe the complex differences between manuscripts, that they are disincentive to critical thought by editors (who are not necessarily textual critics), that for the inexperienced they confuse editorial issues, and that even in textual critics they can induce prejudicial, and therefore stultifying attitudes. Nevertheless they are useful in that they direct consideration of the critical attitudes and thus the practices of editors when they engage in the activity defined by my dictionary as publishing, that is, giving to the world a literary work by an earlier author, previously existing in manuscript. If I may say so, it is timely that editorial attitudes and the circumstances that form them should be considered. I must share any blame assignable in this situation for failing to make clear, in the introduction to *Piers* A, that this was not a do-it-yourself kit for theorizing about editing but an account of a single editor's predicament and his attempts to resolve it. It did not sufficiently emphasize the qualifying effect of the kind of text the editor is 'giving to the world.'

It is worth a moment to consider how great the variety, merely of Middle English texts, actually is when seen from an editor's point of view. The literary work of art (*Troilus*, of course), and *Boece*, the record of an attempt first to understand and then to replicate in a language quite inadequate for the purpose one of the most intellectually sophisticated and elegantly written of philosophical works, are only two instances, albeit in extreme contrast, of support for a generalization that almost every Middle English text poses a distinct editorial problem. Think of the *Brut* of Layamon who, in Ben Jonson's reported words about Shakespeare, 'writ no language,' or *King Horn*, where the possibility of memorial transmission has to be allowed, or *The Scale of Perfection*, of which some copyists appear to have been adepts in mystical ascesis, capable of technically improving the discourse, or Wycliffite texts, where it seems there was continuous editorial adaptation by copyists themselves progressively more radical evangelists. Every such distinctive situation, and there are many more, qualifies the editor's attitude and should in principle define his objective and determine his procedures, his treatment of the manuscript evidence.

Another qualifying circumstance is the state of a text as a composition. Did its author consider it ready to copy and formally publish it, as Chaucer did *Troilus*, or is it from its condition evidently unfinished, as are the large works we call *The Canterbury Tales* and the C version of *Piers Plowman?* Further, is the text absolute, or one of a succession of revisions, or even merely suspect of revision, like *Troilus?*

Then there is the state of preservation of a text. Any editor's attitude to the manuscript which uniquely preserves his text is bound to differ from that of one whose text survives in sixteen or sixty copies. He may believe it to be larded with errors of transcription and riddled with deliberate substitutions. Whatever his opinion it must still, axiomatically, differ from the first exemplar and is thus 'bad,' and moreover indeterminably 'bad'; yet in preserving the work, however imperfectly, it is necessarily 'good.' Where a text survives in many copies there is a relativity: every copy will necessarily differ to some extent from the authorial examplar; those that seem to the editor, for whatever presumptive reason, to differ least become 'good' and are welcomed as evidence of the physical features, that is the language, of their original. There is another significant circumstance of preservation: Where a text is preserved in many manuscripts, do these show the features of a manuscript tradition, or of several traditions? In the case of *Piers Plowman*, for example, it is the existence of identifiable manuscript traditions that points to two occasions on which Langland was willing to allow his poem to be copied.

Texts have physical features and represent, for our purpose today, historical events: the text of any manuscript is a syntagma of language more or less accurately reflecting one that was assembled on a past occasion. If its editor's objective is to recover its original features then every surviving copy is 'good' in the sense that it may afford evidence to that end. To think of a manuscript as 'good' in that it provides evidence of 'how the poem was first read'[1] is not a primarily editorial consideration; it might be of interest to literary historians if the evidence, at least for Middle English, were not almost invariably so jejune. As for the notion of scribal variation in a manuscript having value as 'contemporary commentary, line-by-line, upon the quality of the poetry that it transmits,[2] the essence of such commentary fits easily into half a dozen sentences and is banal. And as for scribal participation 'in the activity of a poem, often at a high level of intellectual and even creative engagement,'[3] I have yet to come upon an instance of this in the case of a great work. It is my observation that if we depended on scribes for our literary insights into the Middle Ages we would be in a bad way. More to the point, scribal variation can direct an editor with alert literary sensibility toward the stylistically notable features of his text.

Every one of those differentiating circumstances is bound to have a part in forming an editor's attitude to, and treatment of his manuscript. The circumstance that ought to affect an editor's procedures most radically will appear from a review of the processes of editing.

One set of these applies to all classes of text, even the drabbest and most prosaic. Its most elementary component operation corresponds to what we do every day to correct typographical error in newspapers and books. A text does not make sense; its language is evident garble, non-words, non-grammar. We make correction, restore the text, conjecturally, by the way, through inference from context. In the preparation of manuscripts for publication a next stage; also elementary, is identification of evident miswritings like metathesis and dittography. Then there are contextually unacceptable readings such as miscounts, miswriting of Roman numerals, wrong pronoun numbers. These processes, eliminating the simpler kinds of unconscious copying error, are effectively applicable to all classes of text, including those uniquely preserved. The reading that the editor substitutes for the one in the manuscript when applying them is determined by inference from the acceptable surrounding context. To apply them he needs some acquaintance with the subject of his text, a command of its language, and enough respect for its author to believe that what he originally wrote made sense. If he is competent in these particulars, so far so good.

Next comes the identification of unconscious scribal substitution that has left the text at least somehow meaningful. It is a fair guess that in uniquely preserved texts a considerable amount of such substitution goes undetected, to be editorially sanctioned by a little, or more than a little, wrenching of lexicography and distortion of Middle English syntax. The taxonomy of this kind of variation resembles that of speech error, which is not surprising, considering that the medieval scribe sounded the copy he picked up as he read it and wrote from auditory as well as visual recall. I do not know of any analysis of such variation that satisfactorily covers a variety of texts. There is much information about it embedded in books like Louis Havet's *Manuel de Critique Verbale* and Pasquali's *Storia della Tradizione e Critica del Testo*. But theoretical knowledge is no real substitute for sustained observation of its occurrence at the level of visible variation, that is, variation of individual manuscripts from the subgroup or group reading.

In an ideal world one would be able to draw a line of distinction here between the two kinds of process involved. But precisely because unconscious variation could and did produce intelligible readings the two cannot be clearly demarcated. A text survives in a number of copies. In one or more lines of their descent aberration, unconscious error, has produced a succession of plausible variations. To those unfamiliar with scribal ways such repeated differentiation of readings takes on an appearance of system, of design; it looks deliberate. So the editorial situation changes, though it should not, from one of eliminating unconscious error to one of absolute identification of originality between rival readings, as if there were a question of deliberate substitution.

One notable Chaucerian instance of this situation has been the CUL Gg 4.27 text of *The Legend of Good Women*, a manuscript in terms of our title both 'good' and 'bad.' The manuscript has genuine status from its unique preservation of what is pretty certainly an authorial revision of the *Prologue*. The larger lineaments of the revision are clearly discernible, and from these the manuscript has acquired what Robinson called 'peculiar authority.' This has been extended to several hundred distinctive G readings on a smaller scale, many of which would be plausible if not subject to comparison. Editors have tended to accept most of them as Chaucerian and to give them the standing of revisions, or even of unrevised authorial readings superior to the corresponding readings in the other manuscript tradition. In fact the majority are scribal aberrations; only a few have the appearance of deliberate substitution.[4]

The other Chaucerian instance, notorious rather than notable, is that of the Hengwrt and Ellesmere copies of *The Canterbury Tales*, both held to be 'good' manuscripts. One reads that, of the two, Hengwrt is 'generally agreed to contain the best text'[5] and that Ellesmere was 'quite extensively edited . . . in a highly intelligent and responsible manner. . . . There can be no question of the intrinsic superiority of Hengwrt as a witness to what Chaucer wrote. . . . It is, for the most part, an editor's dream.'[6] In fact the two copies were differentiated not deliberately but by combinations of mechanical error and unconscious substitution of plausible readings in both traditions.[7] They are equally 'good' and equally 'bad.' To apply these terms to them impedes critical thinking.

The second editorial process takes up where, to the extent of an editor's perception, unconscious variation of all kinds has been dealt with. It is effective only in application to literary works of art of such distinctive excellence that considerable differences of style exist between the modes of composition of the poets and those of their copyists. The postulate of excellence implied in that restriction seems hard for some to grasp. I have seen it described as 'trusting to explanations of the imaginative process that stress the mysterious integrity of its expressive power'; such trust is said to constitute an act of faith and is thus (again I quote exactly) 'distinct from the acts of literary judgement that alone are integral to editorship.'[8] I am at a loss to understand what 'the acts of literary judgement' in that stricture were thought to be, but the expression seems to suggest a notion that the excellence of a literary work is somehow detachable from its language, as if style, and form, and meaning did not exist in and by virtue of the physical features of a text, its language. This last proposition, that they do so exist, which sums up the findings of a couple of generations of stylisticians, and of those modern literary critics capable of writing analytically about style, has nothing romantic about it. Stylistics are not mysterious, merely difficult. The whole effect of a poem is the product of, and undetachable from, the detail of its language. The salient poem, the great literary work of art, is produced not by 'the practitioner of a divine mystery'[9] but by a craftsman. His aptitude may well be exceptional in both nature and degree, and is certainly to be distinguished from mere verbal resource, from fluency, but it is a human phenomenon, and its results are susceptible of analysis. The distinctiveness of the style of a great poet and the possibility of characterizing it are a main premise of textual criticism, by which I mean the differentiation of authorial and scribal readings after elimination of mechanical error and demonstrably unconscious variation from the text. That premise distinguishes textual criticism sharply from impressionistic criticism, from unparticularized response to a literary work, indeed from any response to literature that ignores its own source or cause. It is also a premise of stylistics.

My literary critic begins with a presumption that poets as a class care about the details of their language, their style. That presumption, abundantly supported by what poets have recorded since they began to write about themselves, and by observation of poets at work, corresponds to Roland Barthes's distinction between poets and, for instance, those who are impelled to write about them, *écrivains* and *écrivants*:

> L'écrivain est celui qui *travaille* sa parole . . . et s'aborbe fonctionnellement dans ce travail. L'activité de l'écrivain comporte deux types de normes: des normes techniques (de composition, de genre, d'écriture) et des normes artisanales (de labeur, de patience, de correction, de perfection). . . . L'écrivain est le seul, par définition, à perdre sa propre structure et celle du monde dans la structure de la parole . . . Cette parole est une matière (infiniment) travaillée.[10]

In respect for the detail of poetry, and thus for the poet's craft, literary criticism and textual criticism at their best are undistinguishable.

To be sure, their terminology differs here. The literary critic writes of the 'grammar of the style' of his poem, that is, the particulars in which it differs from both prose and the style of other poems; the textual critic has thus far employed the old-fashioned term *usus scribendi*, 'customary way of writing,' to express the same concept. Both expressions postulate distinctiveness, the quality of style which the poet attains by the craftsmanship of detail. The difference is in the objective: the critic of style analyses the poet's language in order to account for its effects; the textual critic applies the results of such analysis to identification of damage sustained by the poem, of un-authorial, that is, uncharacteristic, elements in the received text. There is not, then, a matter of evaluating competing readings against a 'Platonic idea' (*sic!*) of how the great poet wrote.[11] The key word is 'analysis,' and analysis of describable physical data.

As far as Chaucer and Langland are concerned the condition for such analysis is favourable. Their editors need not, as has been suggested, take comfort from 'an idealist belief that even amid the welter of fragmentary details history has left us, there abides a gleam of light that beams across the ages.'[12] That suggestion, not-withstanding its engaging echoes of *Abide with Me, Lead Kindly Light, Rock of Ages* and Tennyson's *Follow the Gleam*, is incorrect. In Chaucer's case the welter is only apparent, a consequence of Manly and Rickert's unhappy attempt to classify the manuscripts of *The Canterbury Tales*: the data for making grammars of Chaucer's style in his various poems are actually abundant. With *Piers Plowman* it is easy to illustrate the huge preponderance of unquestioned readings from which the grammar of the style of the poem can be described. I use the B version, of which, as Skeat's edition showed, the archetypal form is almost always confidently recoverable. Donaldson and I professed to identify, in that archetypal text, some 760 unoriginal readings, that is to say, corruption in eleven per cent of its 7,200-odd lines; that leaves considerable text as evidence for the grammar of the style of the poem. To apply another measure; the poem consists of 71,000-odd words; if one allows each suspect reading two words the number of words deemed unoriginal is just over two percent. These rough figures are deliberately conservative; if they were refined they would argue even more strongly for the abundance of serviceable data. This is then no matter of 'claiming to be able to discover an original text from the fragments and vestiges that history has left us.'[13] The bulk of the physical structure of this text is intact.

Now it must be considered abstractly just what the editor of a great literary work of art sets out to recover by means of textual criticism. In the plainest and most general terms his objective is the physical features of his poem as they stood in the exemplar first copied by another hand than the author's. The historical event constituted by the literary work of art occurred in that moment.

This is what I earlier had in mind when I said that the editorial circumstances of every text are distinctive. No one would debate that every one of Chaucer's works sets a special editorial problem. But let me talk about that which I know best, the *Piers Plowman* situation. And let it be recalled that I was the one who first wrote that Langland's revision of his poem was continuous and unsystematic. Close and sustained experience of textual transmission excludes, for me, the notion that the minor differences in the texts of *Piers Plowman* manuscripts are the products of repeated and frequent copyist consultation of the poet's working copy.

Such consultation would a priori be a physical improbability because of what it implies about working conditions. It is ruled out by the demonstrable existence of manuscript traditions. A manuscript tradition identifies itself when a number of manuscripts agree so substantially in the texts they present as to make evident their descent from an exclusive common ancestor. This happens three times with the *Piers Plowman* manuscripts. A manuscript tradition originates when an author causes or permits his personal copy of his work to be reproduced; at that moment he loses control of the reproduction he sanctioned, which thereafter generates successive descendants, often in discernible relationships.

Manuscript traditions have a direct bearing on the philosophical concept of the texts of a poem: they are evidence that the authorial texts are not modern editorial ideas. Each tradition exists because there was once a tangible, readable object which the poet (or in the instance of *Piers C* a literary executor) will willing to let be copied. There were thus definitive points, for however long or short a time, in Langland's realization of the artistic conception that drove him to write. Even those *Piers Plowman* manuscripts that might be called 'bad' because their texts seem to have large elements of scribal substitution are valuable as evidence for the occurrence of such moments, evidence of those historical events that one has tried to recover, and are thus 'good.'

But that ambivalence must be correctly understood. It is not the same as the ambivalence of the 'bad' manuscript that uniquely preserves a text. For the 'past,' the historical event, is as near as we can, by the best use of intelligence, bring it. Thus, while any one of the relatively complete manuscripts of *The Canterbury Tales*, if it were the sole surviving copy, would 'be' the poem for us, the situation is otherwise. And the radical difference, the possibility of comparing the physical features of the texts in several or many manuscripts, constitutes an intellectual imperative.[14]

15
Criticism, Solecism: Does it Matter?

Some years ago it struck me as an interesting project to compare the handling of their common central situation, the pursuit of a reluctant male by an ardent female, in the anonymous fourteenth-century romance *Sir Gawain and the Green Knight* and Shakespeare's *Venus and Adonis*; I fancied that I might learn something about the relation between tone and meaning from two excellent poets' handling of that rather special situation. I never got to make the comparison; to prepare myself for it I read the critical literature of the works, and the effect of doing so was to turn me from the poets to their critics, and to some elementary considerations of method. The respective disagreements between critics over these two poems proved to be extreme, and I could only wonder whether this was an inevitable situation.

I suppose my concern with method relates to my particular generation of university teachers of English, which has never been allowed to take the character of its occupation for granted. I entered the university near the end of an age of respect for authorities, great academics of the immediate past. My teachers, students of Kittredge, Klaeber and W. P. Ker, used to refer familiarly to those men, but their names never failed to induce awe in us. We saw ourselves as puny successors to a race of giants, and our first adjustment was to come to terms with our own insignificance. Then even before we had fully formed our attitudes to our profession it was subjected to various challenges: from Dr I. A. Richards, from Downing College and its magazine, and from the great American critics. Precipitated from hero-worship into reappraisal of our newly formed professional selves and their preconceptions we could take none of the approaches or methods that we had inherited for granted. In the new situation there was an absence of assurance, either from the support of authority or from a sense of knowledge of right procedures. And now in recent years, as if that were not enough, the changes in our own society and the world have given fresh point to a question which every professional student of literature must at some time have asked himself: wherein lies the validity of our occupation?

The old answer, that the value of our study lies in the training of minds and the increase of knowledge, cannot be immediately bettered. But it seems impossible not to wonder how well we serve that purpose in promoting or condoning the proliferation of discordant opinions, however ingeniously, learnedly, plausibly argued. Might not the disagreement be a symptom of deficiency in our methods? To be sure, the study of literature, because of its subject and the nature of its medium, is among the most difficult of all branches of learning. But is it really so difficult that it cannot be made more efficient? There should in principle, one presumes, be right and wrong ways of thinking about any given set of phenomena, even about a poem centuries old; and if that presumption is sound, then the right ways efficiently followed should lead to results not necessarily identical—since differences, merely, between the personalities of individual critics would rule that out—but necessarily congruent, differing only as various aspects of the same critical and interpretative truth.

How far the criticism of my two poems is from instancing such congruency I shall now show. My quotations throughout are direct and authentic, but I will not locate or identify them because no good purpose would be served by doing so; I have also refrained from using immediately recent material as possibly too fresh in people's minds.

I begin with *Sir Gawain and the Green Knight*. Here there is agreement in one particular at least, about the excellence of the poem. I read that 'it is one of the great poems of the Middle Ages in English, which is to suggest that it is greater than nearly all poems except a few by Shakespeare'. It is said to have 'an almost flawless structure'; 'it has superlative art in its fashioning; it is mature, deliberate, richly seasoned'; it exhibits 'sophisticated familiarity with varied aspects of aristocratic life and thinking'; 'a gracious comedy of manners is enacted' in it; it is 'one of the few undoubtedly aristocratic poems of the English Middle Ages extant'; 'even Chaucer's *Troilus* is less consistently courtly than *Sir Gawain and the Green Knight*'. There has been corresponding speculation about its author: whether the poem's 'exquisite deftness of touch and the over-all polish' must not mean that he was 'a courtier, man of leisure and learning, at ease among people of refined tastes', possessing 'the intimate awareness of one who had been born to high estate and "gentilesse"'. In any event, says a modern book, 'certainly in tone *Sir Gawain* is the most continental of English romances'; 'the urbanity of the poem . . . looks forward to the courts of the Medicis and Elizabeth'; the highest possible praise, it appears.

No doubt everyone I have just quoted would instantly agree on the need for judicious praise in literary criticism, that praise should be not excessive but appropriate, and conferred for appropriate reasons. But not all can have observed that need, for with agreement about the excellence of the poem the consensus ends; the rarity of further agreement implies that in some cases at least the poem was admired for the wrong, for inappropriate reasons. The high praise plainly registers the affective capability of the poem, but the same capability may have impeded its understanding and assessment. Anyone who openly argued that a poem which engages him power-fully must be correspondingly excellent in all respects, or that those elements of a poem which engage him most powerfully are necessarily its most significant elements, would be smiled at. As soon as we express such propositions nakedly their fallaciousness is evident. But how often are they expressed? How often do they operate, unexpressed and subconsciously, to cloud critical judgement?

Very often, I suspect, in the case of *Sir Gawain*. We call the poem a romance. For a start the various, more specific characterizations applied to it have been such as to put that very broad and barely classificatory label to severe strain. At one extreme it has seemed merely entertainment, a form of 'play' in the sociological sense; at the other a deeply symbolical spiritual document. We can disregard the former description as not literary; the latter would at least historically be a genuine possibility. The variety of views between is consider-able. For instance I read that 'the primary purpose of the poet is to show what a splendid man Gawain was, . . . what a perfect knight can do when he is forced to face the unknown', but otherwise that 'the focus of the story is on the extension and consequences of [Gawain's] blunder, which is misuse of heroic, or courtly ritual'; and that the poet 'utilises a magnifying lens to throw into sharp focus the assumptions of romance, revealing . . . the weaknesses as well as the strengths of the knightly code'. A qualification of the second view runs to the effect that 'the subject of this romance is romance itself', that the poem expresses 'an ambivalent attitude to the romance ideal', the limitations of which 'were a particular fourteenth-century concern', and that the poem is actually 'a gently satiric anti-romance'. I also find references to its 'high comedy', to its 'quintessentially human' or 'rich but delicate comedy', to the 'spirit of comedy' in which its central action develops. It is 'essentially a comic poem', even though 'from the standpoint of romance' it 'has been a tragedy'. The poem, this characterization goes on, 'is thus both a tragic romance . . . and an unromantic comedy'. This view is rhetorically impressive, but elsewhere I find a contrary view, that the romance contains 'not the slightest questioning or probing of the social values of the artistocratic caste'.

This last opinion is not, however, widespread. The majority of interpretations assume that the principal and most significant motive of the romance is some kind of demonstration, of which the central agency is the testing of Gawain, especially in the three successive assaults the lady makes on his 'virtue'. But there is no general agreement about the subject of the demonstration, about what precise quality in him is being tested. In one view, confidently expressed, the temptations are simply an exemplum of admirable behaviour: 'Gawain resisted the Lady because he was the man he was, one deeply committed to the ideal of chastity'. In another, asserted with equal confidence, the subject of the test is Gawain's 'loyalty to his host', the Lady's husband. The virtues specifically at stake are his 'courage, honour, loyalty and courtesy'. This second view is supported by an ingenious adjustment of moral values: 'The term *synne* is used [in the text] with reference to unchastity, but according to the logic of Gawain's thought we see it to be in effect, a venial sin, more important for its implications of secular failure than in itself . . . the betrayal of [the husband] . . . is . . . the truly heinous offence to be avoided'. The critic who found the poem both a 'tragic romance' and an 'unromantic comedy' senses no problem of selection: the Lady's temptations test Gawain in many respects, 'not only continence and a bargain with the host but courtesy, loyalty and the dangers of sin'. The temptations have also been read as social and literary criticism. Because they reverse the male and female sex roles they have been held to stand what is called the courtly love convention on its head and thus to imply 'satire of the deification of women'; 'these scenes are high-style parody of a discredited literary convention' or (in the same essay) 'gentle mockery of manners mistaken for morals'.

There is a corresponding variety of opinions about the meaning of the romance. It will be recalled that one reader thought it merely playful entertainment. Another finds in it a remarkably general moral, that 'if we wish to act to our highest capacity we must be loyal to those who deserve our loyalty. In a word we must be obedient to our station and our social duty'. Yet another discerns a more specific intention in the poet, to contrast the 'incipient corruption' of 'Arthur's young court' 'in matters of sex and loyalty' with the 'morally superior' court of Bercilak. Recalling that it is the latter's wife who conducts the temptation we may think that reading poorly supported by the actual text. There is one even more remote: the temptation of Gawain proceeds according to the specified stages of hamartiology, as 'widely applied to the legends of the Saints', and is 'congruent with the patristic tradition'; the romance is deeply symbolical of spiritual truths, a 'drama of the human soul' on its journey through life, in which the two ladies in the castle 'represent the two personified aspects of the Christian Fortuna'; they and the Lord of Hautdesert are 'agents of Divine Providence'.

One response to the situation I have sketched is to interpret it as an invitation to syncretism. This I find in an appraisal of the poem which describes it as 'reflecting a many faceted solidity which is both comic and serious. It is meant to entertain and to some extent teach a sophisticated audience. It is a combination of secularism and religion, of the marvellous and the real, of the subjective and the objective, of the decorative and the direct, of the vague and the clear, of courtesy and horror, of the elevated and the plain.' By admitting so many possibilities of categorization that description certainly registers the difficulty of the work. Another response, to assert stoutly that 'There is nothing problematical in the poem', may seem self-delusive. A third, my own, is purely one of dismay at such lack of agreement.

Lest this situation should be thought peculiar to medieval studies, I quickly turn to *Venus and Adonis*, about which there is also some diversity of critical opinion. Shakespeare criticism, however, scores one point: some of its exponents have been bold enough to allow that this might be an unsuccessful poem. As long ago as 1817 it was called 'hard, glittering and cold'; later in that century it was judged 'a model of what a young man of genius should not write on such a subject'. In our time it has been found 'uninspired and pitilessly prolix', 'destitute of feeling for the human situation', 'a manufactured poem, consistently constructed for the market'. 'Desperate, indeed, is the word for *Venus and Adonis* as a whole . . . there is strain, there is conceit, there is bad taste.' 'Shakespeare falls between the serious and the comic.' The poem 'shifts disconcertingly from frigid conceits to moving pathos'. 'This wavering is symptomatic of [the author's] lack of perfect control.' The poem is 'an exercise in versifying'. Against these views are set clean contrary ones. It has been called 'the first rank product of a mind which for the variety and excellence of its fruits has never been surpassed'. It has seemed 'a great work of release, an assertion of natural energies', or 'the paean of the young poet, singing the song, not of Ovid, but of his native countryside, a song of earth, the song of a new nation . . ., the song of youth'. It has (somewhat inconsistently) been said to be 'a complete artistic success, despite some flaws or weaker passages. . . . all things work together'. The same critic writes of 'the imaginative unity of the poem . . . in its view of elemental and human passions as a feast for the mind and spirit: as sometimes moving and sometimes amusing, but always offering an absorbing living spectacle'. How splendid that sounds—until one tries to conceive the precise nature of such 'imaginative unity' and see the description as a denial of formal significance to the poem.

Critics have had difficulty in identifying its effect. It has been called 'a kind of verbal painting', and less imprecisely, 'a series of beautiful and voluptuous pictures'. It has been characterized as both a 'verse romance', and an account of Adonis's revenge on Venus for her destruction of his mother Myrrha. Various critics have found in certain tonal elements of the poem effects other than of gravity; these they have variously identified. For one 'the rhetorical burlesque and the comic characterization of the legendary lovers travesty Neoplatonic notions of love'; the words and actions of Venus 'burlesque Renaissance styles' and 'romantic literary conventions'. For another there is 'obvious farce inherent in the representation of the Goddess of Love's failing to arouse passion in a mortal youth'. Shakespeare's intention (the term is used without evident unease) was 'to write a sensuous, sophisticated farce'. No matter with respect to accurate use of critical terms that Adonis is killed; our little farce is rounded with a death. For a third critic, indeed, the poem contains 'the spirit of . . . a romantic, that is to say Shakespearean comedy'. A fourth calls it 'a sparkling and sophisticated comedy'; even 'the verse itself is comic'. Someone else writes of the poet's 'almost satiric' outlook, and finds his use of hyperbole 'ironic'; and still another sees the poem as 'the expression of the most savage irony known to him in literature'. Predictably the poem also acquires the label, 'wry, ironic comedy'. Still, the death of Adonis is troublesome. For the proponent of the 'verse romance' notion it is 'a result of inherent antipathies in nature'. For the discoverer of the 'spirit of comedy' in the poem the metamorphosis of Adonis serves to put off grief, to make 'the story light as a bubble and keep it floating'. For the reader who found the poem 'sparkling' and 'sophisticated' the grief of Venus is distanced 'by making her speeches burlesques of conventional sixteenth-century Elizabethan complaints'. It comes as no surprise then to find the poem called 'a tragicomedy of love'. But against these views is the stern pronouncement that the 'dominant impression of *Venus and Adonis* is not really of a "jocosity"'. Someone has actually called it 'essentially a tragic poem'. To round off these differences there is an ingenious interpretation which identifies in the changing stage of mind of Venus 'an Aristotelian anagnorisis'.

A corrective voice reminds us that the poem is 'not a comedy or a tragedy. It is not a drama' but the narration of a myth; it 'interprets life through a fictional paradigm'. The author of that cautionary view does not specify what aspects of life the paradigm interprets, but such information is forthcoming from other sources. One pronounces the poem as 'didactic a piece of work as Shakespeare ever wrote' and reads it as an allegory of the destructive agency of 'sensual love', naturally symbolized in Venus, while Adonis (the unloving) is 'reason in love, all truth, all good'. For another interpreter the poem, somewhat vaguely, 'allegorizes the generative impulse in its proper and improper force'; for another it is 'a metaphysical commentary on the destruction of good by evil'; for a third the boar which kills Adonis is 'death, the eternal hunter'.

There is still more. *Venus and Adonis* has been described as a 'wholly impersonal' work. It is, however, also searched for autobiography. Its 'confused emotional quality' may relate to the poet's 'revulsion from the physical fact of sex'. Elsewhere I read that Adonis stands for the young man of the first fourteen sonnets; his similar reluctance to propagate, 'and the close parallels . . . in respect of imagery and theme make it certain that the connexion exists'. Or the poem is the work of a commercial dramatist intent on proving himself a sophisticated gentleman; it makes 'a claim to social dignity for its author'.

Is it presumptuous to see the critical situation of these two poems as evidence of the inefficiency of a procedure of trial and error, assertion and counter-assertion (with occasional compromise) and no better assurance of correctness than the absence of contradiction? I do not know whether these situations are typical. The poems are peculiarly difficult, and such conflict of opinions as they have generated may not represent the best products of the professional or expert study of English literature. Even so, is it either inevitable or appropriate that the study of any literary topic, however difficult, should result in such chaos?

The answer ought to be that it is not. Obviously literary study can never develop an exact science: the affective element in our apprehension of literature excludes that possibility at the outset. The peculiar sensibility which initially drew most of us to our pre-occupation is not subject to measurement, and its operation, indispensable to all kinds of literary study, can be tested for accuracy only by individual re-enactment of the experience of a literary work. But as I understand literary criticism the operation of that sensibility is only one element of the critical process, namely a source of its data. A second, which subjects those data to description, analysis and explanation, is properly a reasonable, an intellective activity. Even if literary criticism were no more than the rationalization of subjective responses, it is manifest that such rationalization could be more or less skilful, more or less rational. It does not follow from the presence of a subjective element in a mental activity that subjectivity should there have free rein; if anything the contrary implication has force: such a situation calls for intellectual regulation of the subjectivity.

The beginning of such discipline in our study would be avoidance of certain solecisms of critical logic. When a critic of *Venus and Adonis* writes of the poem that 'we are struck by a certain note of cold sensuality which not all of Shakespeare's artistry can efface' his use of the term 'efface' makes critical nonsense out of what might be a valid insight. When a discussion of the same poem asserts, after maintaining its lack of unity of effect, that nevertheless 'Shakespeare was wholly successful in what he set out to do' the implicit *petitio principii* vitiates the exposition: the possibility of a truth of literary history that underlies the situation being identified is reduced. Critical perception is dimmed by a fog of fallacious argument, of unauthorized inference, of unsystematic synthesis. Yet even for us students of literature it should be possible to maintain distinctions between an assumption, a proposition and a hypothesis in the development of a discussion, or to understand what is meant by implication or by absolute proof, and what is involved in an assessment of probabilities.

Another possible control of subjectivity would be regulation of the use of evidence. There can, for instance, be no justification for critical assertions made in defiance of the text they relate to, but they are not uncommon, and they lead to misinterpretation. There is nothing in the actual text of *Sir Gawain and the Green Knight* to suggest the 'incipient corruption' of 'Arthur's young court'; indeed the poet expressly sets the action in the first, the golden age of Arthur's court. So one argument about the meaning of the poem is imperfectly founded. Someone tells us that 'Read as a chastity test the temptation makes Gawain practically a subject for canonization', whereas the poet states that Gawain was in great danger of succumbing, and was saved only by the grace of the Virgin Mary, patroness of chastity. So an argument about the subject of the testing, and thus of the poem, is poorly based. We read that Adonis was killed 'through the motiveless malignity of the wild boar'; the beast's *méchantise*, however, consisted in defending himself against a hunter and his pack of hounds. So an alleged similarity between Shakespeare's poem and *Hero and Leander* is reduced. Or we read that 'with the death of Adonis lust triumphed', in disregard of the thirty-line-long curse upon love which Venus pronounces beside his corpse.

Such practices I call critical solecisms. Another kind, at least as grave, is disregard of significant external information. Here is an instance. Part of the argument advanced for *Venus and Adonis* being a comedy is that 'the verse itself is comic'. Four lines in particular are singled out: these, we read, are 'so banal . . . that one must explain their flatness as the result of either ineptitude or of dramatic propriety'. Their banality, supposing it to be genuine, was quite missed by a contemporary poet who was evidently impressed by the passage where they stand, for he made their content the subject of a substantial poem (not comical) and even echoed them in its title. That fact questions, to say the least, the modern critical response. Disregard of external information can lead to the basing of arguments on erroneous historical and critical generalizations. This occurs in the case for the comic or anti-romance quality of *Sir Gawain*. Its proponent, correctly observing that Gawain's crestfallen return to Camelot is likely to provoke a smile at his expense, then generalizes that 'comedy is not the stuff of which romance heroes are made'. Apart from Gawain's not being actually 'made' of comedy, he has forgotten the 'comedy' in the careers of beloved romance heroes like Horn and Havelok and William of Palerne and Perceval, and Bevis whose mother checks him by seizing hold of his ear (to name instances only from Middle English). Gentle ridicule of the hero can be part of the effect of romances; the case thus lacks foundation. To turn back to *Venus and Adonis*, a part of the argument for its being a comedy has been that 'the tradition that Shakespeare followed was demonstrably comic'. But as far as I can ascertain *Venus and Adonis* was only the third English poem of its kind; of its two predecessors one only might possibly be called 'comic'; even that ends with a drowning and a suicide. The argument from tradition is thus not very strong. Much solecistic generalization has to do with the term 'Ovidian'; one cynically wonders how many of its users have read Ovid even in translation; certainly not the one who writes of the goddess and the boy that 'the events in the poem retell their Ovidian romance'. Such patent factual and critical inaccuracy is probably less misleading than the more insidious historical inaccuracy resulting from derivative generalizations. I have in mind the use by some critics of the term 'Ovidian' as if it explained everything about *Venus and Adonis*. Unless they mean by it no more than 'erotic' it explains nothing for me: the effects of the poem are remote from any that I can sense, or find identified by classical scholars, in *Metamorphoses*.

Another possible control of subjectivity would be a more disciplined use of critical terms. If I understand correctly, the terminology of criticism is the instrument of contact between its affective and intellective elements: identifying the subjective response by naming it contributes one set of the matrixes indispensable to the rational understanding and logical explanation of the phenomenon which is the poem. Therefore precision of identification of affects, that is the precise use of critical terms, and correctness of interpretation must be directly related. Moreover, such precision can itself operate as an intellectual control since it implies discrimination by comparison and should thus direct critical thinking to the logical relation of notions. By contrast the wider the application of a term of description or classification, the less its descriptive or classificatory value must become. Thus it is relatively uninformative to describe the absence of solemnity as comedy, or to identify a pathetic with a tragic effect. But still worse, the inappropriate use of such terms has a kind of stultifying absoluteness whereby that which is not tragic must be comic, and so on. A spurious logic of criticism is set up in which there is no middle term, no range of subtly differentiated effects between those extremely differentiated kinds. Sometimes the particular consequence is absurdity, as in the portentous assertion that the death and metamorphosis of Adonis were 'not intended to arouse tragic emotion', or in the waggish comment about the close of *Sir Gawain* that 'from the standpoint of romance the poem has been a tragedy', where the intended meaning must have been 'disaster'. In general however the slovenly use of critical terms produces simply dull confusion: identical responses by various critics imprecisely named appear to be conflicting; disagreement is multiplied, and the growth of understanding retarded.

Good logic, scholarly accuracy, and the precise use of critical language would improve situations like those just above. But the ultimate control of subjectivity must be through maintenance of a critical point of view, that is through consistently thinking about a poem in terms of its mode of existence. Some gross failures to do this will show what I mean. Someone calls the Lady of Hautdesert 'an honest English rose'; someone with apparent solemnity writes that Gawain's having fended off her sexual advances is 'To . . . the glory of British literature'; someone apparently not familiar with the English observes that 'the icy, petulant Adonis is an English gentleman'; someone describes Venus as 'a forty-year old countess'. Such unilluminating nonsense could not be seriously written by anyone who kept in mind that a personage in a literary fiction exists only as an experience in the reader's imagination.

The critical point of view implies several presumptions of special relevance to our two poems: that a poem has by logical definition a normative meaning; that a successful poem functions by the interaction of all its parts; and that the whole significance of the unity of a poem, its 'meaning', is a product of relation between the inherent possible significance of what is represented and the quality of feeling generated by the mode of representation in the most general sense. In terms of such presumptions no interpretation of either poem ought to be acceptable which leaves any part of it out of account. But in the case of both our poems a main difficulty for critics has been the satisfactory correlation of all their respective parts.

The central problem seems to be one of tone. Both poets have elected to represent an essentially ludicrous situation. Cardinal elements in the action of *Sir Gawain*, and the whole action of Shakespeare's poem, are of a kind to have inherent significances, an a priori value, and to set up particular expectations of treatment. The question is how each poet valued the action in question, what meanings and feelings he sensed in it. These are essential parts of the whole meaning of the works and will reveal themselves principally in the tone of their representation, from which the attitudes of the poet to his subject and his audience might be inferred.

The critical disagreements, and the frequency of the term 'ambivalence' in discussion of both poems, point to the difficulty of each. But here too there is an elementary logic. For genuine ambivalence in a poem is either deliberate, in which event it is a function of the meaning of the poem, or unintentional, in which event it may well register fluctuation or imperfect realization of the poet's response to this subject, with whatever implications.

Critics of *Venus and Adonis* have at least recognized that their problem is one of tone: the necessary deliberateness of Shakespeare's conflation of two fables from *Metamorphoses*, which radically changes the relation of his two personages, directs attention to his attitude to the action. They have identified tonal discords; the difficulty has been to account for them, for example to discover a significant relation between general elevation of the narrative through stylistic elaboration and occasional naturalism of an extreme character. Essentially laughable incident is reported in richly beautified language, with punctuations of grotesquerie. What the critics have not squarely faced is a choice of obligations: to reconcile all parts, to relate the various mixtures of effect, or to accept the implications of that being impossible about the poet and the poem.

In the case of *Sir Gawain* it may be that tones have simply been mis-heard, and the poem misread in consequence. The complexity here results from the poet's predicament as a narrator in representing Gawain's temptation. This must appear not merely genuine but extreme. The Lady's advances must seem irresistible and Gawain must nevertheless resist them; moreover, in his character as the knight of courtesy *par excellence* he must resist with grace: he cannot reject his temptress brutally or sharply. No doubt that combination of requirements taxed the poet. A second complicating circumstance derives from the alliterative tradition in which the poet worked. This afforded him an exceptional resource of vocabulary, to be sure, but its terms had been developed for derring-do, not for his delicate, even awkward amatory topic. And Gawain's accumulated reputation as an amorist will not have helped; the poet had to insist on his chastity if there was to be any element of doubt over the outcome of the temptation. Such insistence would be bound to affect his tone.

Critics in general hold the poet to have acquitted himself well: the temptation scenes, they write, exemplify lightness, subtlety and social poise; they are conducted with 'exuberant humour' in a 'romping style'; the talk between Gawain and the Lady is 'gay . . . banter'; the poet is 'as sophisticated as the cosmopolitan Chaucer'.

But even cursory comparison with the most nearly similar situations in Chaucer's poetry casts doubt on such opinions and sends one back to the text of *Gawain*; a realistic examination of the Lady's manner of proceeding, which seems not calculated to succeed, makes to seem dubious the 'sophistication' of the temptation scenes (which, one then recalls, have been read as a satire of traditional attitudes to love). Her unmistakable offers of herself make the game too easy; her mention of her husband will put off Gawain by bringing the moral notion 'adultery' into his mind; telling him she is helplessly infatuated with him will more likely make him shy away from emotional responsiblity than undertake it; she even tries to constrain him, and reproaches him for being a backward lover. One can see why an Edwardian critic gallantly excused her for her failure as 'in-experienced'.

Indeed the inexperience, when one compares the management of these scenes with Chaucer's representation of, for instance, the seduction of Criseyde by Diomede, might seem to be the poet's. The difference of psychological realism between them is of the same kind, if not of the same degree, as that between Mr B.'s attempts on Pamela's virtue and the seductions in *Les Liaisons Dangereuses*.

There is a further element of difficulty in the temptation scenes of *Sir Gawain*: the pietistic and moral expressions. Delighted to have Gawain prisoner at her mercy in his bed the Lady praises the Heavenly Lord for her good fortune; she begs God to reward Gawain for his small kindness in kissing and talking to her; when she leaves him for the time being with a loving kiss the two commend each other to Christ. In the second episode the poet plainly states that the Lady's temptations were designed to persuade Gawain to wrongdoing; Gawain, in the third episode, is described as anxious lest he should commit sin. These are strange words and notions to find in a 'courtly', 'sophisticated', 'aristocratic' poem; taken together with Gawain's angry self-justification at the end of the second beheading scene, a stock antifeminist topos echoing Jerome against Jovinian, they might rather suggest a clerkly, moralistic attitude. And that suggestion could redirect the interpretation of the romance. It might turn out that the social gloss of the poem is not so knowledgeably applied as has been argued. If so we should be the better critics for giving the poem appropriate praise.

It is of course easy to write destructive criticism as I have been doing. But there is a kind of criticism which both destroys and is constructive, namely self-criticism, and my task would have been harder or even needless if some of the writers from whom I have quoted had exercised this. Their sensibility and in some cases their learning are impressive. But their affirmations, denials and counter-affirmations can set up a confusion which, rather than stimulating the young judgement, may create a false impression of the supremacy of the affective element in literary study. I would rather see sensibility, the capacity for strong response, taken for granted and the intellectual element in criticism fostered. Not very long ago an educational bigwig was quoted in the press as proclaiming that our students nowadays are too sophisticated to be taken by the hand and shown the 'beauties' of literature. Perhaps so, perhaps not. But in any event they need more than ever to be taught to think acutely and reasonably about it, even if only so that they may become proficient in thinking acutely and reasonably about other matters. It might seem our business as teachers and critics both, to learn this ourselves so that we may show them the way.

16
Outstanding Problems of
Middle English Scholarship

To begin I will say that in my title the two main senses of the term 'outstanding' come together, for the problems I have in mind are or ought to be prominent, conspicuous; and they remain as yet undetermined, unsettled. In representing them to you I would not wish to seem to imply that I myself am able, either here or in course of time, to resolve them: that would be absurd. I will, however, admit to a claim to be able to identify outstanding problems, and I suppose for that activity I am as qualified as anybody simply from having spent three decades in breaking my head on them. But you will be able to judge the validity of my identifications for yourselves.

They will not take the form of a list of neatly defined research projects of graduated size and difficulty such as one might dream of having in a drawer for one's best doctoral and post-doctoral students. What I plan is to propose to you the existence of a number of large areas of Middle English scholarship which need either investigation or, more often, reinvestigation. My hope will be to communicate my own sense of the need for concern with such areas, in particular so that the implications of leaving a question in abeyance or, *a fortiori*, of pretending that an answer to it exists by saying to oneself, 'Let us make an assumption for practical purposes,' will be more clearly seen.

The first problem is one of texts. However predictable you may find that beginning, the reason is not my preoccupation, but the overpowering circumstance that all the data for our study come from texts, and that the validity of the data relates directly to the authenticity of the texts. The studies of lexicographers, grammarians, literary critics, exegetes or what have you are in the first instance as 'good' as the texts on which they are based. No one is likely to debate that statement. But now I will assert that most Middle English texts are in one way or another bad, and that may seem open to objection. Let me say what I have in mind.

For a start, a text may have been inaccurately transcribed or inaccurately printed through inefficient checking. Human error can never be absolutely eliminated, only reduced, and one may therefore be inclined to discount the possibility of great carelessness in any editor, but the uncertainty remains. Or a text may be incorrectly transcribed through imperfect knowledge of Middle English. In my observation that happened most often in the nineteenth century, and any of the pioneer volumes of the Early English Text Society is likely to be faulty in this way; but I recently found examples of glaringly ignorant mistranscription in a publication dated 1971.[1] The safeguard against such kinds of error is effective though tedious: more checking, in the first instance by editors, in the second by any user of a text to whose arguments its detail is important.

It is a more serious deficiency of texts that they have an unwarranted appearance of reliability. This is to some extent natural: merely by being in print they assume authority beyond that of manuscript. Such authority is both powerful and insidious, and cannot in my observation be abolished by proclamation. The only defence against it is experience of what scribes can do to texts. That deficiency is particularly important in the case of any work uniquely preserved. The lack of other copies for comparison both operates as a limitation on the editor (who may indeed never have worked on any other manuscript), and puts scholars at the mercy of the single scribe as evaluated by that editor. And that scribe's necessarily postulated errors, we should recall, may quite likely be only the last of a succession of such events.

But what seems to me the worst feature of the situation respecting the texts of Middle English literature is exemplified in some of the most important, which we use most often and cherish most, namely that the editions which present them are not open, an 'open edition' being one where the editor makes available all the evidence needed to check his conclusions and decisions. Let me leave Gower aside, for I cannot make sense of Macaulay's Introduction to the *English Works*. Chaucer will be instance enough. There is no open edition of any of his works, as far as I know. Root's *Troilus* looks open: it has a critical apparatus at the foot of the page. But in fact this records only a selection of variants.[2] His classification of manuscripts is not substantiated, and the spellings of his text are silently selected from one of two copies—unless he rejects the spelling of both.[3] Manly and Rickert's *Canterbury Tales*, with its six volumes of apparatus to two of text, looks as if it ought to be open but I do not find it so. Because they edited by recension[4] (and I abstain from describing the logic of that)[5] the accuracy of their classification of manuscripts is vitally important. But it does not seem possible to tell from their tables of manuscript groupings whether the agreements which they treated as evidence for such groupings are in original, or unoriginal readings, or both kinds—and of course agreement in original readings is not evidence of genetic relation, but, rather, evidence that the manuscripts in agreement are correct copies of the same poem at that point.[6] And it does not seem clear whether the spelling of their text is that of an actual manuscript or not.[7] As for Robinson, his citation of variants is highly selective,[8] and the text of his edition is arbitrarily eclectic in all particulars and disingenuously so to boot, for it purports to have been constructed upon principles.[9] I say that from knowledge, having had occasion to examine his treatment of 3000 lines of Chaucer's text, with access to full manuscript variants. Robinson had flair and a nose for an original reading; it may be that candid and systematic, or I should say 'open' editing, would in many cases come to the same answers as he did. But it would be assessable by the editor's peers, and thus not potentially deceptive. As things are, the editorial judgment of Robinson and of other Chaucer editors can be assessed only by procedures so discouragingly laborious that for practical purposes we tend to accept it. Yet there are grounds for suspecting it, such as Root's conviction of revision in *Troilus*[10] when all but one of his items of evidence could be accounted for by scribal agency,[11] or Manly and Rickert's presentation of a number of evidently scribal variations as possible authorial revisions.[12] One grew up with Robinson's edition and retains a sentimental affection for it. But his cryptic and unassessable text has been the subject of close stylistic criticism (we do not know how many 'soiled fish of the sea'[13] it might contain), and has elicited elaborate structures of interpretation which might have taken other directions had full information about textual variation been readily available. Withholding such information has denied the majority of scholars experience of what scribes can do to texts, and they have the more uncritically accepted poorly based proposals of authorial revision.

That Robinson's modernization of the manuscript spelling has conferred on many generations of undergraduates an illusion that Chaucer's Middle English is easy is probably not calamitous. Even when the same illusion encourages grammatical ignoramuses to write truculently about Chaucerian versification, or about Chaucer's Englishness and modernity, not much harm ensues because the error of such writers is manifest to the knowledgeable. But it is a serious matter that Robinson's silent manipulation of the rhythm of Chaucer's four- and five-stress lines,[14] combined with the common editorial practice of withholding information about minor manuscript variation, has gravely retarded understanding of Chaucerian versification. The fact of the matter is that the manuscripts of Chaucer's poetry abound in minor variation which either certainly or possibly affects the syllabic value of the line. From its nature much of this variation is not the result of slovenly copying but was prompted by scribal concern, whether deliberate or unconscious, with rhythm. Moreover there is a perceptible general relation between the date of manuscripts and the kind and extent of syllabic variation in them. This must relate to scribal understanding of grammatical final *e*. The minor variation indicates that there were scribes who understood the grammar of that inflection or were anyway aware of its value to the rhythm and copied it pretty faithfully; others appear to have dimly sensed its importance and put it everywhere; for still others it was apparently soundless, an orthographical flourish. It will have been scribes of the second and third sort such as had an ear for the music of verse who introduced syllabic variation to smooth the rhythm. I surmise that correct appreciation of their treatment of the Chaucerian line could make a major contribution to agreed understanding of its character. And I am sure that the minor variation which constitutes that treatment can be used to improve our far-from-adequate understanding of the difficulties which fifteenth-century art poets evidently experienced with versifying musically.

Having begun my observations on the problem of Middle English texts with an assertion that most of them are in one or another way bad, I take leave of it with an admission that I have no quick practical remedy to propose. In my time I have had very few postgraduates with both the aptitudes and the temperament to make first-rate textual critics, and the amount of work that needs doing is enormous. There are even some Middle English works of manageable size like *Horn* and *Orfeo* which have never yet been edited in any real sense of that term. Perhaps the right beginning of the correction is to cultivate mistrust of texts.

Another outstanding general problem with some acute particular bearings is that of ascription, of authorship; here too there is implicit an opposition between faith and reasonable doubt. Dealing with so many unsigned and undated works, we find it more comfortable, once an ascription has been sanctioned in print, to forget how slender the evidence for it was, and how subjectively this was interpreted. A little time with Skeat's *The Chaucer Canon* or Brusendorff's *The Chaucer Tradition* can refresh the memory. Or take the rondeau at the end of *The Parlament of Fowls*, attested in only three of the fifteen authorities for the poem, in one of those three copied in another hand, in the other two incomplete. Skeat, whose reconstruction of the rondeau is what editors print, does not discuss it in *The Canon*; Brusendorff, accepting Chaucer's authorship, explains its absence from most copies by omission, though he finds the necessarily assumed frequency of such omission 'strange.'[15] In pointing out this situation I am not preparing to reject from the Chaucer canon any or all of the lightly supported works commonly ascribed to him, or which he does not himself claim to have written. I am reminding myself that I accept his authorship of those poems partly from habit (I first encountered them in a book called *The Works of Geoffrey Chaucer*), partly because I have faith in my own taste which finds in them the Chaucerian savour (though of course they will themselves have had a part in forming my notion of that savour), and partly on the logically bad ground of *argumentum e silentio*, that I do not know of any other fourteenth-century poet who could have written them. I cannot reasonably claim support for Chaucer's authorship of such poems from their appearing in manuscripts which also contain works more securely ascribable to him, if I reject yet other poems in those manuscripts as unChaucerian on subjective grounds.

The fact of the matter is that no one has worked out a rationale of ascription. Certainly none is detectable in the discussions of authorship of Middle English literature by the first three or four generations of our predecessors in the field. And it may be that none was developed in more recent times simply because the unwieldiness and mass of the earlier publications induced acquiescence in the views about authorship there expressed. How ill-equipped we are with precedents of logic to apply to this problem should appear from the circumstance that no one has systematically refuted Ethel Seaton's ascription, in 1961, of a dozen poems commonly held to be Chaucer's, including *The Legend of Good Women* and its Prologues, to a Sir Richard Roos (c. 1410–81/2)[16] to whom in MS Harley 372 a translation of Alain Chartier's *Belle Dame Sans Merci* is ascribed.[17]

There are, to be sure, some opinions so preposterous that it may seem not worth the effort to oppose them, and Miss Seaton's claims for Roos as a poet may have that character. But the circumstance that they could be put forward at all is a commentary on the fabric of assumptions which they challenge, on the quality of the reasoning by which the works she reassigns were previously otherwise ascribed. We reject her claims because we *feel* them to be preposterous, but we do not seem to have developed a logical technique to show their nonsensical quality.

A rationale of ascription will have to be developed if one particular and particularly important authorship problem, that of the four poems in MS Cotton Nero A.x, is to be solved. Whether they are by one or several poets is a matter of some importance to the literary history of the fourteenth century as well as to interpretation of the poems themselves. But the importance of the problem has not brought out the best in those so far attempting it. Discussion has been marred by argument from inaccurate data, such as asserting that an expression or a usage is peculiar to a text or class of texts when it is not so, by ignorance about the practices of alliterative versification, about Middle English grammar, about medieval rhetoric. There is absurd false inference: for example that when a homonym appears with different meanings in two poems those poems must be by different authors. There are other faults of logic. I find an assumption that a conclusive proof one way or another might be afforded by selected classes of data, 'key' data: but in fact it should be apparent that to identify such data effectively one would have to know the answer to the problem. Then there is the fallacy of the authorial composite personality, which appears in arguments for common authorship. This operates as follows. By merely acquiescing in the possibility of common authorship, as one reads the poems one hypothesizes consciously or otherwise an impressionistic construct of the personality and art of a single poet. Thus differences in texture and structure between the four poems can appear as evidence of the poet's versatility, and so on. Then one proffers this construct as proof of common authorship, which of course it is not; correctly repre-sented, it is an individual's judgment that nothing in the authorial personalities suggested by the several poems seems to him repugnant to a hypothesis of common authorship. It can be no more conclusive than an equally plausible presentation of the opposite view would be.

This is not a satisfactory situation. No argument on either side of

this question of common authorship has been so effectively conducted as to amount to a demonstration. Moreover, whether the
issue, one way or another, is in fact susceptible of convincing
demonstration does not seem theoretically determinable to me. How
can we assess the strength of the initial presumption of common
authorship set up by attestation in the same unitary manuscript, in
the same hand, and in the same or a very similar dialect? I would
judge that the tests have not yet been devised. So the immediate
problem of scholarship here is to study these poems effectively in
terms of that major unknown quantity, resisting always the pressure
of what Newman called 'the irritation which suspense occasions.'[18] A
part of that effective study will have to be revaluation of most earlier
work.

Another general class of problems, outstanding in both senses of
the term, is the chronology of Middle English literature. I do not
suggest that this will ever be fully ascertainable. But the problem is
less forbidding if viewed in its several aspects. There are the many
anonyma from all parts of the period, sometimes already crudely
datable from the terminus *a quo* of an identifiable source of known
date, or one *ad quem* of the language or handwriting of the
manuscript where they occur. There are long works like *Piers
Plowman* of which we know the approximate period in which it was
written, and the likeliest sequence of versions, but have not yet
closely dated any version, notwithstanding the numerous evidently
topical references more or less confidently identifiable in each. There
is the matter of the serial dating of many of Chaucer's works within
the canon both absolutely and in relation to the datable works. A
possibility of improvement exists in all these instances. It must begin
with a review of earlier arguments, and since the dating of texts is of
primary importance in literary history, and the literary history of the
English Middle Ages has yet to be well written, there is urgency. A
review, a reassessment must necessarily improve a situation now
characterized for the most part by acquiescence in received dates,
about many of which thinking hardened more than a generation ago.
But there can also be sharpening of detail. A fair amount of new
information applicable to source study, especially of religious texts,
has come to light in the last thirty years; the collections of specimens
of dated vernacular hands available for comparison in the great
libraries grow steadily if unobtrusively; and our lexicographical
information increases, at least in quantity. There is room for

improvement in the use of topicality, to which I shall presently turn. As for the dating of Chaucer, there reassessment will serve best by throwing into prominence the degree to which the traditional calendar of his works rests on subjective judgment, and thus disturbing complacency about his chronology. I strongly suspect that there are datings with no better basis than some forceful scholar's measurement of the works concerned against his *idea* of Chaucer, an *idea*, moreover, directly relatable to that scholar's historically and philosophically conditioned personal background. *The Second Nun's Tale* comes to mind, classed as 'early' because of its 'immaturity of style and the closeness of the translation.'[19] Did the style seem immature—a quality not as far as I know demonstrated—because of feeling that it would have been unenlightened of Chaucer to write a pious work in his middle, let alone later, career?[20]

In this matter of dating Chaucer's poetry the suggestion of authoritative, agreed conclusions reached by the best kind of argument which editorial blandness and the veneer of print convey is gravely misleading. In fact the quality of the argument was often undistinguished; many discussions came nowhere near agreement but simply lapsed; and it could happen that the rhetorical skill of a proponent rather than the excellence of his evidence would establish his opinion. The whole body of evidence for the general sequence of composition on which we base our conception of Chaucer's development as an artist needs to be reconsidered. As far as I know there has been no attempt of real scope on the subject since Tatlock's youthful work in 1907.[21]

One class of evidence for dating medieval literature is topical reference. Topical allegory is of course not peculiar to medieval literature, but it has peculiarly acute importance in our period for dating and indeed interpretation. It has not, on the whole, been successfully used. There is dispute at all stages: sometimes about whether a particular text actually contains a topical allusion, or where the presence of one is accepted, about its reference. The limitations of evidential force when an unmistakable topicality exists in one of several versions of a poem but not in another are sometimes not understood correctly. The status of the *argumentum e silentio* is not correctly appreciated: thus, if Gower had been writing *Miroir de l'Homme* after 1381, he would certainly have mentioned the peasant uprising of that year.[22] There is a presumption that the correspondence of a topical allegory to its reference must be exact, and so because of his youth the Black Knight of *The Book of the Duchess* cannot 'be' John of Gaunt (and so—one might go on to argue—the poem we have cannot be the one Chaucer calls *The Death of Blanche the Duchess*); and a presumption that topical allegory must have single or limited reference, so that Lady Meed in *Piers Plowman* cannot refer to both Alice Perrers and the corrupting power of money; and a presumption that topical allegorization functions rigidly, so that if in a Prologue to *The Legend of Good Women* Alcestis is asked to take the book in which she will figure to the Queen, she cannot also 'be' the Queen' the relationship between topicality and time in a dreamvision poem is misconceived through the presumption that the textual sequence of topical animadversion must necessarily be the same as the historical sequence.

I cannot think where authorization for any such presumptions might be found and it occurs to me that they may either have been carried back from more modern literature, where they might conceivably apply—the close topical correspondences of *Absalom and Achitophel* come to mind—or they can originate in the use of terms like *is* or *is equated with* or *stands for* instead of historically appropriate ones like *suggests, calls to mind*, whereby the user becomes as it were trapped in a system of unhistorical concepts by his ill-chosen vocabulary. The importance of correctly appreciating topical allegory will not be uniform; in some cases it will be secondary, in others (I am thinking of the courtship in *The Parlament of Fowls*) crucial. But every case is a grey area in Middle English scholarship, and they should be clearned up, above all in the understanding that a situation can exist where the presence of topical allegory is unmistakable and where nevertheless its precise reference cannot be recovered. Recognition of such situations should be the minimum of acceptable agreement.

A circumstance contributing to the continued existence of such grey areas has been that information about the detailed history of the period, especially about minor non-political and non-military figures, and about social, political, and religious conditions is scarce or hard to come by quickly. Because of their scope the standard histories contain relatively little such information; they are often too general to be effectively related to works of literature; or else what they say is generalized from those works, and not always expertly; and their detail is subject to challenge, as happened not long ago with respect to the date of Blanche of Lancaster's death.[23] The situation has been improved by some outstanding special studies: Yunck's *Lineage of Lady Meed*,[24] Leff's *Heresy in the Later Middle Ages*,[25] Mann's *Chaucer and Medieval Estates Satire*[26] come to mind; for me at any rate they have illuminated the literature of the late fourteenth century. Now I would like a book of comparable quality on the court and court life in the reigns of Edward III and Richard II, and a biographical dictionary of the minor figures in fourteenth-century England, for the number who did not make the *Dictionary of National Biography* or have come into prominence since its publication is not inconsiderable; and a handbook designed to identify the particulars of historical, legal, and social information needed for the effective study of Middle English literature and to furnish or at least direct me to it. I would—if I may be extravagant—like a history of the English episcopacy in the fourteenth century, if only to discover whether Langland or the author of the relevant Oxford History of England volume was right about it.[27]

But seriously, I believe that the importance of studying Middle English literature, especially that of the fourteenth century, in terms of its contemporary world, in all senses of that expression, can hardly be exaggerated. Medievalists have not just to learn about, but also to keep in constant view, how radically the Middle Ages and their points of reference differ from our own time and its values, lest insights into our common humanity obscure the differences. There is room for improvement: this can range from discouraging unhistorical nonsense like calling the accomplishments of Chaucer's Squire 'lady like,' and checking the tendency to impressionistic or subjective criticism, to deepening understanding of the attitudes of the major poets (I have those bishops in mind). Some of the contribution to this particular need will have come from historians; it is up to us to make them responsive to it. In other cases there could be collaboration between a historian and a literary persons, potentially a very stimulating arrangement.

Beyond the problem of strengthening the historical basis of Middle English studies lies that of writing the literary history of the period. By that I do not mean the kind of writing which achieves little more than a chronologically or otherwise organized succession, presented as discourse, of authors and what is known of their lives, and of literary works, along with descriptive summary accounts of the latter and desultory, often derivative and outmoded critical opinions. The examples of this kind are what have made 'literary history' a

pejorative term. What I have in mind, and what should in my
judgment be our ultimate common objective, to which by any activity
as medievalists we can contribute, is the systematic explanation of the
succession of literary phenomena and classes of phenomena
comprised under the heading Middle English literature. Another
way of seeing this would be as an undertaking to account for the
formation and development of the English literary tradition, in the
understanding that everything written in England (and not necessarily in English), or available for Englishmen to read or hear,
between the Conquest and 1400, had some significant bearing on that
development. We have no literary history of the period in those
senses, and none, I think, in immediate prospect. But it seems to me a
realizable ideal.

To achieve it, that is to enable the effective generalizations
required, the first step must be investigation or reinvestigation and
improved understanding of several large topics. I will specify some
which I have identified.

One is the development of the English verse system ('metre') after
the Conquest. Here I will flatly assert that a fresh approach is called
for, and that it will have to begin with agreement on a system of
notation or anyway on a set of terms, if it is to achieve anything.
There are specific questions to answer. What are the theoretical and
the physical differences between the versification of the early Middle
English lyrics and that of their Provençal models? What is the
explanation for the considerable variety of stanza forms to be found
in Middle English poetry, notably in verse on political and historical
topics? Which came first, the systematic attempts to combine the old
alliterative measure and the naturalized imported one, as in the
Summer Sunday stanza,[28] or the application of the alliterative long
line for written composition? What precisely differentiates Chaucer's
Book of the Duchess line from the French octosyllabic? Does such
difference throw any light on his use of the longer ('decasyllabic')
line? Whose use of that longer line in couplets induced Chaucer to
adopt it? What is the significance of Langland's choice of the
alliterative long line, presuming him to have wanted a national
audience?

There is also need for a new study of the poetry in the alliterative
long line to replace Oakden's book,[29] now virtually obsolete. That
study should begin with re-editing, or at least recollation of a
considerable number of the texts. It should also in any analyses

include allowance for the factor of possible scribal corruption as Oakden did not; this will matter particularly in the use of data from texts uniquely preserved to determine alliterative patterns. And in this study, because of the importance of ready access to statistics about vocabularly usage and word collocations, it would be very desirable, supposing that the programme for dealing with multiple spellings were not too problematic, to have a computerized alphabetical word list and a concordance.

A quite different class of subject calling for a definitive study is *fine amour*. This topic is clouded by uncertainty, and extreme views about it have been expressed in reaction to earlier misconceptions, so that there is even an impression of the misconceptions being about something that did not exist. But they relate to an actual phenomenon: that Andreas is relatively unimportant historically and C. S. Lewis was mainly wrong does not negate it. One knows just enough about it to perceive the complexity of its history of change.[30] *Fine amour* may seem to belong in the province of Romance studies. But for the understanding of Middle English poetry, exposed to its varying influences over at least three centuries, we need the kind of synoptic history which the Romance scholars active in the subject may be too specialized to produce, one concerned particularly with transmission and dissemination. And if the evidence forces upon the historian of *fine amour* as the conclusion of his account Troilus's jibe at lovers, *in nouncertayn ben alle youre observaunces*,[31] that in itself will be a salutary corrective of extreme views.

The last topic I shall mention requiring investigation to promote the writing of the literary history of the Middle English period can be called 'influences.' I have already referred in two connections to that of Provençal poetry; two others of immense importance are those of Anglo-Norman and continental French literature. The situation differs radically in the two cases.

About the influence of Anglo-Norman (later more properly Anglo-French) literature very little has been done. In the individual cases where editors of Middle English texts have been forced to take account of corresponding Anglo-Norman works there has been activity to the extent of carrying out comparisons. But I do not know of any general examination of relationships. There are circumstances which discourage the conduct of one: that Anglo-Norman composition tends to inordinate length; that some Anglo-Norman texts are still unedited; that the to surveys of Anglo-Norman literature written in English offer poor inducement. But in the nature of things there must, during the three centuries from 1100 to John Gower's death, have been not merely Anglo-Norman 'influence,' by the provision of models for composition in English, but also constant interaction. The co-existence in England of two vernaculars which merely on the showing of MS Harley 2253 were by 1300 of equal status at least outside the royal court and its periphery ought to be conclusive evidence that this is a topic worth serious attention.

By contrast the influence of the Middle French poets has received a great deal of attention in the particular respect of what is called Chaucer's 'debt' to them, to the extent that there are now lists of the most minute verbal and notional resemblances. But the activity has not been well conducted. The alleged resemblances have not, as far as I know, been analysed or classified; the terminology used to denote them is often prejudicial; there has been insufficient allowance for the possibility of memorial derivation and of accidental resemblance resulting from use of common sources, or the treatment of similar topics, or of medieval commonplaces. There is resistance to the notion of reciprocal influence. I have no doubt that the derivativeness of Chaucer's early poetry, which in some respects is undeniable, has been exaggerated with regard to specific borrowing of detail. The subject should be reopened; we must not be cowed by the names of Kitteredge and Lowes into taking their assertions on faith or, for that matter, into accepting the suggestion of the density of reference to French sources in Robinson's notes at its face value.

The question of influence should also be considered more broadly in at least two ways. Consideration should be extended beyond identifying resemblances of language or narrative situation to comparison, for instance, of the quality of the sensibility in French and English poems of corresponding topic and kind, and of attitudes assumed by the French and English poets in approximately similar literary situations, and of the quality of tone and of the texture in the two poetries. And it should consider influence not just particular case by case but in the light of all known instances seen together as elements of a selective cultural assimilation. The results might be some generalizations more interesting and significant than the two or three threadbare ones at present available.

It is time now for me to cut short my list, but I have said enough to establish its tenor: that much of our predecessors' work in Middle English scholarship, from which we might think of ourselves as going forward, is poorly based and was not very well conducted; therefore our first understanding problem is reassessment and correction. It has a corollary: that we must not tolerate, in ourselves or others, shortcomings such as have invalidated some previous scholarship.

We must require, in all cases first of ourselves, the highest standards of Middle English grammar and lexicography, never scanting this primary essential because of the demands of other exacting skills upon us. We must neither be confused by massively detailed representations into equating a multiplicity of bad argument with a good one nor proffer arguments characterized by mass or novelty rather than quality. We must both rigorouly observe the logic of inference in our own work and demand its observation of others. We must respect the theorem of inconclusiveness imposed upon medieval scholarship by the anonymity or datelessness of so many of the works we deal with, observing the restriction it imposes on historical and critical activity where unresolved and possibly unresolvable issues are in question. And we must acquire and require such elementary skills in critical thinking as will safeguard both against Bradleian or 'creative' criticism and against critical solecisms like one I read recently, that Troilus's style 'is perfectly consistent with his character even to the extent of revealing some subtle aspects of his motivation.' By such and similar means we may with luck protect our work from being too quickly discredited in its turn, and what matters more, strengthen the tradition of English medieval studies.

Notes*

1 The Autobiographical Fallacy in Chaucer and Langland Studies

1 For a collection of passages where this occurs see M. W. Stearns, 'A Note on Chaucer's Attitude toward Love', *Speculum*, XVII (1942), 570–4.

2 An extended illustration of this conviction that one 'knows' one's author as an actual person is afforded by A. L. Rowse's *William Shakespeare: a Biography* (London, 1963). One instance of how the conviction operates in this book must suffice. Of the sonnets Rowse writes (p. 198), 'there is no doubt that Shakespeare experienced it all: he was too direct and natural, too straight and true a writer for it to be otherwise'.

3 It is the theme of L. Spitzer, 'Note on the Poetic and the Empirical "I" in Medieval Authors', *Traditio*, IV (1946), 414–22, esp. p. 419, f.n., where he applies it to Villon's *Testaments*.

4 G. L. Kittredge, *Chaucer and His Poetry* (Cambridge, Mass., 1915), p. 48.

5 Following the lead given by A. S. Jack, 'The Autobiographical Elements in Piers the Plowman', *JEGP*, III (1901), 393–414. This was taken up by J. M. Manly, 'The Authorship of *Piers Plowman*', *MP*, VII (1909–10), 135ff. For a summary of the discussion see M. W. Bloomfield, 'Present State of *Piers Plowman* Studies', *Speculum*, XIV (1939), 222ff.

6 E.g. by J. S. P. Tatlock, *The Mind and Art of Chaucer* (Syracuse, 1950), p. 30: the dreamer of *The Book of the Duchess* 'is in no sense Chaucer himself'; by K. Malone, *Chapters on Chaucer* (Baltimore, 1951), p. 24: 'Chaucer's love-sickness . . . is not to be taken as genuine. It is a conventional device.'; by B. Kimpel, 'The Narrator of the *Canterbury Tales*', *ELH*, XX (1953), 84: the narrator 'is a literary device'; by J. Lawlor, *Piers Plowman: An Essay in Criticism* (London, 1962), pp. 281, 285.

7 Tatlock, *The Mind and Art of Chaucer*, p. 62; Malone, *op cit.*, p. 55; and cf. D. M. Bevington, 'The Obtuse Narrator in Chaucer's *House of Fame*', *Speculum*, XXXVI (1961), 295.

---

*The absence of uniformity in the reference systems of these notes reflects the various house styles of earlier publishers. I have let them stand to reduce the risk of new error, that is, to protect such accuracy as I initially attained. G.K.

8 Bevington, *loc. cit.*

9 Tatlock, 'The People in Chaucer's *Troilus*', *PMLA*, LVI (1941), 88n. Bevington (*loc. cit.*) refers to 'the poet's own portly stature'.

10 Tatlock, 'The People in Chaucer's *Troilus*', p. 88n; *The Mind and Art of Chaucer*, pp. 17, 65.

11 Tatlock, 'The People in Chaucer's *Troilus*', p. 88n. His opinion receives approval from Stearns, *op. cit.*, p. 571.

12 B. H. Bronson, 'In Appreciation of Chaucer's Parlement of Foules', *University of California Publications in English*, III (1935), 197.

13 M. Galway, 'Chaucer's Sovereign Lady', *MLR*, XXXIII (1938), 145–99, esp. p. 197; 'Chaucer's Hopeless Love', *MLN*, LX (1945), 431–9.

14 Malone, *op. cit.*, pp. 78–9.

15 R. Blenner-Hassett, 'Autobiographical Aspects of Chaucer's Franklin', *Speculum*, XXVIII (1953), 797–8.

16 S. F. Damon, 'Chaucer and Alchemy', *PMLA*, XXXIX (1924), 782–8.

17 J. M. Manly, *Some New Light on Chaucer* (London, 1926), pp. 246–8.

18 R. S. Loomis, 'Chaucer's Eight Years' Sickness', *MLN*, LIX (1944), 178–80.

19 F. N. Robinson, *The Works of Geoffrey Chaucer* (2nd ed., Cambridge, Mass., 1957), p. 793.

20 B. F. Huppé, 'Historical Allegory in the Prologue to the "Legend of Good Women"', *MLR*, XLIII (1948), 393–9. See also W. E. Weese, 'Alceste and Joan of Kent', *MLN*, LXIII (1948), 474–7.

21 *Some New Light on Chaucer*, p. 242.

22 P. Aiken, 'Vincent of Beauvais and Chaucer's Knowledge of Alchemy', *SP*, XLI (1944), 371–89.

23 A. H. Bright, *New Light on 'Piers Plowman'* (Oxford, 1928); and see also his 'Langland and the Seven Deadly Sins', *MLR*, XXV (1930), 133–9.

24 Lawlor's care in this respect deserves to be noticed. See, e.g. *op. cit.*, pp. 281, 285, 313, 319.

25 J. R. Hulbert, '*Piers the Plowman* after Forty Years', *MP*, XLV (1947–8), 221.

26 Lawlor, *op. cit.*, p. 315.

27 For discussion of these see Bloomfield, *op. cit.*, p. 223.

28 Malone, *op. cit.*, p. 27.

29 Kimpel, *op. cit.*, p. 85.

30 B. H. Bronson, *In Search of Chaucer* (Toronto, 1960), p. 30.

31 W. W. Lawrence, *Chaucer and the Canterbury Tales* (Oxford, 1950), p. 28.

32 J. R. Kreuzer, 'The Dreamer in the *Book of the Duchess*', *PMLA*, LXVI (1951), 547.

33 B. H. Bronson, '*The Book of the Duchess* Re-opened', *PMLA*, LXVII (1952), 878.

34 *Ibid.*

35 C. A. Owen, 'The Role of the Narrator in the "Parlement of Foules"', *College English*, xiv (1952–3), 265.

36 R. Baldwin, *The Unity of the Canterbury Tales* (Copenhagen, 1955), p. 67.

37 S. Manning, 'That Dreamer Once More', *PMLA*, lxxi (1956), 541.

38 Bronson, '*The Book of the Duchess* Re-opened', p. 871.

39 Kimpel, *op. cit.*, p. 86.

40 H. Lüdeke, *Die Funktionen des Erzählers in Chaucers epischer Dichtung, Studien zur Englischen Philologie*, lxxii (Halle, 1928); R. Crosby, 'Oral Delivery in the Middle Ages', *Speculum*, xi (1936), 88–110; 'Chaucer and the Custom of Oral Delivery', *Speculum*, xiii (1938), 413–32; H. J. Chaytor, *From Script to Print* (Cambridge, 1945), ch. vi, 115ff.

41 E. Faral, *Les Arts Poétiques du XIIe et du XIIIe Siècle* (Paris, 1924), p. 259.

42 There seems no real need to insist that a medieval poet would wish to do this. But see B. H. Bronson, 'Chaucer's Art in Relation to His Audience', *University of California Publications in English*, viii (1940), 15.

43 Lüdeke, *op. cit.*, pp. 145–6.

44 I am aware that the accuracy of this statement is not specifically demonstrable with respect to Chaucer and Langland. But I cannot envisage any other situation. Of Chaucer at any rate there is a reasonable presumption that his patrons and public were to be found at court. About Langland's patrons we know nothing, but to me his poetry seems too hard to have earned him much of a living in the market place. Its nature and quality, in my opinion, imply an educated and intelligent audience, and therefore, presumably, one which (unless he had independent means) in some way maintained the poet.

45 J. W. H. Atkins, *English Literary Criticism: The Medieval Phase* (London, 1952), p. iii; E. R. Curtius, *European Literature and the Latin Middle Ages* (London, 1953), pp. 452, 455.

46 I have in mind the authorial profession of humility discussed by J. Schwietering, *Die Demutsformel Mittelhochdeutscher Dichter* (Berlin, 1921), and the classical method of satirization called *memorabilia*. An attempt to identify the latter in *Piers Plowman* can be found in J. Martin, 'Wil as Fool and Wanderer in *Piers Plowman*', *Texas Studies in Literature and Language*, iii (1962), 535–48.

47 The important generalizations by Spitzer must be most carefully qualified with respect to the dream-vision. For instance the assertion, 'we must assume that the medieval public saw in the 'poetic I' a representative of mankind, that it was interested only in this representative rôle of the poet,' (*op. cit.*, pp. 415–16) would apply to many dream-vision poems only in the second instance, to the extent that it is true of all medieval literature.

48 Support for these statements will be found in G. Kane, *Piers Plowman: The Evidence for Authorship* (London, 1965), pp. 53ff.

49 'Robert or William Longland?', *London Mediæval Studies*, I (1948 for 1939), 437ff.

50 Faral, *op. cit.*, p. 151.

51 Thus Bronson's anxiety ('*The Book of the Duchess* Re-opened', p. 878) about a Chaucerian audience being 'misled' would be met.

52 The existence of this kind of involvement has, of course, been recognized, e.g. by C. A. Owen, *op. cit.*, pp. 267, 269, and notably by E. T. Donaldson, 'Chaucer the Pilgrim', *PMLA*, LXIX (1954), 928–36, esp. p. 935. Bronson's dissenting view (*In Search of Chaucer*, p. 28), seems to result from treating the relation between Chaucer and his narrator out of the context of medieval narrative; I would call his argument by reference to *Gulliver's Travels* anachronistic.

53 Martin, *op. cit.*, p. 535.

54 Spitzer, *op. cit.*, p. 416.

55 *Ibid.*, p. 421.

56 Bronson, *In Search of Chaucer*, p. 67.

57 As Chambers ('Robert or William Longland?', pp. 450–60) maintained.

2 Chaucer and the Idea of a Poet

1 '*The English Works of John Gower*', ed. G. C. Macaulay, II. *EETS* Extra Series LXXXII, London, 1901, p. 466, lines 2941*–7*.

2 *Prologue to the Legend of Good Women* in *The Works of Geoffrey Chaucer*, ed. F. N. Robinson, Second Edition, Cambridge, Mass., 1957, p. 492, lines F422; 423; G410, 411.

3 *Le Dit de La Panthère d'Amours*, ed. H. A. Todd, *SATF*, Paris, 1883, pp. 31 ff.

4 *Oeuvres Complètes de Eustache Deschamps*, VII, ed. G. Raynaud, SATF, Paris, 1891, pp. 266–92.

5 *Op. cit.*, pp. 270–2.

6 *Op. cit.*, p. 266.

7 H. Schless, '*Transformations: Chaucer's Use of Italian*', in *Geoffrey Chaucer*, ed. D. Brewer, London, 1974, pp. 184–223.

8 Guillaume de Machaut, '*Le Livre du Voir Dit*', ed. P. Paris, *Société des Bibliophiles François*, Paris, 1875, pp. 223, 224.

9 *Op. cit.*, pp. xiv, xxviii–xxxi, and G. Cohen, '*Le Voir Dit* de Guillaume de Machaut', *Les Lettres Romanes*, I, 1947, pp. 99–111.

10 *Le Voir Dit*, pp. xix–xxvii. See also 'Dictionnaire de Biographie Française', ed. J. Balteau *et al.*, III, Paris, 1939, pp. 742, 743, and Cohen, *op. cit.*, p. 100.

11 For a more recent affirmation of the same view see Cohen, *op. cit.*, p. 111.

12 *Le Voir Dit*, p. 189.

13 *Op. cit.*, p. 186, and compare p. 195.

14 *Op. cit.*, p. 135.

15 *Op. cit.*, p. 119.

16 *Op. cit.*, p. 209. Compare *Chanterai por mon corage*, lines 51–6, in J. Bédier and P. Aubry, *Les Chansons de Croisade*, repr. New York, 1971, p. 114.

17 E. Hoepffner, ed., 'Oeuvres de Guillaume de Machaut'. *SATF*, Paris, 1908, I, pp. xix–xxi.

18 *Le Voir Dit*, pp. 155, 156.

19 *Op. cit.*, pp. 110, 111.

20 *Op. cit.*, p. 184, for example.

21 *Op. cit.*, p. 348.

22 J. Wimsatt, 'Chaucer and French Poetry', in Brewer, *Geoffrey Chaucer*, p. 119.

23 *Le Voir Dit*, p. 102 and compare p. 68. The Chaucer poem in question is ' Merciles Beaute ', III, *Sin I fro Love escaped am so fat*, in "Works", p. 542.

24 T. Wright, 'Political Poems and Songs', *Rolls Series* XIV, I, p. 325, and 'The Political Songs of England from the Reign of John to that of Edward II,' Camden Society VI, London, 1839, p. 142.

25 See D. Schueler, 'Age of the Lover in Gower's Confessio Amantis', *Medium AEvum* XXXVI, 1967, p. 155.

26 v 160, 312 in G. Kane and E. T. Donaldson, ed. *Piers Plowman: The B Version*, London, 1975, pp. 315, 326. The Armentières in question is near Lille in the Département du Nord, in territory that was ceded to the Count of Flanders by the French king in 1369 (E. Perroy, *The Hundred Years War*, London, 1965, p. 154). The other two are in Eure and Marne. Peronelle's name of origin appears to derive from the last ('Dictionnaire de Biographie', p. 742). Langland could hardly have known this.

27 See *Le Voir Dit*, pp. 27, 28.

28 *Works*, p. 226, lines 212–20.

29 *Op. cit.*, p. 124, lines 2188–2202.

3 Chaucer, Love Poetry and Romantic Love

1 This venture into alien literary history is a gesture of gratitude to E. Talbot Donaldson for his 'Myth of Courtly Love' (*Ventures* 5[1965]: 16–23), which shocked me out of slothful acquiescence in the received opinions about the subject and set me trying to find out for myself. Other things apart I found that curiosity about the subject is no novelty. Here is John Gower anticipating Jean Frappier (note 25 below): *De fin amour qui voet savoir l'istoire/Il falt q'il sache et bien et mal suffrir;/Plus est divers qe l'en ne porra croire.* (*Balades*, XLVII, 15–18, in *The Complete Works of John Gower, The French Works*, ed. G. C. Macaulay, Oxford, 1899, p. 375).

2 Roger Boase, *The Origin and Meaning of Courtly Love: A Critical Study of European Scholarship* (Manchester: Manchester University Press, 1977), pp. 129, 130.

3 *LGWP* F544, G534. Chaucer references are to *The Works of Geoffrey Chaucer*, ed. F. N. Robinson, 2d ed. (Boston: Houghton Mifflin Co., 1957).

4 Fol. 102*b*, col. *b*, line 37. The passage is printed in J. A. W. Bennett and G. Smithers, *Early Middle English Verse and Prose*, 2d ed. (Oxford: Clarendon Press, reprint ed., 1974), p. 50, line 268. And see *MED* s.v. *amour* n.(1)(c). This use takes away some of the force of Jean Frappier's argument in *Amour courtois et table ronde* (Geneva: Droz, 1973), p. 96, that we should reserve *fine amor 'à la sacralisation que l'on sait d'un amour en principe adultère.'* The marriage of Floris and Blauncheflor was made, it could be said, in heaven.

5 *Can vei la lauzeta mover*, lines 9, 10, in Moshé Lazar, ed., *Bernard de Ventadour . . . Chansons d'Amour* (Paris: Klincksieck, 1966), p. 180.

6 *Poets of the Minnesang*, ed. Oliver Sayce (Oxford: Clarendon Press, 1967), p. 95. For a translation of the poem see *Walther von der Vogelweide, Sprüche, Lieder, der Leich*, ed. P. Stapf (Wiesbaden: Vollmer, n.d.), pp. 306–11.

7 *RR* 4703ff.

8 *TC* 1.232–59.

9 See for example, Frappier, *Amour courtois et table ronde*, pp. 13, 15, 21, 22, 29, 30, and especially 93, 94. Frappier's essays seem to me the most authoritative writing on the subject.

10 Many of these were actually copied in Italy. See J. H. Marshall, *The Transmission of Troubadour Poetry*, Inaugural Lecture Delivered at Westfield College (University of London), 1975, p. 5. There is a traditional opinion that Chaucer is unlikely to have known Provençal; for a contrary view see Robert M. Estrich, 'A Possible Provençal Source for Chaucer's *Hous of Fame*, 300–310,' *MLN* 55 (1940): 342–9.

11 See P. Meyer, 'Mélanges de poésie Anglo-Normande', *Romania* 4 (1875): 374–80; and M. Dominica Legge, *Anglo-Norman Literature and Its Background* (Oxford: Clarendon Press, 1963), pp. 33–61.

12 See Patricia Thomson, 'The 'Canticus Troili': Chaucer and Petrarch,' *CL* 11 (1959): 318–28.

13 Bertran de Born, *Domna, puois de me no·us chal*, lines 67, 68, in Albert Stimming, ed., *Bertran von Born: Sein Leben und seine Werke* (Geneva: Slatkine Reprints, 1975), p. 120.

14 Here is the answer to the question put by Giraut de Bornelh nearly a century after Guillaume in a poem of regret for the decay, as he saw it, of an ideal courtly world: '*Don es lo tortz issitz/D'elas malrazonar/No sai.— De cals, d'elas o dels amans?*' ('Where the crime of speaking ill of ladies has come from I do not know. From whom, themselves or the lovers?') *Per solatz revelhar*, lines 37–9, in Adolf Kolsen, ed., *Sämtliche Lieder des*

Trobadors Giraut de Bornelh (Halle: Niemeyer, 1910), 1.416. It was, so to speak, an original sin of the cult.

15 '*Qui vid anc mais penedensa/faire denan lo pechat?/On plus la prec, plus m'es dura;/mas si'n breu tems no·s melhura,/vengut er al partimen.*' *Lo tems vai e ven e vire*, lines 31–5, in Lazar, *Chansons d'amour*, pp. 233–4. Compare Walther, *Poets of the Minnesang*, p. 96, lines 15–19: '*Frowe, ich trage ein teil ze swære:/wellest du mir helfen, sōhilf an der zīt./sī aber ich dir gar unmære,/daz sprich endeliche; sōlāz ich den strīt,/unde wirde ein ledic man.*' ('Lady, the share I am carrying is too heavy. If you are willing to help me, help in good time. But if I mean nothing at all to you, say that once and for all. Then I shall give up the effort, and become a free man.')

16 *Poésies complètes du troubadour Peire Cardenal (1180–1278)*, ed. René Lavaud (Toulouse: Privat, 1957), pp. 2–5.

17

De totz los bens qu'en amor so,/ai ieu ara calque plazer,/car ieu ai mes tot mon esper,/mon penssar e m'entencio/en amar dompna coind'e bella,/ e soi amatz d'una piucella,/e quan trob soudadeira gaia,/deporte mi cossi que·m plaia;/e par tant non son meins cortes/ad amor si la part en tres./Amors vol ben que per razo/eu am mi donz per mais valer,/et am piucella per tener;/e sobre tot qe·m sia bo/s'ab toseta de prima sella,/qand es frescheta e novella,/don no·m cal temer que ja·m traia,/m'aizine tant que ab lieis jaia/un ser o dos de mes en mes,/per pagar ad Amor lo ces. Amors m'envida e·m somo, lines 11–33, in A. H. Schutz, ed., *Poésies de Daude de Pradas* (Toulouse: Privat, 1933), pp. 70–1.

De Pradas is rarely anthologized or discussed. I first came upon this poem in the Estrich article referred to above (note 10). Schutz grouped it with 'Chansons Plaisantes ou Satiriques,' and John Newton, in 'Clio and Venus: An Historical View of Medieval Love', called it a 'humorous song'. F. X. Newman, ed., *The Meaning of Courtly Love* (Albany, N.Y.: SUNY Press, 1968), p. 33. But a fairly recent history of Provençal literature does not credit de Pradas with a sense of humour: '*Son expression amoureuse est d'une simplicité, d'une banalité qui n'engagent jamais l'homme.*' R. Lafont and C. Anatole, *Nouvelle Histoire de la Littérature Occitane* (Paris: Presses Universitaires de France, 1970), 1.137.

18 They were quoted out of context by A. J. Denomy, *The Heresy of Courtly Love* (Gloucester, Mass.: Peter Smith, 1947; reprint ed., 1965), p. 24.

19 Jean Leclercq et al., eds., *Sermones super Cantica Canticorum 1–35, S. Bernardi Opera* (Rome: Editiones Cistercienses, 1957), 1.144.

20 See John Fox, *A Literary History of France: The Middle Ages* (London: Benn, 1974), pp. 121–8, 180–3.

21 See note 11 above. C. B. West, in *Courtoisie in Anglo-Norman Literature* (Oxford: Blackwell, 1938), pp. 123–9, allowed the possibility but discounted the likelihood of much direct Provençal influence in England in

favour of Northern France. By whichever channel, Gower's *Cinkante Balades* (ibid., p. 123) in all particulars of content as distinct from form and organization read like an early-thirteenth-century period piece.

22 See Theo Stemmler, *Die Englischen Liebsgedichte des MS. Harley 2253* (Bonn: Universitätsbibliothek, 1962). This remarkable dissertation seems a conclusive demonstration of Chaytor's proposal of direct Provençal influence on the early English lyric: H. J. Chaytor, *The Troubadours and England* (Cambridge: Cambridge University Press, 1923), passim.

23 *The Fair Maid of Ribblesdale*, lines 83–5, in G. L. Brook, *The Harley Lyrics* (Manchester: Manchester University Press, 1948), p. 39. Chaytor (*The Troubadours and England*, pp. 115–16) quotes this passage with Provençal analogues.

24 Compare Frappier, *Amour courtois et table ronde*, p. 95; Fox, *A Literary History of France*, pp. 123, 124.

25 Compare Frappier, *Amour courtois et table ronde*, p. 93:

'*On n'interprète Jaufré Rudel ou Bernard de Ventadour en dissertant sur Guillaume de Machaut, sur Chaucer ou sur Charles d'Orléans, comme si du XIIe siècle à la fin du Moyen Age il s'agissait toujours du même 'amour courtois'. A l'intérieur de ce concept global et trop flottant, il faut savoir discerner d'assez nombreuses variétés.*'

Frappier's discussion of Andreas (pp. 81–7) is a much-needed corrective of earlier opinions, especially that of C. S. Lewis, about the importance of *De amore*.

26 See, e.g., ibid., pp. 15, 28–30.

27 Ibid, pp. 13, 14, 94.

28 Ibid., pp. 17–19, 21.

29 Ibid., pp. 13, 14, 81.

30 A stage in such a devaluation might be the 'satirical romance.' See the discussion of *De Guillaume au Faucon* and *Flamenca* by S. N. Brody: 'The Comic Rejection of Courtly Love,' in *In Pursuit of Perfection: Courtly Love in Medieval Literature*, ed. Joan M. Ferrante and George D. Economou (Port Washington, N.Y.: Kennikat Press, 1975), pp. 238–46.

31 Frappier, *Amour courtois et table ronde*, pp. 13, 16–18, 21, 22.

32 The revelation comes at line 10535. Guillaume de Lorris et Jean de Meun, *Le Roman de la Rose*, ed. Félix Lecoy (Paris: Champion, 1970), 2.71.

33 *Donna me prega, perch'eo voglio dire*, lines 21ff., in Guido Favati, ed., *Guido Cavalcanti: Le Rime* (Milan: Ricciardi, 1957), p. 214; ibid., p. 305.

34 Conon de Béthune, the last of the conscious imitators of the troubadours, died about 1220; and the most notable thirteenth-century practitioner of *fine amour* poetry, Thibaut de Champagne, in 1253.

35 Daniel Poirion, *Le Poète et Le Prince: L'évolution du lyrisme courtois de Guillaume de Machaut à Charles d'Orléans* (Paris: Presses Universitaires de France, 1965), p. 192.

36 Poirion (Ibid., pp. 195ff.) argues in extenuation that Machaut wrote relatively little complimentary verse to his patrons. But the subservience is implicit in his having written the kind of poetry they and their ladies wanted in the times he lived in.

37 Guillaume de Machaut, *Le Livre du Voir Dit*, ed. P. Paris (Geneva: Slatkine; reprint ed., 1969), p. 61. On the court poet as a lover see, e.g., Normand Cartier, 'Le Bleu Chevalier de Froissart et Le Livre de la Duchesse de Chaucer,' *Romania* 88 (1967): 241–2.

38 Poirion, *Le Poète et Le Prince*, pp. 199–205, in a both judicious and sympathetic discussion of *Le Voir Dit*, is hard put to it to bring Machaut out of the matter well. His perorations on pp. 200 and 205 are more ingenious than convincing, and, as far as Chaucer's reading of *Le Voir Dit* goes, are totally anachronistic. See above, pp. 26–30.

39 *LGW* F 546, G 536. In G, incidentally, Alceste is not *kalender . . . To any woman that wol lover bee* (lines 542–3) but *calendier . . . Of goodnesse* (lines 533–4).

40 Here is Gustave Cohen in a 1951 broadcast on Radio Française: "'Le Voir Dit" *a, comme son nom l'indique, l'accent même de la vérité, le son passionné et un peu triste de la dernière aventure d'un barbon amoureux d'une audacieuse'. La Poèsie en France au Moyen-Age* (Paris: Richard-Masse, 1952), p. 100.

41 See Alfred David, 'Literary Satire in the *House of Fame*', *PMLA* 75 (1960): 335. The most notable particular is Chaucer's profession of un-aptness for or inexperience in love. See *House of Fame* 612–40, *Parliament of Fowls* 157–68, and especially *TC* 2.13 and 3.43, 44, where he uses the actual term *sentement* of Machaut's *Qui de sentement ne fait* (see note 37). In *Prologue to the Legend of Good Women* Alcestis represents the Dreamer as not wanting to be a lover (F 490, G 480). The profession of inexperience seems to have amused Chaucer; note how the Squire, that '*lovyere*' . . . '*fressh as is the month of May*,' deploys it as a *recusatio* in his tale (F 278–82).

42 *Les Chansons de Conon de Béthune*, ed. A. Wallensköld (Paris: Champion, 1921), pp. 17–18.

43 Pierre Bec, *La Lyrique française au Moyen Age* (XIIe–XIIIe siècles), vol. 2 (Paris: Picard, 1978), 2.60–1, 63–4.

44 Ibid., vol. 1 (Paris: Picard, 1977), pp. 122–3.

45 Collected in Karl Bartsch, ed., *Romances et pastourelles françaises de XIIe et XIIIe siècles* (Leipzig, 1870; reprint ed., Wissenschaftliche Buchgesellschaft, 1975), vol. 1, *Romanzen*, pp. 3ff.

46 Specimens are to be found in Bec, *La Lyrique française*, 2.13–20.

47 Collected in J. Bédier and P. Aubry, *Les Chansons de Croisade* (Paris: Champion, 1909; reprint ed., New York, 1971).

48 There are two very different specimens in Bec, *La Lyrique française*, 2.20–2.

49 See R. H. Robbins, ed., *Secular Lyrics of the XIVth and XVth Centuries* (Oxford: Clarendon Press, 1952), pp. 18–25.

50 The scholarship of Chaucer still lacks an informed, disinterested and synoptic study of his relation to Ovid.

51 *MED* s.v. *binden*, v., 3, 4, 5, 11.

52 For the notion that the operation of the intellect is disturbed by love see, e.g., *On the Properties of Things: John Trevisa's translation of Bartholomeus Anglicus De Proprietatibus Rerum I* (Oxford: Clarendon Press, 1975), pp. 101, 102.

53 *Bo* 2, m. 8, lines 13–16, translating '*Hanc rerum seriem ligat/Terras ac pelagus regens/Et caelo imperitans amor*' (*Boethius . . . The Consolation of Philosophy, with an English Translation by S. J. Tester* (Cambridge, Mass.: Loeb Classical Library, new ed., 1973), p. 226, lines 12–15).

54 *MED* s.vv. *kinde*, n., 5b; *laue*, n., 2, 3.

55 *MED* s.v. *kinde*, n. 8 (*a*): 'Nature as a source of living things . . . often personified.' The Trevisa quotations are especially good instances of that meaning.

56 *MED* s.v. 8(*c*).

57 *Adan, mout fu Aristotes sachans*, lines 5–6, in A. Langfors et al., eds., *Recueil général des jeux-partis français*, SATF (Paris: Champion, 1926), 2.63.

58 See R. W. King, 'A note on 'Sir Gawain and the Green Knight,' 2414ff.,' *MLR* 29 (1934): 435, 436.

59 Thomas Brinton, *The Sermons of Thomas Brinton, Bishop of Rochester (1373–89)*, ed. Sister Mary Aquinas Devlin (London: Camden, 3d ser., no. 86, 1954), vol. 2, sermon 69, p. 318; sermon 54, p. 245: '. . .*non est nacio sub celo ita de adulterio diffamata sicut nacio Anglicana*'. Compare what Alcestis says to the Dreamer in the Prologue to the *Legend* about men who *do nat but assayen/How many women they may doon a shame;/ For in youre world that is now holde a game* (F 487–9, G 477–9).

60 *The Physician's Tale*, of course.

61 *Second Nun's Tale* 8.156, 231.

4 The Liberating Truth: The Concept of Integrity in Chaucer's Writings

1 Charles Muscatine, *Poetry and Crisis in the Age of Chaucer*, Notre Dame, 1972.

2 Alfred David, *The Strumpet Muse: Art and Morals in Chaucer's Poetry*, Bloomington, 1976. See esp. pp. 36, 239.

3 Since writing this lecture I have found most welcome support for my position in an essay by the late Rosemary Woolf, 'Moral Chaucer and Kindly Gower', in *J. R. R. Tolkien, Scholar and Storyteller: Essays in Memoriam*, eds. Mary Salu and Robert T. Farrell, Ithaca, 1979, pp.

221–45. There is also George R. Stewart, 'The Moral Chaucer', in *Essays in Criticism by Members of the Department of English*, University of California, Berkeley, 1929, pp. 91–109.

4 See pp. 50 ff., and notes 16, 17.

5 See for example Normand Cartier, '*Le Bleu Chevalier* de Foissart et *Le Livre de la Duchesse* de Chaucer', pp. 241f.

6 IV 1505, and compare 1491ff. Chaucer references are to *The Works of Geoffrey Chaucer*, ed. F. N. Robinson, 2nd edn, Cambridge, Mass, 1957.

7 See for instance Judson B. Allen, *The Friar as Critic*, Nashville, 1971, p. 60 n. 18 and below, p. 264, n. 20.

8 This is clear from the friar's use of the name as a term of discredit in *It is but a dido, . . . a disours tale*, in XIII 172. *Piers Plowman* references are to G. Kane and E. T. Donaldson, *Piers Plowman: the B Version*, London, 1975, unless otherwise indicated.

9 Beryl Smalley, *English Friars and Antiquity in the Early Fourteenth Century*, Oxford, 1960, pp. 130, 131. It is intriguing to speculate what Chaucer, if he read Boccaccio's De *Genealogia*, made of that man's attempt to justify Vergil's invention (Charles G. Osgood, ed. and transl., *Boccaccio on Poetry*, New York, repr. 1956, pp. 67–9).

10 Beryl Smalley, *The Study of the Bible in the Middle Ages*, Oxford, 1941, pp. 216, 217; Allen, *The Friar as Critic*, pp. 58, 59.

11 Smalley, op. cit., p. 217.

12 See for example *Piers Plowman* B Prol. 60, 61; x 197; XIII 75; XIX 221; xx 125, 368.

13 III 1919, 1920 I ne have no text of it, as I suppose,
But I shal fynde it in a maner glose.

14 Sydney Armitage-Smith, *John of Gaunt*, London, 1964, pp. 460, 461, adduces evidence which suggests that Gaunt fathered a daughter on a maid of honour of Queen Philippa either before or during his marriage to Blanche of Lancaster. He argues for the earlier event, but either interpretation would support my point.

15 G. Kane, *Piers Plowman: the A Version*, London, 1960, I 132 (B I 145); IV 101 (B IV 114); VII 62 (B VI 68) where the word has the sense of *O.E.D. Truth*, sb. 9b, 'Conduct in accordance with the divine standard; spirituality of life and behaviour'. This use is frequent in B where once (I 131) *truþe þat is þe beste* actually replaces A's *perfite werkis* (I 120). The *Dictionary*'s earlier *Cursor Mundi* citation under s.v. 4, 'Disposition to speak or act truly or without deceit; truthfulness, veracity, sincerity; formerly sometimes in wider sense: Honesty, uprightness, righteousness, virtue, integrity', is mistaken. This use refers to the Deity, and would belong with the one in *Pearl* 495, *al is trawþe þat he con dresse* (*Pearl*, ed. E. V. Gordon, Oxford, 1953, p. 18). The meaning here is of

an infinite quality of God and belongs in a classification where there is no
implication of a possibility of moral deficiency.

16 Instances are B vi 96; xiii 359; xv 310; xix 194.

17 The uses occur at B xi 152, 156, 159(i), 162, 164; xii 287, 290, 292. The
meaning here is a contextual specialization of *O.E.D.* s.v. 4, 'Honesty,
uprightness, . . . integrity', synonymous with *soopnesse* in xi 147, the
quality for which the 'righteous heathen' Trajan was saved.

18 See note 15 above for examples.

19 *O.E.D.* s.v. 8, but the example there cited belongs under 9b:

> to louen þi lord leuere þan þiselue;
> No dedly synne to do, deye þei3 þow sholdest,
> This I trowe be truþe, B i 143–5

'This, I am confident, is spirituality of life and behaviour.' More satisfactory examples, however, occur at B iv 157; v 277; xv 414; xx 161.

20 *O.E.D.* s.v. 9a: see A vii 94 (B viii 112). Langland also allegorizes this
sense, as in A ii 86 (B ii 122) and notably in B xix 261, 333, and xx 53, 56.

21 *O.E.D.* s.v. 10b; cp. e.g. A i 97, 122.

22 For example, the enlargement of the meaning of *trouthe* and its acquisi-
tion of status as an abstract term appear from Chaucer's use of it in
Lenvoy de Chaucer a Bukton (*Works* p. 539) as a doublet for
sothfastnesse. *Sothfastnesse* is his term for translating the philosophical
abstraction *veritas* or *verite* in *Boece* and *Melibee*, with only one exception (*of ful sad trouthe* for *solidissimae veritatis* in *Boece* v pr. 6, 169).
This exception, and his use of *trouthe* in glosses (iii metre ii, 16, 22 and iv
metre i, 16: with the last, *of cleer trouthe*, compare *of cler sothfastnesse*
for *perspicuae veritatis* in iv pr. 4, 185) support the appearance.
Langland's equivalent to *sothfastnesse*, which he uses only once in B, of
the Second Person of the Trinity (xvi 186) is *soopnesse*, generally in
personified abstraction, but once (xi 147) to denote the *trouthe* for which
Trajan was saved. In *Sir Gawain and the Green Knight trawþe* once
unmistakably signifies an elaborately conceived wholeness of
personality, 'integrity', but with a markedly religious and specifically
devotional quality (*Sir Gawain and the Green Knight*, ed. J. R. R.
Tolkien and E. V. Gordon, 2nd edn, rev. Norman Davis, Oxford, 1967,
p. 18, lines 625ff.) In *Confessio Amantis trouthe*, variously the philosophical abstraction and its realization in personal integrity, is the
principal virtue—*lief To god and ek to man also*—commended by
Aristotle to Alexander,

> For if men scholde trouthe seche
> And founde it not withinne a king
> It were an unsittende thing.
> The word is tokne of that withinne.

(*The English Works of John Gower*, ed. G. C. Macaulay, II, EETSES 82, London, 1901, VII, 1723ff.) This is the *trouthe* Richard is enjoined to cherish in the envoy to *Lak of Stedfastnesse* (*Works*, p. 537). The subject is touched by Willi Héracourt, '*What is trouthe or soothfastnesse?*', *Englische Kultur in sprachwissenschaftlicher Deutung, Max Deutschbein zum 60. Geburtstag*, Leipzig, 1936, pp. 75–84, and by Geoffrey Shepherd, 'Make Believe: Chaucer's Rationale of Storytelling in *The House of Fame*', in *J. R. R. Tolkien, Scholar and Storyteller*, pp. 216, 17.

23 I have not come upon discussion of this conception as such in the ancient philosophers, though it seems likely to have existed. Seneca once refers to *religio, pietas, iustitia et omnis alius comitatus virtutum consertarum et inter se cohaerentium* (*L. Annaei Senecae ad Lucilivm Epistvlae Morales*, ed. L. D. Reynolds, Oxford, 1965, II, p. 332, lines 2, 3). Horace's *integer vitae scelerisque purus* (*Q. Horati Flacci Opera*, ed. H. W. Garrod, Oxford, 1912, Odes I, 22 line 1) comes to mind and looks like a reflection of Stoic teaching, but his lexicographer disappointingly glosses *integer* here *pius, innocens* (Dominicus Bo, *Lexicon Horatianum*, I, A–K, Hildesheim, 1965). The conception is occasionally suggested in the twelfth-century compilation of maxims mainly from Cicero's *De Officiis* and *Seneca's De Beneficiis* called *Moralium Dogma Philosophorum*, of which at least 15 Latin and two French manuscripts have survived in England. (John Holmberg, ed., *Das Moralium Dogma Philosophorum des Guillaume de Conches*, Uppsala, 1929, and see J. R. Williams, 'The Quest for the Author of the *Moralium Dogma Philosophorum*', *Speculum* XXXII, 1957, pp. 736–47 and Richard Hazelton, 'Chaucer's *Parson's Tale* and the *Moralium Dogma Philosophorum*', *Traditio* XVI, 1960, pp. 255–74.

24 St Thomas Aquinas, *Summa Theologiæ*, vol. 13, ed. and transl. Edmund Hill, New York, 1964, Ia 94,2, pp. 92, 93: '*Anima enim hominis in statu innocentiæ erat corpori perficiendo et gubernando accommodata, sicut et nunc; unde dicitur primus homo factus fuisse in animam viventem, id est corpori vitam dantem, scilicet animalem. Sed hujus vitæ integritatem habebat, inquantum corpus erat totaliter animæ subditum in nullo ipsam impediens.*' The translator notes, 'The English word 'integrity' has come to have a sense too restricted to morals, and a limited corner of morals at that, to serve to translate *integritas* in this context.'

25 *Summa Theologiæ*, vol. 26, ed. and transl. T. C. O'Brien, New York, 1965, Ia2æ, 82,1, pp. 30, 31. *Works*, p. 493.

26 *Prologue to the Legend of Good Women* G 414, *Works*, p. 493.

27 Verses 21–4: '*Inuenio igitur legem, volenti mihi facere bonum, quoniam mihi malum adiacet: condelector enim legi Dei secundum interiorem hominem: video autem aliam legem in membris meis, repugnantem legi mentis meæ, & captiuantem me in lege peccati, quæ est in membris meis. Infelix ego homo, quis me liberabit de corpore mortis huius?*' The con-

nexion with original sin appears in the *Glossa Ordinaria: 'Secundum interiorem*. Ambrosius. *Quia caro ex adam traducitur peccatum in se habet; si anima traduceretur et ipsa haberet, quia anima ade peccaui. Si vero anima peccatum in se haberet, homo non se cognosceret.'* and in the *Postilla*: '*Quoniam mihi malum adiacet. quia magis promptus est homo ad perficiendum malum in opere quam bonum, propter corruptionem nature.'* (*Biblia Sacra Cum Glossa Ordinaria Walafridi aliorumque et interlineari Anselmi Laudunensis*, Basel, Froben and Petri, 1498, vol. vi.

28 John viii 32: '*Si vos manseritis in sermone meo, vere discipuli mei eritis, et cognoscetis veritatem, et veritas liberabit vos.'*

29 Nicholas de Lyra, *Postilla* on John xviii 38, *Quid est veritas?*: '*Non querit diffinitionem veritatis set querit que est illa veritas cuius virtute et participatione homines efficiuntur de regno christi. Intellexit enim per hoc in quodam generali aliquid dominium existens extra communem modum hominum. Et hoc est verum si intelligatur determinate et magis in particulari: quia veritas diuina filio appropriatur. Veritas per quam homines in presenti efficiuntur de regno Christi est quedam impressio et participatio veritatis diuine.*'

30 *Ioannis Saresberiensis Episcopi Carnotensis Metalogicon*, ed. Clemens C. Webb, Oxford, 1929, iv, 39, 942a lines 3–7: '*Est autem primeua ueritas in maiestate diuina. Alia uero est, que in diuinitatis consistit imagine, id est in imitatione. Omnis enim res tanto uerius est, quanto imaginem Dei fidelius exprimit; et quanto ab ea magis deficit, tanto falsius euanescit.*'

31 John xviii 38 and *Lenvoy de Chaucer a Bukton*, line 2, *Works*, p. 539. Chaucer's apparently frivolous use of a scriptural quotation here should not suggest lack of respect for its subject. Compare Dante echoing Luke xxiii 46 and Psalm xxx 6 in the lyric,

> Ne le man vostre, gentil donna mia,
> raccommando lo spirito che more.

(K. Foster and P. Boyde, ed., *Dante's Lyric Poetry*, Oxford, 1972, i, p. 52), and, for other instances, op. cit. ii, p. 87, note 1–2.

32 So it appeared in the mid-fifteenth century to Denis the Carthusian, interpreting John xviii 38: *Doctoris Estatici D. Dionysii Cartusiani Opera Omnia in Unum Corpus Digesta*, Montreuil, 1901, xii, p. 587. I have heard this commentator described as highly conventional.

33 Sister Mary Aquinas Devlin ed., *The Sermons of Thomas Brinton, Bishop of Rochester (1373–89)*, *Camden Third Series*, vols LXXXV, LXXXVI, London, 1954, ii, p. 496. Evidence that Brinton did not compose all the sermons in the collection there published does not bear on this very personal one (See the review by H. G. Richardson in *Speculum* xxx, 1955, pp. 267–71). Brinton had taken *veritas liberabit*, the *thema extraordinarium* of his last sermon, as a motto when he came to the see of

Rochester (Devlin op. cit., pp. 496, 7). This subject in its spiritual implication was in the air. There is no need to account for Chaucer's alertness to it as a distillation of Boethian philosophy, and a historical unlikelihood that Chaucer in the balade *Truth* intended 'reference to a great world force, which under any condition, independently of the actions of men, will deliver the world and redress its evils'. (So B. L. Jefferson, *Chaucer and the Consolation of Philosophy of Boethius*, Princeton, 1917, repr. New York, 1965, pp. 116ff, 119.)

34 Chaucer, *Parson's Tale*, x 393, 486, 560, 565, 566, 611–17, 638, 643, 644, 736, 874–86.

35 *Summa Theologiæ Ia2æ*, 82, I (vol. 26, p. 30) and see C. Vollert, 'The Two Senses of Original Justice in Medieval Theology', *Theological Studies* V, 1944, pp. 16, 17.

36 *Hugonis de Sancto Charo . . . Tomus Sextus in Evangelia . . . in quo declarantur sensus omnes*, Venice, 1732, p. 341, col. 1.

37 Pp. 72, 73.

38 *Postilla* on John viii 34, *Qui facit peccatum seruus est peccati*: '*In opere autem peccati homo mouetur contra illud quod est sibi proprium, quia uiuere secundum rectam rationem est proprius hominis motus. . . . In peccato autem homo mouetur contra rectam rationem, et ideo licet peccatum sit voluntarium; tamen in ipso consistit maxima seruitus.*'

39 *Metalogicon*, IV 39, 942a line 21: *Veritas autem est lux mentis et materia rationis*.

40 *Moralium Dogma Philosophorum*, p. 71: '*Satis enim nobis persuasum debet esse, etiam si deos omnes celare possimus, nichil tamen auare, nichil libidinose, nichil inconuenienter esse faciendum.*' See also note, p. 193: *De Officiis*, the source of this passage, reads *incontinenter esse* etc. Compare *Parson's Tale*, x 144: *lo, what Seneca . . . seith. . . .* '*Though I wiste that neither God ne man ne sholde nevere knowe it, yet wolde I have desdayn for to do synne.*' Compare p. 69 above.

41 *Lotario dei Segni (Pope Innocent III) De Miseria Condicionis Humanae*, ed. Robert E. Lewis, Athens, Georgia, 1978, p. 129: '*Nusquam est quies et tranquillitas, nusquam pax et securitas; ubique est timor et tremor, ubique labor et dolor.*'

42 *Parson's Tale*, x 141–55. In Pennaforte the two citations of 141–5 appear in inverse order, and the Parson's second one is attributed simply to *Philosophus*. Robinson notes (*Works*, p. 769) that the citation in 466–8 is from *De Clementia*. See Robert C. Fox, 'The Philosophre of Chaucer's Parson', *Modern Language Notes* LXXV, 1960, pp. 101, 102. Elsewhere in *The Parson's Tale* (484, 534–7) the *philosophre* is Aristotle. (A. C. V. Schmidt, 'Chaucer's "philosophre": a Note on "The Parson's Tale" 534–7', *Notes & Queries* CCXIII, 1968, pp. 327, 328.) See also Harry M. Ayres, 'Chaucer and Seneca', *Romanic Review*, x, 1919, pp. 1–15.

Seneca was 'very popular throughout the Middle Ages, when he was considered to be almost a Church Father because of his supposed correspondence with St Paul'. Roberto Weiss, *Humanism in England During the Fifteenth Century*, Oxford, 2nd edn, 1957, p. 132.

43 See for instance Epistle 48, *Epistvlae Morales*, I, pp. 124–7.

44 *Sermons of Bishop Brinton* II, p. 497.

45 *Works*, p. 537.

46 I 477–541.

47 II 99–130.

48 III 1178–1204.

49 VI 91–102.

50 This struggle produces, according to Alfred David (op. cit. p. 36) 'the greatness of *Troilus* and of much else in Chaucer's poetry'.

51 See Jill Mann, *Chaucer and Medieval Estates Satire*, Cambridge, 1973, passim.

52 I 183–8.

53 The notable instances are Monk, Friar, Prioress, Man of Law, Physician, Merchant and Guildsmen. The attributes of Knight, Parson and Plowman seem almost systematically opposed to the vices for which those classes are criticized in estates satire.

54 Morton W. Bloomfield, *The Seven Deadly Sins*, Michigan, 1952, pp. 175, 6.

55 B Text v 137–81, 385–440.

56 Anger, for instance, successively confesses to the hatred between friars and beneficed clergy, malice and envy in a nunnery, and tale-bearing in a monastery. Sloth has sinned as a man neglectful of his religious duties, as a parson ignorant through neglect of his duty, as a laggard debtor, a breaker of vows and maker of bad confessions, an employer behind with paying his servants, unappreciative of the kindnesses of his fellow Christians, wasteful of his substance, a person idle in his youth.

57 See Charles Muscatine, *Chaucer and the French Tradition*, Berkeley, 1957, pp. 204–13.

58 Compare *Piers Plowman* B x 298–304.

59 See John Alford, 'Some Unidentified Quotations in *Piers Plowman*', *Modern Philology* LXXII, 1975, p. 399.

60 *Vos qui peccata hominum comeditis, nisi pro eis lacrimas & oraciones effuderitis, ea que in delicijs comeditis in tormentis euometis* (*Piers Plowman* B XIII 45α). John Alford (private communication) suggests a connexion with Osee 4.8 *Peccata populi mei comedent*. I am not aware that this quotation has been identified.

61 See for example Dean S. Fansler, *Chaucer and the Roman de la Rose*, repr. Gloucester, Mass., 1965, pp. 162–74; Mann, op. cit., pp. 38, 39, 42, 46, 49, 124–6; Muscatine, *Chaucer and the French Tradition*, pp. 204, 205.

62

> *quis Papiae demorans castus habeatur,*
> *ubi Venus digito iuvenes venatur,*
> *oculis illaqueat, facie praedatur?*
> *Si ponas Hippolytum hodie Papiae,*
> *non erit Hippolytus in sequenti die.*

Confession of the Archpoet lines 30–4 in F. J. E. Raby, *The Oxford Book of Medieval Latin Verse*, Oxford, 1959, p. 264.

63 I 3307–9, 3655–6.

64 VII 155. See *O.E.D.* s.v. I 1.

65 I 165. That is the primary sense of the expression: see *M.E.D.* s.v. *fair* adj. 1a: 'Pleasing to the sight; good to look upon; beautiful, handsome, attractive: (a) of persons, more often of women but freq. of men', and *maistri(e* n. 3(f) *for (the)* 'to a well-nigh unequalled degree, as well as possible, very much, very'. As it became apparent to the hearer from the detail that this sense was inappropriate (198–202) he would look for another one, but having heard 166–97 he could not entertain the notion that the Monk's spirituality was being praised. The rest of his description (203–7) would confirm the exclusion.

66 I 3734; IV 1950–54. Compare Woolf, 'Moral Chaucer and Kindly Gower', p. 231: 'one of the most striking characteristics of [Chaucer's] narrative technique is the effect of continuous moral probing and of a sure and delicate sense of decorum, which never fail unless Chaucer contrives a deliberate breach.'

67 IV 2187–2206.

68 Verses 21–4.

69

> 'Allas', quod Haukyn þe Actif man þo, 'þat after my cristendom
> I ne hadde be deed and doluen for dowelis sake!
> So hard it is', quod haukyn, 'to lyue and to do synne.
> Synne seweþ vs euere.'
>   *Piers Plowman* B XIV 323–6.

70 The prayer at V 1031–79 and the reference to the temple at 1306 make this clear. The conception of pagans with knowledge of a supreme deity (such as is invoked or addressed at 842, 865–92) would be familiar enough. On the quality of the oath see Woolf, op. cit. p. 240.

71 *O.E.D.* s.v. *Truth,* sb. 2.

72 B XII 287 ff. Chaucer's representations of the after-life of Arcite (I 2809, 10) and Troilus (V 1808–27) imply his awareness of the interest.

73 IV 1839, 40. Compare *Parson's Tale* 858: '*And for that many man weneth*

that he may nat synne, for no likerousnesse that he dooth with his wyf, certes, that opinion is fals. God woot, a man may sleen hymself with his owene knyf.'

74 *Sermons* ii, p. 245: *'possunt confessores esse infideles, si sibi confessis non dicant solidas veritates vt eos conuertant a pessimis viis suis.'*

75 vii 113, 115, 125, 131, 135, 148, 151, 155, 166, 170, 178, 193, 208.

76 vii 95–7. The text does not show that she had gone or been sent away at 202, 203 where *he caughte hire by the flankes, And hire embraceth harde, and kiste hire ofte.* This circumstance calls to mind *Physician's Tale* vi 72–102, and specifically 67, 68: *Swich thynges maken children for to be To soon rype and boold, as men may se.*

77 vii 91, 251.

78 *Sermons* ii, p. 274: *'in peccato [sunt] quattuor detestanda, scilicet vilitas macule, reactus (sc. reatus?) pene, quantitas offense, et elacio inobediencie.*

79 v 1479.

80 viii 1044–6.

81 *O.E.D.* s.v. *Truth*, n. 2, 'One's faith or loyalty as pledged in a promise or agreement'.

82 *O.E.D.* s.v. *Integrity*, 3b and cp. *Truth*, n. 4.

83 *O.E.D.* s.v. *Truth*, n. 9.

84 i 46. The *trouthe* ascribed to Palamon in *The Knight's Tale* (i 2789) is specifically that of a 'servant' in love, and therefore no more than constancy of affection. Troilus is commended for his *trouthe*, along with other excellences, including *wisdom*, but by Pandarus (*Troilus and Criseyde* ii 160); and the reader has already observed Troilus's defects of personality. His *trouthe* is sexual constancy. As for his *wisdom*, that is never apparent. Here, as elsewhere, Pandarus is lying.

85 *The Legend of Good Women*, 1890, *Works*, p. 510.

86 *Moralium Dogma Philosophorum*, p. 73: *'ut in fidibus musicorum aures uel minima sentiunt, sic nos, si uolumus esse acres uitiorum animaduersores, magna sepe intelligemus ex paruis: ex occulorum obtutu, ex remissis aut contractis superciliis, ex mesticia, ex hilaritate, ex risu, ex locutione, ex contentione uocis, ex summissione, ex ceteris similibus facile iudicabimus, quid eorum apte fiat quidue ab officio discrepet.'*

87 x 46, 47. The word *tale* can mean simply 'discourse'. For the tone of *myrie* see *Piers Plowman* B xiii 436–56.

88 The question is an old one that has elicited widely various answers. Some are sketched in 'Chaucer's Retraction: a Review of Opinion', by James D. Gordon, in *Studies in Medieval Literature in Honor of Professor Albert Croll Baugh*, ed. MacEdward Leach, Philadelphia, 1961, pp. 81–96, and in 'Chaucer's 'Retraction': Who Retracted What?' by Angus Cameron in *Humanities Association Bulletin* xvi, 1965, pp. 75–87. There

is a more recent study, 'Chaucer's 'Retractions'; the Conclusion of *The Canterbury Tales* and its Place in Literary Tradition', *Medium AEvum* XL, 1971, pp. 230–48 by Olive Sayce.

89　*Piers Plowman* B x 444.

90　This state of mind, a product of the development of the doctrines of divine justice and grace against the background of the Augustinian concept of predestination, had an intellectual basis which will have made it particularly distressing to a person of intelligence and sensibility, and hard to escape. It is like that identified by Carré in Fulke Greville's early seventeenth-century *Treatie on Humane Learning*, a 'passionate concern with individual salvation in the midst of a world that appeared politically and intellectually on the brink of collapse. . . . The teaching of Calvin and of Seneca combine to urge even graceful courtiers like its author to abandon all hope in philosophy and to clutch the austere comfort of religious stoicism.' (Meyrick H. Carré, *Phases of Thought in England*, Oxford, 1949, p. 220. The resemblance is strikingly apparent in the final chorus of Greville's *Mustapha*,

Oh wearisome condition of Humanity,
Borne vnder one law, to another, bound:

with its clear references to Romans vii 21–4 and Innocent's *De Miseria*. (*The Works in Verse and Prose Complete of . . . Fulke Greville, Lord Brooke*, ed. Alexander B. Grosart, III, repr. New York 1966, p. 416.)

91　'*Nullus sibi blandiatur et dicat quia "Deus non in finem irascetur, neque in eternum indignabitur," set "miseraciones eius super omnia opera eius," quia cum iratus est, non "obliviscitur misereri," nec quicquam eorum que fecit odit. Assumens in argumentum erroris quod ait Dominus per prophetam: "Congregabuntur in congregacione unius fascis in lacum, et clauden-/-tur in carcerem, et post multos dies visitabuntur." Homo namque peccavit ad tempus; non ergo omnes puniet in eternum. O spes inanis, o falsa presumpcio!*' The terrible feature of Innocent's argument against universalism (the passage is headed '*Quod reprobi nunquam liberabuntur pena*') or even against undue confidence in divine grace and mercy, is the construction he puts on the 'comfortable words', the scriptural passages which might seem to offer hope to sinners: '*Predestinatis . . . Deus irascitur temporaliter. . . . De quibus illud accipitur: "Non in finem irascetur" et cetera. Reprobis autem Deus irascitur eternaliter.*' 'It is with the elect that God is wrathful for a time only.

Of them it is that this "He shall not be wrathful forever" is understood. With the reprobated, however, God is angry for eternity.' *De Miseria*, p. 217, lines 1–11, 22–5.

92　B xv 47–50; xx 69, 70.

93 See p. 29, note 60 above.

94 As far as I know the history of this subject has yet to be written. The chapter 'Poetry and Theology' and the excursus 'Early Christian and Medieval Literary Studies' in E. R. Curtius, *European Literature and the Latin Middle Ages* (tr. W. R. Trask, London, 1953, pp. 214–27 and 446–67) bear on it, as does a very interesting article by Glending Olson, 'Medieval Theory of Literature for Refreshment', *Studies in Philology* LXXI, 1974, pp. 291–313. Langland, referred to in this article on p. 303, had reservations about the subject, if I gauge his tone in XII 20 correctly, and he was writing religious verse. But cp. p. 68 above, and p. 264, n. 16.

95 Such as those advanced by Boccaccio in Book XIV of the *De Genealogia Deorum*.

96 *Piers Plowman* C VI 92–101 (W. W. Skeat, ed., *The Visions of William concerning Piers the Plowman . . . Text C, EETS* 54, London, 1873. All time not spent in pursuit of salvation is time lost. The Dreamer's interlocutors do not trouble to comment on his confession or expression of hope for grace. Reason says bluntly. 'I advise you, hasten to begin a commendable way of life, beneficial to the soul'; Conscience adds, 'Yes indeed, and persevere in it'. See pp 130 f. and p. 281 notes 31, 32.

97 *Works*, p. 536. This poem, beginning with a clear reference to Seneca's eighth epistle (*Epistvlae Morales* I, p. 14) and transforming its *vera libertas* (op. cit. p. 16, lines 2, 4) in the refrain that quotes John viii, to which it progresses by a succession of Boethian maxims and the religious commonplace of life as a pilgrimage, could be called an expression of Christian stoicism in the sense of Note 90 above.

98 This is the traditional interpretation of John viii 31, 32: 'Dicebat ergo Iesus ad eos, qui crediderunt ei, Iudæos: Si vos manseritis in sermone meo, veri discipuli mei eritis, & cognoscetis veritatem, et veritas liberabit vos.' The *Catena* ascribes it to Augustine: 'From what shall the truth free us, but from death, corruption, mutability, itself being immortal, uncorrupt, immutable?' (*Catena Aurea: Commentary on the Four Gospels Collected out of the Works of the Fathers by S. Thomas Aquinas*, IV, i, Oford, 1865, p. 303. It appears little different in the *Postilla* on John viii 33: *Et veritas liberabit vos quia in presenti veritas fidei liberat a seruitute culpe . . . et in futuro a seruitute miserie quando ipsa creatura liberabitur a corpore mortis,*' and is restated in the fifteenth century by Denis the Carthusian: '*liberabit, id est liberos faciet a servitute peccati et dæmonis, et in resurrectione liberabit a servitute poenæ et mortalitatis.*' (op. cit., p. 434.)

99 Denis the Carthusian, op. cit., p. 434. The context seems to require treating *influens* as a transitive verb, notwithstanding the dictionaries: it seems to be used for *infundens*. The alternative translation, 'abounding in grace', would make *gratiam* a somewhat recondite accusative of respect.

100 Sayce, 'Chaucer's 'Retractions'', pp. 245, 246, concludes that Chaucer in
     his prayer for forgiveness and intercession was 'not expressing a conven-
     tionally pious attitude' but 'ironic and humorous detachment. . . . Far
     from being a personal confession of literary sin, it is a conventional
     structural motif which is used as a vehicle for the expression of opposing
     æsthetic standpoints. By means of irony and humour Chaucer presents
     the problem in all its complexity.' The point is in identification of the
     problem: of Chaucer's personal salvation. Whatever knowledge he may
     have had of retractions and confessions by other poets such as he cites
     would have made his own a little less humiliating rather than induced a
     mindless conformity to convention. And if he had a sense of irony as he
     wrote his *retracciouns* this will have come from the superior knowledge
     of the vanity or worse of his works, which negated his sense of
     achievement, of artistic fulfilment: *Sapientia enim huius mundi stultitia
     est apud Deum.* As to the 'humour' of the presentation, I cannot see any.
     Rather I sense pathos in the statement, not least when perversely it
     breaks into a perfect specimen of the verse line that Chaucer had devised
     or naturalized, *and many a song and many a leccherous lay.*

5 Philosophical Chaucer

1 That is to say, a system in which explanations of the nature of man's
   existence are prescribed, and speculation about it is discouraged or
   prohibited.
2 There is a sympathetic account of these processes of intellectual history in
   Gordon Leff, *Paris and Oxford in the Thirteenth and Fourteenth
   Centuries*, New York, 1968, pp. 222–55.
3 I find an intriguing similarity between the Ockhamite concept of *potentia
   absoluta* which essentially denies human intelligence the capacity to distinguish between good and evil, justice and injustice, and an oriental one
   described by Norman Powell Williams in *The Ideas of the Fall and of
   Original Sin* (London 1927, reissue 1938, p. 5), of an absolute which
   transcends both sets of concepts.
4 In this particular the difference between the pre-Reformation and the
   modern ethos is immense. It lodges in our concept of the absolute importance of a sense of achievement for the attainment and retention of a
   successful, a 'viable' personality.
5 The Anglican furore of the mid-seventies was not long in subsiding. And
   just now, in 1987, we have an essentially doctrinal confrontation between
   the Pope and the episcopal hierarchy of America.
6 Gordon Leff, *Heresy in the Later Middle Ages*, Manchester, 1967, I, p. 2,
   and *passim.*
7 Even taking account of the conventions of the dream-vision kind,

Chaucer actually flaunts his religious writings. His claim to have rendered Innocent's dismal tirade, and the *Second Nun's Tale*, and 'Orygenes upon the Maudeleyne' is prominently asserted. (*Prologue to the Legend of Good Women* G 414–417: Chaucer references are to F. N. Robinson, ed., *The Works of Geoffrey Chaucer*, Second Edition, London, 1957.) In this situation the important possibility that the *De Miseria* translation was made between writing and revising the *Prologue to the Legend* suggests itself. And the *Parson's Tale* by itself unmistakably indicates his interest in conduct, for it is an amazingly perceptive analysis of the motives of behaviour, the 'pathology of the moral life'. This phrase is Bernard Williams's: *Moral Luck: Philosophical Papers, 1973–80*, Cambridge, 1981, p. 38.

8 It still seems necessary to proclaim the quality of that intelligence. If it were apparent for no other reason, then the fact that all his literary production and his huge learning were a 'spare time' achievement would attest it. In this achievement I do not know of any medieval layman without a patron who can rival him.

9 *Nun's Priest's Tale*, 3234–51.

10 One main element in making a translation is the actual understanding of the intellectual content of the work being attempted. I believe that the style of *Boece* and Chaucer's translation procedures reflect an initial difficulty, even occasional frustration, in attempting that understanding. Much of the persuasion of *De Consolatione* is effected by its elegant Latinity. Boethius's bald arguments seem no better or worse than others on the subject, and may have disappointed Chaucer. For an important discussion of how Chaucer proceeded see Tim William Machan, *Techniques of Translation: Chaucer's Boece*, Norman, Okla., 1985.

11 It is easy, in the pleasure of experiencing Chaucer's representations of clerical figures, to forget with what minute precision, as Jill Mann has shown, they reflect the detailed and systematic criticisms of estates satire. This is true even of his Parson, who is compounded of the good opposites of the shortcomings of parish clergy there listed. Moreover the terms by which Chaucer creates him evidence extreme familiarity with the terminology of religious reform.

12 By Robert Payne, but as Skeat once wrote, 'I have lost the reference'.

13 See note 23, p. 254 below.

14 Cicero in *Twenty-Eight Volumes, XXI, De Officiis*, transl. Walter Miller, Loeb Library, Cambridge, Mass., 1975, p. 17.

15 The sense of degradation, infection, is hard to conceive nowadays. I have not found reference to original sin in the new *Book of Common Prayer*, but here is how a historian of the subject describes the conception of it as late as the sixteenth century. 'The sin of Adam, which is the sin of mankind, is regarded as a perennial fountain of filth and uncleanness which is perpetually bubbling up in black streams of perverted and

degraded impulse, manifesting itself not merely in those acts which the moral law stigmatises as sinful but in all the daily, hourly, momentary acts, even though in appearance innocent or virtuous, performed by the unconverted man.' Williams, *The Ideas of the Fall*, p. 433. Cp. pp. 51–3 above.

16 This was demonstrated anew by the late Judson B. Allen in *The Ethical Poetic of the Later Middle Ages: A decorum of convenient distinction*, Toronto, 1982. This was the one acceptable defence of poetry.

17 *Op. cit.*, p. 9.

18 *Piers Plowman* B xi 86–106 implies this.

19 *De Officiis*, p. 274.

20 This concept was imaginatively very powerful. Judson Allen conveniently illustrates this: Statius led by Vergil's prophecies to believe in Christ; Vergil himself reverenced as at least a prophet; Ovid a Christian saint; Plato, entombed, a 'confessor', by the text of a golden plaque on his breast, which read 'Credo Christum de virgine nasciturum, pro humana genere passurum at die tercia resurrecturum.' (*The Friar as Critic: Literary Attitudes in the Later Middle Ages*, p. 60, n. 18).

21 Allen, *Ethical Poetic*, p. 5.

22 *Op. cit.*, p. 54.

23 The latter term has been recently defined by Bernard Williams, *Ethics and the Limits of Philosophy*, Cambridge, Mass., 1985, p. 72.

24 There is nothing in Chaucer as explicit as the questioning of the doctrine of original sin, and by implication, divine justice, set up for condemnation by Dame Study in *Piers Plowman* B x 108–11, or the Ockhamite *Quare placuit? Quia voluit* of xii 216 by which Ymaginatif dismisses the question why only one of the thieves at the crucifixion was saved. But there are Canterbury pilgrims who instance the absolute effects of original sin, their souls lost in 'the body of this death' (see note 27, p. 254 above). And there is a remarkable set of injunctions addressed to a god in the *Prologue to the Legend of Good Women* (G 318ff.) which might be thought to the point.

25 *Parson's Tale* 144, *De Officiis* p. 306, *Moralium Dogma* p. 71; and see note 40, p. 256 below.

26 Chaucer's most outrageous illustration of this condition is the absolute cynicism of the Pardoner, expressed in his *Prologue*, notably lines 424–53.

27 A nice debating point is whether the *Prologue* Friar or the Pardoner should have this place. Each applies exceptional aptitudes to unmistakably reprehensible ends. I suppose that the Friar should, for his perversion of the sacrament of penance, bear the greater guilt.

28 On this set of concepts see Robert Nozick, *Philosophical Explanations*, Cambridge, Mass., 1981, pp. 411ff.

29 *De Officiis*, p. 148, closely reflected in *Moralium Dogma Philosophorum*, for which see note 86, p. 259 above.

30 The outstanding examples are Monk, Somonour and Pardoner; the Monk's ugliness is accentuated by calling him *a fair for the maistrie*, which

means 'exceptionally handsome', before the details of his repulsive appearance are given. When, however, it is dramatically necessary for a character to be personable, as in the case of the Friar, Chaucer, disregards the convention.

31 This is how I read *The Shipman's Tale.*

32 Thus: peaceful conduct is absolutely admirable, violence is not, but if in the Europe of 1938 pacifism had been a governing principle of conduct, violence and thus evil would have prevailed. In opposing Hitler some value was sacrificed.

33 For instance, in the Monk and the Wife of Bath.

34 In one instance at least of public concern there was a predicament: this had to do with the morality of engaging in war. It was possible to define circumstances in which warfare would be lawful, but any many who took part in a war failed in charity when he raised his sword against his enemy. See James Muldoon, *Popes, Lawyers and Infidels*, Philadelphia, 1979.

35 So *For he hadde geten hym yet no benefice* (*Prologue* 291) may carry a sting in the suggestion that the Clerk, unlike the other clerk on the pilgrimage, the Parson (480), had no sense of pastoral mission. His Aristotelian studies were self-indulgent, self-gratifying.

36 p. 362. Compare p. 57 above.

37 *Ethical Poetic*, pp. 5, 55.

38 See note 28 above.

39 Lawyers and spendthrift lords were then as now fair game, but the dishonesty of Manciple and Reeve is nevertheless deplorable. One recalls, also, that they are being admired for their contrivance by someone who supported the monk in his views about claustrality.

40 It is of course possible that Chaucer had in mind harm done to the *mayde childe . . . yit under the yerde* (95–7) who was present during the handling and kissing. The possibility is implied in two passages from *The Physician's Tale: Swich thynges maken children for to be To soone rype and boold* and *Of alle tresons sovereyn pestilence Is whan a wight bitrayseth innocence* (67, 68 and 91, 92). Cp. p. 259, note 6.

41 *Melibee* can be read as an extended exercise of such a reduction.

42 *An non habet potestatem figulus luti ex eadem massa facere, aliud quidem vas in honorem, aliud vero in contumeliam?* (*Romans* 9.21); *Fidelis autem Deus est, qui non patietur vos tentari super id quod potestis, sed faciet etiam cum tentatione proventum ut possitis sustinere.* (1 *Corinthians* 10.13).

43 *Introduction to the Pardoner's Tale*, 295 and *De Officiis*, p. 122.

44 Bernard Williams, *Moral Luck*, especially Chapter 2, pp. 20–39.

6 Music Neither Unpleasant nor Monotonous

1 The expressions are *freke, gome, lede, renk, segge, wye,* and *warpen . . . word* as in *Ech a word þat he warp* (v.86).

2 Compare *For þow shalt yelde it ayein at one yeres ende* (VI.43), *Wiþ gile þow hem gete ageyn alle reson* (XVIII.334); *And as chaste as a child þat in chirche wepeþ* (I.180), *Whan I come to þe kirk and knele to þe Roode* (V.105); *For he þat yeueþ and yarkeþ hym to reste* (VII.80), *And er he gyue any grace gouerne first hymselue* (V.51); *But sooþnesse wolde noȝt so for she is a Bastard* (II.24), *Hendiliche heo þanne bihiȝte hem þe same* (III.29). Quotation is from G. Kane and E. T. Donaldson, *Piers Plowman: the B Version*.

3 *The Vision of William concerning Piers the Plowman*, ed. W. W. Skeat (10th edn. rev., Oxford, repr. 1968), pp. xxiii, xxxix, and *The Vision of William concerning Piers the Plowman in Three Parallel Texts*, ed. W. W. Skeat (3rd impression, Oxford, 1969), ii, lxi.

4 *The Vision of Piers the Plowman . . . Text B*, EETS, os 39 (repr. 1930), p. xli.

5 George Saintsbury, *A History of English Prosody*, i (London, 1906), pp. 167, 168. Saintsbury simply misread the interpolation about teaching in English in Trevisa's Higden. Trevisa's points are that boys learn their grammar faster nowadays, and that ignorance of French is increasing. Saintsbury may not have realized that the grammar which they studied, whether in French or English, was Latin grammar. Any literate Middle English text is a demonstration that vernacular grammar could in that period (as indeed today) be interpreted through the study of Latin. As to the surviving inflexions, their rôle in Chaucer's verse line, and their remarkably correct use in manuscripts like Ellesmere, Hengwrt, and the Trinity College Cambridge B.15.17 manuscript of *Piers Plowman* imply knowledge somehow transmitted by teaching, not just preserved by ear.

6 Dorothy Everett, *Essays on Middle English Literature* (Oxford, 1955), p. 48: 'The greatness of *Piers Plowman* does not obscure its comparative lack of art, . . . it still remains evident that its writer (or writers) felt no compulsion to polish his work.'

7 As does Chaucer's, for instance in *House of Fame*, 1096, 1098.

8 See J. A. Burrow, *Ricardian Poetry* (London, 1971), pp. 34, 35 for an important insight in respect of this.

9 'The poet reaps his triumphant reward because he has set himself so many obstructions to overcome.' S. Chatman, *A Theory of Meter* (The Hague, 1965), p. 207. Compare Robert Frost's 'Writing free verse is like playing tennis with the net down'. (Address to Milton Academy, Milton, Massachusetts, 17 May 1935.) My two colleagues who severally told me of and located this quotation have my thanks.

10 Compare J. Lawlor, *Piers Plowman: an Essay in Criticism* (London, 1962), p. 190: 'the chief characteristic is the entire absence of any tension between the demands of speech (and thus sense) on the one hand, and a theoretically unvarying metrical pattern on the other'; p. 191: 'There can be no question of discrepancy, whether delicate or strident, between a theoretically unvaried scansion and the actual demand of speech and

sense—that discrepancy . . . for which the older term 'modulation' may be preferred'; p. 223: 'There can be no juggling within the phrase, and thus no scope for those skills of inversion and transposition which can contribute markedly to our pleasure in the foot-counted line. . . . The 'prosody' of Langland does not allow patterned diction.'

11 See, for example, R. W. Sapora, Jr., *A Theory of Middle English Alliterative Meter with Critical Applications*, Speculum Anniversary Monographs, i (1977), p. 20; 'Non-stressed, non-alliterating syllables are not metrically significant', and p. 45: 'Some stress alternations occur in lines where both stressed and non-stressed readings would result in metrical lines. The method I have adopted in such cases is to assign or not assign metrical emphasis so as to produce the least complex reading, the only exceptions being those cases where the more complex reading seems to reflect the sense of the line better than the less complex one.' Any formulae that might emerge where such opinions and procedures are in force will bear little relation to the lines of poetry.

12 The figure *paromoeon* was held to exist by virtue of the alliteration falling on the first syllable regardless of stress. (C. B. Kendall, 'Bede's *Historia ecclesiastica:* The Rhetoric of Faith', in J. J. Murphy, *Medieval Eloquence* (Berkeley, 1978), p. 159.) For the passage in *De Schematibus* to which Kendall seems to be referring see *Rhetores Latini Minores*, ed. Carolus Halm, Leipzig, 1863 (Minerva reprint 1964), p. 610. Heinrich Lausberg (*Handbuch der Literarischen Rhetorik*, 2nd impression, Munich, 1973, i 478) had interpreted Bede's examples similarly.

13 That is the pattern created by, within the line, the interplay of lexical stress, the phrase rhythm which will modify this, semantic stress, and possibly awareness of a rhythmic norm, and externally, the tone, emotional colour, and pace of the context. See, for discussions, e.g. O. Jespersen, *A Modern English Grammar*, i (Heidelberg, 1909), pp. 150 ff., G. Leech, *A Linguistic Guide to English Poetry* (London, 1969), pp. 103 ff., Chatman, *A Theory of Meter*, pp. 52 ff.

14 There are conveniently gathered references to phoneticians' studies of these phenomena in Chatman, *A Theory of Meter*, pp. 34 ff.

15 'What determines the metrical structure is the phrasing imposed by sense and normal stress.' W. Nowottny, *The Language Poets Use* (London, 1962), p. 109; and cf. n. 13 above. In *Piers Plowman* no aids are needed to 'pick out the stressed syllables' (T. Turville-Petre, *The Alliterative Revival* (Cambridge, 1977), p. 17). The notion that this was one of the conventional functions of alliteration seems supported by (and may indeed derive from) the absence of modulation in a great many lines of Middle English alliterative verse. But whether one charitably assumes that the writers of such verse thought themselves conventionally bound to produce relentlessly 'regular', metronomically accented lines, or judges them insensitive versifiers, their limitations are apparent. In Langland's case the choice is between assuming his inability to meet the formal demands of the verse

convention and allowing him technical virtuosity which transcended them.

16 Chatman, *A Theory of Meter*, p. 224.

17 See, for instance, E. Salter, *Piers Plowman: an Introduction* (Oxford, 1962), pp. 21, 22: 'his general practice is to refuse alliteration the dominance it so often has in other contemporary works'. She may, however, be referring to Langland's style, his sparing use of 'exotic, colourful terminology', rather than his technical performance. Lawlor, *Piers Plowman: an Essay in Criticism*, p. 223: 'Langland's is emphatically a poetry to be read aloud—and, at that, stated, not intoned' is perceptive. Most recently Turville-Petre (*The Alliterative Revival*, p. 60) writes of Langland's use of grammatical words to alliterate: 'The result of this practice is to distort the basic rhythm of the alliterative line much more radically, and much more daringly, than anything attempted by the author of *Gawain*. Langland . . . brings his verse much close to prose. . . . Paradoxically, in his flouting of prosodic norms, Langland is more consciously moulding his verse form than the author of *The Destruction of Troy*, who is always content with the most regular metrical patterns.' Notwithstanding the unfortunate terms 'distort' and 'flouting', there are signs of understanding the mode of function of Langland's alliterative line in that quotation. But the same writer seems to find difficulty in reading the poem, or possibly is differentiating reading from scanning it: 'There is at times doubt about the stress-pattern of the line, so that the reader has to hesitate and go back over the line to discover its structure' (ibid., p. 59).

18 I use the term subjectively. The indeterminacy of Langland's historical and grammatical final *e* compels this. See *Piers Plowman: the B Version*, pp. 215, 216, n. 184.

19 By 'scan' I mean read expressively in accordance with the metrical accents of the line, and taking account of the existence of stresses intermediate between light and heavy.

20 'The phrase is a single intonational unit, and the accent forms its center. . . . Any stressed syllable bears a potential for accent; whether that potential is fulfilled will depend on broader conditions of meaning and emphasis. . . . Accent is the prominence which one syllable in an uttered phrase receives when it is the center of the pitch contour; it is not fixed to the word but to the phrase.' Chatman, *A Theory of Meter*, pp. 57, 58.

21 It was identified by Marie Borroff, *Sir Gawain and the Green Knight: A Stylistic and Metrical Study* (New Haven, 1962), p. 171.

22 Compare Turville-Petre, *The Alliterative Revival*, p. 48.

23 Leech, *A Linguistic Guide to English Poetry*, p. 107.

24 Specifically of prepositional phrases: 'annititur semper praepositio sequenti dictioni et quasi una pars cum ea effertur'. (*Institutiones Grammaticae*, in H. Keil, *Grammatici Latini*, iii (Leipzig, 1859), p. 27). It

would not take much reflection to see the extensions of the principle to other kinds of phrase.

25 Lines with this feature are not uncommon: see, for instance, v.33, 269, 381; ix.143; xiii.74, 336; xiv.296; xvii.350.

26 Turville-Petre, *The Alliterative Revival*, p. 17. The error again is a legacy from Saintsbury: 'The alliteration is not unfrequently a real set-off, and no mean one.' (*History of English Prosody*, i, 186.) By 'set-off' he means 'adornment, decoration or ornament'. See *OED*, s.v. i.

27 'All artistic conventions are devices for creating forms that express some idea of vitality or emotion. Any element in a work of art may contribute to the illusory dimension in which such forms are presented, or to their appearance, their harmonization, their organic unity and clarity; it may serve many such aims at once. Everything, therefore, that belongs to a work is expressive; and all artifice is functional'. S. Langer, *Feeling and Form* (New York, 1953), p. 280.

28 *Handbuch der Literarischen Rhetorik* ii. 885: 'Die Wortanfangs-Alliteration tritt auf: i) vorwiegend lautmalend im Satzkontext, so die Wiederholung des Wortanfangs *s*- zur Wiedergabe des Zischens der Schlangen . . . 2) vorwiegend gruppierend (auch als Vokal-Alliteration) in der Abfolge koordinierter kommata.' He refers, naturally, to good practice; what is criticized in, for example, *Ad Herennium*, iv.xii is pointless and excessive alliteration. (*Ad C. Herennium de Ratione Dicendi*, ed. with an English translation by H. Caplan (Cambridge, Mass, 1954), pp. 271–3.) For a sketch of classical attitudes and practice see J. Marouzeau, *Traité de stylistique appliquée au latin* (Paris, 1935), pp. 42–7.

29 See, for example, I. A. Richards, *Practical Criticism* (London, 1929), pp. 217, 218; Nowottny, *The Language Poets Use*, p. 112; Chatman, *A Theory of Meter*, p. 198 (he properly recalls Richard's precedence by quoting him); Langer, *Feeling and Form*, p. 28.

30 The force of this principle in application to statements of moment and concern should appear from the consideration that pattern can confer an illusion of significance upon nonsense as in some nursery rhymes.

31 Saintsbury, *History of Prosody*, p. 192.

32 There is hyperalliteration in the speech of another liar, Hawkyn: see, for example, xiii.304, 310, 311.

33 See iv.88, 89, 92, 93, 95, 97.

34 See xi.19, 20, 22, and compare 35.

35 See xvii.141, i.141, xvii.287, xix.350 and xvii.83–5 respectively.

36 For a small sample of the variety of effects Langland obtained with hypernormative vocalic alliteration see i.9, 65; v.164; xi.27; xiii.353; xiv.165; xviii.372, 419.

37 See Lausberg's classification, n. 28 above. The function is like that of *annominatio* (Lausberg, ii. 885), a kind of analogy, *argumentum a simili* (ibid. i. 254), and an 'intellektueller Aufmerksamkeitserreger' (i. 323).

Compare W. Empson, *Seven Types of Ambiguity* (2nd edn., London, 1949), pp. 11, 12, and Nowottny, *The Language Poets Use*, p. 5.

38 See *Piers Plowman: the B Version*, p. 138.

39 For examples of even more elaborate patterning see xiii.87 and xx.306 with four alliterating syllables before the pause and then secondary alliteration, and xiv.137 with deferred pause and two secondary alliterations.

40 He uses it, for example, at ii.112, 160; vii.103; x.401.

41 See, for instance, Prol. 58; i.43; iv.176; vi.63; x.333; xii.16; xv.178, 541; xvi.237; xx.12.

42 Compare, for intance, v.503; xiii.258; xv.420; xvii.100; xx.306.

43 Compare, for instance, iii.72; vi.99; x.419; xiii.368; xv.48; xvii.254; xviii.341.

44 See Kenneth Burke, 'Lexicon Rhetoricae', in R. W. Stallman, *Critiques and Essays in Criticism: 1920–1948* (New York, 1949), p. 235.

45 Langland's making each in turn bear the name Warren suggests that this word had unfavourable connotations, but it is hard to be confident about them. The word means 'a piece of land enclosed and preserved for breeding game'. (*OED*, s.v.1. The first citation is from *Piers Plowman* B Prologue, 163.) Maybe it carried some of the odium of such institutions. The difference of scale discourages connecting it with the family name of the earls of Surrey, even though the career of John de Warenne (ob. 1347) was unprincipled enough.

46 For instance by A. C. Spearing in 'Verbal Repetition in Piers Plowman', *JEGP* lxii (1963), 722–37.

47 *A History of English Prosody*, i. 185,186.

48 This is in the best medieval tradition. Compare the following: 'il domine son talent, discipline son style, conserve le contrôle de ses moyens d'expression. Il en résulte un surprenant alliage d'intensité et d'artifice, une extraordinaire combinaison de la sincérité avec les procédés. Le tout est beau, délectable à l'intelligence du lecteur aussi bien qu'à l'oreille de l'auditeur; n'oublions d'ailleurs pas que, de son temps, le lecteur est aussi, et d'abord, auditeur: la qualité des sons est nécessaire pour que l'idée pénètre en l'esprit, la musicalité ne se peut séparer de la vérité. Art subtil, dans lequel seuls les plus grands excellaient.' (Dom Jean Leclercq, 'Sur le caractère littéraire des sermons de S. Bernard', in *Recueil d'études sur Saint Bernard et ses écrits*, iii (Rome, 1969), p. 199.)

7 Poetry and Lexicography in the Translation of *Piers Plowman*

1 E. A. Nida, 'A Framework for the Analysis and Evaluation of Theories of Translation,' in R. W. Brislin, ed., *Translation: Applications and Research* (New York, 1976), pp. 51–2.

2 W. Winter, 'Impossibilities of Translation,' in W. Arrowsmith and R. Shattuck, eds., *The Craft and Context of Translation* (Austin, Tex., 1961), p. 73.

3 J. Mathews, 'Third Thoughts on Translating Poetry,' in R. A. Brower, ed., *On Translation* (New York, 1966), p. 67: 'One thing seems clear: to translate a poem whole is to compose another poem.'

4 Compare W. V. Quine, 'Meaning and Translation,' in Brower, *On Translation*, p. 148: 'Empirical meaning is what remains when, given discourse together with all its stimulatory conditions, we peel away the verbiage. It is what the sentences of one language and their firm translations in a completely alien language have in common.'

5 *'There is no completely exact translation,'* W. Winter, 'Impossibilities of Translation,' p. 69. Compare J. C. Catford, *A Linguistic Theory of Translation* (London, 1965), pp. 93–103, and H. C. Triandis, 'Approaches toward Minimizing Translation,' in Brislin, *Translation*, pp. 229–30.

6 George Steiner, *After Babel* (London, 1975).

7 Quoted by E. S. Bates, *Modern Translation* (London, 1936), p. 107. For a modern equivalent, see Catford, *A Linguistic Theory*, p. 25.

8 Steiner, *After Babel*, p. 303.

9 Bates, *Modern Translation*, p. 124. Compare D. S. Carne-Ross, 'Translation and Transposition,' in Arrowsmith and Shattuck, *The Craft and Context*, p. 6: 'True translation is much more a commentary on the original than a substitute for it. Like criticism, to which it is closely allied, its role is interpretative.'

10 For that notion see L. Ray, 'Multidimensional Translation: Poetry,' in Brislin, *Translation*, p. 262.

11 Compare Georges Mounin, *Les Problèmes Théoriques de la Traduction* (Paris, 1963), pp. 278–9.

12 R. Jakobson, 'On Linguistic Aspects of Translation,' in Brower, *On Translation*, p. 233.

13 Compare Steiner, *After Babel*, p. 28.

14 F. L. Saran, *Das Übersetzen aus dem Mittelhochdeutschen* [now in at least its fifth impression], revised, B. Nagel (Tübingen, 1967), instances some of the difficulties of translating that language into modern German.

15 A corresponding approximation would be Nevill Coghill's Chaucer translations, *A Choice of Chaucer's Verse* (London, 1972) and *The Canterbury Tales* (London, 1977). Like their originals they are lively and readable, and being in verse have in a sense a corresponding external form. They also reproduce with fair accuracy the abstractable content of their originals. But the verse is twentieth-century, and the feeling is more Coghill's than Chaucer's.

16 Several important ones are given in J. F. Goodridge, *Piers the Plowman:*

William Langland: Translated into Modern English with an Introduction (reprinted: London, 1975), p. 21.

17 *A New English Dictionary on Historical Principles* [hereafter *N.E.D.*], ed. James A. H. Murray (Oxford, 1888–1928), s.v. 'Shall' 8.a.

18 *Piers Plowman* references are to G. Kane and E. T. Donaldson, *Piers Plowman: the B Version*.

19 *N.E.D.*, s.v. 'Shall' 3.

20 *N.E.D.*, s.v. 'Shall' 5.a.

21 *N.E.D.*, s.v. 'Will' v.^{1} or "Will" v.^{2}1.

22 *N.E.D.*, s.v. 'Will' v.^{1}6.

23 *N.E.D.*, s.v. 'Will' v.^{1}10. The dictionary gives no instance of this sense, 'expressing determination, persistence and the like,' before Caxton, but it is clearly present here and in the other resolutions of amendment at v, 69, 226, 301, 455.

24 *N.E.D.*, s.v. 'May' v.^{1}1, 2; *Middle English Dictionary* [hereafter *M.E.D.*], ed. Hans Kurath (Ann Arbor, Mich., 1954), s.v. 'mouen' v. (3) 1, 2.

25 See E. Salter and D. Pearsall, eds., *Piers Plowman* (London, 1967), p. 61, note to ll. 2, 3: 'I dressed myself in rough clothes, like a shepherd, in the garb of a hermit of secular life.' Failure to value the contrast led these editors to mistranslate the preceding line where *shepe/shep* however spelled means 'sheep,' not 'shepherd.' This is an old error, found in one family of C manuscripts, and hallowed in Skeat's note to the line. Elsewhere, however, the Dreamer specifically describes his customary dress as clerical habit, *longe clothes* (Salter and Pearsall, *Piers Plowman*, p. 78, l. 41).

26 So Goodridge, *Piers the Plowman*, p. 262: '*In the garb of an easy-living hermit*, i.e., one who did not keep his cell. . . . Shepherds and hermits were dressed alike.' How Goodridge knows this he does not reveal, but the poet appears not to have thought so: he presently writes of 'easy-living' hermits that they *Cloped hem in copes to ben knowen from opere* (Prol., 56), 'to look distinctive.' The *copes* here are clerical dress (*M.E.D.* s.v. 2): see C revision (*The Visions of William concerning Piers the Plowman: Text C*, x, 210, 211, *clothed hem in copes*
clerkus as hit were, Other on of som ordre.

27 To judge by examples in *N.E.D.* and *M.E.D.*, use of *appose* with an adverb of manner is not very common. When this does occur (see *M.E.D.*, s.v. "ap(p)osen" 1.(a) for examples) the adverb (*with wordes strongue . . . streite, sad & sar, weel*) most often implies an effect on the person interrogated. If, however, *soopliche* here is an extension of such modification it is so extreme as to appear a trope.

28 It is intriguing to speculate whether the slovenly expression was designed to contribute to the impression of the speaker's main trait. But this may just be colloquial syntax: compare, *May no peny ale hem paie ne no pece of bacoun, But if it be fressh flessh ouper fissh yfryed* (vi, 309, 310).

29 *his goode wille* (xviii, 212).

30 Compare also *Tho was he Iesus of Iewes called, gentile prophete, And kyng of hir kyngdom and croune bar of þornes* (xix, 48, 49) and *Ther nede haþ ynome me þat I moot nede abide And suffre sorwes ful soure, þat shal to Ioye torne* (xx, 46, 47).

31 How subtly the poet is able to vary this might be illustrated from the difference of response to Haukyn's account of his sinful state in Passus xiii of the B version, which evokes compassion in the spirit of xiv, 325, '*So hard it is,*' '*quod haukyn,* '*to lyue and to do synne,*' and to the same passages, incoporated with relatively little modification, into the confessions of the sins in the C revision.

32 *M.E.D.*, s.v. 'leaute' n. assigns the first meaning 'Uprightness, honorableness, honesty; truth; justice, fairness' to this word. It is often used in contexts of public behaviour such as government and courts of law. There is another, lexicographically very problematic personification of *lewte* at xi, 84. In xx, 348, the problem is of another kind: the need to translate *Hende speche* as 'the natural instinct not to disoblige,' or 'the desire to be agreeable,' neither of which will do as the name of a personification.

33 *feiþ may noȝt haue his forþ, hire floryns go so þikke.* The translation is authorized by either *M.E.D.*, s.v. 'forth' adv. 1, in which case the expression is elliptical (sc. *haue his wei forþ*), or s.v. *ford* n. 2 (b) '*haven* ~ "be allowed freedom of action"'.

34 '*I falle in floryns*', *quod þat freke,* '*and faile speche ofte.*' See *M.E.D.* s.v. 'fallen' v.24c.

35 Thus 'Lady Meed,' Mede, the central figure of Passus ii–iv, signifying various aspects of the social change to a monetary society which Langland found generally destructive of integrity, would strictly need several modern names to match the development of her representation. The personifications *Conscience* and *Ymaginatif* have even more complicated identities deriving from medieval notions of psychology and not reproduceable by single terms.

36 Matthew 22:14, *Multi enim sunt vocati, pauci vero electi.*

37 At least one such expression, *dyngen upon Dauid* (iii, 312) where *dyngen* is a verb used of threshing with a flail (*dyngen vpon sheues*, vi, 141) is instanced in an earlier piece. The slack parson in *The Papelard Priest* complains that he is obliged to leave a good party to *dyngen opon dauyd wyt a dirige* (*London Mediaeval Studies*, ii, i [1951], pp. 34 and 44, l. 56).

38 Compare *my buzard love* in *Loves Diet*, l. 25 (*The Poems of John Donne*, ed. H. J. Grierson [reprint ed.: London, 1958], i, p. 56).

39 See *N.E.D.*, s.v. 'Thrave, Threave.' This would have been a fully live metaphor in the fourteenth century.

40 The problem of translating puns is solemnly discussed in Catford, *A Linguistic Theory of Translation*, pp. 94ff.

41 See for example H. Lausberg, *Handbuch der Literarischen Rhetorik* (Munich, 1973), p. 322: "*Die annominatio* (Paronomasie) ist ein (pseudo-)

etymologisches Spiel mit der Geringfügigkeit der lautlichen Änderung einerseits und der interessanten Bedeutungsspanne, die durch die lautliche Änderung hergestellt wird, andererseits. Hierbei kann die Bedeutungsspanne bis ins Paradoxe gesteigert werden. Die so hergestellte Etymologie . . . zwischen den beiden Wörtern wird dem Publikum als eigene Arbeitsleistung vom Autor zugemutet.'

42 *M.E.D.* s.v. 'acces(s)e,' n. 1. This ingenious *annominatio*, incorporating metaphor, is a refinement of the earlier form of the line, *aftir al þis surfet an axesse he hadde* (*Piers Plowman: the A Version*, V, 201). The pun-evoking word *excesse* was apparently a new importation; Langland's B-text use of it probably antedates all the dictionary examples. One C scribe apparently did not believe in it and substituted *excessus*; at least two scribes in the B tradition wrote *accesse* in its place. None of this makes translation any easier.

43 See *M.E.D.* s.v. 'lithen' v. (2), v. (3), and *N.E.D.* s.v. 'Lithe' v.^{2}, v.^{3}

44 See M. Marcett, *Uhtred de Boldon, Friar William Jordan, and Piers Plowman* (New York, 1938).

45 See *M.E.D.* s.v. 'jordan' n.

46 See *M.E.D.* s.v. 'juste' n. The two meanings derive ultimately from the same Latin etymon. Langland could have known this.

47 How much of this most careful creation of the poet comes across in translation it is hard for anyone who knows the original poem to judge; for him the Dreamer has a vital existence of which he is bound to be aware even when reading a translation.

48 See *M.E.D.* s.v. 'harlot' n. 3b for the fifteenth-century and apparently earliest recorded uses of the word mean female prostitute. Its primary fourteenth-century sense was abusive of the male sex, as in Old French.

49 See *M.E.D.* s.v. 'boie' n. (1) 4 for the fifteenth-century development of the meaning "male child, boy, youth."

50 Goodridge, *Piers the Plowman*, p. 213. The usage is emotional, not perfunctory: the feeling can be observed in children striving to form and formulate conceptions of magnitude or scope. Compare for example Prologue 211, 212, *an hundred . . . Sergeantz . . . at þe barre*; III, 123, *She makeþ men mysdo many score tymes*; III, 145, 146, *She may neiȝ as muche do in a Monþe ones As youre secret seel in sixe score dayes*; III, 181, *Thow hast hanged on myn half elleuene tymes*, V, 368–70 *I haue . . . Sworen . . . There no nede was nyne hundred tymes*; V, 425, *þus tene I trewe men ten hundred tymes*. The numbers are both arbitrary and conveniently alliterative, but they become poetically significant once selected; we recognize their 'rightness after the event.' Compare Kenneth Burke, '*Lexicon Rhetoricae*,' in R. W. Stallman, *Critiques and Essays in Criticism: 1920–1948*, p. 235.

51 Strictly speaking the 'heel' of a meat pie, the bottom crust. Anyone with experience of the commercial British product will know that this part of it is, to say the least, unpalatable.

52 Bates, *Modern Translation*, p. 99: 'Translators may be divided into four kinds: those who neither use nor need dictionaries; those who need them and use them; those who need them but don't use them; those who would like them but have to do the best they can without. Sixteenth-century translators belonged to the last class; our contemporaries to one or other of the other three classes.' There is probably no Middle English scholar in the first of those classes, and there should not be any in the third.

53 Goodridge, *Piers the Plowman*, p. 30. The word embarrasses him, and he puts it in quotation marks.

54 *N.E.D.* s.v. 'Young Man, Youngman' 2b. Compare Goodridge, *Piers the Plowman*, p. 50.

55 *N.E.D.* s.v. 'Stock' sb. 1d: Goodridge, *Piers the Plowman*, p. 78, 'pairs of stocks.' With *stokkes* correctly translated *loke no3t þerafter* assumes its correct sense, 'do not look back at them in longing.'

56 *N.E.D.* s.v. 'understand' v. 6a; Goodridge, *Piers the Plowman*, p. 175. His mistranslation of the verb extends to *by so*, which must mean 'provided that.'

57 *M.E.D.* s.v. 'breden' v. (2) b, 'spread out,' here 'become broad' from O.E. *brǣdan*. The activity of *M.E.D.* 'breden' v. (3) 'breed,' is not shown by its Middle English lexicography to be reprehensible, and anyway town pigs breed like country pigs. The reference is to the consequence of gluttonous feeding, made possible by abundantly available pigswill, not to mention the content of the medieval town gutter. Compare Goodridge, *Piers the Plowman*, p. 41.

58 *M.E.D.* s.v. "hoven" v. (1) 2; compare also *N.E.D.* s.v. "Hove" v.[1]2; Goodridge, *Piers the Plowman*, p. 31.

59 This is the form of the half line in Skeat's B text (W. W. Skeat, *Piers the Plowman* [reprint ed.: London, 1930], XIII, 299), and its spelling *losse*, historically better as *los* or *loos*, might seem misleading. But *M.E.D.* under 'los' n. (2) cites *losse* among variant spellings.

60 Compare Goodridge, *Piers the Plowman*, p. 160, where mistranslation of *losse* leads to further error: translation of the purpose clause signalled in *þere-by to* as one of result.

61 Goodridge, *Piers the Plowman*, p. 185.

62 Goodridge, *Piers the Plowman*, p. 228.

63 It means 'profited.' See *N.E.D.* s.v. 'Win' v.[1]6c, 'to get gain, make profit.'

64 As does Goodridge, *Piers the Plowman*, p. 57.

65 As does Goodridge, *Piers the Plowman*, p. 31.

66 'In any translation one has to face the problem of the extent to which what he is to translate is culture-specific (emic) or universal (etic). It is easy to see that etic concepts, such as fire, moon and sun, produce fewer translation difficulties than emic concepts, such as the Greek concept of *philotimo* or the Anglo-American concept of *fairness*.' H. C. Triandis, 'Approaches toward Minimizing Translation,' p. 229.

67 See I, 20; XII, 77; XIV, 147; XV, 557; XVII, 245; XIX, 449; XIII, 15; XV, 104.

68 Compare the meanings of *clergie* in Prol. 116 and III, 165, and XII, 85, where the suggestion is of not much more than the literacy needed to read the Mass-book.
69 Goodridge, *Piers the Plowman*, p. 248.
70 Goodridge, *Piers the Plowman*, p. 63.
71 Steiner, *After Babel*, p. 269.

8 The Perplexities of William Langland

1 Compare Gordon Leff, *Heresy in the Later Middle Ages* (Manchester, 1967) 1:330, 2:411.
2 Lines 127–29. My *Piers* quotations are from Kane (London, 1960) for A, from Kane-Donaldson (London, 1975) for B, and from Skeat (Oxford, 1886) for C.
3 F. R. H. Du Boulay, *An Age of Ambition* (London, 1970), pp. 66, 67. Compare *Piers Plowman* C 6.70 ff.
4 Quoted by G. R. Owst, *Literature and Pulpit in Medieval England* (Cambridge, 1933), p. 558.
5 Owst, pp. 291–3.
6 F. N. Robinson, ed., *The Works of Geoffrey Chaucer*, 2nd ed. (Boston, 1957), p. 252.
7 B 10.305, 306. See Morton Bloomfield, *Piers Plowman as a Fourteenth-century Apocalypse* (Brunswick, N. J., 1961), pp. 68–73.
8 A Prologue 63, 64; B Prologue 66, 67; C 1.64, 65. In C the expression in the first of these lines is made more violent: *But holy churche & charite choppe adoun swich shryuers.*
9 Bloomfield, pp. 78 ff.
10 W. H. Pantin, *The English Church in the Fourteenth Century* (Cambridge, 1955), pp. 159, 160.
11 Bloomfield, p. 80.
12 Lines 18 ff. The passage recalls Chaucer's representation of a similar attitude in 'The Summoner's Tale' (1919–28).
13 See above, pp. 50 and 254, 255, Notes 15–20.
14 *De officio regis*, cited by Leff, 2:543. There is a scribal error in Leff's footnote: the text actually reads '*Nec est fingendum ministerium huius differencie verborum nisi quod rex gerit ymaginem deitatis Cristi, sicut episcopus ymaginem sue humanitatis.*'
15 'This World Fares as a Fantasy,' lines 97–100, Carleton Brown, *Religious Lyrics of the XIVth Century* (Oxford, 1924), p. 163.
16 If Langland was, as seems likely, acquainted with Innocent's tirade against the intellect, *De studio sapientum* (Robert E. Lewis, ed., *De Miseria Condicionis Human* [Athens, Georgia, 1978], pp. 109, 110), then

the pathos of the Dreamer's ambition is deepened by the quotation of Prov. 25:27 at 15.55, with which Innocent makes play.

17 An example is B 14.60, 61:

if þow lyue after his loore, þe shorter lif þe bettre:
Si quis amat christum mundum non diliget istum.

18 This is a handy moment to write of Morton Bloomfield's *Piers Plowman as a Fourteenth-century Apocalypse* that it taught me more about *Piers Plowman* than any other single book. Detail after detail of his scholarship continues to fit into place. Here one might notice his intriguing information about the dates forecast for Antichrist's arrival (pp. 92, 93).

19 Leff, 1:138.

20 Compare Elizabeth Kirk, *The Dream Thought of Piers Plowman* (New Haven, 1972), pp. 118, 119.

21 See Ceslaus Spicq, *Saint Paul: Les épîtres pastorales* (Paris, 1947), pp. 57, 58: '*qui omnes homines vult saluos fieri et ad agnitionem veritatis venire*'; '*qui dedit redemptionem semetipsum pro omnibus.*' Origen came to the belief by another route. See Jean Daniélou, *Origen*, trans. W. Mitchell (New York, 1955), pp. 287–9. But compare p. 60 n. 91.

22 For an early fifteenth-century instance see Leff, 1:397, 398.

23 Quoted by Spicq, *Saint Paul*, p. 57: '*omnia quaecumque voluit fecit: ergo omnes salvat.*'

24 '*Rectitudo est quod vult et rationale est omnino quod fiat sibi.*' Adam of Woodham, quoted by Leff, 1:298.

25 Used as an argument by Truth in the debate of the Four Daughters of God at 18.149.

9 Langland and Chaucer: An Obligatory Conjunction

1 A notable exception is Charles Muscatine, *Poetry and Crisis in the Age of Chaucer* (Notre Dame, Ind.: Notre Dame University Press, 1972). John Burrow makes a few occasional comparisons of the two in the course of arguing his thesis in *Ricardian Poetry* (London, Routledge, 1971). See pp. 35–45, 115). After submitting the title of the lecture upon which this essay is based I received an advertisement of David Aers, *Chaucer, Langland, and the Creative Imagination* (London: Routledge, 1980).

2 Introduction to *The Pardoner's Tale* 6.295.

3 The difficulty is to keep the other aspect of the work constantly before the mind's eye. From its character *Piers Plowman* will be best understood as always and indivisibly both a poem and a religious document. It will be harder to keep the historical perspective in Chaucer's case.

4 That is, the treatment of Chaucer's personages as if they were historically actual, not impressions created by complexes of linguistic norms. Every author who writes about people doubtless strives to create in his readers an illusion to that effect, but the business of criticism is to account for the successful illusion, not to indulge the fancy by play within it. The label of the fallacy is to some degree unfair to Bradley. See Katherine Cooke, *A. C. Bradley and His Influence in Twentieth-Century Shakespeare Criticism* Oxford: Clarendon Press, 1972).

5 In cold print this has an alarming look of rash generalization about a subject as yet very imperfectly explored. It rests principally on the findings of Charles Thurot published in *Extraits de divers manuscrits latins pour servir à l'histoire des doctrines grammaticales* (Paris, 1869; reprint, Frankfort on the Main: Minerva, 1964), and on a discussion by James J. Murphy, 'Literary Implications of Instruction in the Verbal Arts in Fourteenth-Century England,' *Leeds Studies in English 1* (1967): 119–35. Since delivering the lecture on which this essay is based, I have learned from Alastair Minnis of David Thomson, *A Descriptive Catalogue of Middle English Grammatical Texts* (New York: Garland, 1979). My presumption was that from the limited choice of available Latin grammars (Thurot, *Extraits*, p. 94) the same basic texts would have been used in fourteenth-century English elementary education whether lay or clerical.

6 Dorothy Owen, *Piers Plowman: A Comparison with Some Earlier and Contemporary French Allegories* (London: University of London Press, 1912), p. 127, referred to 'a common stock of allegorical material' identifiable in *Piers Plowman*, part of which 'was probably supplied to French and English poets independently by the commentaries on Scripture and other theological and educational works.' No doubt the allegory in *Piers Plowman* could have been assembled from such works. But more likely it was the tradition of versifying religious allegory established by the earlier French poets and massively realized by de Deguileville that suggested the general form and texture of *Piers*.

7   *Une vision veul nuncier*
       Qui en dormant m'avint l'autrier.
       En veillant avoie lëu
       Considere et bien vëu
       La biau roumans de la Rose.
       Bien croi que ce fu la chose
       Qui plus m'esmut a ce songier
       Que ci apres vous vueil nuncer.

   Guillaume de Deguileville, *Le Pelerinage de vie humaine*, ed. J. J. Stürzinger (London: Roxburghe Club, 1893), lines 7–14.

8 Guibert de Nogent used the term *expositio tropologica* to describe his

commentary on the prophets and Lamentations (manuscript, University of North Carolina, fols. *1a, b*).

9 See note 7 above. The passage there quoted is not in the second version of the *Pelerinage*, but this contains at least two references to the *Roman*, at lines 2084 and 13200–92 (John Lydgate, trans., *The Pilgrimage of the Life of Man*, ed. F. J. Furnivall, Vol. 1, Early English Text Society, extra series, no 77 (London, 1899); Vol. 2, Early English Text Society extra series, no. 83 (London, 1901).

10 I refrain from locating such possible echoes in the hope of provoking a reaction, corrective or in support. Although nothing in the text of *Piers Plowman* suggests Langland's approval of poetry on profane subjects, there is an a priori likelihood that he was exposed to it.

11 *Piers Plowman* B 11.101, 102:

þyng þat al þe world woot, wherfore sholdestow spare
To reden it in Retorik to arate dedly synne?

For the sense of *reden* see *OED* s.v. *Read*, v. 14. *Piers* quotations are from George Kane and E. Talbot Donaldson, eds., *Piers Plowman: The B Version* (London: Athlone Press, 1975); and from W. W. Skeat, ed., *The Visions of William concerning Piers the Plowman . . . Text C*, Early English Text Society, no. 54 (London, 1873).

12 *The Squire's Tale* 5.37–40.

13 *Piers Plowman* B 15.372–6:

Grammar, þe ground of al, bigileþ now children,
For is noon of þise newe clerkes, whoso nymeþ hede,
That kan versifie faire ne formaliche enditen,
Ne nauȝt oon among an hundred þat an Auctour kan construwe,
Ne rede a lettre in any langage but in latyn or englissh.

See *MED* s.v. *formal* adj., *formalli* adv. For the identity and authority of the speaker see 15.16–39 above. Thurot (*Extraits*, pp. 103–21) discusses some thirteenth- and fourteenth-century approaches to grammar which may have been in Langland's mind. See also B. L. Bursill-Hall, *Speculative Grammars of the Middle Ages* (The Hague: Mouton, 1971), and E. J. Ashworth, *The Tradition of Medieval Logic and Speculative grammar* (Toronto: Pontifical Institute, 1978).

14 George Saintsbury, *A History of English Prosody from the Twelfth Century to the Present Day*, 1:166ff. See p. 266, n. 5.

15 5.1793–6.

16 B 12.16. The line is quoted in context below, note 22.

17 2.620–4.

18 Lines 167, 168.

19 2.47–9.
20 B 9.99–104:

> He dooþ best þat wiþdraweþ hym by daye and by nyȝte
> To spille any speche or any space of tyme . . .
> Tynynge of tyme, truþe woot þe soþe,
> Is moost yhated vpon erþe of hem þat ben in heuene;
> And siþþe to spille speche þat spire is of grace
> And goddes gleman and a game of heuene.

The speaker, Wit, 'Intelligence,' and the context indicate the seriousness of what might otherwise seem a fanciful description, and imply Langland's lively sense of the character and dignity of language. That seriousness is further shown by his use of *spire* here to recall *Acts* 2.3, *dispertitae linguae tanquam ignis*, the emblems of conferment of the gift of tongues. See *O.E.D.* s.v. *Spire* sb.[1], 5, 'elongated or pointed shoot or tongue of fire or flame', and the quotation from Mirk's *Festial*.

21 2.523–26 and compare 3.1101–1103.
22 Ymaginatif, the reflective faculty, is speaking to the Dreamer (B 12.16–24):

> 'þow medlest þee wiþ makynges and myȝtest go seye þi sauter,
> And bidde for hem þat ȝyueþ þee breed, for þer are bokes ynowe
> To telle men what dowel is dobet and dobest boþe,
> And prechours to preuen what it is of many a peire freres.'
> I seiȝ wel he seide me sooþ, and somewhat me to excuse
> Seide, 'Caton conforted his sone þat, clerk þouȝ he were,
> to solacen hym som tyme; so I do whan I make.
> *Interpone tuis interdum gaudia curis*
> And of holy men I here,' quod I, 'how þei ouþerwhile
> In manye places pleyden þe parfiter to ben.'

The Dreamer's defensive answer is designedly wilful and wayward, or disingenuous. By the expression *to solacen hym* he misrepresents his authority: the completed distich specifies a reason other than that implied by the Dreamer: *ut possis animo quemvis sufferre laborem* (M. Boas and J. J. Botschuyver, eds., *Disticha Catonis* [Amsterdam: North Holland Publishing Co., 1952], p. 159). Moreover the Dreamer's 'labour, toil, exertion' is the actual composition that he has just represented as recreational, and earlier (11.86ff.) had conceived of as a corrective mission. His second excuse, in which he associates himself with the saints of Christian legend, is meant to seem outrageous. The circumstance that the poem continues for almost as long again after the Dreamer's 'self-justification' has a further bearing on the character of this.

23 See E. R. Curtius, *European Literature and the Latin Middle Ages*, trans. W. Trask (London: Routledge, 1953), pp. 162–5, for the schema of 'outdoing.' Compare Harold Bloom, *The Anxiety of Influence*, Oxford 1973.

24 *Thebaid* 12.816, 817, in *Statius with an English Translation* by J. H. Mozley (London: Loeb Classical Library, 1928), p. 504.

25 *Inferno* 4.101, 102, in Dante Alighieri, *La Commendia secondo l'antica vulgata a cura di Giorgio Petrocchi* (Rome: Mondadori, 1966), 2:69, 70.

26 *The House of Fame* 1.143, 144; *The Parliament of Fowls*, lines 698, 699.

27 The implications of this statement are bound to seem debatable to some, and I have to allow that at the level of higher theology the argument for hope of salvation was as solid as it had even been in the history of the Church. My reading of preachers and poets suggests that in the popular mentality of the later fourteenth century this was not the case. See p. 260, notes 90, 91.

28 I have argued this at more length in *The Liberating Truth: The Concept of Integrity in Chaucer's Writings* above, pp. 61, 62 and p. 257, n. 60.

29 B 11.84–107. The speaker is *lewtee*, a 'good' character, whose name in *Piers* unless contextually particularized has a general sense, 'observance of, respect for the law,' as, for example, at *Prologue*, line 122, 2.21, 48, 3.291. See E. T. Donaldson, *Piers Plowman: the C Text and its Poet*, Yale Studies in English, no. 113 (reprint, Hamden, Conn.: Shoe String Press, Archon Books, 1966), p. 89. That Lewtee's reading of the *Non oderis* quotation (it resembles Leviticus 19.17) here is limited and potentially misleading appears from the misapplication of *fratres* and from the apparent misattribution to *þe Apostle*. The latter, however, with its corrective singular *fratrem*, attaches it to Charity in clear association; cf. 1 John 4.20: '*Si quis dixerit quoniam diligo Deum, & fratrem suum oderit, mendax est.*' Langland repeatedly associates *loue and leaute* as at B 3.291, 11.145, 167. And compare 11.171, *Lawe wiþouten loue, . . . ley þer a bene!*'

30 B 19.1: *Thus I awaked and wroot what I hadde ydremed*; 19.481: *And I awakned þerwiþ and wroot as me mette.*

31 C 6.1–103.

32 The Dreamer is represented as at length acknowledging that he has *tynt tyme and tyme mysspended* (lines 92, 93). By the convention of the genre that waste and misapplication of his time was the writing down of his dreams, an activity variously reprehensible because neither *lowable and leel*, thereby profitable to his soul, nor necessary (*for þer are bokes ynowe*), but actually sinful because it involved his living on the charity of his friends, in effect begging, which to Conscience seemed *nouht parfytnesse*. Moreover the language of the admission calls to mind how according to Wit, 'Intelligence,' *Tynynge of tyme* is the thing in the world most hated in heaven, and with it *to spille speche*, the spoiling of language (see note 20 above).

33 See note 29 above.
34 B 5.187 and 15.44–50 come to mind with their suggestion that Langland
    might have endowed the Dreamer with what he considered his own
    besetting sins of anger and pride.
35 See note 28 above.
36 See, e.g., J. S. P. Tatlock, 'Chaucer's *Retractions*,' *PMLA* 28 (1913):
    521–9; John M. Manly and Edith Rickert, eds., *The Text of the Canterbury
    Tales* (Chicago: University of Chicago Press, 1940), 2:471, 472; O. Sayce,
    'Chaucer's 'Retractions': the Conclusion of *The Canterbury Tales* and Its
    Place in Literary Tradition,' 230–48.

10 Langland and Chaucer II

1 They seem to me to have more in common than Langland has with any of
   the alliterative poets, or Chaucer with Gower.
2 Illustrations beyond Faral can be found in Giovanni Mari, *I Trattati
   Medievali di Ritmica Latina*, *Memorie del R. Instituto Lombardo di
   Scienze e Lettere*, xx, viii, Milan, 1899, pp. 373ff.
3 I do not find this spelled out in what pass for literary histories of
   fourteenth-century English poetry.
4 Considerable loss can be presumed in each case. Chaucer, employing the
   established convention of the dream vision, lays claim to many hymns for
   the feast days of love, that is, presumably, lyrics in the French forms; only
   a few survive. (*Prologue to the Legend of Good Women* F422, 423)
   Langland makes no such claim, but because the A version of *Piers
   Plowman* is altogether accomplished writing we presume an earlier
   apprenticeship. *William of Palerne* comes to mind. Its translator was
   called William, and it is now and again remarkably like *Piers Plowman* in
   turn of style and metre. When I first aired this notion years ago I was
   sharply told by philologists that there were linguistic reasons why
   Langland could not have written *William of Palerne*. I accepted this
   because I did not know then what scribes could do to the language of texts.
   The possibility should be examined.
5 *House of Fame* 1096. I take the expression to imply 'not associated with',
   or 'inappropriate for serious and learned subjects.'
6 That Chaucer invented this verse form cannot be ruled out, but is
   unlikely. For a French decasyllabic or (with feminine rhyme) hendeca-
   syllabic couplet was in use for narrative until the mid-thirteenth century,
   and Machaut (James Wimsatt points out to me) used it for at least four
   complaintes. The stroke of genius was, if he saw any of the French
   instances, to adopt and adapt the form.
7 See above, pp. 80 ff. *William of Palerne* intrudes a little into this generalization. The metre of that poem waits for a sensitive analysis.
8 By this I mean a metre written to be, or written as if to be read aloud, in

which, accordingly, rhetorical and dramatic stresses dominate, and the abstract beat of the norm is not consciously sensed.

9 Many of what we call Chaucer's minor poems have elaborate stanza forms which will in themselves have been trials of strength. The metres of *Anelida and Arcite* look like experiments. For a *tour de force* there is the Clerk's envoy at the end of his tale. (1177–1212) That it is a model *sirventes* in *coblas unissonans* is unlikely to be an accident.

10 See above, pp. 87 ff. It would need more than a note to illustrate this stylistic feature adequately, but here are a few example. The logic of discourse changes at the caesura in B III 171, 257; a syntactical unit runs from caesura to caesura in v 160b, 161a; from caesura to the line end after the next caesura in v 290b–1, 423b–4; the caesura serves to punctuate at x 173, 346, 467; it sets off a parenthetic statement at x 460; introduces a resumptive subject at x 365, a resumptive object at III 167; it enables parataxis at x 388; contributes to an effect of colloquial speech in IV 1–5, v 302, 303; enables parallelism at v 217, 310–12; and chiasmus at v 177, 284.

11 See notes 12, 27, pp. 267, 269 above.

12 For instance see *Knight's Tale* 2605, *Legend of Good Women* 635 ff.

13 see above, pp. 84, 85.

14 *Piers Plowman* B xv372. This heartwarming opinion of the importance of grammar goes back a long way: see *Seneca in Ten Volumes V, Ad Lucilium Epistulae Morales*, p. 360.

15 This effect is what Jacobson had in mind when he spoke of 'The poetic resources concealed in the morphological and syntactic structure of language, briefly, the poetry of grammar, and its literary product, the grammar of poetry.' (Roman Jacobson, 'Closing Statement: Linguistics and Poetics', in *Style in Language*, ed. Thomas A. Sebeok, Cambridge, Mass., 1960, p. 375. For the bearing of this principle on textual criticism see pp. 211 ff. above.

16 As part of the whole matter of the style of our poets, this is a huge subject. The principle both exploit is that the physical and logical forms of organized statement are simultaneously experienced. Thus, when there is anormative character in either or both those forms 'tension' is created. This becomes a component of the semantic and emotional experiences of the statement. I illustrate from the point where Pandarus is near to completing his reduction of Criseyde's defences.

"Good adventure, o beele nece, have ye
Ful lightly founden, and ye konne it take;
And for the love of God, and ek of me,
Cache it anon, lest aventure slake!"
    Troilus and Criseyde II 288–291

All artifice apart, here is what Pandarus's statement says: 'Beautiful niece, without effort on your part you are in a fortunate situation which will not necessarily continue. Whether you benefit from it depends on yourself. I put an emotional charge on you to take advantage of it quickly.' Between the logic of the statement in that naked form and the grammar into which Chaucer has cast it for Pandarus to speak there is no correspondence; in fact the syntax conceals the nature of his argument. The first component, *Good aventure . . . have ye Ful lightly founden*, which ought to have the status of a principal clause, is made to be the apodosis of a conditional construction, and to depend on *and ye konne it take*, 'if you know how to grasp it'. The last component, *lest aventure slake*, is made a negative clause of purpose, 'so that the luck does not run out'; this is governed by the imperative *Cache it anon* which contains Pandarus's objective. So the good fortune (Troilus's love) is grammatically made to seem contingent on Criseyde's capability, as it is not, and the continuation of the good luck is made to seem contingent on her undertaking an (unspecified) course of action implied in the imperative. A responsibility which does not actually exist is put upon her by the syntactical misrepresentation; it is intensified by the presence between the conditional clause and the imperative of an emotional interjection.

17 Both are amazingly proficient. For the interest of contrast there are in Langland's case the hurried summary at the end of *Piers Plowman* B Prologue (217–31) and the solemnly deliberate prayer of Repentance after the Great Confession (B v 450–505), and in Chaucer's the 'let's get on with the story' haste of the Canterbury *Prologue* 30–42 and the portentously deliberate opening stanza of *Troilus and Criseyde*.

18 Chaucer's advantage here is considerable in that straightforward narrative possesses a contextual time. Thus in *The Knight's Tale* Palamon's seven years of imprisonment, which get less than a dozen lines (1451–61) seem dreary enough; the concept 'prisoner' substitutes for extended development. But the fifty weeks between Theseus's proclamation of the tournament and the day itself, which get more than six hundred lines (1850–2491), pass swiftly in the sense of heightened anticipation. This is a different kind of control from Langland's. In *Piers Plowman* a statement like the Dreamer's *Coueitise of eiȝes . . . folwed me fourty wynter and a fifte moore* (B xi 46, 47) conveys little if any sense of the passage of time. But in B xii 139ff, in a discourse by Ymaginatif who has been the Dreamer's loyal companion for fortyfive years (xii 3), we readily accept, as from the time of the Old Law, a prophecy of the Incarnation which in its turn is briskly followed (146ff) by reference to the birth of Christ as an event of the past.

19 The other controlling circumstance is context itself, for this, and with it the poet's tone, determine the particular nature of the receptivity in which we experience the physical features of a poem. We 'interpret the rhythm . . . into "attributes" congruent with the situation.' (Winifred Nowottny, *The Language Poets Use*, London, repr. 1968, p. 115) But the physical

features of the text have a reciprocal function: 'the sound-structure makes the reader feel, as an immediate experience, what the sense of the words call up.' (*op. cit.* p. 14) In that complex process the syllabic length of words in a passage is significant because of the presence of secondary stress in polysyllables; syntactical structures because of the different rates of apprehension of simple or compound or complex or paratactic grammatical relation; the arrangement of clauses within sentences because each disturbance of absolutely logical sequence, whatever else it does, enforces a change of pace.

20 For the Chaucer figures, which should be taken as approximate, see Joseph P. Mersand, *Chaucer's Romance Vocabulary*, New York, 1937, pp. 40–3. The *Piers* figure is my estimate. The exact size of the vocabulary of this poem will be available when the three texts have been lemmatized.

21 I have in mind particularly III 284–330; IV 47–109; XIII 328–41, 362–98, but the whole enclosing context (274–405) has this quality; and XV 165–94, 531–73.

22 This I have observed in generation after generation of students, even as the subject matter has become progressively more remote.

23 Instances are *House of Fame* 729–863 and the Wife of Bath's *Prologue*; *Miller's Tale* 3708–43 and *Reeve's Tale* 4024–45; *Troilus and Criseyde* II 1406–59; *Troilus and Criseyde* IV 834–47.

24 For instance V 300–5, 526–36, 630–3, 639–43 and X 5–139.

25 Langland did not invent this particular collocation, which comes from the alliterative satire tradition of the earlier fourteenth century. Compare *to dyngen opon dauyd wyt a dirige* in *The Papelard Priest* (A. H. Smith, 'The Middle English Lyrics in Additional Manuscript 45896', *London Mediaeval Studies* II i (1951), p. 44 line 56). The association with threshing appears clearly in *Piers* B VI 141, *dyngen vpon sheues*. Langland's distinction is to have implied in the expression both a rebuke to parsons over-concerned with farming their glebe, and a reference to the spiritual food to be obtained from strenuous occupation with the Psalter.

26 See above, p. 100. Langland's use of vocabulary awaits expert study in the light of Middle English lexicography.

27 *Se ce songe n'ai bien songie, Je pri qu'a droit soit corrigie De ceuz qui songier miex saront Ou qui miex faire le pourront. Tant di aussi que, se menconge I a aucune que a songe Soit repute, quar par songier Ne se fait pas tout voir noncier.* Guillaume de Deguileville, *Le Pelerinage de Vie Humaine*, ed. J. J. Stürzinger, London, 1893, p. 422 lines 13517–24.

28 Macrobius, *Commentary on the Dream of Scipio*, transl. William Harris Stahl, New York, 1952, p. 90.

29 *Pelerinage de Vie Humaine*, p. 1 lines 9–13. He simply writes *Bien croi que ce fu la chose Qui plus m'esmut a ce songier Que ci apres vous vueil nuncier.*

30 This first inner dream runs from B xi 5–406. The key lines are 146, 147 where Trajan says of Gregory that *he wilned to my soule Sauacion for soopnesse þat he seiȝ in my werkes.*

31 The second inner dream occupies B xvi 19–167. The term *loue dreem* (20) is used to mean 'ecstasy. ecstatic experience of the love of Christ' in *The Minor Poems of the Vernon MS.* ii, ed. F. J. Furnivall, EETS 117, 1901, p. 449 line 20.

32 Compare John Burrow: 'Sceptical criticism has produced no good reasons to doubt that Langland is portraying his own circumstances at the time of writing.' (*Medieval Writers and Their Work: Middle English Literature and its Background 1100–1500*, page 45.

33 It is hard not to associate Queen Anne with the composition of at least the *Prologue* to *The Legend of Good Women*.

34 There were Gower, a landowner of leisure called 'moral' for his estates satire verse, Strode, called 'philosophical' (*Troilus and Criseyde* v 1856, 1857), presumably the Merton philosopher turned lawyer (one recalls that lawyers were technically clerks), Vache and Scogan and Bukton to whom Chaucer wrote verse missives in the Dantean manner. (For these see K. Foster and P. Boyde, *Dante's Lyric Poetry*, I, *The Poems*, Oxford, repr. 1972, pp. 2–30, 148–58, 194–202.) Already this begins to look like a coterie. It is altogether probable that Chaucer had a circle of informed readers, the older of whom would have grown in literary sophistication along with his poetry. On its fringes one imagines the Clanvowes and Usks.

35 Yet one reads, 'When Chaucer speaks of himself, he displays the same personality which is implicit in the rest of his poetry—in the 'innocent' tone, especially, which gives to the irony its peculiar, personal flavour.' (Burrow, *op. cit.* p. 46.)

36 '*Allas*', *quod Haukyn þe Actif man þo*, '*þat after my cristendom I ne hadde be deed and doluen for dowelis sake! So hard it is*', *quod haukyn*, '*to lyue and do synne. Synne seweþ vs euere.*' B xiv 323–6.

37 He is the hero of *Der Ackermann aus Böhmen*. Recent editions of this work are by L. L. Hammerich, Copenhagen, 1938, and Gunther Jungbluth, Heidelberg, 1969.

11 Conjectural Emendation

1 This essay is based on a paper read to the Oxford Medieval Society on 3 March 1966.

2 *Beowulf with the Finnsburg Fragment*, ed. A. J. Wyatt, rev. R. W. Chambers (Cambridge, 1948), p. xxvi.

3 Ibid.

4 E. Vinaver, *The Works of Sir Thomas Malory* (Oxford, 1948), i, pp. xcii–xciii.

5 A. E. Housman, *Selected Prose*, ed. J. Carter (Cambridge, 1961), p. 29.
6 Ibid.
7 Compare Housman, p. 43.
8 Quoted by A. Dain, *Les Manuscrits* (Paris, 1949), p. 151.
9 *Johnson on Shakespeare*, ed. W. Raleigh (London, 1931), p. 60.
10 Vinaver, op. cit., p. xciii. Compare Housman, pp. 105, 106, and K. Sisam, *Studies in the History of Old English Literature* (Oxford, 1953), p. 30, n.
11 U. T. Holmes, reviewing E. B. Ham, *Textual Criticism and Jehan le Venelais* in *Speculum*, xxii (1947), 469.
12 R. P. Wülker, quoted by Sisam, op. et loc. cit.
13 Housman, p. 105.
14 Ibid., p. 43.
15 Vinaver, p. xciii.
16 Compare Housman, p. 43:

'the average man, if he meddles with criticism at all, is a conservative critic . . . He believes that the text of ancient authors is generally sound, not because he has acquainted himself with the elements of the problem, but because he would feel uncomfortable if he did not believe it.'

17 P. Maas, *Textkritik*, 3., verbesserte und vermehrte Auflage (Leipzig, 1957), p. 10.
18 *Les Manuscrits*, p. 159.
19 *Textkritik*, p. 13.
20 *Textkritik*, p. 13:

'Natürlich ist es viel schädlicher, wenn eine Verderbnis unerkannt bleibt, als wenn ein heiler Text zu Unrecht angegriffen wird . . . die nicht bezeichnete Verderbnis schädigt den stilistischen Gesamteindruck.'

21 *Studies*, p. 39.
22 *Textkritik*, p. 33:

'Konjektur, 'richtig' oder 'falsch,' [ist] ein wesentlicher Teil der examinatio, d.h. der Prüfung, ob der überlieferte Text der beste ausdenkbare ist oder nicht'; and p. 13: 'jede Konjektur reizt zur Widerlegung, durch die das Verständnis der Stelle jedenfalls gefördert wird.'

23 *Studies*, p. 44.
24 Compare Sisam, *Studies*, pp. 36–7:

'A defender of the manuscript readings . . . might argue that the scribes were well trained, and that they knew more about Old English usage, thought and tradition than a modern critic can. I doubt if this holds good for the earlier poetry.' Textual criticism is in debt to Dr Sisam for giving this doubt the support of his authority.

25 Housman, p. 51.
26 F. W. Hall, *A Companion to Classical Texts* (Oxford, 1913), p. 151.
27 *Textkritik*, pp. 11–12, esp. p. 12. His general discussion implies a third criterion, the consensus of competent judgement, 'die Übereinstimmung aller Urteilsfähigen,' adding that this is 'freilich ein schwer zu umgrenzender Begriff': on p. 13 he writes, of conjectural readings, 'nur die besten werden sich durchsetzen'.
28 Maas, *Textkritik*, p. 13: 'die Texte als die Grundlage jeder philologischen Forschung sollten so behandelt werden, dass über den Grad der Sicherheit, der ihnen zukommt, möglichste Klarheit herrscht.'
29 *Textkritik*, p. 13.
30 Housman, p. 145.
31 *Textkritik*, pp. 11–12.

12 The Text of *The Legend of Good Women* in *CULS* MS Gy 4–27

1 The collation was carried out by Janet Cowen of King's College London; the text is one she and I have prepared for an edition of the poem.
2 F. N. Robinson, *The Works of Geoffrey Chaucer* (London, 1957), p. xxxix. The scholarship of the subject has been very conveniently summarized in *The Poetical Works of Geoffrey Chaucer: A Facsimile of Cambridge University Library MS Gg. 4.27 with Introductions by M. B. Parkes and Richard Beadle* (Cambridge, 1980), iii. 46–56.
3 These are the groups: TrG, 8 agreements after line 2000; TrA^{3}G, 6 after 2200; STrA^{2}G, 7 after 2000; TrA^{3}A^{2}G, 5 after 2000; StrA^{3}A^{2}G, 8 after 2000. These readings are excluded from the present analysis because of the possibility that they are present in G by scribal 'correction'.
4 The spelling of the lemmata from which G's reading varies is Robinson's, unless our text differs. Variants peculiar to G are as spelled in the manuscript. Variants of groups in which G figures have the spelling of the manuscript first in the cited order of sigils.
5 These he first inadvertently omitted, and then, when he noticed his error, copied out of place without signalling that fact.
6 Robinson reads *He*, but G's omission is evidence for original *Hym*.
7 The subject of many Cockney jokes. Langland may have been exploiting it in his alliteration of [f] with [ð] and [θ].
8 The analysis leaves a residue of differences between readings of G and the large family for which plausible explanations have not recommended themselves. They are the following (G's reading is the second): 964, 2563

called/*clepid*; 1170 *dere/leue*; 1560 *hir/it*; 1911 *caste/caughte*; 1978 *Phedra leve syster/leue systyr Phedra*; 2119 *assure/ensure*; 2214 *wrecched/wreche* (*so Rob.*); 2367 by/with; 2618 And/zero; 2676 to/a.

9 Compare Parkes and Beadle, op. cit., p. 54.

10 I have not been able to find where Robinson gives this information.

11 Again, if these readings are scribal, the agreements are by coincident variation. They are mainly in one or to readings; the exceptions are STrA¹G, 9; SG, 5; PG, 5; TrA¹G, 4. All agreements are in trivial variation.

12 He actually ventured a silent conjectural emendation *metri causa* in G Prol. 189, where the manuscript reads *adam made*. The readings G 271 *me* (MS *ne*) and G 398 *this* (MS *his*) are apparently typesetter's errors: they are absent from the first edition. It is not clear whether G 374 *be* (MS *he*) is an emendation for 'sense' or someone's error. The original was certainly *he*: compare F 388.

13 Robinson, p. 913.

14 This is a very elegant instance, identifiable as such from a Gower quotation: *Thei thoghten wel sche hadde be In hire astat of hih degre. Confessio Amantis* II. 1224, quoted in *MED*, s.v. *Degre* n., 4 (a).

15 There is the same variation at 502/490; see below, p. 57.

16 Robinson (p. 913) records his unease and gives or even adopts conjectural emendations by earlier editors. But he presumably thought of the passage as revised, and so it looks as he prints it in his text. How many persevere at referring to his critical notes?

17 The subgroups are TrA¹, which over the whole poem agree in about 300 unoriginal variants, and STrA¹, which agree in 37 unoriginal variants.

18 Compare Parkes and Beadle, op. cit., p. 47.

13 John M. Manly (1865–1940) and Edith Rickert (1871–1938)

1 The important reviews were those by Carleton Brown, *MLN* 55 (1940): 606–21; Dorothy Everett, *RES* 18 (1942):93–109, and *YWES* 21 (1940):46–50; and R. K. Root, *SP* 38 (1941):1–13. Manly's apologist Germaine Dempster singled out Root's review as especially perceptive ('Manly's Conception of the Early History of the *Canterbury Tales*,' *PMLA* 61 (1946): 379–415); Brown's was in fact also penetrating. The language of all was gentle, but Root's hostility can with hindsight be detected.

2 The process is well described in G. Pasquali, *Storia della Tradizione e Critica del Testo*, 2d ed. (Florence: F. Le Monnier, 1952).

3 There is even resistance to the process, as if our poets had been careless of the form and meaning of their verse, and their medieval readers content

with texts that sometimes made bad sense or bad verse. Some of the blame for this lies with George Saintsbury (see *A History of English Prosody*: ref. pp. 77, 78 and 266 n. 5), some with French textual critics two generations ago (on whom see J. Fourquet, *Le Paradoxe de Bédier*, University of Strasbourg Faculty of Letters Publications, fasc. 105 [Paris, 1946]). But the notion that textual criticism is frivolous or self-indulgent will always have an appeal for those who find its conditions intellectually too demanding.

4 John M. Manly and Edith Rickert, eds., *The Text of the Canterbury Tales Studied on the Basis of All Known Manuscripts* (Chicago and London: University of Chicago Press, 1940), 1.150. Parenthetical text and note references are to volume and page of this edition.

5 This is a trap for the inexperienced, but in fairness the suggestion of inconsistency between the account of collation in 2.10 and the description of the contents of the apparatus (5.v) is not real: it is quickly apparent that language variants do not figure in the latter. It was clearly impracticable to admit them.

6 Of course, when that process which, as a hypothesis, is by definition provisional, has been carried out, the archetypal text of the manuscript has to a large extent effectively been recovered. This is such an obvious consideration that I continue amazed at never having seen it expressed.

7 This was apparently the *Student's Chaucer* first issued in 1895 by the Clarendon Press and often reprinted. It was a confidently edited text: Skeat observed (p. 719) that 'there are very few doubtful readings in the Canterbury Tales' and listed thirty-three (pp. 731, 732). He did not signal emendations.

8 Either they changed their views about this, or they did not have any clearly formed views. Compare 2.22, 23, 26 and 2.419. In the first place 'individually trifling variants' are said to have classificatory value, to indicate 'the original text-tradition' better than striking variants; in the second agreement between a number of such variants is ascribed to coincident variation.

9 Carleton Brown (*MLN*, pp. 609, 610) sensed involvement in 'contradictions and discrepancies' here.

10 The system of symbols set out at 2.44, 45 makes this impracticable.

11 See note 36 below.

12 See above, p. 180 and n. 36 below.

13 Its greatest exponent in our time, Paul Maas, spent more than a generation refining its techniques, already well developed by classical editors. His essay *Textkritik* first appeared in 1927 in Gercke and Norden's *Einleitung in die Altertumswissenschaft*; he several times modified and supplemented it. The last impression appeared in 1960. See p. 287 n. 17.

14 Dempster, "Manly's Conception of the Early History of the *Canterbury Tales*," p. 414.

15 This was noticed by Brown (*MLN*, p. 620) and by Everett (*RES*, pp. 108, 109).

16 A. E. Housman, *Selected Prose*, p. 43. The passage is quoted on p. 287, n. 16 above.

17 Maas, sec. 13; cf. Housman, *Selected Prose*, pp. 35ff.

18 Much information about scribal habits was available in the 1930s. In particular, F. W. Hall's *Companion to Classical Texts* (Oxford: Oxford University Press, 1913) provided analysis of mechanical error; J. J. Griesbach, *Novum Testamentum Graece*, 2d ed. (London, 1796), B. F. Westcott and F. J. A. Hort, *The New Testament in the Original Greek* (Cambridge and London: Cambridge University Press, 1881), identified kinds of variation prompted by scribal response to the text being copied. See also p. 209 above.

19 19 See below, pp. 192 ff.

20 As was suggested by E. T. Donaldson, *Chaucer's Poetry*, 2d ed. (New York: Ronald Press, 1975), p. 254.

21 *Procul recedant somnia Et noctium phantasmata; hostemque nostrum comprime Ne polluantur corpora.* The lines are from "Hymn for Compline," *Te lucis ante terminum*, F. J. E. Raby, ed., *The Oxford Book of Medieval Latin Verse* (Oxford: Oxford University Press, 1959), p. 48, See *Breviarium ad Usum Insignis Ecclesie Eboracensis, Surtees Society*, vol. 71 (London, 1880), col. 5. I am obliged to my colleague J. S. Wittig for pointing out their aptness here.

22 *RES*, p. 96.

23 3.465, 466: notes to D 1693, 1695.

24 See *OED*, s.v. *As* conj. 9, *MED* s.v. *as* conj. 2a; *OED* s.v. *Be* v. 16, *MED* s.v. *ben* v. 8; also T. Mustanoja, *A Middle English Syntax* (Helsinki, 1960), p. 465.

25 *OED*, s.v. *That* conj. ii.2, 'Introducing a clause expressing the cause, ground or reason of what is stated in the principal clause.' Compare, e.g., *Me is þe vvrs þat ich þe so*, E. G. Stanley, ed., *The Owl and the Nightingale* (London: Nelson, 1960), line 34; *Two dayes þer fastinde he yede þat non for his werk wolde him fede*, W. W. Skeat, ed., *The Lay of Havelok the Dane*, 2d ed., rev. K. Sisam (Oxford: Oxford University Press, 1973), lines 865, 866; and *To him heo hadde gret envie þat he so riche heo* (sc. *sholde beo*), C. d'Evelyn and A. J. Mills, eds., *The South English Legendary*, EETS, o.s. 235 (London, 1956), p. 282.

26 Likely usages would be *I hote*, *I bidde*, or imperative *do way* or *do so*. I cannot recall *I seie* in such a use.

27 See, for instance, 2.84, 102, 157, 201–202, 238–39.

28 F. N. Robinson, ed., *The Complete Works of Geoffrey Chaucer* (Cambridge, Mass., Houghton Mifflin, 1933), p. xxxiii.

29 *Confessio Amantis* 5.4787, 4788 and 7716, 7717: *The English Works of John Gower*, vol. ii, EETS, o.s. 82 (London, 1901), pp. 77, 163.

30 So Larry D. Benson, "The Order of *The Canterbury Tales*," *Studies in the Age of Chaucer* 2(1981):77–120, and Charles Owen, "The Alternative Reading of *The Canterbury Tales*: Chaucer's Text and the Early Manuscripts," *PMLA* 97 (1982):237–50.

31 Whether or not Chaucer knew the term, it is a *sirventes* in the form *coblas unissonans*.

32 F. N. Robinson, *The Works of Geoffrey Chaucer*, 2d ed. (Boston: Houghton Mifflin, 1957), p. 712.

33 If I read the apparatus correctly, these are He Ne Cx^1Tc^2 (the editors' group *b*), To (?)Ld^1 Ry^1 (in the editors' group *d**), Ha^2 (in the "*cd* line") and Se (in group *d**). In Se the lines are at the foot of the page in the main hand. The classifications are from the descriptions of the manuscripts. I have been unable to translate them meaningfully into the genetic scheme for *The Miller's Tale* (3.128).

34 There is a suggestion in the variants that the original of 1007, 1008 read *Wo was his herte . . . And with a sorweful chere*.

35 Cf. *OED*, s. vv. *Win* v.[1] 7d and *Spur* sb. 3a.

36 For a start the Manly and Rickert collations, which survive, will have to be checked for correctness: we know nothing about the training of the 'very large staff' who produced them, and not all fifteenth-century Chaucer manuscript hands are easy. If the check is favourable, the next step is to etablish a norm for collection of variant groups by provisional determination of originality in the largest possible number of places. That sounds formidible, but should not be hard in most instances, as Skeat (*Student's Chaucer*, p. 719) observed. Only then comes the collection of the groups formed by agreement in variation from that text. This will be best done in the first instance separately for each formal section of the poem. Here the *codices deteriores*, copies of surviving copies, will identify themselves and are to be eliminated. Now at length the variant groups can be examined with respect to persistency and congruency, with allowance for the essential likelihood of convergent variation (by both coincidence and contamination) and taking into account that in genetic schemes it is possible for a single manuscript to have the status of a family. It may turn out that no significant classification is possible. If, on the other hand, a aystem of groupings sufficiently well defined to be recognizable as stemmatic should prove discernible, the result will have great value, for simply by its existence as a consonant hypothesis it will confirm the effectiveness of the first one, the provisional identification of originality. It will also enable identification of authorial revision to be undertaken with less danger of begging the question.

14 Good and Bad Manuscripts: Texts and Critics

1 B. A. Windeatt, ed., *Geoffrey Chaucer*: Troilus & Criseyde (London and New York: Longman, 1984), p. 33.
2 Ibid.
3 Derek Pearsall, "Editing Medieval Texts: Some Developments and Some Problems," in Jerome J. McGann, ed., *Textual Criticism and Literary Interpretation* (Chicago: University of Chicago Press, 1985), p. 103. Pearsall goes on to propose that the activities of scribes, 'the first literary critics, . . . provide a wealth of insight into a contemporary or near-contemporary reading of a text (and therefore into the text itself), into the tastes of the age and the expectations of readers.' He has the advantage of me there: I was not vouchsafed such insight in ten years and more of reading manuscript variations. His proposition implies that copyists, men occupied with earning a poor living by the formation of letters on a page, were in a position, or indeed were qualified, to think in any significant critical sense about what they were copying. As for the 'high level of intellectual and even critical engagement,' its height is relative to the level of the base. A scribe copying Lydgate might well seem to soar by variation.
4 See pages 163–167 above. For unmistakable cases of sophistication in the transmission of Chaucer texts see pp. 193, 194 above.
5 Norman Blake, The Canterbury Tales *by Geoffrey Chaucer Edited from the Hengwrt Manuscript* (London: Arnold, 1980), p. 6.
6 Pearsall, 'Editing Medieval Texts,' pp. 93, 94, 96.
7 Discussed above, pp. 193–196. Blake's 'generally agreed,' which suggests informed consensus, actually refers to uncritical acquiescence in Manly and Rickert's proposition of an 'intelligent editor' of Ellesmere. That editor is the child of their relative inexperience of scribal substitution. It lives on in Blake's edition and does mischief to those who embrace and cherish it. Witness, for instance, Blake's unhappy defence of the contextually induced variant *complyn/couplyng* as 'union, i.e. harmony' (p. 167, note to line 4163), for which there is no shred of lexicographical evidence. On the scribal character of *couplyng* see p. 189 and p. 291 n. 21 above.
8 Pearsall, 'Editing Medieval Texts,' p. 101.
9 Ibid., p. 99.
10 Of the two the poet (*écrivain*) is the one who shapes and fashions his utterance . . . and gives himself over entirely to the effort of exercising that function. The poet's activity implies two types of standard: technical standards of arrangement, of literary kind and form of style; and craftsman's standards, of hard work, persistence, perfectionism. . . . It is only the poet, by that definition, who loses the outlines of his own identity and

the shape of the world in the structure of words he is setting down: this is produced from a raw material shaped with immeasurable effort. Roland Barthes, *Essais Critiques* (Paris: Éditions du Seuil, 1964), pp. 148, 149.

11 Pearsall, "Editing Medieval Texts," p. 95.

12 Lee Patterson, 'The Logic of Textual Criticism and the Way of Genius,' in McGann, ed., *Textual Criticism and Literary Interpretation*, p. 86.

13 Ibid.

14 The comic irony of a situation where this has actually to be proclaimed is evident in the anomalous postures of those who, rejecting the imperative, take refuge in the shelter of the 'good' manuscript, for intance, Hengwrt, superior 'not only in its more accurate representation of a flexible, idiomatic and successful metrical practice . . . but also in numerous readings of a substantive and significant nature. . . . an early and uneditorialized manuscript of uncontestably high quality' (Pearsall, 'Editing Medieval Texts,' pp. 94, 96). How do they attain to such a particularized and evidently deeply held conviction?

16 Outstanding Problems of Middle English Scholarship

1 I will not name living persons whom I cite in terms like this: no good purpose would be served by embarrasing them publicly. My examples are genuine enough.

2 Robert Kilburn Root, *The Book of Troilus and Criseyde* (Princeton, 1926; rpt. 1954), pp. lxxxvii, lxxxix.

3 *Ibid.*, pp. lxxxi, lxxxii, lxxxv.

4 John M. Manly and Edith Rickert, *The Text of the Canterbury Tales* I, xii; II, 40.

5 *Piers Plowman: the B Version* p. 17, esp n. 10. ;on, *Piers Plowman: the B*

6 See above, pp. 179 ff.

7 Manly and Rickert, I, x.

8 F. N. Robinson, ed., *The Works of Geoffrey Chaucer*, 2nd ed. p. xliv.

9 *Ibid.*, p. xxxvi.

10 Root, pp. lxx ff.

11 This is my considered opinion as a textual critic.

12 Manly and Rickert, II, 495 ff.

13 See Fredson Bowers, *Textual and Literacy Criticism* (Cambridge, 1959), pp. 29, 30.

14 Robinson, p. xli. The objection is not to emendation for the meter, but to the withholding of information about individual instances.

15 Aage Brusendorff, *The Chaucer Tradition* (London, 1925), p. 288.

16 Ethel Seaton, *Sir Richard Roos* (London, 1961), pp. 125–28.

17 *Ibid.*, p. 244.

18 John Henry Newman, *The Idea of a University*, ed. Martin J. Svaglic (New York, 1960), p. 56.

19 Robinson, p. 755. One may also ask whether close translation is necessarily a feature of the early stage of a career.

20 An example of such feeling is to be found in Manly and Rickert's extraordinary note on *The Parson's Prologue* and *Tale* (*The Text of Canterbury Tales*, IV, 526, 527). This is worth reading as a demonstration of how prejudice or preconception can cloud the mind.

21 John S. P. Tatlock, *The Development and Chronology of Chaucer's Works*, Chaucer Society, Second Series, 37 (London, 1907; rpt. Gloucester, Mass., 1963).

22 *Ibid.*, p. 224.

23 See J. J. N. Palmer, 'The Historical Context of the Book of the Duchess: A Revision,' *Chaucer Review*, 8 (1973–4), 253–61.

24 John A. Yunck, *The Lineage of Lady Meed* (Notre Dame, 1963).

25 Gordon Leff, *Heresy in the Later Middle Ages*, (Manchester and New York, 1967).

26 Jill Mann, *Chaucer and Medieval Estates Satire* (Cambridge, 1973).

27 May McKisack, *The Fourteenth Century: 1307–1399* (Oxford, 1959), pp. 295–302.

28 See Russell Hope Robbins, ed., *Historical Poems of the XIVth and XVth Centuries* (New York, 1959), pp. 98–102.

29 J. P. Oakden, *Alliterative Poetry in Middle English* (Manchester, 1930–5).

30 When I wrote this I did not know of the work of Moshe Lazar and Jean Frappier, especially the latter's *Amour Courtois et Table Ronde* (p. 247, n. 4 above).
317–21.

31 *Troilus and Criseyde* 1, 337.

Index